VINCENT DE PAUL, THE LAZARIST MISSION, AND FRENCH CATHOLIC REFORM

Vincent de Paul, the Lazarist Mission, and French Catholic Reform

ALISON FORRESTAL

OXFORD
UNIVERSITY PRESS

OXFORD
UNIVERSITY PRESS

Great Clarendon Street, Oxford, OX2 6DP,
United Kingdom

Oxford University Press is a department of the University of Oxford. It furthers the University's objective of excellence in research, scholarship, and education by publishing worldwide. Oxford is a registered trade mark of Oxford University Press in the UK and in certain other countries

First Edition published in 2017

Impression: 1

Published in the United States of America by Oxford University Press
198 Madison Avenue, New York, NY 10016, United States of America

British Library Cataloguing in Publication Data
Data available

Library of Congress Control Number: 2016960745

ISBN 978–0–19–878576–7

Printed in Great Britain by
Clays Ltd, St Ives plc

Acknowledgements

It is a pleasure to express my gratitude to those who have helped in the production of this book. Megan Armstrong, Joe Bergin, Jennifer Hillman, John Rybolt, CM, Seán Smith, and Ed Udovic, CM, read the manuscript or sections thereof, and it benefited greatly from their opinions. Simon Hodson and Ruth Manning generously gave me copies of their doctoral dissertations, while Barbara Diefendorf furnished me with a copy of a particularly useful document at a key moment in research. Paul Henzmann, CM, Bernard Koch, CM, and Claude Lautissier, CM, were enormously helpful in sharing their knowledge of the Parisian archives of the Congregation of the Mission when I first began my research on Vincent de Paul there. My teaching colleague at NUIG, Enrico Dal Lago, offered valuable encouragement as I reached a conclusion, while he and my other colleagues in History at the university have maintained a wonderfully supportive and convivial atmosphere in which to research and write in the decade since I joined them. Siubhan Comer saved me a great deal of work by producing a map of Lazarist houses for the volume, as did Cathal Smith in editing its bibliography. I also acknowledge appreciatively the financial support for my research that I received from the British Academy Small Grants scheme, the NUIG Millennium Fund, and the Irish Research Council Research Fellowship scheme, as well as the NUI's Publications Grant for the cost of indexing. Finally, and most of all, I would like to thank Dave Gillard for his patience and understanding throughout the production process.

Contents

Abbreviations

AAE	Archives des Affaires Étrangères, Paris
Abelly, *Vie*, i–iii	Louis Abelly, *La Vie du venerable servant de Dieu Vincent de Paul*, 3 vols (Paris, 1664)
ACMP	Archives de la Congrégation de la Mission, Paris
AD	Archives Départementales
AN	Archives Nationales, Paris
Arsenal	Bibliothèque de l'Arsenal, Paris
ASV	Archivio Segreto Vaticano, Rome
Bib. Maz.	Bibliothèque Mazarine, Paris
BNF	Bibliothèque Nationale, Paris
BSG	Bibliothèque Sainte-Geneviève, Paris
CCD, 1–14	Paul, Vincent de. *Saint Vincent de Paul. Correspondence, Conferences, Documents*, ed. Jacqueine Kilar et al. 14 vols (New York, 1985–2014)
CED, 1–14	Paul, Vincent de. *Saint Vincent de Paul. Correspondance, Entretiens, Documents*, ed. Pierre Coste, 14 vols (Paris, 1920–5)
Coste, *Saint*, i–iii	Coste, Pierre. *Le Grand Saint du grand siècle: Monsieur Vincent*, 3 vols (Paris, 1931)
SCPF	Archivio Storico de Propaganda Fide, Rome
SOCG	Scritture originali riferite nelle congregazioni generali (Original papers discussed in general congregations)

Map. Lazarist Houses Established in France (excluding Paris), 1625–1660

This list does not include the supposed houses of Alet and Montpellier, often counted amongst the foundations of this period: for further information, see Ch. 8, n. 30 (Alet), and n. 21 (Montpellier).

Introduction

I

Few individuals have become more associated with the drive in the Catholic church to improve religious devotion and discipline in the post-Reformation period than Vincent de Paul. References to his involvement in works of mission, charity, and clerical training crop up habitually in surveys of 'the refashioning of Catholicism' during the sixteenth and seventeenth centuries, which reassert his importance to reform and renewal without further ado.[1] The 'cheerful and modest' de Paul, as Diarmaid MacCulloch characterizes him, smiles from their pages, as the broad spectrum of his activities, and the enthusiasm with which he and his keenest supporters participated in them, are used to provide brief examples of the diverse practices that were put in place to shape religious devotion during the Catholic Reformation.[2]

More generally, these survey works earn their worth by drawing on the extraordinary wave of modern scholarship that has advanced the traditional agenda for research into the early modern Catholic church, in the process transforming our understanding of its development. Notably, for France, it is now widely recognized that while the disruption of the Wars of Religion (1562–98) meant that the drive for Catholic reform began later there than elsewhere, once it was set in motion it reached levels of intensity and creativity over the first six decades of the seventeenth century which were unmatched in any other region. Yet, while historical analysis of the Catholic Reformation in France and elsewhere has moved forward in leaps and bounds in recent decades, study of de Paul has not kept pace, and he remains uneasily located within these advances in knowledge and interpretation. For information on his life and work, historians still depend mainly on the standard biography produced by the Vincentian Pierre Coste, the triple volume *Le Grand Saint du grand siècle*, even though it is now close to a century since this was published.[3]

[1] Bireley, *Refashioning*, 42, 94, 104, 134, 141–2. See also the mentions in Po-chia Hsia, *Catholic Renewal*, and Wright, *Counter-Reformation*.

[2] MacCulloch, *Reformation*, 646. For an identical earlier sketch of the 'smiling' de Paul, see Delumeau, *Catholicism*, 58.

[3] Coste, *Saint*, i–iii. In the seventeenth century, members of the Congregation of the Mission were generally known as Lazarists (and are often still recognized as such in France), but they are now more commonly identified as Vincentians.

In this book, de Paul stands out compellingly as a figure of remarkable energy, ingenuity, and resourcefulness in Catholic Reformation France, whose experiences offer priceless insights into the shifts in fortune, function, and style that shaped the French church in this formative period: he was the founding superior general of a congregation of secular missionaries commonly known as the Lazarists, and his interests ranged unusually widely and into some of the most important areas of religious reform and renewal over more than forty years of this period. But, just as importantly for a new analysis of his activities, until his death on 27 September 1660 he did not act alone, but worked indefatigably and productively with a broad set of male and female associates in efforts to influence the character of devotional belief and practice within the church. In telling the story of de Paul's efforts to institute and expand the Lazarists, this book therefore examines the development of a missionary operation whose multifaceted features and workings amounted to a significant enterprise for reform, and evokes new answers to questions on its origins, organization, functioning, and impact. It offers a wholly fresh perspective on the challenges and opportunities that the contemporary environment offered to an individual of vision and pragmatism in gathering the resources, devising the structures, and forging the relationships that enabled him to express his devotion and to promote its like amongst others.

At the time of its publication, Pierre Coste's work represented a major breakthrough in Vincentian scholarship, because he strove to take a more rigorously historical approach to de Paul's life than earlier biographies of the saint. Thus, Coste made important corrections to previously supposed facts, relating to, for instance, de Paul's date of birth, family, and early education. The three volumes of *Le Grand Saint* also bulged with extracts from newly discovered letters by de Paul as well as other documents from the Lazarists' archives, most of which had rarely or never before reached a general audience.[4] Since then, the work has proved valuable in providing a basic chronology and sense of de Paul's occupations for modern historians. It describes his activities as the founder and superior general of a major congregation of secular clergy which began to carry out formal missions in rural areas of France in 1625, that is, to complete organized tours of parishes in order to deliver religious instruction, administer the sacraments, and establish confraternities of charity. It outlines the expansion of the group's remit to include clerical retreats and the management of seminaries to train clergy (clerical formation); it recounts the foundation of confraternities of charity for aiding the sick poor, which were modelled on an original that de Paul instigated in Châtillon-lès-Dombes in 1617, and pays close attention to two in particular: the first, known as the Ladies of Charity, comprised women of high social rank at the *Hôtel-Dieu* hospital in Paris; the second, which de Paul co-founded in 1633 with Louise de Marillac, was the Daughters of Charity, whose less elevated members committed to living in community as they too cared for the sick poor.

[4] Coste was the editor of thirteen volumes of de Paul's correspondence, conferences, and other documents relating to the Lazarists, Daughters of Charity, and the confraternities of charity, published between 1920 and 1924 (a fourteenth volume included an index of the collection): *CED*, 1–14.

For all its merits, however, Coste's text is characterized by assumptions and omissions that ultimately render its analysis of de Paul unsatisfactory. Most obviously, Coste proved reluctant to query some of the more dubious tales associated with de Paul despite their lack of historical credibility (notably his supposed Corsair captivity), with the result that these retain their place in the popular derivative biographies published since his own.[5] A more fundamental flaw arises, however, from Coste's willingness to treat what he judged to be de Paul's accomplishments as the organizing principles for all the actions which preceded them. As a result, his dedication to affirming that de Paul was the principal advocate and organizer of religious devotion in France from the 1620s until his death led him to make claims about his actions that are supported only by hyperbole and narrow sets of evidence. Furthermore, it led Coste to mistake an oversupply of descriptive information for proof of argument, so much so that de Paul is often unmentioned for long sections in the text before his decisive influence on events is once again proclaimed.

Ultimately therefore, *Le Grand Saint* takes quite a conventional approach to the life of a religious founder. For Coste, de Paul possessed an extraordinary and often singlehanded ability to lead others in all kinds of major works of charity, resurrect clerical standards in France, supervise multiple missionary campaigns, and act as a watchdog against heresy: all talents and achievements that could really be explained only by the blessings of the providential God in whose name he acted.[6] Although, therefore, the names of those with whom de Paul established contact through his work are to be found at every turn in the text, they are consistently presented in positions of subordination to his farsighted and inspired leadership, as beneficiaries of his direction, and as patrons in thrall to his virtue. Subsequent biographies have manifestly failed to overcome these failings, despite legitimate efforts to ascribe parity to Louise de Marillac in the foundation of the Daughters of Charity.[7] More broadly, they are also symptomatic of the cursory attention that Coste paid to the wider religious, social, and political context in which de Paul moved, thereby neglecting, in other words, to situate and assess his 'great saint' in the context of the 'great century'. But is it really realistic to present de Paul in this manner? Even at the time that Coste wrote, historians of France celebrated what they termed the 'religious renaissance' of early seventeenth-century France, and pointed to the myriad of figures that actively shaped its dynamic character, from the mystic Barbe Acarie, to the theologian and cardinal Pierre de Bérulle, and the ascetic reforming bishop of Cahors, Alain de Solminihac.[8] Recent studies have adjusted

[5] Guillaume, *Vincent de Paul*; Pujo, *Vincent de Paul*. For further comment on the captivity, see Ch. 1, section I.

[6] Coste, *Saint*, iii, 568: 'C'est sa gloire unique entre tous les grands hommes que la Bienfaisance ne puisse rien concevoir et rien tenter qu'il n'ait d'avance et en quelque façon embrassé dans l'immensité de ses initiatives. On dirait qu'il a atteint les limites mêmes de la charité et que l'homme désormais ne saurait aller au-delà.'

[7] Pujo, *Vincent de Paul*, *passim*; Román, *Vincent de Paul*, esp. 460–2.

[8] These included but were not restricted to: Brémond, *Histoire*, ii, 193–262; Faillon, *Olier*; Sheppard, *Acarie*; Sol, *Solminihac*.

this perspective, to highlight the breadth of reform initiatives and the broad base of sources from which these drew their energy and resources, while also emphasizing the high level of engagement by a varied set of actors, male and female, lay and clerical, in them. How should we assess de Paul's standing, in the light of such contributions to knowledge?

II

It would be disingenuous to claim to be the first to recognize the deficiencies described above. Within the Congregation of the Mission itself, scholars such as John Rybolt and Bernard Koch have made sterling efforts to encourage the reassessment of aspects of de Paul's life and Lazarist history, specifically through their unearthing of documents shedding light on the devising of internal rules and routines, practices of community prayer, and financial affairs.[9] Similarly, José Román has incorporated Miguel Pérez Flores's sensitive scrutiny of Roman sources relating to the Congregation's approval by the papacy in 1633 into his biography of de Paul, though he otherwise relied overwhelmingly on well-known documentation from the Congregation's own archive, and yields few groundbreaking insights.[10] Fellow Vincentian André Dodin has offered a series of notable publications on de Paul's spirituality, ranging from its biblical and other sources to his views on miracles, Mariology, and charity. While often very perceptive, Dodin usually wrote with a theological outlook, often with a devotional readership in mind. He also relied unquestioningly on a traditional chronology, narrative, and interpretative framework. This included inflating de Paul's achievements beyond credibility; for instance, Dodin concluded that de Paul dominated the decisions on appointments to benefices made by the royal Council of Ecclesiastical Affairs, of which he became a member in 1643. This is despite a conspicuous lack of archival research to support Dodin's judgement; as a result, his compositions regularly fall short of the standards expected of a rigorously historical text.[11]

Outside Vincentian ranks, a handful of scholars have sought to address precise aspects of de Paul's work. Susan Dinan has explored his role in the germination of the unusual confraternal structure of the Daughters of Charity in her study of their early history, explaining convincingly the measures that de Paul and Marillac took in insisting to church authorities that it was not a traditional enclosed order, but a

[9] See, for example, Koch, 'Dernières Années': 144; Rybolt, 'Codex Sarzana'; Rybolt, 'Two Unpublished Documents'. Rybolt has also published, with Luigi Mezzadri and José-Maria Román, a multi-volume survey history of the Vincentians, although most of the discussion in vol. i deals with the period after de Paul's death: Mezzadri and Rybolt, *Vincentians.*

In the same vein, see Edward Udovic's excellent translation of and commentary on the funeral oration delivered by Henri de Maupas du Tour two months after de Paul's death: Maupas du Tour, *Funeral Oration.*

[10] Pérez-Flores, 'De l'Équipe missionnaire'; Román, *Vincent de Paul, passim.*

[11] Dodin, *De Paul and Charity*, 41. For further examples of Dodin's work, see especially his *L'Esprit Vincentien* and *François de Sales.*

confraternal body whose members lived in community.[12] Since Dinan's main focus was the work that the Daughters pursued during their early growth, however, she did not pursue de Paul's relations with the group in any depth beyond this issue. In turn, Pierre Blet has queried the conventional assumption that de Paul was directly responsible for numerous episcopal appointments in the 1640s and 1650s, reminding readers of the multiple influences that could be brought to bear on the crown's decision-making process. Yet he did not consider the possibility that de Paul might have exercised sway over appointments to other types of royal ecclesiastical benefices, or indeed to presentations in the gift of other patrons, such as members of the French nobility.[13] Both he and Dinan, moreover, analyse distinct areas of de Paul's activity in isolation; while the cumulative impact of their contributions is therefore important in assessing de Paul's contribution to Lazarist history and church discipline, it is still piecemeal.

Both of these studies also engage to some extent with a scholarly trend that should be a priority in assessing any aspect of de Paul's activity, that is, the involvement of multiple constituencies in shaping religious change in the church. Historians of France have long been amongst those who urge that religious change in the wake of the Council of Trent (1545–7, 1551–2, 1562–3) should be examined from an angle that is greater than that of the institutional and clerical. One of the major fruits of this approach has been a growing body of research into the rich diversity of religious experience amongst those commonly categorized as *dévots*. These most active of French Catholics in the seventeenth century included lay members of both sexes, as well as consecrated women and clergy of many stripes, united mainly by their common desire to shape society according to Catholic precepts of devotion and morality. However, those who originally promoted the notion that the French church benefited from a religious renaissance justified their opinions mainly on the basis of the extraordinary contributions to spirituality and theology made by a selection of privileged *dévot* individuals such as Bérulle and the Capuchin monk Benet of Canfield, author of the *Rule of Perfection* (first published in 1609 but available in manuscript from at least 1592).[14] Unfortunately, this led them to define reform so narrowly that it became for the most part a rebirth that seemed confined to a cohort of spiritual sophisticates, gifted ecstatics, and mystics during the 1590s and early 1600s. Though he was rarely considered a primary figure of influence or import, de Paul was often lumped in with these as a disciple of the teaching on priestly spirituality that Bérulle disseminated orally and in writing.

More positively, these studies have emphasized the fact that the early manifestations of religious creativity and change became visible first outside the official hierarchical leadership of the French church, and pointed to the significance of

[12] See particularly Dinan, *Women and Poor Relief*, 42–53. See also Brejon de Lavergnée, *Histoire*, 205–7, which revisits this issue in summary fashion and within the context of the Daughters' growth over the seventeenth and eighteenth centuries.

[13] Blet, 'Vincent de Paul'; Darricau, 'L'Evêque'; but especially my *Fathers, Pastors and Kings*, 67–9.

[14] Cognet, *Spiritualité française*; Dagens, *Bérulle*; Optat de Veghel, *Canfield*. For a slightly later example, see Cochois, *Bérulle*.

informal circles of devotion and spiritual exchange in giving rise to them. Since then, the work of Benedict and Diefendorf, amongst others, has confirmed that although the protracted crisis of the civil wars delayed the evolution of the reform movement in France, the roots of religious revival lay deeply in the trauma endured during the years of the militantly anti-Protestant Catholic League in the 1580s, and were at least partially a response to it. Classical expressions of League piety—ascetic penitential practices, penitential processions, confraternities, and eucharistic adoration—were early expressions of the Catholic Reformation that matured in the seventeenth century.[15] Indeed, Denis Richet has proclaimed that the League, though politically vanquished, emerged victorious in the seventeenth century, as its social asceticism, advocacy of the Tridentine decrees, and emphasis on eucharistic devotion were transformed into a mass of vocations, organized missions to the faithful, and moral campaigns to purify the streets.[16] From this it can be gathered that anti-Protestantism was a foundational component of the reform movement as a whole, but also that initiatives to restore the Catholic religion to its pre-eminence often arose and functioned without institutional support, at least initially. Furthermore, it has become apparent that the shaping of Catholic beliefs, practices, and structures for a new age also featured substantial lay agency from an early stage, and that official reforms by members of the episcopate only took hold much later.[17]

The contribution that lay people made to the creation and implementation of ambitions for religious and moral discipline has therefore become a critical question for the history of reform within France, as it has for other regions. One effect of this has been that traditional works concentrating on bishops and dioceses are not as common in the literature of reform as they once were. Instead, scholars have attempted to marry study of such members of the clerical hierarchy and the 'ordinary religion of the people' within a diocesan perspective, so that they are viewed in relation to each other rather than in isolation.[18] Others have tackled the question of lay influence in the decades after the civil wars from entirely new perspectives. Notably, studies of Catholic reform outside France indicate that the features of religious activities were often the results of active alliances between those outside the upper echelons of the church hierarchy. In his sweeping study of Catholic revivalism, *The Europe of the Devout*, which incorporated eastern France as well as further afield in the Low Countries, Germany, and Italy, Louis Châtellier has identified particular social types, in this case, urban and aristocratic lay elites, who banded together into devotional Marian sodalities with the encouragement of members of the Society of Jesus during the period of Catholic

[15] Benedict, 'Catholic Response'; Cassan, 'Laïcs, ligue et réforme'; Diefendorf, *Penitence*, chs 1 and 2. See also Tingle, 'Origins of Counter-Reform Piety'.

[16] Much of Richet's work remains untranslated. A key article, 'Sociocultural Aspects', is printed in translation in Forster and Ranum (eds), *Ritual, Religion and the Sacred*. For a larger selection of his writings, see Richet, *De la réforme*.

[17] Hayden and Greenshields, *Six Hundred Years*, 103–46.

[18] Hoffmann, *Church and Community*, Luria, *Territories of Grace*; Peyrous, *Réforme catholique*; Sauzet, *Contre-réforme et réforme*.

Reformation.[19] The Netherlands, like France, experienced several decades of political upheaval and fragmentation in the fallout from the Protestant Reformation, only for the southern provinces to emerge by the early seventeenth century as a 'bulwark of the Counter-reformation'. Judith Pollmann has found that the dynamic partnerships formed between religious clerics and laity belonging to social groups 'of the middle', mainly meaning returning exiles and those who occupied posts in local government, were absolutely essential to this process. She has concluded that these invested so heavily in education and religious infrastructure and mobilized so enthusiastically in a variety of devotional sodalities that they succeeded in generating a religious culture and identity distinct from their northern neighbours.[20]

For France, Alain Tallon has subjected the elusive association known as the Company of the Holy Sacrament, founded in Paris in 1627, and of which de Paul was a member from around 1635, to searching scrutiny, uncovering the manner in which its largely lay membership dominated the decision-making that saw it mount measures attacking the vices of sin and ignorance, such as duelling, drunkenness, and prostitution. His research highlights the fact that those associated with religious change in this period frequently expressed their zeal collectively, but he also demonstrates that the Company's members were remarkably independent of episcopal oversight in doing so.[21] This was partly because a sufficient number enjoyed the kind of private wealth and political offices that made it possible to organize their ventures to improve society without the support or approval of bishops. Equally importantly, the social composition of the members that Tallon has identified is very revealing, for they tended to represent the upper reaches of French society. Those who founded the Company were a duke, a future prelate, and a Capuchin friar, but it included many representatives of the *robe* nobility within its ranks.[22]

This finding is supported to some degree by the work of Barbara Diefendorf on female religious activism from the League period through to the height of reforming zeal in Paris. She has singled out a category of female social 'elite' who took the initiative in shaping religious practices after the wars, leaving the church's hierarchy uncertain of the wisdom of permitting even women of wealth and social rank to dictate the terms under which female religious life should be organized.[23] This elite included some women whose families were part of the old nobility, but

[19] Châtellier, *Europe of the Devout*.

[20] Pollmann, *Catholic Identity*, 158. See also the excellent works of Marc Forster on south-west Germany in which he has argued that local communities played a dynamic part in shaping Catholic identity, and that religious beliefs and practices were largely the products of popular tastes and demands rather than the prescriptions of higher church or state authorities: *Counter-Reformation*; *Catholic Revival*.

[21] French scholarship has also borrowed heavily from the innovative research on confraternities carried out for other regions, especially Venice and Florence. Particularly influential works include Black, *Italian Confraternities*; Flynn, *Sacred Charity*; Terpstra, *Lay Confraternities*.

[22] Tallon, *Compagnie*, *passim*.

[23] Diefendorf, *Penitence*, *passim*. See also her '"Give us back our children"', and for a more traditional approach, Rapley, *Dévotes*.

also incorporated the wives and daughters of men who had acquired noble status by serving as presidents of sovereign courts in the capital or in other senior royal offices that conveyed the privileges of nobility, and a significant number closely related to councillors in the courts or officers in noble households. Thus, while much of Pollmann's work concentrated on male agency in the shaping of religious culture in the southern Netherlands, Diefendorf's investigation has uncovered a high level of female involvement in this process within Paris. She has offered a further welcome contribution to knowledge of the activities of *dévotes* by mapping the forty-eight new religious foundations that they funded, joined, and visited between 1604 and 1650, and has provided some insights into the main figures and relationships that underpinned these ventures.

Of further relevance to this study is the interaction of these kind of individuals and groups with the crown. Inspired by devotion, but not limited to participating in the liturgical elements of such, some *dévots* were highly and explicitly political, heavily involved, for instance, in the efforts to dislodge Cardinal Richelieu and redirect crown policy regarding the Habsburgs and the Huguenots in the 1620s (culminating in the failed coup led by the queen mother in November 1630).[24] But they did not all share a common political perspective and many were not overtly political at all. Even so, this did not mean that they were isolated from political affairs, or that they had no political significance whatsoever. A cluster of studies by Armstrong and Nelson, amongst others, has affirmed that the Bourbon crown took a major role in the design of religious infrastructure for a new age in the seventeenth century. Motivated by piety and political sense, Henri IV, Marie de Medici, and their successors sought to enhance the links between the monarchy and the church by channelling reform initiatives that had originally emerged independently of them. Such tactics led them to lavish their favours on new religious foundations. Further potential for royal impact on the structures and discipline of the church lay in the power that the crown could wield over church goods and offices. Joseph Bergin has written extensively on the crown's efforts to exercise its right to episcopal patronage over the seventeenth century in publications that reveal the close connection between the establishment of the Bourbon monarchy's authority and the revival of the Catholic church.[25] Within the workings of this structural relationship, even those *dévots* who steered clear of direct political roles and engagement might recognize the benefits to be accrued by engaging with the negotiations that led to the filling of church posts and the organization of ecclesiastical goods under royal control.

Amongst these, Bergin counts Vincent de Paul, who appears fitfully in his analysis of the 1640s, when the crown established a Council of Ecclesiastical Affairs to manage its benefices. However, this does not reveal a great deal about de Paul's activities therein, for he was not the main focus of Bergin's attention. More positively, his study offers a vital critical perspective on the workings of the Bourbon monarchical state and the growing complexity of the administrative

[24] Maillet-Rao, *Pensée politique*, esp. part III. [25] Bergin, *French Episcopate*.

machinery that characterized it. Many other publications have thrown light on specific aspects of the 'administrative state', in which political and social integration were primary goals. These have often acknowledged that the crown was obliged to cooperate with traditional social elites in striving to achieve these goals, particularly when it did not possess the ability to achieve them without their willingness to step in to assist.[26] Tim McHugh has noted this effectively in his work on the establishment of the Parisian general hospital in the late 1650s, in which de Paul and other *dévots* had an interest. He has demonstrated that the crown did not wish to maintain this institutional project independently, and could not have done so even if it had; instead, it formally instituted the venture through royal decrees that amalgamated existing institutes of public charity, and depended on the willingness of a configuration of devout and wealthy subjects to take charge of its organization and direction thereafter, in the interests of public piety and order.[27] This suggests, therefore, that it is particularly enlightening to seek such co-dependencies in affairs of religion, or at least in those which had a religious dimension. Furthermore, it points to another aspect of relations between *dévots*, as yet underexplored in the French context; that is, the manner in which connections between parties could function through use of the crown's fiscal structures, and the appropriation of its financial resources and practices.[28]

III

The trends in the scholarship of French Catholic reform described above might appear to render a study of an individual cleric not merely unfashionable but downright archaic. It is certainly true that they have led to a decline in the production of conventional biographies, and research on individuals now habitually focuses on a specific element of their thought or activity, Stéphane-Marie Morgain's works on Bérulle's political theology and his quarrels with the Carmelites (for whom he acted as perpetual visitor from 1614, having been instrumental in establishing them in France some years earlier) being worthy exemplars.[29] However, contrary to what might be supposed, these trends provide more reason

26 In his study of the Burgundian system of justice, for instance, James Farr has used the evidence of trials for sexual transgression to characterize ideology within the judiciary as an expression over time of the crown's desire for social control. For Farr, these cases reveal a judiciary that was sharply influenced by the Counter-Reformation in the seventeenth century, and therefore increasingly loyal to an ideology of hierarchy and patriarchy: Farr, *Authority*, *passim*. See also Collins, *State*; Kettering, *Patrons, Brokers and Clients*.

27 McHugh, *Hospital Politics*, 83–109.

28 Most notably, various kinds of *rentes*, which might be the annual returns or annuities on private capital invested in government securities over set periods of time, or the investments or loans themselves.

29 Morgain, *Bérulle et les Carmélites*; Morgain, *Théologie politique*. See also Ferrari, *Figures de la contemplation*. For a further study of Oratorian relations with the crown, see Williams, *French Oratorians*. Benoist Pierre's biography of *Père* Joseph takes a broader perspective on its subject's life, but its principal aim is to capture the formation of the apostolate of a militant and politicized *dévot*: Pierre, *Père Joseph*.

than ever to focus attention on an individual such as de Paul. Just as excessive attention to a few key figures of reform easily produces a distorted picture of both their own contributions and the church that they were seeking to improve, so too their neglect underplays what an individual could achieve in specific circumstances and in collaboration with other people and groups. If it is assumed, and there is good reason for doing so, that an individual could not transform a religious system on their own, then the importance of both internal and external influences on the articulation and achievement of their goals is impossible to ignore. It is a fundamental contention of this book that de Paul's rise and contribution to reform can only be explained when assessed within the unique conjuncture of circumstances that pertained in France at this time. That researchers now highlight the vibrancy and active pursuit of reform initiatives by a variety of *dévots* within French society should not lead us to downplay de Paul, but to situate and assess him anew within the workings of this dynamic environment.

Overall, the early modern era saw deeply significant transformations in the role and understanding of Catholic institutions and practices.[30] In establishing an association of clerics whose pastoral work had three major and interrelated strands of responsibility, de Paul witnessed to and helped to shape changes in the organization and pastorate of the French church. Moreover, as the founding superior general of this association, he worked to develop it and to fulfil his own vocational call to be a missionary within it at the same time for many years. A further intriguing characteristic of these efforts is, however, the extraordinary degree of engagement with individuals and groups that it involved. Historians now recognize the importance of collaborative networking in the pursuit of reform in the French church, but few studies methodically chart its functional significance for individuals and groups in the manner of this book. Over more than four decades, de Paul's activities present an unparalleled insight into the combination of ideas, resources, and people that determined the construction and nature of the Lazarist enterprise, and the achievements that he could claim for it. Clerical and lay, male and female, wealthy and poor—de Paul worked with, through, for, and even despite others in pursuing his goals.

The central research questions of this book therefore concern de Paul's efforts to create, characterize, and articulate a distinctive and influential vision for missionary life and work, both for himself and for the Lazarist Congregation, in the French church during this era. Together, its five parts offer an integrated analysis of the sources and resources on which he based this interpretation, the organizing principles that he used to direct its practice, and the strategies that he adopted in order to perpetuate and protect it. It should be noted from the outset, therefore, that the term 'mission' has more than one meaning when it is used in relation to the Lazarists in this book. This is because de Paul used the term to refer to the formally organized and contained 'missions' that the Lazarists carried out in rural parishes, but he also understood it to denote a more traditional apostolic sense that he and

[30] O'Malley, *Trent*, 67.

his fellow Lazarists were 'sent out' or called by God to propagate the Christian faith in specific ways. Two of the titles by which the missionaries were known to contemporaries, therefore, the 'Congregation of the Mission' and the 'Priests of the Mission', evoked both of these interpretations. Neither alluded, however, to a further usage of the term mission then coming into vogue in the Catholic church, which described a formal collection of missionaries in a designated political unit, such as the Jesuit *missio hollandica*.[31]

It is also important to note that the remit of the book is by and large confined to the French hexagon (that is, French territory in Europe), and does not stretch to the few, small, or sporadic forays that de Paul authorized a tiny number of his men to take elsewhere.[32] This is not only for pragmatic reasons, but is justified principally by the fact that the bulk of the development that the Lazarists enjoyed during de Paul's time as superior general was confined to metropolitan France itself, and it was to this that he devoted most of his energy throughout his tenure. Furthermore, although the book is chronologically sensitive, its structure is largely thematically determined. Analysis progresses therefore through the origins, foundation, and early expansion of the Lazarist mission from the 1620s onwards to de Paul's efforts to consolidate his achievements and to protect the Lazarists' position for the future in the 1640s and 1650s. Chapters 1–4 adhere more tightly to a chronological narrative, establishing the basis on which de Paul secured the foundation of the Lazarists in 1625 and their formal approval by Pope Urban VIII in 1633. The rest track the evolution of the three constituent parts of the Lazarists' work, which formed the principal areas of de Paul's interest and activity in the long term: formally organized missions to the rural poor, clerical formation, and the promotion of confraternal welfare.

Of crucial foundational importance to these was de Paul's early immersion in the *dévot* environment, and his initial efforts to apply and adapt the pastoral teachings and practices that could be found there. Part I of the book provides an outline of the circumstances of de Paul's arrival in Paris in 1608. It calculates the debt that his emerging sense of vocation as a missionary owed to the patronage and pastoral experience that he enjoyed over the next decade, while working mainly for his patron employers, the Gondi family, and as *curé* of two parishes (Clichy and Châtillon-lès-Dombes). In the years between 1608 and 1617, de Paul found the perfect testing ground in rural areas to pick out his preferred tools of ministry (sacramental observance, catechesis, and confraternal formation), to advance his pastoral skills, and to settle on a template for the ideal reformed parish.

De Paul's next step was to translate his personal vocational imperative into an institute or organization of missionaries who were dedicated to evangelizing the rural poor (their mission) through the completion of formal missions in their parishes. Part II orientates analysis around de Paul's actions in bringing into being three essential constituents that would secure the position of the 'Priests of

[31] Bossy, 'Catholicity'; Clossey, *Salvation and Globalization*, 15.

[32] To Italy, Poland, Ireland, Scotland, North Africa, and Saint-Laurent (modern day Madagascar). These await further research, but the starting points are relevant chapters in Coste, *Saint*, ii, chs 24–7, 39.

the Mission', at the centre of an enterprise of reform: endowment, structure, and ethos. In illustrating that de Paul was deliberately pushing the boundaries of conventional clerical life in enacting his vision, Chapter 4 offers critical insights into the competitive nature of clerical ministry and the governmental priorities of church authorities in these years. Chapter 5 then investigates the ethos that de Paul devised to distinguish the 'Priests of the Mission' from other clerical groupings. At the time that he established the community, others like Adrien Bourdoise and Bérulle were doing likewise in Paris, and existing orders such as the Capuchins and Jesuits were beginning to expand their numbers and pastoral operations in France. Groups like these possessed ideological frameworks composed of regulations, values, and works which they developed to form and protect their identities.[33] For the Lazarists, de Paul drew inspiration from a range of spiritual and pastoral sources to construct an ethos, that is, a code of missionary qualities and practices that he believed would enable them to assert their singular character as humble instruments of God's charity.

In Part III, attention turns to the expansion of the original remit of rural missions to a more diverse portfolio of pastoral work from the 1630s. Seminaries are amongst the most important products of the Catholic Reformation in France and elsewhere during the Tridentine period, and de Paul was one of the earliest and most successful innovators in this domain in France. His decision to permit the Lazarists to assume responsibility for ordinand retreats and seminaries is of acute importance in exploring his ability to expand their work so that it tackled reform on a second front. However, the chapters also investigate the ways in which he dealt with other key challenges in building up the specialism of clerical formation: the devising of a robust institutional model for clerical training at the Lazarist motherhouse in Paris, and the foundation and funding of houses to advance its work in the provinces. For the second of these, they train a critical eye on the origins, features, and fruits of the relations that de Paul cultivated with founders and donors to expand the Lazarist infrastructure. Barbara Diefendorf has exposed the intense pressure that even the most devout benefactors in Paris could exert on the structure and operation of the female convents that they endowed or supported,[34] and the negotiations that de Paul was obliged to entertain in order to develop the Lazarists' work reveal that he was subjected to similar pressures, occasionally with extraordinary implications for its future.

[33] The Capuchins established 285 foundations in France between 1589 and 1643, 229 of them before 1625, while the number of Jesuit foundations in France in 1610 stood at 45, with 1,379 fathers attached to them: Fouqueray, *Histoire de la compagnie de Jésus*, iii, 151–2; Le Bras, *Études*, i, 203; Mauzaize, *Capucins*, vol. v; Mauzaize, *Le Rôle et l'action*, vol. i; Wittberg, *Rise and Fall*, 197.

[34] Diefendorf, '"Give us back our children"'. For similar evidence from outside France, see especially Mary Laven's lively study of female religious in early modern Venice, where patriarchal efforts to reform conventual life so that it reflected Tridentine ideals were often thwarted by the convents' deep embedding in the social and political soil of the republic. Efforts to render the walls less porous by the enforcement of enclosure, for instance, found little popularity among the nuns, their families, or their friends, for whom the convents acted less as sites of exclusion and detachment than as zones of sociability: Laven, *Virgins*.

This theme also features in Part IV of the book, which studies the collaborative nature of de Paul's activity as a Lazarist missionary from other perspectives. Chapter 9 examines the long-term impact of his realization that confraternities offered a means to organize and promote female religious expression. Though the promotion of confraternal charity duly became the final constituent of the Lazarist pastorate, scholarship on this aspect of de Paul's work has concentrated almost entirely on one particular confraternal grouping, the Daughters of Charity. Little attention has been paid to the wider confraternal membership as a whole, and in particular to the significant personal opportunities that these vehicles of pastoral care offered to de Paul. Most recently, in examining the works and goals of female elite piety in these years, Diefendorf has argued persuasively for a shift from the acts of heroic asceticism associated with League piety towards a more active engagement with works of charity in the 1630s. Her discussion of this change is designed 'to bring these women out of Monsieur Vincent's long shadow', or, in other words, to counter what might be called the 'Coste narrative'.[35] Unfortunately, although meritorious for its exposure of female charity, it has the undesirable effect of erasing de Paul from events almost entirely. Chapter 9 of this book turns a spotlight back onto de Paul by explaining how, over time, the confraternities became the principal means through which he engaged with lay women. Indeed, it affirms that for a small inner circle of consoeurs (members of the confraternity at the *Hôtel-Dieu* hospital), the works of charity gave rise to an extremely unusual, privileged, and productive affinity with de Paul that led them to make common cause with him in all three spheres of the Lazarist enterprise. Chapter 10 then takes analysis further to assess the ways in which de Paul carried his preference for communal performance of Christian acts of piety and morality into associations that he did not found, promote, or run himself, so that he acted uniquely as a point of connection between the Lazarists, the Ladies, and the influential Company of the Holy Sacrament.

In providing a map of the relationships that de Paul cultivated to develop the Lazarist institute, and to realize his own call to missionary work through it, Parts III and IV portray a highly interconnected individual who was, by the 1640s, poised to consolidate his position within the reform movement. Part V scrutinizes the extent to which de Paul realized two aspects of this potential. Thanks to royal patronage, he was elevated to the new royal Council of Ecclesiastical Affairs in 1643, while the Richelieu family handed him direct rights over appointments to the benefices of two major abbeys and a priory during the 1640s and 1650s. Chapter 11 proves that both opened up new avenues to answer his desire to populate the church with devout clergy; it also confirms that the horse-trade of ecclesiastical appointments at court in particular forced major tests on him. In acceding to the Council, de Paul was a beneficiary of the Bourbon state's ability to function as 'an engine of social advancement' and 'the dispenser of social status', but did his elevation assist him in other ways?[36] His admirers have usually

[35] Diefendorf, *Penitence*, 26. [36] Bercé, *Absolutism*, 45.

assumed that his supreme humility enabled him to achieve all his wishes in this domain, but a detailed reading of the evidence unearths a more complex dynamic between virtue and practicality in de Paul's use of networks and intelligence to achieve his goals.

Chapter 12 discloses that networks and intelligence also played key parts in de Paul's efforts to quash the Jansenist movement. From the early 1640s, as Anthony Wright has contended, the debate that ensued over its ideas irreparably fractured the basic unity of the reform movement.[37] Luigi Mezzadri has detected the theological distinctions that distanced de Paul from adherents to the Jansenist cause, but Chapter 12 casts its net more broadly to establish that de Paul's attitude and actions should be assessed in terms of ethos, reputation, and legacy.[38] It explains how de Paul fought to reassert control over his own reputation and the missionary ethos of the Lazarists against Jansenist attacks, in a bid to ensure that the Congregation retained sufficient legitimacy in the church to survive its founder's death. The new division amongst *dévots* complicated his ability to do so, because it was replicated in the collaborative network that he had established through missions and clerical formation. It therefore became essential that de Paul adapt accordingly, by forming new, dispute-specific, alliances on the strength of shared opposition to Jansenism.

IV

The materials available for the tracing of de Paul's efforts to implement his vision of mission are diverse and plentiful. The primary resources are the gargantuan archive composed of his surviving letters, sermons, memoirs, and notes for the conference talks that he regularly delivered to his associates in the Congregation, and less regularly to the women of the confraternities in Paris. They also include many precatory and regulatory documents, such as the 1625 contract of foundation and the 1633 papal bull of approval, which provide the kind of keystone evidence necessary to track the development of de Paul's understanding of the Lazarist mission, and his efforts to describe and regulate it. De Paul's letters, meanwhile, are an unparalleled resource for the thought and activities of a *dévot* in seventeenth-century France. Sustained and methodical study of their contents as well as the pattern of his communications with a huge range of correspondents across France offer a wealth of information and insights about his ideas, interests, and activities, and the manner in which he steadily built the Lazarist infrastructure of works and houses from the 1620s.

Although these letters are gratifyingly substantial in number, it is still necessary to take account of the fact that only a fraction of those originally composed have survived. Relatively few of the letters that de Paul wrote before 1625 are extant, but successive decades have left a far more abundant legacy, partly because he wrote many more as he began to expand the range of the Lazarist works from missions to

[37] Wright, *Divisions*, 180–2. [38] Mezzadri, *Fra giansenisti*.

seminaries, and to set up Lazarist houses in the provinces. Within these sets too, of course, some years offer a greater number of missives and other writings than others, and it follows that it is easier to study the chain of some events, and to identify the characteristics and fruits of certain relationships, than it is for others. It must, of course, be recognized that the profusion of sources is not necessarily a measure of their real significance. For example, de Paul meticulously maintained correspondence in the later 1620s with the head of the Pluyette family, which held the right to student scholarships at the first residence of the Lazarists, the former college of Bons-Enfants.[39] However, while this may shed light on one of the financial burdens that the new association assumed when de Paul accepted the college, it is of negligible significance when compared to the acute issues that determined the structure and pace of its early growth, such as the financial arrangements for the enormous Gondi endowment and the fulfilment of the missions that it specified, or the devising of a strategy to seek papal approbation of the new community.

Furthermore, this book deals with some specific areas of de Paul's activity that are rarely or ever mentioned in his surviving letters, either because the letters which did contain such references are now lost or because he did not wish to put his views in writing. A further complication with the uncovering and piecing together of evidence is the fact that de Paul often did not simply wield a pen to seek information, express his views, or exert influence, but relied on oral communication to make his mark. This is certainly the case in regard to his time on the Council of Ecclesiastical Affairs, when he sometimes used private approaches and covert conversations to pursue his objectives. To compensate for these kinds of limits, the findings of this study also rely on close analysis of a broad spectrum of sources. Amongst the most important of these is the *vie* of de Paul published by a long-time associate, the bishop of Rodez, Louis Abelly, four years after his death.[40] Sensitivity to Abelly's hagiographical intentions is essential in judging the contents of his text, however, for it was sponsored by the Lazarists, and was intended to be the first step in seeking de Paul's canonization. Indeed, Abelly is a prime source of some of the most pervasive myths perpetuated about de Paul. Readers of this book will find that those tales which impinge on the effective analysis of his thought and activities are confronted at appropriate points within its chapters.

Finally, in a work that privileges the functions that collaborative relations and networking assumed in achieving religious goals, the benefits of harvesting from the many relational sources preserved in a cross-section of ecclesiastical and state archives cannot be understated. Traditional studies of de Paul have tended to restrict their sources to internal documents held in Vincentian archives, but the evidence of such documents as the letters, memoirs, decrees, contracts, and minutes used in this study helps to piece together the components and evolution of de Paul's mission work, as well as to rethink its relationship to the wider currents of reform and the concerns of the royal regime. They are instrumental in plugging gaps in de

[39] For evidence of this correspondence, see *CCD*, 1.

[40] Abelly, *Vie*, i–iii.

Paul's own testimony, and in offering the means to counterbalance the partiality of Abelly's perspective on events. Most importantly, the information and opinions aired by individuals such as Cardinal Mazarin, royal councillors, *parlementaires*, rival clergy, and other contemporaries on de Paul and the Lazarists are not presented through the prism of de Paul's words. They, therefore, provide alternative means from which to examine his ideas, his actions, and his impact over the course of decades, and are, whether positive or negative in hue, indispensable to the task of positioning him anew within the history of Catholic reform in France.

PART I

A WEALTH OF RESOURCES

1
A Foothold in Paris

I

In the 1650s, the headquarters of the Congregation of the Mission at Saint-Lazare, Paris, was a prominent feature of the French ecclesiastical landscape. A bustling centre of Catholic piety, it accommodated a large resident community of priests, brothers, and seminarians, while also attracting a regular stream of visitors to its main entrance on the rue du faubourg Saint-Denis. Many hoped to encounter the elderly man whose name had become synonymous with Saint-Lazare, for he had resided there for nearly three decades, throughout which he had managed the ever growing portfolio of works in which the Congregation's members engaged. The range and complexity involved in supervising these was belied by the modest quarters that Vincent de Paul enjoyed at the motherhouse, where he habitually used just two rooms to work and rest. Dressed for function rather than comfort, his bedchamber was unheated and uncurtained, and contained only a wooden table, two straw-bottomed chairs, and a bedstead with a rough straw mattress. The room in which he received visitors was just as sparsely decorated.[1] Both, however, were the nerve centres of Lazarist government, and the locations from which de Paul took stock of past events and issued advice and directives, while keeping his primary focus on the future of the Congregation.

The origins of the Lazarist enterprise were, however, far less auspicious than its distinguished status in the 1650s might imply. The operation for which the motherhouse was the epicentre was the culmination of a lifetime's work by de Paul, who had first arrived in Paris some fifty years earlier, in 1608. Thereafter he spent the majority of his life in the city, venturing from it only on short trips or to minister in parishes for a few months. Over time, Paris was to become a generous source for many of the resources on which de Paul built the Lazarists, and he was to earn garlands for his contribution to the invigoration of ecclesiastical life within its bounds and beyond. Yet, in 1608, de Paul was a young unknown, no more likely than any other of the countless ecclesiastics drawn to Paris for their livings in the early 1600s to rise from anonymity to fame or even to find the kind of foothold within society that might allow this ascension. The initial attractions of Paris for a young impecunious priest are easy to understand: as the capital city of the monarchical realm and the de facto capital of the French church, it was a place of

[1] Abelly, *Vie*, iii, 273.

potential and opportunity, with a vibrant religious life and complex ecclesiastical infrastructure. Before de Paul entered through its gates, his options were limited, and he hoped that Paris would provide, as he confided in his mother not long afterwards, a clerical livelihood, of the sort that would eventually allow him to enjoy 'an honourable retirement' close to his family.[2] As yet, he was unaware that his proposed interlude in the city would eventually stretch into a lifetime.

The assumption of residence by a young priest was not likely to cause a ripple in a large city already thronged with clergy, however momentous a step it was to the individual who took it. For de Paul, it was a major transition, since he arrived in Paris without having an established patron on whom to rely for favours, and with only limited funds to maintain himself until he could find a source of income. In these regards, he was similar to any young cleric with a decent education but few other means of advancement in a competitive environment. At the same time, however, de Paul was not wholly unprepared for what Paris offered. Although he was of rural origin, he had already spent a great deal of time in urban environments, and had become accustomed to the hustle and bustle of city life. He had spent his childhood in the rural setting of Pouy parish in Dax diocese, south-west France, but, in an era when many did not travel far beyond their home place, he had then moved to the town of Dax before settling in Toulouse. He even managed to fit in a short, though memorable, trip to the Eternal City of Rome during these years.

Before proceeding further, it is worth noting that de Paul's movements before he reached Paris are quite difficult to chart, particularly since it is impossible to verify precisely where he was or what he was doing between 1605 and 1607. In his letter to his mother, he alluded to some 'misfortunes' that he had recently experienced, although it is not clear to what he was referring. Some assume that this was a reference to a notorious 'captivity' period of the years 1605–7, but it may simply refer to de Paul's failure to make much headway in gaining a benefice and income to date. In any case, the veracity of his captivity has been subject to much debate, with the scholarly assessment in recent years leaning towards scepticism about the authenticity of the episode. Indeed, the debate is now arid, in the absence of new and decisive archival discoveries.[3] A far more fruitful line of enquiry, for our purpose, is to focus instead on what we know with greater certainty of de Paul's pre-Parisian activities, with a view to discovering the extent to which he was prepared for his entry to religious and social life in the capital. On what resources could the young priest draw to establish himself after his arrival? And at what level might he expect to operate in the hierarchy of church life?

[2] *CCD*, 1: 15–17, de Paul to his mother, 17 February 1610.

[3] A detailed evaluation of the alleged captivity is to be found in Román, *Vincent de Paul*, 69–83. Román cautiously endorses the story, yet acknowledges that it is not possible to make a definitive judgement, and that de Paul's whereabouts during this missing period ultimately remains a mystery. For a crisply sceptical assessment, with which I am in agreement, see Poole, 'Formative Years'.

II

The third of six siblings in a moderately well-off and socially respected peasant family, de Paul left his birthplace in Pouy between 1593 and 1595 to attend school in Dax.[4] It was quite normal for a reasonably secure peasant family such as the Pauls to educate one son, perhaps with the hope that he would ultimately be ordained to the socially elevated state of priesthood. Thus, in 1596 de Paul took the tonsure and minor orders. Louis Abelly painted these events as evidence of de Paul's desire to 'give himself totally to God as a cleric', but this ascribes a maturity to the decision that was probably not present. Indeed, the steps had no great significance in themselves; they were taken by many young boys, often younger than de Paul, who did not subsequently seek full priestly orders, but were able to seek certain ecclesiastical benefices on the basis of their clerical status.[5] Even so, de Paul now needed to leave Dax if he was to pursue his education further, so he moved to the much larger urban centre of Toulouse to attend a university that had a distinguished record in learning since its foundation in 1229. In the Faculty of Theology, there were seven chairs, three of royal foundation, and four held by members of the Carmelite, Dominican, Augustinian, and Bernardine religious orders.

As a thriving university city and the seat of the local archbishop, Toulouse housed a much larger and more diverse population of 40,000 than the small town of Dax. A significant portion of its inhabitants were clerical, for it was home to a substantial ecclesiastical officialdom, including the archiepiscopal entourage of Cardinal François de Joyeuse, the canons of Saint-Étienne cathedral and Saint-Sernin basilica, university theologians, and Inquisition officials. As the Wars of Religion came to a close, the city saw a dramatic growth in the number of religious communities, as orders such as the Recollects (1601) and the Third Order of the Dominicans (1603) built monasteries supported by the donations of its residents.[6] Furthermore, as early as 1590 when he had convened a provincial synod, Joyeuse had attempted to bring a Tridentine flavour to religious practices in the diocese. In addition to presiding over several diocesan synods, he conducted pastoral visits between 1596–7 and 1602–4, in an effort to re-establish order in parishes that lacked resident *curés* and regular sacramental observance; during nearly forty years of warfare, over 100 churches had been pillaged, damaged,

[4] The family owned and farmed three blocks of lands that covered almost 11,000 m^2 (their house was known as Ranquines), while also renting plots of lands close by in Lachine. De Paul's eldest brother, Jean, farmed the latter until his death (before 1626), while two other brothers, Bernard and Dominique (the latter was also known as Gayon and Menion), lived on the homestead. Biographers usually claim that neither married, but Dominique certainly did, and fathered at least two children with his wife, Jeanne de Quillac. De Paul's sisters married local farmers: AD des Landes, GG1; *CCD*, 13a: 75–7. See also n. 14.

[5] Abelly also recorded an incorrect date for the event (19 September 1596): Abelly, *Vie*, i, 10; *CCD*, 13a: 1–3.

[6] The city authorities agreed to accept Henri IV as lawful monarch in 1596, shortly before de Paul made his way there: Finley-Croswhite, *Henri IV*, 137; Schneider, *Public Life*, 172.

or destroyed.[7] Adding further colour to Toulouse's religious life were the hordes of bestaffed pilgrims who passed through it every June on their way to the shrine of Santiago de Compostela. With the added bonus of a traditionally cosmopolitan student body, this was an ideal location for a young cleric such as de Paul to seek ordination and complete his studies.[8]

Amongst the early biographical details of de Paul's life, it is particularly instructive to note the type of university education that he received, since it offered him a solid grounding in theology. In total, de Paul spent seven years studying theology at the University of Toulouse, and received his bachelor degree in October 1604.[9] Like other students, he ultimately completed an oral interview before a panel of faculty members on his general knowledge of his chosen discipline, as well as a public debate lasting at least three hours on a topic of his choice (*tentativa*). To reach the point of examination, a candidate normally studied for five years, although this could be interrupted or extended, as it was in de Paul's case. At Toulouse, as at other French universities, students were expected to be able to demonstrate competence across the major areas of their discipline, but professors were given free rein to teach what they wished, with no requirement that a topic receive full coverage. In addition, students were required to act quite independently in acquiring their theological expertise outside the lecture hall, and to devote considerable time to study in private. For this reason, it is not essential to determine who de Paul's professors were or in what ways they influenced him intellectually. It is more important to know that his learning was dominated by scholastic theology, with instruction usually given in dogma and casuistry. The Scriptures, citations from which were prominent in de Paul's later writings, were generally given much less emphasis in teaching, and in most universities students were left to read them alone, with the aid of a printed biblical *apparatus*. While de Paul's education in Dax would have provided him with some Latin, and while his lectures were delivered in Latin, his professors at Toulouse did not supply the tools of biblical exegesis to their charges, and although the university had had a reputation in the early sixteenth century for Humanist learning, it was not normal for theology students to receive instruction in Hebrew or other ancient languages of biblical scholarship there.[10]

The formal permission that the university gave to de Paul in 1604 to expound the second book of the *Sentences* of the renowned twelfth-century theologian Peter Lombard was probably a reflection of what he chose to defend in his *tentativa*, as

[7] Baccrabère, 'Pratique religieuse'; Forrestal, *Fathers*, 39.

[8] It is difficult to gauge exact student numbers, and estimates vary dramatically. Numbers declined from a high of at least 4,000 in the early sixteenth century to 1,000 on the eve of the French Revolution: Schneider, *Public Life*, 31.

[9] Abelly, *Vie*, i, 12. In 1624, legal documents also credited de Paul with a licentiate in canon law, but this was probably an honorific title that he attained when appointed principal of the college of Bons-Enfants, a college of the University of Paris, in that year: *CCD*, 13a: 71, 73.

It is possible that de Paul spent a short period of time at the University of Zaragoza during these years, as Abelly and Collet suggested, but the evidence to support the claim is far from incontrovertible: Abelly, *Vie*, i, 10; Collet, *Vie*, i, 9. See Poole, 'Formative Years', and Román, *Vincent de Paul*, 41–64, for summaries of the evidence.

[10] Brockliss, *Higher Education*, 59, 73–4, 190–1, 230–4.

well as a reflection of the fact that the *Sentences* was the principal text used for commentary in the Faculty.[11] This approval is significant because it indicates that de Paul possessed a high standard of competence in particular aspects of scholastic theology, which certainly challenges the often cited view that he was an uneducated peasant. Critically, because the second book of the *Sentences* is a treatise on grace (including creation, the fall, and sin), de Paul was well prepared thirty years later to evaluate the Jansenist debate over grace that almost paralysed the French church.[12] In gaining his degree, de Paul had passed through what was probably the most rigorous course of study and examination that French universities of the period offered, in contrast to courses of study for degrees in law, for example, which were far easier to complete.[13]

De Paul's acquisition of the right to expound the *Sentences* suggests that he may have intended to proceed towards a career in university teaching or even that he had actually spent some time teaching at the university in Toulouse, perhaps assisting an established professor in late 1604 and 1605. This would have been a requirement for those seeking to proceed to the next qualification in theology, the licence. While studying, however, de Paul had added a further string to his bow by gaining pedagogical experience in teaching young boys. A university education did not come cheaply and, after his father's death in 1598, de Paul had funded his studies, as many students did, by part-time tutoring.[14] Then, around 1598, he accepted a similar kind of teaching position in Buzet, a village approximately 15 miles north-east of Toulouse. He appears to have had both the knowledge and aptitude for the post, because, once there, he began to attract students from notable families in the town and its hinterland. In time, de Paul returned to Toulouse, with his students in tow; this permitted him to continue his studies, which appear to have been interrupted while he struggled to recover financially, and presumably emotionally, from his father's death.[15]

During his years of study, de Paul decided to commit himself to ecclesiastical life. He was ordained in September 1600 and, although he was under age (at 20 rather than 24), he was in possession of 'a proper canonical title', meaning that he had a guaranteed means of support.[16] This was the parish of Tilh in Dax diocese, but a rival claimant to the title meant that de Paul was forced to travel to Rome to fight

[11] Bigonneau, 'Études de Saint Vincent de Paul'. The attestations for de Paul's degree in theology and leave to expound the *Sentences* were used by Abelly, but were lost by the time that Collet published his study in 1748. Collet noted that they had been dated 12 October 1604: Abelly, *Vie*, i, 12; Collet, *Vie*, i, 10–11.

[12] See Ch. 13. [13] Brockliss, *Higher Education*, 33–4, 74, 79–81.

[14] While in Dax, de Paul acted as tutor to the children of a local judge called Comet, who was related to his mother through marriage. De Paul's mother, Bertrande de Moras, came from a notable family in Ortheville, south of Dax. One of her brothers, Jean, was an *avocat* in the presidial court in Dax from 1593 to 1614. He was married to Jeanne de Saint-Martin, whose brother Louis, a *counseiller* in the presidial court of Dax and *sénéchal des Landes*, was married to the sister of Monsieur de Comet, Catherine. I am indebted to Bernard Koch for this information, based on his research in AD des Landes, Série H, subsérie E2 (registre 2).

[15] Abelly, *Vie*, i, 12.

[16] *CCD*, 1: 4–8. In contrast, Pierre de Bérulle, although 25 years old, had only received the three minor orders by this time: Morgain, *Théologie politique*, 46.

his cause in 1600 or early 1601, although ultimately unsuccessfully. Regardless of the outcome, de Paul's trip to Rome made a lasting impression on him, perhaps especially because 1600 was a Jubilee Year, the twelfth such in Christian history.[17] Three million pilgrims travelled to Rome to gain indulgences through participation in a variety of virtuous acts, including visits to the basilicas of St Peter, Paul, John Lateran, and Paul-outside-the-walls. De Paul may have mingled with the crowds, and surely took part in the jubilee rituals.[18]

III

De Paul's ordained status, education, and pedagogical experience were useful attributes for a young man in search of a career, but they did not automatically open doors when he reached Paris in 1608. Naturally, his first priority on arrival was to find a means of livelihood, but he was disadvantaged in the competitive world of clerical preferment by his relative lack of ministerial experience, particularly since he had never served in a parish. It is even conceivable that de Paul's impecuniosity at this time might have led those around him to believe an accusation of theft against him, from which he was not exonerated for some years because he refused to defend himself. A succession of authors from Abelly onwards have proved eager to use this tale to portray a man who trusted humbly in God's ability to see through the petty anger, spite, and lies of men to the purity of truth. But it is of dubious provenance, and the three accounts of it are entirely inconsistent.[19] More instructively, it is clear that de Paul possessed sufficient common sense to realize that it would be wise to seek out opportunities where he could associate with those who might provide him with means to earn his ministerial living and to enhance his prospects. As a result, soon after his arrival in Paris, he began to lodge in Saint-Germain, a quarter which held a concentrate of royal palaces and households as well as major religious establishments such as the Abbey of Saint-Germain. His tactic did not yield results for a time, however, and he initially struggled to settle in Parisian society, despite the fact that the city was then, just ten years after the enactment of the Edict of Nantes, undergoing an astonishing resurgence in religious fervour that might have created openings for him.[20] This

[17] *CCD*, 1: 111, de Paul to François du Coudray, 20 July 1631: 'O Monsieur, how fortunate you are to walk on the ground where so many great and holy individuals have trod. This consideration moved me to such an extent when I was in Rome thirty years ago that, although I was burdened with sins, I could not help being moved even to tears.'

[18] Chalumeau, 'Vincent de Paul'.

[19] Most decisively, in his own accounts de Paul emphatically stated that he was not the accused. While it is possible that he said so in order to deflect admiration from himself, there were many other occasions when he recounted a positive moral tale in the first person. When he used the third person to do so, it is usually possible to prove that he was not speaking about himself through reference to other instances when he spoke personally about the subject: *CCD*, 11: 305; Abelly, *Vie*, i, 23; Collet: *Vie*, i, 29.

[20] Abelly maintained that de Paul had travelled to Paris to deliver an important secret message orally to Henri IV, on the request of Cardinal Arnaud d'Ossat, bishop of Bayeux and diplomatic agent of the crown in Rome. There is little more to this than a posthumous effort to demonstrate de Paul's ability to impress influential associates by his trustworthiness and perhaps to forecast his later entrance into

development was characterized rather mockingly by one resident, the diarist Pierre de l'Estoile, as 'the latest novelty', and manifested as a surge in the number of entrants to convents, an influx of new religious orders representing the international flavour of the Catholic Reformation, and a proliferation of collaborative projects amongst devout Catholics to construct churches and convents.[21]

Perhaps the most spectacular manifestation of the developing climate of religious zeal was Henri IV's decision in 1603 to pardon the Society of Jesus and to allow them to return to areas of France from which a number of *parlements*, led by the Gallican *parlement* of Paris, had expelled them in 1594. Although the *parlementaires* continued to associate the Society with the doctrine of tyrannicide and 'foreign' papal loyalties, the pardon paved the way for a series of royal favours that were designed to demonstrate the king's Catholic credentials as well as the Jesuits' loyalty to the new regime, and enabled the order to expand considerably the number of its houses and colleges in the realm over the next fifty years.[22] At Henri's death, they were given his heart to display at the college of La Flèche, founded in 1603 by his gift.[23] The first Bourbon monarch did not lose opportunities to patronize other religious orders for the same end, blatantly, some argue cynically, targeting those that had proved most intransigently resistant, in Paris and other urban centres, to his claim for the throne in the early 1590s. The Capuchins, for instance, received several tokens of his affection after he took them into his formal 'protection and care', for he approved at least five new friaries in 1600.[24] Henri IV also channelled reform tendencies that had originally emerged independently of monarchical action amongst devout laity. The monarchy's quest for revival relied on a mutually dependent relationship with their aspirations for religious renewal and for the return of the Gallican Catholic church to a position of cultural eminence unrivalled by Protestantism.[25] Thus, in 1602, the king issued letters patent for the foundation of a convent of Capuchin nuns at the request of Marie de Luxembourg, duchess of Mercœur and widow of the duke of Mercœur, one of the last League leaders to submit to the new regime, and requested that the first stone of the convent, located in Paris, be laid in the name of his daughter Élisabeth.[26]

Other members of the royal family were equally inclined to support religious institutions and ventures. Amongst them was the king's former wife, Marguerite de Valois, whose household was situated on rue de Seine in Saint-Germain from 1607. While Marguerite was known particularly for her patronage of the arts and for the receptions that she held at her palace, she was also greatly attached to works of piety.[27] In the final years of her life, she established an elaborate routine of devotion

hallowed political circles. Anyway, the cardinal died in 1604, four years before de Paul was supposed to have received his assignment. Abelly may have realized that this was a significant flaw in his story, and he did not mention Ossat in the second edition of his work in 1668: Abelly, *Vie*, i, 20 (1664); Abelly, *Vie*, i, 22 (1668).

21 L'Estoile, *Journal*, i, 207.

22 Martin, *Jesuit Mind*, 43–63.

23 Nelson, *Jesuits and the Monarchy*, 97–9.

24 Mauzaize, *Histoire*, 6–7; Diefendorf, 'Henri IV, the *Dévots*'.

25 Cognet, *Spiritualité française*; Dagens, *Bérulle*; Diefendorf, *Penitence*.

26 Diefendorf, *Penitence*, 118–19, 122.

27 Viennot, *Marguerite de Valois*, 218–21.

and generous benefactions to charitable causes, evoked in a lamentation written on her death in 1615 from the perspective of the throngs of mourning poor that she had assisted.[28] Two decades later, in his *Les Éloges et les vies des reines, princesses, dames illustres en piété*, Hilarion de Coste described her round of religious rituals, which included attending mass three times daily and receiving communion three times weekly. Marguerite visited the chapel of Notre Dame in St Victor's church each Saturday, while on feast days such as Holy Saturday and on her birthday, she went to local hospitals, and had her almoners deliver linens for patients. She also required them to distribute alms to the poor and sick on a regular basis at the entrance to her palace, for she 'employed most of her revenues charitably to the feeding and maintenance [of the poor]'.[29] To cap, Marguerite partook in what was a marked feature of the religious practice of well-born women at this time, the according of financial favours to 'diverse churches and several monasteries'. Beneficiaries included the Jesuits of Agen, for whom she founded a college, and the Augustinian nuns of Saint-Germain, for whom she built a convent, while the Carmelites, Cordeliers, Augustinians, and others all received 'annual liberalities'.[30]

While living in Saint-Germain, de Paul met a number of members of Marguerite's household, and these contacts eventually led him to join them in employment in early 1610, as one of her eleven almoners. He duly took up residence on rue de Seine, opposite her palace.[31] In particular, he may have been indebted to one of the household officers, Charles du Fresne, sieur de Villeneuve, for his good fortune; however, it is possible that he was also recommended by the bishop of Dax, Jean-Jacques du Sault, who had until recently been Marguerite's first almoner, and with whom de Paul was in contact about a title to a benefice around this time.[32] De Paul's modest circumstances demanded that he explore all possible sources for clerical income, and this imperative did not much diminish in urgency after he was appointed almoner. It provided him with only a moderately rewarding annual salary of between 100 and 200 *livres* until he left Marguerite's employment to become parish priest of Clichy just north of Paris in late 1611.[33] However, the post also offered a security of tenure with which de Paul was previously unfamiliar, as well as greater social and ecclesiastical status. It was not a sinecure, and he joined Marguerite's other almoners in carrying out her pious obligations to the city's religious life, distributing alms and visiting hospitals that she patronized. To the

[28] *Complaintes et regrets des pauvres sur le tombeau de la Reine Marguerite*.

[29] Coste, *Éloges*, ii, 308: '. . . ayant employé charitablement la plupart de son revenu à leur nourriture et entretiennement'; Merki, *Reine Margot*, 424–5; Viennot, *Marguerite de Valois*, 223.

[30] Coste, *Éloges* ii, 308.

[31] It remained de Paul's official address until at least 7 December, 1612: *CCD*, 13a: 24. See also Viennot, *Marguerite de Valois*, 215.

[32] Du Sault promulgated the letters of fulmination which enabled de Paul to take possession of a new benefice, the abbey of Saint-Léonard-de-Chaumes in autumn 1610: AD de Charente-Maritime, 3E1203, fos 229r–230v; Jacques, *Cospeau*, 114.

[33] Biographers have generally suggested that de Paul joined the household in 1609, but he was not listed amongst the staff paid for the final quarter of 1609 (unfortunately the only list for the period extant in Marguerite's household accounts), and he did not mention that his circumstances had changed for the better in the letter that he wrote to his mother in February 1610: AN, KK180, fo. 112r; *CCD*, 1: 15, de Paul to his mother, 17 February 1610.

fore amongst these was the new hospital of the Brothers of Charity in the quarter, which had been founded in 1602 by Marie de Medici, and for whom Marguerite bought a new house in 1606.[34] Subsequently, while de Paul was in her employ, she presented the church of St Peter to the Brothers, and laid the foundation for a new hospital building that she agreed to construct in 1613.[35] In enacting Marguerite's wishes, de Paul simultaneously had opportunity to express his own; those who visited the hospital could obtain attractive papal indulgences newly awarded to the order in February 1607 to augment the popularity of devotional charity; Abelly mentioned twice that de Paul went 'meticulously to visit, serve and exhort the poor sick' while almoner; if he did so on Sundays he gained a 100-day indulgence, if on other days he was rewarded by the remission of sixty days of penitence.[36]

IV

All of the evidence suggests that, although he was gainfully employed, de Paul struggled to find financial stability during this period. He remained so keen to do so that he was even doggedly determined to gain the income from a significant benefice that might supplement his ministerial salary. The benefice in question was the ancient Cistercian abbey of Saint-Léonard-de-Chaumes, located in the diocese of Maillezais in western France.[37] Founded in 1036, from 1609 it had been held by the archbishop of Aix, Paul Hurault de l'Hôpital, who was keen to divest himself of the responsibilities attached to it.[38] When he offered it to de Paul, the poorly resourced priest must have relished the prospect of holding a prestigious abbatial benefice. In reality, it turned out to be a can of worms that brought him legal expenditure rather than material return. Even so, he fought for six years to retain its title and accede to its income, before finally relinquishing his claim in

34 The Brothers of Charity was amongst several new religious orders dedicated to the 'active spirituality' characteristic of the Catholic Reformation, and a prime manifestation of *dévot* piety in seventeenth-century France. Originally founded by the Spaniard John of God (1495–1550) in Grenada around 1535 as a confraternity of lay brothers destined to care for the sick, its members took the three solemn vows of poverty, chastity, and obedience, as well as a fourth specially applicable vow of hospitality to the sick poor (which referred to warm receptiveness, rather than hospital premises): Evennett, *Spirit*, *passim*. For a general history of the Brothers, see Monval, *Frères hospitaliers*. On the foundation of the Hospital, see Bib. Maz., Ms 1792, 'Actes relatif à la Congrégation de S. Jean de Dieu . . .', 1–12, 66–73.

35 This eventually opened in 1631. De Paul also acted as an agent for the crown in the transfer of 15,000 *livres* to the hospital in 1611. For further details, see Forrestal, 'Catholic *Dévot*'.

36 Abelly, *Vie*, i, 21, and ii, 208; Bib. Maz., Ms 1792, 'Actes relatif à la Congrégation de S. Jean de Dieu', 61–3.

37 This was founded in 1036 by Othon, duc d'Aquitaine: Combaluzier, 'L'Abbaye de Saint-Léonard-de-Chaumes'.

38 According to Abelly, Henri IV, prompted by Cardinal d'Ossat, offered the abbey to de Paul in reward for his successful execution of his diplomatic mission on his return from Rome in 1608. But the story of the mission has already been shown to be false, so the most active protagonists in the negotiations for the abbey appear to have been Hurault and de Paul himself. Although the crown approved Hurault's donation in June 1610, there is no evidence to suggest that the king had ordered it: Abelly, *Vie*, i, 20; Audiat, *Saintes*, 180–5.

November 1616. His tenacity reflected the fact that the holder of this benefice stood, in theory, to profit from a handsome return per annum; moreover, it was a distinguished title that elevated its holder to the ranks of an elite of ecclesiastics that controlled the French church's properties and institutions through the practice of *in commendam*.

In his pursuit of the abbey, de Paul demonstrated a pragmatic willingness to use the tried and tested mechanism of benefice holding *in absentia* to forge his livelihood. Despite numerous objections to the practice that enabled absentee titleholders to accumulate dioceses and abbeys *in commendam*, such as that most famously made by the abbot of Cîteaux at the Assembly of Clergy in 1579, he was simply following the example set even by the most reform active of French bishops such as François Sourdis of Bordeaux. As Joseph Bergin comments, 'the one thing' that most bishops of this period had in common was their recourse to the 'spoils system' of benefices, and at least 44 per cent of the bishops nominated between 1589 and 1661 already held one or more abbeys or priories *in commendam*.[39] Archbishop Hurault was amongst those who collected multiple benefices. A former Huguenot, he had converted to Catholicism in the early 1590s in the wake of Henri de Navarre's conversion. Sent to Provence as a royal commissioner in 1594–5, he allied with the *parlement* of Aix to force the virulently Leaguer Archbishop Génébrard of Aix into exile in Avignon and Burgundy, and was rewarded for his efforts with the archiepiscopal title itself in 1599.[40] In May 1610, Hurault acquired the abbey of Saint-Léonard from the Huguenot Gabriel Lamet, *seigneur* of Condun and Chausse and *échevin* in La Rochelle, and lost little time in attempting to put it to profitable use. But rather than having previously had a personal connection to de Paul, it appears that Hurault established relations with him on the advice of a merchant in Saint-Germain with whom de Paul was friendly, and to whom Hurault initially agreed to lease the abbey's temporal revenues for 3,600 *livres* per annum.[41] Ultimately, the archbishop transferred the abbey in its entirety to de Paul, and he entered into full possession on 16 October.[42]

Clearly, Hurault was keen to divest himself of the abbey quickly, though he was equally anxious to ensure that he did not lose out in the deal. In the final arrangement, de Paul was obliged to maintain the lease with the merchant, effectively meaning that he could claim the temporal revenue of 3,600 *livres* for himself. From this, he was obliged to pay Hurault an annual pension of 1,200 *livres*, until he could provide him with a benefice and 1,200 *livres* annually, which he was to do by the close of 1613.[43] This would be far less painful than the 3,600 *livres* specified in the first contract, and de Paul might have considered the

[39] *Collection des procès-verbaux des assemblées générales*, i, 127; Bergin, *French Episcopate*, 93–4, 291; Forrestal, *Fathers*, 19–23.

[40] Bergin, *French Episcopate*, 380, 642.

[41] This was Arnault Doziet, who lived on the same street as de Paul: AN, Minutier Central, LXXXIV/52, fos 265r–266r; *CCD*, 13a: 8–11.

[42] The transfer took place on 17 May, and a papal bull of nomination confirmed this on 27 August: AD de Charente Maritime, E 1203, fos 229r–230v.

[43] *CCD*, 13a: 12–16.

reduction a net gain, for in theory it would leave him with the tidy sum of 2,400 *livres* annually. However, Hurault proved adamant that the exchange of the abbey be made on the condition that it was restored to the glory that it had enjoyed before being destroyed by Huguenot forces during the civil wars.[44] De Paul had to ensure that the ruined chapel was rebuilt so that 'divine service may be chanted and celebrated there' by two monks from the Cistercian order of Cîteaux who would reside on the grounds. He was also required to furnish the monks, one of whom was to act as the abbey's prior, with ceremonial 'vestments and pewter chalices . . . silver chalices, a cross and whatever is necessary'.[45]

De Paul must have known that the abbey was in a poor state when he signed the contracts, but he did not have an opportunity to see his prize until October. It cannot have been a gratifying sight, for all that remained of the church was 'a few corners of walls' which did not shelter even one altar. The other monastic buildings, including the cloisters, were reduced to 'hovels' or 'foundations and remnants of walls'. On his return to Paris, it also quickly became evident that the debts that 'bound and burdened' the abbey's titleholder were to inhibit his efforts to profit from his benefice. In the first place, he quickly struggled even to pay the pension due to Hurault, who issued a legal challenge to him for the payment of arrears in May 1611.[46] Worse, de Paul was then faced with 'holders and usurpers of the domain of the abbey', and became ensnared in at least one lawsuit to oust their wrongful possession.[47]

The principal claim to the abbey was made by the new Cistercian prior, André de la Serre, who was appointed in October 1610. Initially, La Serre simply sought, in the presidial court of La Rochelle, 'the sums of *deniers*, wheat and wine, wood, oil, wax and other things', and the conclusion of building work mentioned in his letters of provision. Unfortunately for de Paul, La Serre quickly increased his demands, to one-third of the abbey's temporal revenue, amounting to 1,200 *livres*. If this was paid, de Paul would be left with only 1,200 *livres* income per annum from the benefice. Thus, he was left with no option but to counter-attack: he contended that La Serre had no right to any revenue, because he had been illegitimately appointed by the abbot of the Cistercian abbey of Morimond, one of four abbeys affiliated with Cîteaux, when, in fact, de Paul himself should have chosen the prior, in agreement with the abbot of another affiliate of Cîteaux, the abbey of Pontigny.[48] Unfortunately for de Paul, the court rejected this argument and on 11 November 1611 ordered him to pay La Serre 300 *livres*, in recognition of his right to a portion of the abbey's revenue. De Paul appears to have been so hard-pressed for cash that he had to borrow even this sum.[49] Thereafter, the dispute continued to rumble, as

44 Combaluzier, 'L'Abbaye de Saint-Léonard-de-Chaumes'.

45 *CCD*, 13a: 9–10.

46 Hurault may have been especially zealous in the pursuit of his pension because, just six weeks after he gave Saint-Léonard to de Paul, he presented his income from it by usufruct to the cleric Georges Lenfant, *sieur de la Patrière*: AN, Minutier Central, ET/LXXXIV/52, fo. 336r–v, and ET/LXXXIV/54, fos 234r–236v, 269r.

47 *CCD*, 13a: 42.

48 AD de Charente-Maritime, B 1522, fo. 104r.

49 It cannot be coincidental that, just three weeks after the court's judgement on 11 November, de Paul received a loan for almost exactly this amount (320 *livres*) from the Oratorian Jacques

La Serre continued to seek further remuneration from him. Finally, in October 1616, the beleaguered abbot washed his hands of the affair by resigning Saint-Léonard to François de Lanson, royal chaplain and prior of Saint-Étienne-d'Ars on the Île de Ré, for whom he professed 'deep affection' and friendship, but to whom he still did not mind divesting a troubling benefice.[50]

De Paul's failure to emerge victorious from this contest was a harsh lesson in the risks entailed in attempts to use the church's patrimony to build up personal assets, especially when one did not possess the substantial financial backup needed to defend them against competitors in the benefice market. In later years, he liked to warn the Lazarists against the pursuit of lawsuits and benefices, on the basis that these were inconsistent with their devotion to God and unedifying distractions from their mission. Experience, such as that gained so painfully in his effort to realize the full advantages of Saint-Léonard, would also eventually cause him to conclude that energetic combat alone did not win legal battles, but that providence would choose the successes and failures that he and the Congregation encountered in the performance of God's work. In the early 1610s, however, de Paul could not afford to be so discerning. This was not merely because he required an income to survive. He knew that possession of benefices would improve his standing in the church, and at this stage incorporated this conventional rule of upward mobility into his vision of a successful career. For now, de Paul could not allow failures to discourage him from seeking new gains, since the acquisition of titles and income could repay their holder handsomely as easily as they could ruin him. But as his next placements were to demonstrate, material advancement was not necessarily incompatible with spiritual development.

Gasteaud: ACMP, 'Reconnaissance d'une dette de M. Vincent envers Jacques Gasteaud' (copy of the original reconnaissance, which is in private hands). A partial copy is printed in *CCD*, 13a: 24–5.

[50] *CCD*, 13a: 42–4.

2

Early Patrons and Favours

I

Had de Paul been content, he could have remained a royal almoner for the next few years, hoping over time to be promoted to a more prestigious post, and to accumulate dignities and revenues that would supplement his salary and enhance his standing. In late 1611, however, his life began to move in a new direction, when he started to avail himself of connections that became opportunities not only for material stability but also for the expansion of his rather limited pastoral experience. This meant that the relations that he forged in these years could also become the main determinants of the options that would be available to him further in the future. Key reformers amongst Parisian *dévots* were well positioned to use their influence to populate the church with ecclesiastics with whom they shared spiritual sympathies, and whom they judged, as a result, to be zealous in the promotion of the faith. Once in post, an individual imbued with both spiritual curiosity and pastoral alertness would find these placements to be the perfect testing grounds on which to experiment with new tools of ministry, to advance skills, and to gain the insights into pastoral practice that would shape his future. Between late 1611 and the close of 1617, de Paul acceded to three such positions, which produced this rich and remarkable combination of advantages. But while the conventional narrative concentrates on two famous episodes that took place towards the end of this period—those of the confession, sermon, and mission of Folleville (January 1617), and the foundation of the first confraternity of charity in Châtillon-lès-Dombes (August 1617)—Chapters 2 and 3 take a broader approach to it. This chapter sets out the narrative context for the advantages summarized above, so that Chapter 3 can focus on their analysis. First and foremost, therefore, there is the question of relationships: to whom or what did de Paul owe his advancement in these years? A second duly follows: to what kind of environments and experiences did his positions expose him?

II

From November 1611, de Paul passed close to two years as *curé* of the parish of Clichy, approximately 14 miles north of Paris, before joining the noble household of Philippe-Emmanuel and Françoise-Marguerite de Gondi in September 1613, initially to act as preceptor to the couple's three children, and subsequently as spiritual director to Madame. He then spent about seven months as *curé* of Châtillon, an annexe of the parish of Buénans, just north-east of Lyon, in 1617, before returning to his employment with the Gondi. The first and third of these positions were parochial and rural, while the second also involved substantial time in country parishes on the Gondi estates. This commonality was important, for de Paul had been divorced for some time from the world of peasant households and country life, and his reconnection with them for sustained periods of time caused him to orientate his pastoral interests decisively towards rural areas in the longer term, and to identify the values, techniques, and skills needed in them. In the shorter term, the posts also shared another quality, for de Paul owed their acquisition to an individual who was one of the most prominent and influential figures in *dévot* circles: Pierre de Bérulle, the founder of the French Oratory.

By the time that de Paul met him in early 1610, Bérulle already enjoyed exalted status as a theologian, and his establishment of the Oratory, a congregation of secular priests, in 1611 was greeted with widespread approbation. De Paul and he were of similar age, but their careers to date could hardly have differed more. This was partly because Bérulle had benefited from far greater advantages of birth, which had granted him automatic access to the individuals and groups most actively and creatively engaged in religious revival after the wars. These emerged mainly from the Parisian *robe*, many members of which had formerly been attached to the Catholic League, but had since thrown their energy into intense spiritual discussions, theological study, and the foundation of convents and churches. Already socially privileged, these early *dévots* also formed a type of spiritual elite, particularly since they congregated around particular figures of unusual charisma, the most celebrated of whom was the widowed Barbe Acarie, whose capacity for spiritual insight and ascetic virtue was renowned. Despite her sex, which debarred her from a public role of spiritual leadership, Acarie had commanded respect for her sanctity and deference for her words from those who formed her circle of lay and ecclesiastical admirers since the late 1590s. Pierre de Bérulle was her cousin, which enabled him to visit her on a daily basis for over six years at this time. The mystical and abnegationist spirituality to which he was exposed during this period of formation later proved extremely influential on the development of his own thought.[1]

Acarie's circle also consisted of other prominent ecclesiastics, including the Capuchin Benet of Canfield, the Carthusian Richard Beaucousin, and the Sorbonne professors Jacques Gallemant and André Duval, all of whom were distinguished theologians. But the name of Vincent de Paul is not to be found amongst those associated with Acarie, and he was certainly never admitted to the intimate circle of people who formed her confidants or who cooperated with her in schemes such as that which saw the first Carmelite convent established in France in 1602.[2] That he managed to meet with individuals such as Duval who were in the circle was entirely due to Bérulle who introduced him to them. But de Paul's introduction to Bérulle

[1] Dagens, *Bérulle*, 132. [2] Diefendorf, *Penitence*, 102–5.

himself had been made possible by his almonership, the obligations of which required that he visit the sick at the Hospital of Charity to give alms. Bérulle regularly visited the sick there, and in this activity found sufficient common ground with de Paul to take him under his wing. He went on to act as de Paul's spiritual director for a number of years. Significantly too, Bérulle was able to compensate for something else that de Paul lacked: as the son of a former parliamentary counsellor who had been brought up by members of the distinguished Séguier family, Bérulle possessed the kind of birthright that automatically ensured him access to the finest households.[3] Those with whom he chose to consort could expect to derive secondary benefit from the personal advantages that his birth and his growing reputation for holy intellect bestowed on him.

Indeed, so crucial did de Paul's acquisition of Bérulle's attention prove to be that Louis Abelly judged that it was divinely prescient of later events: he briefly alluded in his *Vie* to a prophecy from Bérulle that de Paul would establish a new community of priests, with God's blessing and with great fruit.[4] Most have accepted his words without questioning the circularity of the argument.[5] For example, in the late seventeenth century *Père* Courtin elaborated on Abelly's opinion in his life of Adrien Bourdoise, who founded the community of priests of Saint-Nicolas-du-Chardonnet in the later 1610s. In this account, Bourdoise was said to have met de Paul through Bérulle in 1611, and the three confidants had confessed their hopes for their own futures and that of the Catholic church in France. Bonding over their passion for renewing the quality of the French clergy, they prophetically laid out plans for foundations that came to fruition in the Oratory, the community of Saint-Nicolas-du-Chardonnet, and the Congregation of the Mission, and thus answered 'the extreme needs' of the time. For de Paul, those 'with most need of . . . Instructions were without doubt the poor people of the country, who . . . live for the most part as brutes without understanding and knowledge of the virtues of health'. The solution

[3] Cochois, *Bérulle*, 4–7.

[4] Abelly claimed that Paul lived for two years with the new Oratorian community, but this was impossible since it did not take shape until early 1611 when the six first members began to live close to the Carmelite monastery on the rue Saint-Jacques, where Bérulle acted as one of three ecclesiastical superiors to the nuns. While de Paul would have visited Bérulle there regularly, he would only have stayed there for short periods, if at all. Abelly was probably correct to suggest, however, that de Paul relished the shelter of this environment to reflect on his own future, even if he did not wish to join the community permanently. In later years, de Paul referred to his personal experience of the habits of the Oratorians, and perhaps borrowed the Lazarists' daily recitation of the Litany of Jesus from early Oratorian practices. He also proved quite closely acquainted with Bérulle's activities in 1611, notably his private negotiation with Jean-Baptiste Romillion regarding the combining of the Oratory with the *Prêtres de la Doctrine Chrétienne*, the circumstances of which were well documented in Bérulle's correspondence, but did not circulate widely at the time: Abelly, *Vie*, i, 24; Dagens (ed.), *Correspondance*, i, 126, Jean-Baptiste Romillion to Pierre de Bérulle, 5 February 1611, and 165; *CCD*, 2: 460, de Paul to Bernard Codoing, 24 August 1643; Dodin, 'Saint Vincent et l'approbation des Litanies'; Habert, *Bérulle*, 330–1; Morgain, *Bérulle et les Carmélites*, 245–50.

[5] In his study of the Oratorians, Charles Williams, for instance, draws uncritically on Paul Klevgard's account of the story. Klevgard probably used Coste for his narrative, since he also includes Courtin's words as evidence, in the form of a florid dialogue between the three men concerned: Coste, *Saint*, i, 70; Klevgard, 'Society and Politics', 120–1; Williams, *French Oratorians*, 77. See also Prunel, *Renaissance Catholique*, 50.

was, he concluded, to establish 'a Congregation of good Workers capable of instructing these poor people . . . by Missions throughout Dioceses'. At once, his director praised this idea as heaven sent, and further encouraged de Paul by claiming that it was likely that God would use him to establish the congregation in question.[6]

The hagiographic seasoning of this tale loses its attraction when it is confronted by the fact that de Paul did little in the next few years to act on his newfound knowledge of his calling. Concurrently, however, his relationship with his director was one that did realize much of the potential that it was possible to glean from it. This materialized first when de Paul became parish priest of Clichy. Bérulle did not grant this benefice directly to him, but acted as an intermediary to enable him to obtain it. This was because it was in the possession of one of the men that Bérulle had attracted to his embryonic Oratorian community, François de Bourgoing, who had ministered in Clichy for a number of years before he joined Bérulle in November 1611. Prior to this, Bourgoing barely knew de Paul, but Bérulle held sufficient influence over him to persuade him to resign in favour of a successor for whom he vouched. Clichy's population of 600 was sufficient to keep the most conscientious of *curés* quite busy, and Bérulle obviously believed that de Paul would repay his trust and expectations. His promotion of his *protégé* was therefore a public endorsement of his spiritual competence and pastoral potential.[7]

De Paul moved into the presbytery in Clichy in early November 1611,[8] and proved to be an industrious successor to Bourgoing, who had left the parish in reasonable shape.[9] As Chapter 3 will demonstrate, the parish left a pronounced impression on de Paul's opinion of rural religiosity, and it became a primary reference point in his pastoral vision. In the short term, however, it provided the opportunity to experience what parochial ministry entailed, from organizing devotional rituals and routines to maintaining church fabric. For instance, the dilapidated church of Saint Sauveur and Médard was the weak spot in the parish's devotional life at this time, so de Paul began a series of refurbishments in order to ensure that it provided an adequate venue for services.[10] These included structural

[6] This account dates from 1698: Bib. Maz. Ms 2453, 'La Vie du venerable serviteur de Dieu Messire Adrien Bourdoise', 101: '. . . une Congrégation de bons Ouvriers capables d'instruire ces pauvres gens . . . par des Missions que l'on feroit de côte & d'autres dans les Diocèses'. See also Batterel, *Mémoires domestiques*, i (written in 1729, and drawing on Courtin's 'Vie').

[7] Bourgoing was elevated eventually to the position of superior general in the Oratory when the second holder of that position, Charles Condren, died in 1641: Cloysault, *Recueil de vies*, ii, 1; Ingold, *Essai*, 21.

[8] Bourgoing ceded the parish with papal approval to de Paul in November, and he took formal possession of the parish church on 2 May 1612: *CCD*, 13a: 22–4; Habert, *Bérulle*, 330–1; Dupuy, *Bérulle*, 93.

[9] De Paul left the parish in the care of a deputy until 1626, while arranging an annual pension of 100 *livres*. Abelly proved notably silent about this fact, but his pointed insistence that de Paul resigned his cure 'purely and simply, without retaining any pension' raises the suspicion that he deliberately concealed the unpalatable truth that de Paul by then held two benefices *in absentia*, complete with pension, while also being a full-time employee in a private household. The Clichy deal was finally abandoned in 1630, when de Paul's deputy paid him 400 *livres*: Abelly, *Vie*, i, 27; *CCD*, 13a: 97.

[10] By the time that Pierre Collet published his *Vie* in 1737, the church in 1612 was not just in need of some repair but 'in ruins'; this was a gross exaggeration, repeated by Coste, designed to celebrate de Paul's remarkable ability to restore it and the parish: Collet, *Vie*, i, 38; Coste, *Saint*, i, 74–5.

repairs well as the purchase of items such as a new baptismal font and church bell.[11] However, this work illuminates more than de Paul's concern for the provision of suitable facilities. It needed cash to succeed, and Abelly recorded that de Paul took advantage of donations from wealthy Catholics for this purpose. The relations he established then opened the way towards later patronage of enterprises in which he became involved.

Most immediately, the local *seigneur* was Alexandre Hennequin (1583–1623), whose position required that he bear some of the responsibility for the church's refurbishment.[12] De Paul's acquaintance with him was to prove especially productive in the long term. After his father, Pierre Hennequin, was assassinated with Henri III in 1589, the young Alexandre had been reared under the guardianship of his maternal grandparents, the du Breuil.[13] He was also put under the tutelage of two other relatives: first, his father's cousin, Nicolas Hennequin de Vincy, *seigneur* of Fey and Villecien, who was successively secretary of finances for Charles IX, Henri III, and the duke of Anjou, as well as *maître d'hôtel du roi* for Henri III, before being appointed to the League's council of state by the duke of Mayenne in 1589 (he was also brother to the strongly Leaguer bishop of Soissons, Jérôme Hennequin);[14] secondly, either Michel or Louis de Marillac, who were related to the Hennequin by virtue of the marriage of their half-sister Marie to Nicolas Hennequin de Vincy's brother Réné in 1572.[15] Subsequently, three of de Paul's earliest and most committed collaborators emerged from this extended family: Antoine Hennequin, *seigneur* of Fey and Vincy, and Isabelle Hennequin du Fey, two of the three children of Nicolas Hennequin de Vincy and his wife Marguerite Le Ferron, and their cousin Louise de Marillac, probably the daughter of Louis de Marillac. While it cannot be confirmed that de Paul met the three while resident in Clichy, this appointment provided the initial point of introduction to their familial milieu, and latterly to them.[16] Furthermore, by 1618 de Paul knew the parish priest of Villecien, Jehan Maurice, sufficiently well to ask that he act as rector for the new confraternity of charity in nearby Joigny, even though it was amply populated with

[11] De Paul used parish assets to pay for some of the refurbishments. For example, in 1623, he rented 16.25 *arpents* of parish land to a local farmer for six years in order to pay the master mason or carpenter working on the church: AN, Minutier Central, ET/XLV/32, pièce 68 (23 February 1623). See also Abelly, *Vie*, i, 26–7, and Lecanu, *Clichy-la-Garenne*, 211.

[12] Hennequin had also inherited the *seigneuries* of Mathaux, Montault, and Clichy.

[13] In total, eight of the Hennequin family were clients of the duke of Mayenne, leader of the League and among the last of Henri de Navarre's opponents to admit defeat in 1595: Leviste, *Château Du Fey*, 4; Kettering, 'Clientage'; Mesnard, *Pascal et les Roannez*, i, 47–8.

[14] Another brother, Aimar Hennequin, was bishop of Rennes (1575) and archbishop of Reims (1594): Holt, 'Patterns of *Clientèle*'.

[15] The genealogical details given in Pujo, *Vincent de Paul*, 273n., mistakenly state that Marie de Marillac married Nicolas Hennequin de Vincy. Earlier marriages connected the Marillac to the Hennequin of Clichy, and explain the acquisition of the *seigneurie* of Clichy by the Hennequin: Anne Alligret, daughter of the *seigneur* of Clichy, Olivier Alligret, married Louis Hennequin, grandfather of Alexandre Hennequin, in 1526, while her sister Marie married Guillaume de Marillac, the father of Michel and Louis de Marillac, in 1568. On the Hennequin–Marillac connection, see Aubert de la Chesnaye-Desbois, *Dictionnaire*, 7, cols 249–55.

[16] For further details of their support for de Paul's works, see Forrestal, 'Catholic *Dévot*'.

clerics who could have assumed this duty.[17] This suggests that de Paul had been to the Hennequin *seigneurie* of Villecien regularly.

III

Bérulle was directly responsible for de Paul's introduction to another prominent family in these years, the Gondi.[18] The Oratorian founder's relations with its members were already extensive and solidly established; notably, for a number of years, he had acted as confessor and spiritual director to Monsieur de Gondi's sister Charlotte-Marguerite de Gondi, marchioness of Maignelay, and his Congregation had benefited handsomely from her largesse.[19] In later years, her support for de Paul's initiatives was to grow, if not to the same dizzy heights, at least to the point where she became one of the staunchest patrons of his work until her death in 1650.[20] But de Paul first met her after her sister-in-law Marguerite agreed, on Bérulle's proposal, that he should assume the position of preceptor to her three sons in September 1613. Then, not long after he settled into the household, he became Marguerite de Gondi's spiritual director, either at Bérulle's suggestion or with his blessing. So, for the third time in two years, Bérulle ushered de Paul towards what was a new role. Indeed, it is possible that Bérulle was actually Madame's first choice, and if this was so, stepping into shoes that might have been filled by a man who was increasingly revered amongst *dévots* was another notable promotion in ecclesiastical and social terms for the young de Paul, as well as a further public endorsement of his spiritual talents by his clerical and noble patrons.[21] Ultimately, he remained formally attached to the Gondi household until 1625, save for a short sojourn in Châtillon. During these years, he spent long periods of time in the family's Parisian *hôtel* on rue des Petits Champs in Saint-Eustache parish (and between June 1623 and June 1624 on rue Pavée-Saint-Sauveur in Saint-Sauveur parish), and on their country estates.[22]

[17] Amongst these were the Capuchins, whom Pierre de Gondi established in the town in 1607: Niclas, 'Gondi-Retz', 260; *CCD*, 13b: 27.

[18] Abelly, *Vie*, i, ch. 7; Coste, *Eloges*. Coste's account of Madame de Gondi's life has been translated and printed: Rybolt and Diefendorf, 'Madame de Gondi'.

[19] In 1610, Maignelay had encouraged her brother, the cardinal archbishop of Paris, to order Bérulle to establish the Oratory, and had then donated 50,000 *livres* for its foundation in 1611. Thereafter, she contributed regularly to specific houses, including 6,000 *livres* to the house in rue Saint-Honoré in 1617, and 32,000 *livres* to the house in the faubourg Saint-Jacques in 1629: BN, Clairambault, Ms 1136, 6–7; *Oraison funebre de haute et puissante dame Charlotte Marguerite De Gondy*, 45; Bauduen, *Vie admirable*, 248.

[20] For further details, see my 'Catholic Dévot', and Appendix 3.

[21] Raymond Chantelauze plausibly maintains that Bérulle, having far too many calls upon his time to accept Madame's request that he become her director, suggested that de Paul was perfectly suited to the post. Contrarily, Abelly argued that Madame was so edified by de Paul's modesty, discretion, and charity that she asked Bérulle to oblige him to take care of her conscience. In any case, Abelly, ever eager to emphasize de Paul's modesty, asserted that de Paul only agreed to do so on Bérulle's insistence: Abelly, *Vie*, i, 28–9; Chantelauze, *Vincent de Paul*, 93.

[22] Madame gave birth to her youngest son, the future Cardinal de Retz, in the family *château* of Montmirail in September 1613, and it was probably there that de Paul spent his first days of

Of Florentine descent, the Gondi family was one of the most successful banking and financial families to settle in France during the early modern period, and a position in their household was both highly desirable and prestigious. The family had reached noble status under the stewardship of Albert de Gondi, who earned a marshal's baton in 1573 and became the first duke of Retz in 1581 in reward for service to three French kings. By the time that de Paul entered the household of Albert's son, Philippe-Emmanuel, in September 1613, the family was reaping the harvest of royal favour, especially from their fellow Florentines Catherine and Marie de Medici, and was ranked among the great nobility of the regime.[23] Following his father's death, Philippe-Emmanuel de Gondi married Marguerite de Silly, the eldest daughter of Antoine de Silly, count of Rochepot and baron of Montmirail, and Marie de Lannoy, in 1604. As well as noble titles, both brought immense territorial possessions to their union: estates in Joigny and Rochepot in Bourgogne; in Montmirail in Champagne; in Commercy and Euville in Lorraine; in Folleville in Picardy; in Plessis-Écouis in Haute-Normandie, in Villepreux and Hebergeries west of Paris; in Dampierre in Saintonge; on the Îles-d'Or off the coast of southern Provence.[24]

In the course of their marriage, the Gondis emerged as dedicated *dévot* protagonists, and their liberal benefaction of religious communities, missions, and charitable initiatives proved a suitable complement to their political and social prominence. The paths of their enterprises were smoothed and their initiatives given additional prestige because of the family's near dynastic possession of the (arch)bishopric of Paris from 1568 to 1661.[25] Thus, the couple proved generous supporters of de Paul long before they laid the financial foundations of the Congregation of the Mission. For example, in February 1614, his employers loaned him 1,500 *livres* from 1,800 *livres* which they in turn had been loaned by Anne Brachet, wife of François Luillier, *sieur d'Intervalle*. The money was provided 'to meet the needs of his urgent affairs', probably to fund his protracted lawsuits for the abbey of Saint-Léonard. De Paul never repaid the loan, however, for the couple wiped the slate clean six years later, confirming that they were willing to treat the loan as a gift 'in consideration of his good and agreeable services'.[26] This act is noteworthy because it provides an early indication of their willingness to underwrite the ventures of a man who was not in a position to undertake them without assistance. Simultaneously, it demonstrates that their sponsorship brought him to the notice of similar social types whose attention he would have found more elusive

employment, perhaps assisting at the baby's baptism on 20 September: Chantelauze, *Vincent de Paul*, 38; Vance, *Memoirs*, 13.

[23] Milstein, *Gondi*, *passim*.

[24] Marguerite de Silly brought Commercy, Euville, and Folleville to her marriage. Philippe-Emmanuel de Gondi may also have been *seigneur* of Seurres, which his mother bequeathed to him in 1603: Corbinelli, *Histoire*, 573.

[25] Cardinal Pierre de Gondi resigned the see in 1596 in favour of Monsieur de Gondi's brother Henri (who became the first Cardinal de Retz in 1618). He was in turn succeeded by another brother, Jean-François, and his nephew, Jean-François-Paul de Gondi: Bergin, *French Episcopate*, 632–3.

[26] *CCD*, 13a: 64; AN, Minutier Central, ET/LIV/260 (1 February 1614 and 1 April 1620).

otherwise. In this instance, the loan marks de Paul's earliest recorded contact with the Luillier family, which, like the Gondi, enjoyed the financial resources and social prestige that provided the vital oxygen for new religious enterprises, such as the first Visitation convent founded in Paris in 1619. From the 1620s, its female members were to feature prominently on the list of de Paul's associates.[27]

Over time, the Gondi proved willing to assist de Paul to put plans for his advancement into action by permitting him to help himself to the large number of benefices for which they held rights of presentation. Within six months of his installation in the Gondi household, de Paul became the *curé* of one of these, the parish of Gamaches in the east of Rouen diocese.[28] His nomination provides yet more evidence of benefice collecting on his part, although he did not actually follow through on this one.[29] He did take possession of his next sinecure, however. In May 1615, he became a canon and treasurer of the collegial church and cure of Notre-Dame in Écouis, lying approximately 20 miles west of Gamaches.[30] He took formal possession in September, swearing an oath of fidelity and sitting down to a celebratory dinner with his new canonical companions to mark the occasion.[31] But de Paul clearly never intended to dispense his duties in person; the other eleven canons agreed to allow him to appoint a substitute to do so, but they, along with a co-patron of the church, Pierre de Roucherolles, subsequently became rather aggrieved with his persistent absence, especially since the dean and another canon were also proving less than conscientious in their residence. Just under a year after de Paul's appointment, the chapter ordered the trio to attend the next general chapter meeting, in order to explain their absence. While the other absentees turned up to the meeting on 25 May, de Paul communicated only through letters sent by his employer's wife and her brother-in-law, the duke of Retz (who was a third co-patron of the church), which asked that the treasurer be excused from meeting with chapter members for another two weeks. The chapter consented, but unfortunately the trail runs out at this point.[32]

[27] See Ch. 9, section IV.

[28] Philippe de Gondi held the right of presentation in his capacity as baron of Plessis-Écouis, a *seigneurie* located east of Rouen: Corbinelli, *Histoire*, ii, 572–4, 602. The transcription for de Paul's nomination that is printed in 'Notes et Documents', 495, and in *CCD*, 13: 25–6, fails to note that de Paul attended his act of nomination on 28 February 1614. The original document (AD de Seine-Maritime, G 9574, fos 77v–78r) clearly states, using the standard formula for ecclesiastical acts, that he did so. See AD de Seine-Maritime, G6, G133, and G723 for visitations and maps of the deanery which identify Gamaches as a parochial cure.

[29] The register of episcopal collations observes clearly that de Paul did not honour his presentation, since the entry is abbreviated 'non honata', meaning 'non honorata' (without a title). Although written in another hand, it is a common note in the book of collations, written alongside a number of other entries: AD de Seine-Maritime, G 9574, fo. 77v.

[30] Vautier, 'Vincent de Paul'; Régnier, *L'Église*. Neither Abelly nor Collet mentioned the benefices, either because they did not know about them or did not wish to draw attention to de Paul's holding of multiple benefices.

[31] Ordinarily, a canon was supposed to reside in the college, enabling him to participate routinely in the offices and other rituals held in the church. More particularly, the treasurer was charged with the collection and disbursement of church funds, including alms, donations, and foundations, duties which required careful and consistent attention to the balancing of the accounts for income and expenditure. He was also obliged to preside over the twice weekly chapter assemblies in the absence of the two superior officeholders, the dean and eulogist: Vautier, 'Vincent de Paul', 359.

[32] *CCD*, 13a: 30. On Pierre de Roucherelles (Roncherelles), see Dewald, *Pont-St-Pierre*, 159ff.

De Paul continued to hold the office, but also to reside with the Gondi, until he moved to Châtillon in 1617.[33]

It was natural that Madame de Gondi should intervene to protect de Paul since her husband had appointed him to the canonry in question, but her speaking on his behalf also demonstrates the extent to which her employee had integrated into, indeed become dependent on, her household for his security by this time. He was regularly at the family's beck and call, although mainly of the mother and children, since Monsieur was frequently away on crown business. If we discount the period that de Paul spent in Châtillon and the occasions after that when he began to spend more time ministering on the Gondi estates, he devoted about six years to the education of the youngest and most famous son, the future Cardinal de Retz, inculcating basic Christian doctrine and devotion and the first elements of classical study before his charge entered the Jesuit college of Clermont on the rue Saint-Jacques in 1625, age 12. De Paul probably also tutored his eldest brother, Pierre (later count of Joigny and duke of Retz), who was aged about 7 and soon destined for the Jesuits when de Paul arrived in the household. However, he was likely to have devoted most of his pedagogical attention to the middle child, just 3 in 1613, who would have succeeded his uncle as bishop (or rather archbishop) of Paris had he not fallen victim to a fatal hunting accident in 1622. Furthermore, as a clerical member of the household, de Paul was charged with duties of chaplaincy, ensuring that the routine of devotions, involving practices such as daily household prayers and preparation for feast days, ran smoothly, and that suitable levels of decorum characterized conversation and behaviour.[34] Finally, around the turn of 1613, de Paul's duties became still more onerous when he became the spiritual director of the intensely devout Madame. This provided his first real opportunity to engage intimately in the piety of a *dévote*, as his direction of her faith required him to be familiar with her spiritual thoughts, and that he offer guidance on matters of conscience and religious practice. Over time, their interaction enabled him to develop an insightful appreciation for the depths of female piety, and to begin to acquire the expertise that he would later demonstrate in interpreting the rules of engagement with *dévote* women. In this case, de Paul's relationship with Madame was to flourish in particular because they found a common interest in the spiritual welfare of the tenants of the vast rural Gondi estates; during this period, with her encouragement, he began to minister to these, quickly observing how drastically inadequate the service being provided for them in their parishes was. Amongst the localities in which he ministered was the townland of Folleville, which provided the setting for an event which de Paul later foregrounded as the occasion on which

[33] Strikingly, the chapter's deliberations noted that Roucherolles held the barony of Dampierre, which Jean Corbinelli claimed Philippe-Emmanuel de Gondi had inherited through his mother Claude-Catherine de Clermont, the baroness of Dampierre. It is possible that de Paul may have unwittingly become a pawn in a dispute over the inheritance of Dampierre; Roucherelles may have chosen to dispute his rival's rights of presentation by targeting his appointees, on the pretext that 'the entire ruin of the church and foundation' was threatened because of their failure to fulfil their duties: Corbinelli, *Histoire*, ii, 572–4.

[34] Battifol, *Retz*, 161–2.

the Lazarists were truly founded: there, on 25 January 1617 de Paul famously delivered a sermon on confession in a church crammed with locals, after he absolved the sins of an anguished peasant living in nearby Gannes, who had been too ashamed to confess serious sins for many years.

It was in a different location that de Paul underwent a further experience which stands out proudly in the biographical narrative of his life. His move to the parish of Châtillon-lès-Dombes was sudden: after three years with the Gondi, he left his comfortable situation to move there around May 1617. He did so without informing his employers, who were under the impression that he had simply taken a short trip. Over the years, this has invited the speculation of scholars and devotees alike. As a result, a rather simplistic historical narrative depicts his move to Châtillon as an escape from Madame, in particular, with some even implying that she had developed a romantic attachment over the course of what was an intimate association.[35] Even the most charitable of judges tend to blame her excessive dependence on de Paul for his decision, and lament the fact that she tried to thwart his efforts to answer his true calling to the poor.[36] They take their ammunition from the stricken emotional appeal that she sent to de Paul shortly after he wrote to her husband to let him know of his whereabouts and new position, and assume that she goaded her husband as well as a host of others, including her brother-in-law, the bishop of Paris, into attempting to persuade him to return.[37]

At first sight, it may appear that Madame's reaction to de Paul's departure was that of an aggressively clinging female, hysterically lamenting the fact that her personal spiritual guide was no longer at her side.[38] But it is prejudicial to single out her appeal as the selfish demand of a neurotic who stood between de Paul and his true vocation (especially since he was rather unclear about precisely where his true calling lay anyway). As Diefendorf points out, their relationship measured up to the standards set for spiritual direction at this time. Madame reacted exactly as might be expected: pious women were required to rely on their male director for their spiritual and moral health, and it was therefore unsurprising that she panicked when de Paul departed so quickly. She 'feared losing [his] assistance', for she realized that she would find it difficult, if not impossible, to replicate the relationship of trust that she had built up with him over several years. Just as crucially, Madame worried that, without de Paul, her salvation and the salvation of her family

[35] See, for instance, Coste, *Saint*, i, 114–15, and Román, *Vincent de Paul*, 117. In contrast, Diefendorf adopts a more sympathetic and nuanced interpretation of Madame's conduct, arguing that Madame's distress was based on her conviction that de Paul's departure was an 'enormous loss for her peasants, as well as for her husband, sons, and self': Diefendorf, *Penitence*, 207.

[36] Coste, *Saint*, i, 114–15.

[37] These included Charles du Fresne, who had been secretary and then intendant to Philippe-Emmanuel de Gondi since 1615. He had previously acted as secretary to Marguerite de Valois, and de Paul may have become acquainted with him when he was employed as an almoner in her household: Abelly, *Vie*, i, 38 (summary of de Paul's letter to Monsieur de Gondi), 43–4. Abelly dates the correspondence between de Paul and the Gondi to September and October 1617, but the letters are likely to have been written shortly before. See also Corbinelli, *Histoire*, 609.

[38] Parturier, *Vincent de Paul*, 50.

and residents on her lands would be placed in jeopardy.[39] Indeed, her husband encouraged her to write her plea to de Paul, for he was just as concerned as she was about these dangers, should de Paul refuse to return to the household.[40]

Undoubtedly, de Paul's failure to announce his departure indicates that he knew that Madame would resist it on the grounds that it would retard her further spiritual advancement, and that of her dependants. But this does not explain why he decided to leave, or indeed why Châtillon itself proved such an attractive proposition. To answer the first, it is plain that he was finding his position in the Gondi household unfulfilling: when disclosing his reason for leaving to Philippe de Gondi, he confessed that the many demands on his time there did not enable him to prioritize the work for which he felt the greatest inclination.[41] This, he appeared to feel, was rural pastoral care, on which he could focus if he settled within the confines of one parish. But if so, then why not simply return to Clichy, from which he had still not resigned, and which contained enough residents to exercise his pastoral functions with care and commitment? To understand why de Paul chose to head to a completely new location, which was entirely unfamiliar to him and which had over three times as many communicants, we must look beyond his personal penchant for rural parochial duties, and his relationship with the Gondi, to loyalties that he held elsewhere.[42]

Once more, the answer lies in de Paul's relationship with Bérulle, who exerted a decisive influence on his change of environment; indeed, he was the chief reason why de Paul ended up in Châtillon at all. On the invitation of its archbishop, Denis-Simon de Marquemont, Bérulle had been sending Oratorians to Lyon archdiocese to assist in visitations and missions for a number of years, and they formally established a house in Lyons itself in January 1617.[43] Around the same time as this plan was put in motion, Marquemont raised the prospect that the Oratorians might also found a small house in Châtillon, and suggested that the experienced Bourgoing 'or another of his weight' assume the posts of *curé* and superior of the house, and of superior in Lyon.[44] This made sense strategically, for Bérulle was already in the habit of expanding the Oratory by founding communities outside Paris, in places such as Nantes, La Rochelle, and Rouen. It was also remarkably serendipitous. Bérulle found himself in a predicament because he could not spare one of his own to take up the post, but neither did he wish to forgo it.[45]

39 *CCD*, 1: 20, Marguerite de Gondi to de Paul, September 1617: 'If it were only for a time, I would not have so much pain . . . I am not able to seek or receive assistance elsewhere, because you are well aware that I do not have liberty with a lot of people for the needs of my soul.'

40 Abelly, *Vie*, i, 39, and 44, for another letter on the same subject from Monsieur de Gondi to his wife; *CCD*, 1: 21, Philippe-Emmanuel de Gondi to de Paul, 15 October 1617.

41 *CCD*, 1: 18, de Paul to Philippe-Emmanuel de Gondi, August–September 1617.

42 AN Z 10 241; *CCD*, 13a: 74.

43 Dagens (ed.), *Correspondance*, i, 252, Jean Bence to Pierre de Bérulle, 23 October 1617.

44 In the second edition of the *Vie*, Abelly inferred that the Oratorian superior in Lyon, Jean Bence, had been approached by the chapter of Lyon to supply a *curé*, but Bence only arrived in Lyon in December 1616, well after the archbishop initiated his negotiation with Bérulle. It is, of course, possible that Bence encouraged his superior general to accept Marquemont's offer: Abelly, *Vie*, i, 48 (1668).

45 Marquemont took the precaution of approving the appointment of another priest, Jean Lourdelot, to the cure in January 1617, in case Bérulle proved unable to provide. On 30 March,

On earlier occasions, he had relied on individuals who were familiar with and sympathetic to the Oratory's habits to establish a preliminary presence in new locations, and, in this instance, de Paul provided the timely solution which allowed him to do so again.[46]

For de Paul, the vacancy could not have arisen at a better time. In total, he stayed only about seven months in Châtillon, during which time he instigated the confraternity of charity which was the prototype for those which subsequently became set pieces of Lazarist missionary campaigns.[47] The hagiography declares dramatically that he found a 'parish of perdition' on his arrival, which he turned into a beacon of Christian hope, but the reality was both more complex and more revealing of his ability to tap into the piety that already existed amongst the faithful there.[48] Actually, the parish was in excellent shape. Just three years earlier, the officials of an episcopal visitation had made only minor criticisms of religious services and infrastructure, and had not found any abuses in devotion. After being damaged in the Wars of Religion, the parish church had been repaired in 1607, and contained thirteen side chapels, plus five additional altars.[49] The local community was enthusiastic in its religious practice, and the inhabitants expended both time and money on ensuring that their place of worship was kept amply stocked with the paraphernalia of ritual: for example, the most recently founded of the three confraternities, that of the rosary, possessed a substantial and rich range of linens and ornaments to decorate its side chapel as well as vestments for masses held in it.[50]

What was in poor shape, however, was the local *Hôtel-Dieu*, and it is this fact which provides the clue to de Paul's particular contribution to a parish which was already thriving. According to the visitors, the *Hôtel-Dieu* was in ruins, and its patent inability to deal with the indigent therefore provided a practical incentive for de Paul to organize alternative support for them.[51] But he could not have done so without the commitment of parishioners to alleviate hardships. Further, the condition of the parish that the visitors described demonstrates plainly that he did not appeal to a few people who were desperate for someone to lead them out of a

Lourdelot accepted a canonry at Saint-Paul-de-Lyon, and resigned his cure on 19 April, an exchange which suggests that Marquemont had been informed that Bérulle would be able to supply a *curé*. Lourdelot's successor was not named on the document of resignation, so clearly Marquemont did not yet know who Bérulle would suggest: AD du Rhône, 1G 87 (registre 8), fos 256v, 279r; *CCD*, 13a: 44.

46 Dagens (ed.), *Correspondance*, i, 232, Pierre de Bérulle to André Jousseaume, 27 February 1617.

47 Abelly stated that de Paul arrived in Châtillon in July, but this does not accord with the documentary record of de Paul's activities in the parish. He did, however, take formal possession of the cure on 1 July: AD du Rhône, 4G 121 (registre 81), fo. 319v. For further details of the move, see Forrestal, 'Catholic *Dévot*'.

48 Coste, *Saint*, i, 93–116; Dodin, *Vincent de Paul and Charity*, 23; Román, *Vincent de Paul*, 121–3. Bernard Koch's research is indispensable in dispelling these myths. See his commentaries in *Bulletin des Lazaristes de France*: 'Châtillon-lès-Dombes et Saint Vincent'; 'Châtillon-lès-Dombes. Complements'; 'Châtillon-lès-Dombes et les Femmes'.

49 Many others in the area had not benefited from the same restoration. For example, in Clémencia parish, the church windows were found to be missing, the sanctuary and choir collapsed, and the entrance closed up by a wall: AD du Rhône, 1G 48 [28], fos 261v–262r.

50 Archives Communales de Châtillon, GG121; AD de l'Ain, 3 E 23463, fos 81v–84v; AD du Rhône, 1G 48 [28], fo. 262v.

51 AD du Rhône, 1G 48 [28], fo. 264r.

supposed valley of spiritual darkness; instead, de Paul provided the vibrant religiosity that already existed with an additional form and structure of expression.

The opportunity to do so arose on a Sunday morning around mid-August as de Paul prepared for mass in the church vestry.[52] An event which is so well known requires only a brief depiction here, in order to set the scene for the analysis to follow in Chapter 3. In his accounts of it, de Paul explained that he was called to an isolated house just outside the town to attend to a sick and poor family.[53] When he saw their 'indescribable need', it 'touched [him] to the heart', and propelled him to appeal to his congregation on their behalf; he later celebrated the fact that the hearts of his female parishioners were equally 'touched' with compassion for the afflicted. Later in the day, a meeting was then held in the house of a townswoman, and local women walked to assist the family, so that de Paul, going there with 'an upright citizen', met them as they returned. In turn, he administered confession and communion to members of the family. In the immediate aftermath, he recounted that the women proved inclined to listen when he proposed a format that would enable them to deliver aid in the future:

> I suggested that all these good persons animated by charity to go there might each take a day to make soup, not for those sick persons only, but also for those who might come afterwards, and that is the first place where the Charity was established.[54]

A few days later, the confraternity was formally instituted, and on 24 November the vicar general of Lyon approved the rule that de Paul had devised.[55] By this time, the group had in its possession 'ten plates, six bowls, four big and two little *gondolles* . . . ten bed drapes . . . nineteen serviettes . . . four wooden tablets half a dozen spoons', enough to satisfy the requirements of their rule, and sufficient to feed about six to ten patients comfortably at any given time.[56] At this time, the treasurer reported that she held 32 *livres* and 17 *sous*, most of it taken from the new trunk that the group had placed in the church to solicit donations. De Paul contributed 56 *sous* on 15 December, which members used to buy marzipan and prunes for the patients that they visited the following week.[57]

[52] De Paul is known to have given two accounts of the event to the Daughters of Charity, in 1645 and 1646: *CCD*, 9: 165–6, 192–3.

[53] In 1645, de Paul said that he was called to see a sick poor man, but the entire family was probably in need because of the incapacity of the head of the household: *CCD*, 9: 165.

[54] The timing of the meeting differs in both accounts, but they concur that it took place on the day that de Paul made his plea to the congregation: *CCD*, 9: 193.

[55] ACMP, 'Acte d'Association et Premier Règlement des Dames de la Confrérie', 'Règlement de la Charité', 'Erection de la Confrérie de la Charité de Châtillon'. These are facsimiles of the original manuscripts, because the published transcriptions of the text contain some errors and omissions (*CCD*, 13b: 8–21). The originals are held in the archives of the Daughters of Charity in Châtillon. For the episcopal approbation see AD du Rhône, 1G 48 [28], fos 267v–268r.

[56] ACMP, 'Livre de la Charité des Pauvres de Chastillon', entry for 15 December 1617 (*reçus*) (copy). The original is held in the archives of the Daughters of Charity in Châtillon: 'dix plactz, six escueilles, quattre grandes gondolles & deux petites . . . dix linsseulz . . . dixneuf serviettes . . . quattre tablettes de boies demy douzaine de cuilliers'. A *gondolle* was an oblong vessel for liquids, which did not have a stem or handle.

[57] ACMP, 'Livre de la Charité des Pauvres de Chastillon', entry for 15 December 1617 (*livrées*) (copy).

After this, de Paul did not have time to relish the debut of the confraternity in the devotional and social life of his parish community for more than a few weeks. In the midst of his efforts to establish the new grouping, he was interrupted by repeated entreaties from the Gondi that he return to Paris, and was finally convinced just before Christmas to return to the capital to seek advice about the right course of action. On arrival, he hurried to visit Bérulle, with the result that he was once again firmly ensconced in the Gondi *hôtel* by Christmas day.[58] Why he performed this abrupt volte-face is not certain, but it was probably the fact that the campaign to sway his mind had not diminished in the past few months. No doubt he was apprehensive about leaving Bérulle in the lurch, since it was Bérulle who had asked him to move to the south-east in the first place. But they must have concurred that he owed loyalty to the Gondi, and any anxiety that de Paul had about leaving Châtillon was partially alleviated by the appointment of a competent replacement.[59] Whether he would be able to reconcile his decision to please the Gondi with his own inclinations was a question for another day: as we shall see, his sojourns in Clichy, Châtillon, and on the Gondi country estates had provided plentiful occasion to augment his pastoral experience, and to explore its spiritual meaning in the present and for the future.

[58] Abelly noted that de Paul met with Bérulle on 23 December, and returned to serving the Gondi on Christmas eve: Abelly, *Vie*, i, 44–5.

[59] De Paul resigned the cure at the end of January. Louis Girard was nominated to it on 10 July 1618, and appointed *curé* eight days later. For both acts, see AD du Rhône, registre 81, fos 240v–241r. Only the act of appointment is printed in *CCD*, 13a: 57.

3

Identifying Pastoral Strategies

I

The 'sermon of Folleville' retains a seminal position in the standard narrative of de Paul's life and the history of the Congregation of the Mission. Its original foregrounding can be traced back to de Paul himself, who presented it in his twilight years as the occasion on which the Congregation, not formally founded until 1625, was truly born. By the mid-1650s, he and his companions commemorated its birth annually on 25 January; the fact that this was also the date of the feast of St Paul's conversion was not taken to be just a happy coincidence, but confirmation that this day was one of transformation and conversion, when divine providence led de Paul towards his true calling to found a community of priests devoted to rural evangelization.[1] When Folleville is coupled with the establishment of the first confraternity of charity in Châtillon seven months later, it completely overshadows every other episode of this decade in de Paul's life, giving the impression that there is little to be gained from attempts to draw them out from under its shade.

In consequence, to explain de Paul's spiritual development between his stays in Clichy and Châtillon, biographers have found that a famous story about his 'violent temptation' against his faith forms a convenient basis for a plotline of spiritual turmoil, discernment, and conversion. De Paul is said to have endured an extraordinary period of temptation while living in Paris, which resulted first in his vow to serve the poor, and culminated in his realization in Folleville in January 1617 that he was destined to evangelize the poor country folk of France in imitation of Christ.[2] In describing his troubles, biographers are able to transform their subject rapidly into a missionary, the founder of the Lazarists, and a servant of the poor, for the narrative's power lies in the simplicity of the trajectory and the speed with which de Paul progressed along it. In its classic rendering, it hinges on de Paul's willingness to assume the soul-suffering of a doctor with whom he was acquainted: Abelly recounted that as this individual emerged from a period of darkness in which he was tormented by the allure of sin, his temptation passed into de Paul's soul, and he in turn became tortured by the Devil's attacks upon his faith. At length, 'offering himself to God in a spirit of penance', he decided to write out a profession of faith and placed the paper over his heart, making a pact with God that he would renounce the temptation whenever he placed his hand over it. He also resolved

[1] *CCD*, 11: 162. [2] Abelly, *Vie*, iii, 116; Román, 'L'Année 1617'.

to do the opposite of what the temptation suggested to him at all times. In a resounding finale, Abelly judged the result to be that 'God in his grace drew forth from his servant all the great works he did for the aid and salvation of the poor and for the greater good of the Church.' So, de Paul's sacrifice of his own mental stability, the testing of his resolve to love God and renounce the Devil, and his ultimate victory, produced a man wholly dedicated to God and devoted to serving the poor: this was a model of faith forged in the fires of adversity.[3]

This account obviously serves a useful didactic function, but it is suspiciously similar to other tales of instruction that were commonplace in the laudable life stories of saintly figures at this time. In Germain Habert's 1646 life of Bérulle, for instance, the Oratorian founder was said to have asked God to withdraw his grace from him so that he could bear the spiritual pains and infirmities of a young woman who had relapsed into Protestantism after he had heard her confession. In his perfect imitation of Jesus, Bérulle only felt the burden of his torment lift from his heart when he learned that she had made an act of contrition for her sins.[4] It is not altogether surprising, as a result, to discover that the story of de Paul's temptation is potholed with inconsistencies—indeed, it is unlikely that de Paul was really the subject of the temptation at all—for it was its moral potency rather than its factual accuracy which was regarded as the measure of its value.[5]

From the temptation, scholars proceed with scarcely a pause to the climactic episode of Folleville, partly enabled by de Paul's three accounts of it, in which he acutely contracted a record of happenings that actually spanned a number of years.[6] He first recalled a conversation that he had with Madame de Gondi about her early experience of confession, before proceeding directly to Folleville in January 1617. Some years before this event, he observed, Madame's unhappy experience with an ignorant confessor had led her to carry a note with the formula of absolution written on it in case she met another equally as unprepared to hear her confession. Her unhappy memory of this inspired her to discuss with de Paul how to improve the religious service offered to her tenants. He went on to recall that when they were in Folleville in early 1617 he had administered confession to 'a poor man who was

[3] Abelly claimed that he had been given the details by an unnamed 'trustworthy person', and that it had been verified by others who had been told the tale by de Paul. It has evidently been circulating in this form for a time since Maupas du Tour told a similar version in 1660: Abelly, *Vie*, iii, 117; Maupas du Tour, *Funeral Oration*, 122.

[4] Habert, *Bérulle*, 764–71.

[5] For instance, Jean Mauduit wrongly identifies the doctor as Nicolas de Cöeffeteau, who was an almoner in Marguerite de Valois's household from 1602 to 1611, and *prédicateur ordinaire* to Henri IV between 1608 and 1610. Coëffeteau wrote controversial treatises, and was reportedly ill in 1613, both of which fit the profile of the doctor. But he had never been a diocesan *théologal*, as the doctor had. Further, de Paul recounted that the temptation occurred after the doctor had been a diocesan official, but Coëffeteau did not become one until 1617, when he was appointed suffragan bishop of Metz. He was later the titular bishop of Dardania and bishop of Marseille. More troublingly again, de Paul indicated distinctly when he first told the tale that he was not involved at all in it, but that he simply knew the doctor who had endured temptation: *CCD*, 11: 26–7; Abelly, *Vie*, iii, 116; Coste, *Saint*, i, 68; Mauduit, *Vincent de Paul*, 109; Pujo, *Vincent de Paul*, 45; Urban, *Coëffeteau*, 245. For additional pertinent comments, see Poole and Slawson, 'Temptation'.

[6] For a short but useful summary of the accounts and some of the differences between them, see Poole, 'Origins of the Congregation of the Mission'.

dangerously ill', and 'burdened with sin that he had never dared to declare in confession'. On learning this, the perturbed Madame asked de Paul to preach to the local people 'on how to make a good confession and the need there was for making at least one during their lifetime'. He duly did so, 'point[ing] out to them its importance and usefulness and then I instructed them how to make a good one'. So successful was he that all of the inhabitants made general confessions, and he had to ask two Jesuits to assist him in hearing those of the crowd that gathered, as well as to preach and catechize. And this, de Paul finished, marked the foundation of the Lazarists.[7]

In coupling Folleville so firmly to the establishment of the Lazarists, de Paul concentrated more on its relationship to the subsequent history of the Congregation than on precisely describing the episode itself, and his accounts resonate strongly because they are threaded through with three motifs: the power of providence, the foundation of a mission, and the benefits of collaboration. In securing his narrative on these, de Paul gave a sense of cohesion to events that took place over time, and was able to advance his lesson directly from a starting point of pastoral need to an end point of collaborative mission. In later years, he clearly prioritized Folleville over other incidents of his early career because it enabled him to give purpose to and justify later events. It also became a quintessential example to place before his fellow Lazarists as an incentive to answer collectively the call of their missionary vocation.

At the time it occurred, however, Folleville was far less important than might be supposed for de Paul's sense of self-purpose and behaviour, and it would be misguided to assume that it was the most significant event or experience to shape his outlook at the time that it took place. In its aftermath, he certainly did not display much sense that he had reached a moment of supreme enlightenment which resolved his lengthy wrestle with his conscience: he did not suddenly convert to the life of a missionary, and indeed the only alteration that he made in the short term was his temporary relocation to Châtillon. More importantly again, however, de Paul had not been idle before it took place, but was already engaging bountifully with a set of ideas which were shaping his outlook on rural pastoral care profoundly. Furthermore, his priorities in Folleville—notably the promotion of general confession and the delivery of catechetical instruction—were already becoming essential elements in the repertoire of pastoral practices that he was steadily assembling. Thus, Folleville should be understood as the apex of de Paul's activities between late 1612 and January 1617 rather than as a marker of a new phase or a transition in his vocation. Ultimately, however, its greatest importance lay in its representative character: it was illustrative of the kinds of situations that de Paul had met and was meeting on other estates, and its sequence of events demonstrated the demands that pastoral work made. Indeed, viewed panoramically, the years 1611 to 1618 reveal that de Paul's skills and experience grew intensively, as he enjoyed different

[7] *CCD*, 11: 3–4, 163; *CCD*, 12: 7; Abelly, *Vie*, i, 32. Abelly elaborated on the essentials for the benefit of his readers, for example, introducing direct speech, and emphasizing that the peasant died three days after his confession, indebted to de Paul for his spiritual health.

perspectives as a parish priest and a private clerical employee on large estates composed of multiple parishes. As such, he began to realize what was desirable and possible when one worked within a parish on both a short- and long-term basis.

Because little is known of de Paul's reading on pastoral care during these years his personal reflections on his placements and his activities during them are even more significant to the historian. What can be garnered of his reading upholds the notion that he was sincerely in search of practical guidelines, as well as a spiritual backbone to his efforts to shape the devotion of those who came under his care. Regarding the former, he brought a collection of homiletic sermons by the Spanish Franciscan Diego de La Vega to Châtillon in 1617. *Le Paradis de la gloire des saincts* had been published in 1606, and went through multiple editions thereafter. The sermons within it were designed for use on feast days throughout the year, and were specifically related to doctrines associated with feast days such as Christmas or the Ascension. They were therefore perfect for a parish priest seeking inspiration in technique before he mounted the pulpit. De Paul's copy was published in Paris in 1614, so he did not have this text when in Clichy, but he probably purchased it not long afterwards.[8] Around the same time, he procured a catechism (unidentified), with which he hoped to teach the essentials of faith.[9] The third book known to have been in his possession by 1617 was not explicitly catechetical in nature, but potentially enlightening for its vision of lay sanctity, especially female. François de Sales's *Introduction to the Devout Life* was first published in 1609, to instant acclaim and widespread circulation. Though independently insightful, it mined a seam of spirituality already popularized by the Spanish Dominican Louis of Granada in his works *The Sinner's Guide* and the *Memorial of a Christian Life* during the later sixteenth century.[10]

II

De Paul's sojourn in Clichy is conventionally eclipsed by both Folleville and Châtillon, even though he spent well over twice as long there as he did in his second parish. As a result, its impression on his spiritual development and his expertise in pastoral care is overlooked, despite his own testimony to its positive impact in the long term. In general, this did not incorporate a detailed catalogue of his activities there, but it does reveal that Clichy was the kind of parish in which

[8] The original copy is now missing, but the title page, with de Paul's signature, is in the possession of the Sisters of Charity of Saint-Jeanne-Antide-Thouret in Besançon.

[9] Unfortunately, de Paul did not name this, but it was certainly not one of the popular manuals composed by the Jesuit Peter Canisius in the 1550s. Instead, it was one that had been written initially 'to instruct infidels', but had since been used amongst Christians. Canisius had published a trilogy of catechisms in the 1550s, on the request of Emperor Ferdinand, including the *Summa doctrinae christianae*, the *Catechismus minimus* for younger children, and the popular 'small catechism' or *Parvus catechismus catholicorum* for older children. All went through numerous editions, but the *Parvus* was the most popular of the three.

[10] The *Memorial*, first published in 1555, was amongst de Sales's favourite guides for the lay person. For it, *The Sinner's Guide*, and other works of Louis of Granada, see *Summa of the Christian Life*.

he could hope to promote a fairly rigorous devotional routine. This included obligatory recourse to the sacrament of confession on the first Sunday of the month, which was a far more onerous demand on his parishioners than the annual confession and communion that the Catholic church required; it also implies that de Paul was affected by the pronounced emphasis that many Catholic reformers were beginning to place on the practice of frequent confession.[11] Concurrently, he was likely to have wished to promote regular reception of communion; it invariably went hand in hand with any early seventeenth-century cleric's bid to encourage frequent confession, since the purpose of the penitential sacrament was to ensure that the communicant was cleansed of sin before approaching the eucharist.[12] One of the recommendations, for example, that de Sales made to his readers in his *Introduction* was that they should receive both sacraments every week.[13]

Unlike Folleville, de Paul was never to enlist Clichy as a foundational event in the Lazarists' institutional narrative, but it did lend itself handsomely to another purpose. In Clichy, he did not find himself fighting valiantly against a tide of religious ignorance and careless observance, but standing cheek by jowl for the first time in years with the type of 'poor, common people' to whom he subsequently dedicated the Lazarist mission.[14] His interaction with his flock fundamentally moulded his understanding of rural piety, so the overriding legacy that he took from his time in this well-ordered parish was one of idealism rather than improvement: it offered a template of excellence in religious discipline and virtue. It is apparent from the descriptions that de Paul later provided for Lazarists that he romanticized the religious conduct and collective virtues of the inhabitants, but even if his view of them was a shade more idealistic than realistic it represented the type of rural religiosity that he grew to regard as the model that a zealous missionary or parish priest should strive to promote. He recalled that they were well versed in their devotions, obedient to their parish priest, and unquestioning in their acceptance of the practices that he required them to undertake. He portrayed them as being at peace with their lot, because they fulfilled their obligations to God in work and prayer. The piety of his rural parishioners of 'good heart' was, de Paul affirmed, defined by simple and obedient devotion to the rituals and beliefs of the Catholic church.[15] From them, he confessed, he learned to prize virtues that could be held by peasants even as they lay at risk of eternal damnation, and he was later to marvel

[11] There is no first-hand evidence to support the claim, which was made much later by Abelly and witnesses in the canonization process, that de Paul established a small school for some clerics. There was a school in the parish in 1623, however: ACMP, 'Testament de Claude Gilbert, curé de S. Pierre et S. Denys de Montmartre, 9 octobre 1695' (photocopy of the original, taken from the parish register for Montmartre, dated 16 November 1700). On Trent, see Tanner (ed.), *Decrees*, ii, 712, Sess. XIV, 'Canons concerning the most holy sacrament of penance'.

[12] Tanner (ed.), *Decrees*, ii, 698, Sess. XIII, 'Canons on the most holy sacrament of the Eucharist'; de Sales, *Introduction*, 115. De Sales emphasized that he considered anything less than monthly reception of communion to be insufficient.

[13] De Sales, *Introduction*, 111.

[14] *CCD*, 13a: 219.

[15] *CCD*, 9: 507. De Paul also referred at the same time to a conversation that he had with the bishop of Paris about his charges, probably those residing in Clichy: 'Because I have such a good people, so obedient to all that I say, that I think myself that neither the Holy Father, nor you Monseigneur, are as happy as me': *CCD*, 9: 507.

in sentimental salutations at the rustic candour and humble simplicity by which these kind of people could live.[16]

Because the vast majority of Europe's population engaged in some form of agricultural labour, it was commonplace for churchmen to reflect on their religious conduct; Erasmus' hope that the peasant would recite scriptural verses as he ploughed in the fields was already a famous image of the religious commitment that should be found in the mundane rhythms of daily life, for example, and it resonated in the society in which he lived.[17] Other churchmen regularly drew on New Testament injunctions to emphasize the value of an honest day's work in Christian life, and the role that labour played in distracting Christians from the idleness that gave rise to sinful thoughts and deeds.[18] They did not, however, tend to place a particular premium on either manual work or the work synonymous with the rural peasant livelihood. De Paul's praise of his parishioners is therefore distinctive. He did not single out an ideal 'type' of person, but he ascribed particular virtues to the parishioners' collective religious practice, and inferred that rural existence could best express the devotion that God wished. His first parish and his parishioners became the measures against which all others should be set; they also offered an implicit critique of environments where such piety did not flourish and which were inhabited by individuals who did not emulate the people of Clichy.

The kind of passive acquiescence that the parishioners reportedly exhibited towards their pastor suggests that they were not the type of people that would teach him anything other than that he held unbridled authority over them. Yet de Paul was adamant in claiming, seemingly paradoxically, that he learned much that inspired him in his vocation from their manifestation of these very qualities, for he realized that such sincere parishioners deserved the care of a conscientious and competent *curé*, and it distressed him to admit that he was not so well endowed with these attributes.[19] Indeed, the qualities that he chose to idealize in them were those on which he not only set store but also feared for most of his missionary life that he did not possess. Helpfully, Michel de Certeau identifies a comparable construction of such opposites in the writings of some of de Paul's contemporaries, arguing that it was a strain of devout discourse in seventeenth-century France with origins in fourteenth-century mystical spirituality. In a bid to detach themselves from worldly values and honours associated with higher education and ordination, and to negate themselves, devout clergy denigrated their own privileged status as respected priests by contrasting it with the spiritual superiority of the humble and simple male peasant labourers that they encountered, such as the poor and illiterate

[16] For an example, see de Paul's comments on the peasantry in a conference on simplicity and prudence in 1659: *CCD*, 12: 142.

[17] See the preface (Paracelsis) to Erasmus' 1516 translation of the Greek New Testament: *Novum Instrumentum omne*, unpaginated.

[18] See, for example, Martin's Luther's commentary on Matt. 5, the Sermon on the Mount, in which he draws on 2 Thess. 3: 6–13 to urge Christians to pursue their work quietly and to avoid idlers: Martin Luther, 'The Sermon on the Mount', *Luther's Works*, 21, *passim.*

[19] *CCD*, 12: 276: 'I heard with admiration these peasants who chanted the psalms, not missing a single note. At that point, I said to myself: "You who are their spiritual father, you are ignorant of that"; I was distressed.' (My translation from the original French differs in minor ways from *CCD*.)

'young man in a coach' who became the subject of a letter composed by the Jesuit Jean-Joseph Surin in 1630 and widely circulated for decades afterwards.[20] Another example of this moralizing strategy can be found in the writings of Charles de Condren, who was full of admiration for a cowherd that he met in Compiègne who, although uneducated, possessed true knowledge of Christ.[21] In a similar way, the distinction to which de Paul testified in order to provoke himself to improvement was not one defined primarily by social status, but it did invert traditional cultural hierarchy: collectively, his peasant parishioners became the masters and he the student, as he sought to discover virtue and to move closer to God through them.

III

Removed from Clichy to the parishes of the Gondi estates, it must have appeared to de Paul that the religious habits in them were the antithesis of ideal piety. Long before he heard the confession of the sick peasant in Gannes, he began to notice gaps in the knowledge and practice of the peasantry, and had reached the conclusion that this was partly due to the fact that many of their priests were simply not up to the tasks of ministry. After Madame de Gondi divulged her memory of her own poor experience with a confessor, de Paul became even more alert to the words of priests to whom he made his confession, and was disturbed to learn that what she had endured was far from unusual.[22] In response, by early 1616 at the latest, de Paul had begun to hear the confessions of tenants in Joigny, Montmirail, Villepreux, and elsewhere, but also to offer catechetical instruction to them.[23] These were to become standard elements of every mission that he subsequently conducted or organized.

The observance of the sacraments had been a marked feature of de Paul's liturgical life in Clichy, and a series of three sermons that he wrote between 1613 and 1616 reveal that his fascination was reinforced as he dealt with tenants on the Gondi lands. Two of the sermons were on the subject of communion, doctrinally the most significant of the sacraments, and a rite for which confession was a prerequisite. He composed a third on catechesis, which reflected his resolution to add it to the quiver of methods that should be used in the conversion of souls.[24]

[20] Certeau, 'L'Illettré éclairé'. [21] Amelote, *Condren*, 264–5. [22] *CCD*, 11: 163.

[23] As a result, by the time that de Paul heard the sins of the aged peasant in Gannes, he was an experienced confessor in possession of faculties to absolve from reserved sins: *CCD*, 1: 17–18, Edmond Mauljean to de Paul, 20 June 1616. See also Abelly, *Vie*, i, 28.

[24] Two of the sermons deal with the worthy reception of communion, and linger lengthily on the preparations that should accompany reception of the sacrament. The third sermon, composed in March or April 1616, concentrates on catechesis. My analysis is based on the original manuscripts held in the ACMP, which differ in minor ways from the printed versions published in *CCD*, 13a: 31–42, and allow the reader to track alterations that de Paul made to the sermons as he drafted them. Through this process, it becomes apparent that the sermons on communion are not drafts of one sermon, as some conclude. They contain obvious similarities but are distinguished by notable differences in content. Whether de Paul actually delivered the sermons is uncertain, but a deleted comment in the

Manifestly, as de Paul became more familiar with its practice, he perceived that he should not only encourage the faithful to engage in prescribed devotional practices, but simultaneously ensure that they were aware of the reasons why their faith demanded that they did so. For, 'what profit', he asked in early 1616, 'is drawn from the mass by someone who does not know what it is, or from confession by someone who does not know of what it consists?'[25] Concurrently, the sermons demonstrate that he was already well on his way to categorizing the qualities that he considered to characterize the good Christian, and which he would later assert had been present in the model parish of Clichy. Though he may have deliberately fused Clichy and the virtues at a distance of some years from the parish, he had already recognized that these Christian qualities should be desired, and treasured when achieved, by the mid-1610s.

Catechesis had begun to play a more prominent role in Catholic pastoral practices since the Council of Trent, and de Paul's possession of a catechism reflects this trend. His personal experience of the state of rural piety on Gondi lands did not simply alert him to the problems associated with poor confessional practices, for he noticed more fundamental and wide-ranging issues as he moved amongst the peasants:

> Is it not true that ignorance is so great, that I found myself with christians & catholics, who when I asked if they knew the commandments of God, they responded that they have never been to school, and others that they knew them well to read in the hours (prayers)?[26]

Catechesis should, in his view, remedy deficiencies such as ignorance of the commandments and other essentials of faith, such as 'who merits the title of Christian, the end for which man is created, that there is one God in three persons and three persons in one God . . . the sacraments, and Christian practice'.[27] However, interestingly, de Paul admitted at the time that he was also led towards it by the success with which Protestants had pioneered its use; he recounted that he had witnessed their skill and assiduity in teaching the heretic faithful regularly on Sunday afternoons to discuss their faith 'pertinently, or, better said, perniciously'. These words betray an antipathy to the Huguenot religion that was quite normal for a French Catholic churchman, but they were also tainted with envy. De Paul

introduction to the sermon on the catechism confirms that he composed it for an audience in Joigny, and that he intended it to pave the way for sessions of catechesis to gatherings of children in the area: ACMP, 'Sermon sur le catéchisme', fo. 1r–v, and 'Sermon sur le [*sic*] communion I', and 'Sermon sur le [*sic*] communion II' (unpaginated).

[25] 'Catéchisme', fo. 2v: 'Et puis quel profit tire de la messe celuy qui ne cest [sait] pas ce que c'est, ni de la confession celui qui ne cest [sait] en quoy elle consiste?'

[26] 'Catéchisme', fo. 2r: 'N'est-il pas vray que l'ignorance est sy grande, que je me suis trouvé avec des personnes chrestiennes & catholiques auxquels j'ay demandé s'ilz sçavoyent les commandements de Dieu, qui me respondoyent qu'ilz avoyent jamais esté à l'escole, & d'autres qu'ils les sçavoyent bien lire dans les heures?'

[27] 'Catéchisme', fo. 1v: 'Il enseigne qui est celui mérite le tiltre de chrestien, la fin pour laquelle l'homme a esté créé, comme il y a un Dieu en trios personnes & trois personnes en un Dieu . . . les sacremens, & l'exercices du chrestien.'

accused the Huguenots of stealing 'the catechism to ruin our faith', and urged Catholics to turn the tables on them by seizing back the catechism in order to 'apply it on the wound' to heal it.[28] More positively, he also profited from Catholic role models who had issued this type of rejoinder to Protestant evangelization: in La Rochelle, an area where there had been a real contest between the denominations and where de Paul still held the abbey of Saint-Léonard-de-Chaumes, he had admired the work of a 'good doctor' who had successfully catechized the children of around 1,500 Catholics. This was probably the talented Jacques Gasteaud, one of the Oratorians with whom de Paul forged a relationship during these years.[29]

Throughout all three sermons, the purifying power of instruction is a persistent refrain. In one of the pair on communion, de Paul explained that the well-disposed soul was one that responded to God in love and thankfulness for the gift of his Son, who gave his flesh 'for the life of the world'.[30] Catechesis drew individuals towards God, teaching them to renounce vice and to praise god as they learned of his love for them:

> The catechism teaches us faith, it makes us put our hope in God in our adversities, it makes us love and fear God and our neighbour, secures us against the devil's temptations, renders us safe against the enemies of the faith and ultimately obtains paradise for us.[31]

When extolling the benefits of effective catechesis, de Paul referred to qualities that he would insist he had recognized in the parishioners of rural Clichy. First, he affirmed that it promoted obedience amongst those who completed it, and would form a primary means of ridding them of the 'crass ignorance' and 'blindness' that characteristically plagued those who had never done so.[32] Their obedience would rest on a state of restoration, that is, catechesis would restore participants to a state of openness, indeed to a condition of ignorance, which would dispose them to receiving the sacraments of confession and communion, 'thinking only in [their] heart[s] about emptying the dirt from [their] soul[s] by contrition and making a firm proposition not to offend God anymore'. At first glance, the notion that the successfully catechized might be both knowledgeable and ignorant is paradoxical, but de Paul was describing a form of spiritual childhood, in which their status was defined solely by trust in, respect for, and love of God—a state in which they lived in awe or fear of God.[33] He defined ignorance in two diametrically opposing ways:

[28] 'Catéchisme', fo. 2r: 'l'apliquons sur la playe.'

[29] A native of Niort, east of La Rochelle, and equipped with a doctorate in theology from the Sorbonne (1602), Gasteau was the superior of the Oratorian house in La Rochelle in 1613. He oversaw the provision of pastoral care to the Catholic residents of the city parish of Saint-Jean, where he was *curé*: 'Catéchisme', fo. 2v; Habert, *Berulle*, 330.

[30] ACMP, 'Communion II': 'pour la vie du monde.'

[31] ACMP, 'Catéchisme', fo 2v: 'Le catéchisme nous enseigne la foy, il nous fait metre notre espérance en Dieu en nos adversitez, il nous fait aymer et craindre Dieu & nostre prochain, nous asseure contre les tentations du diable, nous rend asseurez contre les ennemys de la foi & finalement nous obtient le paradis.'

[32] ACMP, 'Catéchisme', fo. 2r.

[33] ACMP, 'Communion II': '. . . pensant seulement en son Coeur vider les ordures de son âme par une contrition et à faire une ferme proposition de ne plus offenser Dieu . . . tout ressouvenir que celui

a positive state of humble malleability, readiness, and candour (actualized in the parishioners of Clichy), and a negative condition in which a filthy soul was damaged by vileness and wilfulness.[34]

Catechesis, confession, and eucharistic practice were, therefore, intrinsically linked in de Paul's pastoral vision and practice in these years, with the first preparing the way for the others. The eucharist was the most august source of divine grace for Christian living, a 'celestial pasture' of nourishment; corrupted souls, de Paul warned, would be troubled by 'an extreme regret . . . which gnaws at their souls because of their unworthiness, unpreparedness, and lack of devotion when they approach this sacred banquet'.[35] To precede it, he began to favour a specialized form of confession, known as the general confession, in which sinners confessed, not merely sins committed since their last confession, but all of the sins that they had committed throughout their life. Absolved of sin, they could then approach the eucharistic sacrament without being paralysed by the type of fear and shame that had caused the peasant in Gannes to hide his sins until persuaded to do otherwise.[36] Most studies do not linger on the significance of this special ritual in de Paul's pastoral programme, but his trust in its efficacy lasted for the duration of his life.[37] He extended its use into a variety of pastoral contexts, and, like catechesis, it was explicitly identified as one of the Lazarists' priorities in the contract of foundation that inaugurated the community in April 1625.[38]

De Paul was, therefore, to become a leading advocate of general confession as a means of ensuring that the faithful admitted all of their sins, approached the eucharist cleansed of sin, and died in the favour of God. He was not, of course, the only or even the first to understand its potential. None of his contemporaries could claim this accolade either. It was Ignatius of Loyola, founder of the Society of Jesus in the sixteenth century, who had proved most attuned to the rite's possibilities. He formalized its place in the Jesuits' conception of conversion and *christianitas* when he included it in the *Spiritual Exercises*. In this seminal text, general confession formed the climax of the first of four weeks of meditations, which

de Dieu, de notre entendement toute connaissance et de notre volonté tout amour que celui de Dieu, considerant qui nous somme et quel est celui que nous recevons.'

34 ACMP, 'Catéchisme', fo. 3r: 'Il faut donc que ceux qui voudront aprendre renoncent aux vices & aux péchés, qui sont comme des ordures de l'âmes, & dans peu de temps ills loueront Dieu d'avoir aprins ce qu'ilz aprendront & ne voudroyt pour tout ce qui est au monde parce que le pris du royaume des Cieux & la' (the sentence ends here).

35 ACMP, 'Communion II': 'cette céleste pâture . . . La peine est pour ceux qui . . . ont un extreme regret et comme un Prométhée qui leur ronge l'âme à cause de leur indignité, indisposition et indévotion qu'ils ont lorsqu'ils s'approchent de ce sacré banquet.'

36 *CCD*, 12: 7, 73.

37 Exceptionally, Alexandrette Bugelli investigates the place of general confession within de Paul's spirituality but concentrates mainly on the theology of reconciliation rather than on the practice of the rite in the circumstances of rural mission: Bugelli, *Vincent de Paul*.

38 Likewise, see requests from the Lazarists to Propaganda Fide for indulgences to be granted to those who completed general confessions. De Paul also encouraged members of the confraternities of charity and the Daughters of Charity to prepare the sick for a general confession of their sins when they visited them to lend aid: *CCD*, 9: 49; *CCD*, 13a: 214, 306, 310–11; *CCD*, 13b: 379–83.

guided the individual through the stages of purgation, illumination, and union that Ignatius hoped would prepare and dispose the soul 'to rid itself of all its disordered affections', and to seek and find 'God's will in the ordering of our life for the salvation of our soul'.[39] From there, the general confession had quickly became widely practised amongst Jesuits as well as a customary element of the spiritual direction that they offered to others.[40] Indeed, Maher suggests that instances of its use can identify persons or groups who were under Jesuit influence, for confraternities such as the Aas incorporated general confession into their initiation rituals, and women who sheltered in the refuges established by the Jesuits and their supporters were obliged to make a general confession on entry.[41] Still, scholars have found it exceedingly difficult to trace the passage of the practice from the more rarefied orbit of Jesuit confessors, seminarians, and well-born Catholic followers to widespread use in the Catholic mainstream, so de Paul's appeal to it from the 1610s provides a noteworthy example of its migration beyond the spheres of Jesuit ministry.

Perhaps de Paul had met Jesuits in Paris, or had studied the *Spiritual Exercises* and decided to adopt general confession. It is also possible that he learned about it from the Oratorians, who were beginning to administer it too, or from its recommendation to readers as an occasional practice by de Sales in his *Introduction to the Devout Life*. What is sure is that de Paul resolved to use a particular definition of the practice, which was a combination of the types that the Jesuits had developed.[42] He envisaged that peasants should confess sins that they had deliberately concealed (itself a sin which should also be confessed), as well as review their entire life so that they could express sorrow for all of the sins that they had committed during it and turn resolutely away from evil. Short of time, he could not hope to ask the penitents to complete the specific exercises that Ignatius of Loyola laid down in the *Spiritual Exercises*, but the objective of the speedier process that he adopted remained identical: the examination of conscience in order to identify and confess sins should result in a closer relationship with God. As his insistence that the stricken peasant of Gannes confess the specific sin that he had hidden confirms, de Paul required that penitents should itemize their sins in order to purge themselves of all that distanced them from God. Yet the ultimate purpose of the confession was not the forensic recounting of infractions, but the acquisition of an overall view of the patterns of error in their lives. In that sense, the rite was an emergency response to sinful situations, and a condensed version of the general confession with which Ignatius of Loyola punctuated the meditations and exercises of his *Spiritual Exercises*.

[39] Ignatius of Loyola, *Exercises*, para. 1.

[40] The Jesuit Constitutions obliged novices to make a general confession before admission to first vows, and Ignatius advised Jesuits to make a general confession every six months: *Constitutions*, paras 65, 98, 200.

[41] Maher, 'Confession and Consolation'. On the Aas, see Châtellier, *Europe of the Devout*.

[42] O'Malley, *First Jesuits*, 137. De Sales, *Introduction*, 49–50.

IV

De Paul's recourse to catechesis and general confession ensures that disappointment awaits those who seek originality in the practices to which he appealed during the initial years of his involvement in rural pastorate. Yet wholesale innovation was not essential when a priest such as he was newly exposed to practices that were current in the church, and was provoked into applying them in ways that he thought suitable for the situations that he encountered. Further confirmation of the potential to be unlocked by adaptation comes from his tenure in Châtillon, where he experimented with a venture that resulted in the first of many confraternities of charity that he promoted in succeeding decades. Confraternities in general were already proving crucial to the impact of the Catholic reform movement internationally; moreover, by using these organizational models to promote particular forms of veneration, rituals, and moral imperatives, clerical groups such as the Jesuits and Capuchins were actually following substantial precedents from Catholic religious practice in the later middle ages. Then, a dense pattern of confraternities had prevailed throughout Europe, along with an almost infinite variety of devotions and works under their banner. Reformers now seized upon them anew to promote regimens of pious rituals and moral habits for their members:[43] In Rome alone, sixty confraternities were founded between 1540 and 1600, mainly by Jesuits.[44] There and elsewhere, they proved notably adept in seizing upon the advantages of formal collective expressions of devotion, and encouraged the development of confraternities that combined common prayer and sacramental practice under the auspices of the Blessed Sacrament, the Holy Name of God, or, from the early 1560s, the Blessed Virgin.[45] Likewise, in the early seventeenth century, the French Oratorians became known for their establishment of confraternities of the rosary in the parishes in which they operated. They hoped to use these to foster loyalty to the church's highest human model of sanctity, and to encourage the faithful to seek the Virgin's protection and intercession as they joined in repeating a compendium of prayers that traced the mysteries of Christ's life, death, and resurrection from the annunciation to the coronation. On his arrival in Clichy, de Paul found one of these amongst the trio of confraternities in his parish. It had most likely been set up just a few years earlier by his predecessor as *curé*, the Oratorian Bourgoing.[46]

From his time in Clichy at the very least, therefore, de Paul was familiar with confraternities as venues for devotional prayer, but they were also used effectively to

[43] The literature on confraternities in the late medieval and early modern period is voluminous. See, in particular: Black, *Italian Confraternities*; Donnelly and Maher (eds), *Confraternities and Catholic Reform*; Flynn, *Sacred Charity*; Gutton, *Confréries*; Terpstra, *Lay Confraternities*; Terpstra (ed.), *Politics*.

[44] Paglia, *Pietà dei carcerati*, 86–7.

[45] Châtellier, *Europe of the Devout*, *passim*; Lewis, 'Jesuit Confraternal Activity'; Maher, 'How the Jesuits Used their Congregations'; O'Malley, *First Jesuits*, 192–9.

[46] Abelly claimed that de Paul founded this confraternity, but Bourgoing appears to have instigated it before he left the parish. In 1623, de Paul converted the confraternity into a confraternity of charity, along the lines of that he had established in Châtillon in 1617: Abelly, *Vie*, i, 27; Lebeuf, *Histoire*, i, 424–5.

advance regular active Christian service to the poor. Again, the Jesuits in particular had been to the fore in encouraging the foundation of confraternities that combined common prayer and sacramental practice with works of mercy.[47] And, although with only moderate success, Archbishop Charles Borromeo had promoted confraternities of the Holy Sacrament and charity in Milanese parishes, in order to implant good habits of piety and moral action.[48] There were plenty of precedents, as a result, for the type of charitable organization that de Paul introduced in his parish. It was not from these, however, that he drew his immediate inspiration for it. Instead, he relied on another manifestation of the Catholic reform movement, the Brothers of Charity. In the first place, the new confraternity's name derived from this order, and specifically from the hospital that the Brothers had run in Rome since 1584, in fulfilment of their fourth vow, which obliged them to care for the sick.[49] De Paul had probably encountered the hospital when he paid a visit to Rome around 1600–1. Secondly, however, he had become more conversant with their work when he paid visits to their hospital in Paris a decade later, and he now chose to exploit the rule that they followed there and in their other hospitals. Crucially, he adapted it to fit a parish setting and to suit the needs of a new set of practitioners, that is, lay women who were neither institutionalized nor clericalized. He divided his rule into ten sections, which included directions for the government of the confraternity and the care of its resources, and instructions on the procedures to be followed when rostered 'servants of the poor' visited the sick in their houses.

The use of terms such as 'servants of the poor' was certainly not exclusive to de Paul or even to the Brothers who also used it, but reflects a general concern for Christocentric charity amongst *dévots* of the period. However, the rule does borrow explicitly from that of the Brothers, for the instructions of both on the provision of clothing, bedding, food, and meals were almost identical in words and sequence, as were their directions for sacramental preparation and provision of devotional reading to patients.[50] Yet de Paul simultaneously refrained from turning the consoeurs into female replicas of the hospitaller religious, and when the rules diverged it was because the Brothers' methods did not suit the needs of the lay confraternal members, or alternatively did not provide any or sufficient guidance for them. For example, the Châtillon rule offered detailed counsel to the inexperienced lay woman on the type of instruction to be given to patients: when the consoeurs first entered the house of a patient, they were told to erect an image of the crucifixion, so that the afflicted could 'consider what the Son of God suffered for him'.[51] Because they aimed to assist the poor spiritually as well as corporally,

[47] Maher, 'How the Jesuits Used their Congregations'; Maher, 'Confession and Consolation'.

[48] Zardin, 'Relaunching Confraternities'.

[49] ACMP, 'Règlement de la Charité . . . ', fo. 1r: 'Ladicte confrérie s'appellera la confrérie de la Charité, à l'imitation de l'hospital de la Charité de Rome; et les personnes dont elle sera principalement composée, servantes des pauvers ou de la charité.' For the vow, see Hélyot, *Dictionnaire*, iv, col. 625. The term used was 'hospitalité', which referred to warm receptiveness, rather than simply hospital premises.

[50] For extended analysis, see my 'Catholic Dévot'.

[51] ACMP, 'Règlement de la Charité . . . ', fo. 3v: 'il considère ce que le Filz de Dieu a souffert pour luy.'

members were asked to lead souls 'by the hand to God', 'exhorting [them] to bear their illness patiently, for love of God . . . to make acts of contrition . . . to resolve not to re-offend God'.[52]

It would be naive to argue that this confraternity broke through the 'circle of exclusions' that restricted female access to most positions of early modern civil, political, and ecclesiastical leadership. Yet it certainly was unusual in the extent to which it advocated for the active agency of lay women in religious devotion. Its members elected their own officers—a prioress, treasurer, and assistant—to administer resources and organize welfare. But most uncommonly for female confraternal participants, each 'servant of the poor' held a vote in all decisions, and their rule required that they meet on the third Sunday of each month to deliberate and pray together before the ballots.[53] It also took cognizance of their liberty to juggle time-consuming duties of charity with household responsibilities, no doubt because de Paul consulted with the members when formulating it, but also perhaps because he remembered the balance of responsibilities that his former employer had maintained amidst the myriad demands on her time. From the moment that the prioress identified a potential patient to the moment that she recorded their death or recovery, they were placed in the nursing care of her associates, who provided clean clothing, basic medicines, and food from provisions purchased by the treasurer. As a result, the consoeurs enjoyed considerable and authentic power over their activities; rather than being a simple and dry rendition of material duties, the rule acted as a charter of rights and obligations, both material and spiritual, with each member holding a stake in the pursuit of its objectives. However flattering this recognition of the input of individuals might prove, of course, it was designed to tie them ever more closely to the communal work of welfare. So too was the rule's encouragement of spiritual kinship, for the family of 'sisters' was asked to listen to exhortations for 'spiritual growth', and discuss issues arising regarding their spiritual progress and welfare activity.[54] In addition, 'the whole Company' was to assemble to confess and celebrate the eucharist four times annually in order to seek God's blessing for their association, on days chosen for their relevance to their sex or their community, such as the feasts of local patron saints Martin and Andrew.[55]

52 ACMP, 'Règlement de la Charité . . . ', fo. 5r–v: 'les mener comme par la main à Dieu'; 'les exorteront à supporter le mal patiemment, pour l'amour de Dieu . . . leur feront faire quelques actes de contrition . . . à se résoudre à ne jamais plus l'offencer'.

53 ACMP, 'Règlement de la Charité . . . ', fos 2r–v and 6r–v. The consoeurs were obliged to engage a male procurator to represent them in legal affairs, and the parish *curé* possessed a vote in the decision-making process. On other female confraternities, see Casagrande, 'Confraternities'.

54 ACMP, 'Règlement de la Charité', fos 6r–v, 9v.

55 The feast of Pentecost would remind the consoeurs of their role as apostles of the Lord; the feast of the Assumption would orientate their thoughts towards the reward given to the Mother of God for her purity, obedience, and servitude. The confraternity was officially established on the feast of the Immaculate Conception of the Virgin Mary (8 December), a further reference to her proposed devotional importance for confraternal members. This feast became a holy day of obligation in 1708, although the doctrine of the Immaculate Conception was not promulgated until 1854: ACMP, 'Règlement de la Charité', fo. 9r–v.

As the opening sentence of the rule declared, charity towards one's neighbour was 'an infallible mark of the true children of God', and the defining message that de Paul wished to pass to the women was that they should serve their divine protector in imitation of the 'humility, charity and simplicity' with which he had reached out to the needy. In turn, when they aided the least of his children, they served him who stood with them in their hunger and sickness.[56] In going on to state expressly that one of the primary objectives of the confraternity was to dispose souls to salvation, de Paul resorted to words which were very similar to those that he had used in his sermon on catechesis just over a year before, when he observed that catechesis would enable individuals to recognize and respond to the love of God manifested in the sacrifice of his Son. Here, however, he meant that the confraternal members should open their lives to God, even at times when they were not engaged in visits. At this point, it is necessary, therefore, to draw attention to the presence of a further explicit influence on de Paul's construction of the confraternal venture: this was the teaching of François de Sales, a copy of whose *Introduction to the Devout Life* had accompanied de Paul to the parish. It would be almost another two years before de Paul would meet de Sales, but so important did he consider the *Introduction* to be to his structuring of female piety that he stipulated that those consoeurs who were able should read a chapter 'unhurriedly and attentively' from it each day. This was because the imitation of Christ should not stop abruptly once they left the bedsides of the sick, but should dictate each waking moment, regardless of whether they were alone, surrounded by family, or immersed in household tasks. Their routines were to be threaded with interior and external acts of devotion, including prayers of thanks and entreaties to virtue, and attendance at mass when feasible. In sum, the benefits of a healthy training in interior piety would become evident in their virtuous conduct, for a tranquil demeanour reflected a soul at peace with the will of the Lord, and replete with the fruits of his love.[57]

In later years, de Paul was to amplify his explicit dependence on de Sales's teaching to justify the involvement of lay women in charitable works, but it is clear that even at this early stage the bishop's published words provided spiritual inspiration, justification, and indirect endorsement for the values and activities enshrined in this prototype confraternity. De Sales taught that 'Devotion must be exercised in different ways by the gentleman, the worker, the servant, the prince, the widow, the young girl, and the married woman . . . the practice of devotion must also be adapted to the strength, activities, and duties of each particular person.' Every vocation was therefore agreeable when united with devotion.[58] As a rallying call to a form of female apostolate through which Catholic women could seek sanctification in the world, de Sales's work dovetailed perfectly with the objectives that de Paul set for each of the 'servants of the poor'; the pursuit of her

[56] ACMP, 'Règlement de la Charité', fo. 1r: '. . . une marque infaillible des vrays enfants de Dieu'; ACMP, 'Règlement de la Charité', fo. 11r. The rule quotes Matt. 25: 40 at this point.

[57] ACMP, 'Règlement de la Charité', fos 9r–10v.

[58] De Sales, *Introduction*, 43–4.

own spiritual perfection and the sanctification of others, through care for their physical and spiritual wellbeing, while still living in society.[59]

From the time that he left Châtillon at the close of 1617, de Paul was to display absolute confidence in the value of the confraternity of charity as a framework for implanting both the means of holiness and holiness itself in individuals and communities. The actions that he took in this parish, and the manner in which he justified them, were the culmination of close to a decade of pastoral experience, during which he began to isolate deficiencies in the service that the clergy provided to the rural faithful and to devise remedies to apply in response, but also to give formal expression to existing devotional inclinations amongst inhabitants. At first glance, the environments in which he spent his time in these years could not have been more dissimilar, seemingly worlds apart in terms of the social status of those he met, the level of material comfort available, the numbers to whom he attended, and their apparent spiritual needs. Yet, all of this was to de Paul's advantage. From Clichy, he drew a template for the thriving parish and devout laity, which he could recall to keep his aspirations for rural religious practice alive. Over time, on the Gondi estates and Châtillon, he enterprisingly tested out related tactics of instruction, sacramental observance, and communal charity; when used in combination, these could form a strategy for conversion and habitual piety that might turn his ideal into reality anywhere in rural France, however long he remained in one place. Equally, de Paul crossed social and geographical boundaries in these years, and by 1618 he straddled domains that were defined and differentiated by geography and the social status of those he encountered within them. Both in terms of his exposure to different modes of life and his ability to act simultaneously in both domains later, this was highly beneficial: he was of rural origin and had lived amongst country people, but had also resided at length in Paris, where he had grown accustomed to urban life in a noble household. In these locales, he ministered to people from distinct groupings in the social hierarchy, and he learned to move between them with a more certain and precise understanding of their spiritual attitudes, knowledge, and appetites. Of course, de Paul's clerical status and education had been vital to his securing access to both environments and the socially differentiated people within them in the first place, and he would otherwise have found it an insurmountable challenge to win opportunities to minister to nobility like the Gondi or rural peasant parishioners, or to attach to Pierre de Bérulle. As a result, in his own person de Paul gingerly bridged the urban and rural worlds of early seventeenth-century people, which offered him an advantage over a contemporary like Bérulle, who was predominantly Paris-based, of illustrious social stock, and generally most at home amongst his own social type. De Paul was beginning to chart his own course, reaching out to people of different backgrounds and circumstances. And while not remaining exclusively amongst any of them, he would ultimately act as a point of contact for them.

[59] ACMP, 'Règlement de la Charité', fo. 10r.

PART II

THE ANATOMY OF A MISSION

4

Founding a Congregation of Missionaries

I

When de Paul returned to Paris from Châtillon, he slipped back into his roles as preceptor and director, reverting officially to the status that he had previously held in the Gondi household.[1] Yet although his return reaffirmed his dependence on the family's patronage, the second stage of his relationship with its members was in reality perceptibly different from the first. The passage of time would reveal that de Paul was deeply impressed by the pastoral ideas and practices to which he had been exposed in the years immediately preceding 1618. For some time, the Gondi lands continued to be the principal laboratory for his experiments in pastoral ministry, and the security of tenure that he enjoyed in the family's employ allowed him some freedom to risk undertaking them, while also providing a means of preserving a sense of common action and purpose with the Gondi themselves. This culminated, shortly before the death of Madame, with the endowment of the Congregation of the Mission in 1625. In charting its course thereafter, de Paul was forced to confront insistently pressing questions, the answers to which would determine the character, functioning, and, critically, the durability of his new mission institute. The most fundamental of these related to the development of a formal organizational structure to support its vocational imperatives. It paired with a second: in the chase to obey these imperatives, what material assets would sustain the labours of his new community? And this, in turn, led to a third: as the new Congregation of missionaries positioned itself amongst the clerical groupings of the church, what kind of reception could be expected from the ecclesiastical authorities and its peers in ministry? The answers to these questions are best gleaned through a composite analysis of the three milestones of the Congregation's early formation process: its initial foundation in 1625, the issuance of papal approval in 1633, and the controversial acquisition of the priory of Saint-Lazare in Paris in 1632.

[1] Coste claims that de Paul did not act as tutor to the children after he returned from Châtillon, but Madame's will expressly refers to de Paul as her confessor and tutor to her children in February 1619, so he must have remained in this role for some time after his return: *CCD*, 13a: 64; Coste, *Saint*, i, 115.

II

Amongst the long-term insights that de Paul gained from his work on the Gondi estates and in Châtillon, one of the most constructive was that he did not need to be a parish priest to improve religious practices. Once he returned to Paris, he began, as a result, to attempt to combine his taste for rural pastorate with a more 'itinerant' approach, and use both confraternities and missions to make his impact on visits to these. Thus, from 1618, he began to found confraternities on Gondi lands, and in the early 1620s he started intermittently to organize small mission-type campaigns, before eventually organizing a congregation for this purpose. In hindsight, the path that he took from the pulpit of the church in Folleville to the notary's quarters may have seemed entirely logical as well as providential to him. Yet, however surely de Paul made his way, he did so quite slowly, moved by his dawning realization that collaborative missions might provide a rewarding means to evangelize the rural population. He ran a small mission-type event with three Parisian clerics on the Gondi estate in Villepreux in February 1618, but there is no evidence that he followed this quickly with another elsewhere.[2] Instead, he devoted attention to the foundation of confraternities on Gondi lands, and he and Madame hoped in the following year that either the Jesuits or Oratorians could be prevailed upon to complete missions there. When neither proved interested, it prompted de Paul to do so, and in an ad hoc fashion. While she remained in reasonable health, Madame encouraged his forays onto Gondi land, before beginning to consider leaving a legacy which would enable him to minister formally and regularly when her health began to decline irreparably.[3]

While ministering to rural dwellers gradually became de Paul's chief concern from this time the Gondi also proved decisive in expanding his horizons. In 1619, Louis XIII appointed de Paul, an 'upright priest of known ability', to the office of chaplain general of the royal galleys, on the recommendation of Monsieur de Gondi, who had inherited the office of general of the galleys of France from his elder brother in 1598.[4] Gondi was paid 12,000 *livres* yearly for fulfilling extensive and demanding duties; he held command over all of the royal galleys which defended French maritime interests in the Levant, and was required to construct and arm them for combat, acquire convicts to man the oars, pay wages to

[2] These were Pierre Berger and Gontiere, both clerical counsellors in the Paris *parlement* (Berger was also a canon of Notre-Dame de Paris), and Jean Coqueret (1592–1655), a theologian of the College of Navarre and principal of the College of Grassins. De Paul may have been introduced to them by a mutual acquaintance, the Sorbonne theologian André Duval: Gueriteau, *Opuscules*, 3–28.

[3] So keen did Madame prove to implement her wish that she purportedly included a provision that 16,000 *livres* should be assigned for this purpose in her will for several years. In the only version that survives, however, she stipulated rather that a sum of 1,000 *livres*, payable annually, should be used to pay the Jesuits or the Oratorians to carry out missions on the estates: Abelly, *Vie*, i, 66; *CCD*, 13a: 64. The will is dated 25 February 1619.

[4] On 16 January 1644, Louis XIV made this appointment permanent on the request of the then general of the galleys, the duke of Richelieu, one of de Paul's patrons: *CCD*, 13a: 337–78. See also Corbinelli, *Histoire*, 570–2, 600.

crew, and lead them into battle. Likewise, when de Paul was appointed chaplain to the galleys, he held authority over the ecclesiastics that served on the vessels when they were in port, and received 600 *livres* annually for his efforts.[5] This meant that he, and others that he recruited, needed to travel to Marseille and Bordeaux periodically. De Paul was also theoretically responsible for galley convicts imprisoned in Paris between their sentencing by the courts and their transport to the ships, and he may have influenced Gondi's decision to lodge them in a house near Saint-Roch church in the faubourg Saint-Honoré in 1618. Certainly this would have been convenient when he became galley chaplain as it allowed him to minister to them more efficiently than if he had to visit those 'weakened by pain and misery' in several prisons around Paris.[6]

De Paul's missions to April 1625 can therefore be divided into those he organized for galley convicts and rural communities, although it is impossible to quantify their number with certainty. There is only one record of a mission to the galleys (in Bordeaux in 1623), and although he acquired missionary faculties to use on Gondi land in the dioceses of Chartres, Sens, and Beauvais, only two specific locations for his rural missions are identifiable: Villepreux (1618) and Montmirail (1621).[7] Mapping the confraternities that de Paul founded is not a foolproof means of identifying mission sites, since he often established a confraternity of charity without holding a mission; for example, he started a confraternity in Montmirail in October 1618, but he seems to have held a mission there only in 1623, which covered the small town of Montmirail itself, and its surrounding villages. However, his privileged access to the Gondi lands was critical to his ability to attract clerics to the missions that he orchestrated, for these offered genuine opportunities for conscientious clerics to practise their pastoral skills on ordinary rural Catholics. In 1623, for instance, several like-minded priests accompanied de Paul to Montmirail, among them the experienced preachers Blaise Féron and Jérôme Duchesne, both doctors of the Sorbonne, and affiliates of Adrien Bourdoise's community in the parish of Saint-Nicolas-du-Chardonnet.[8] Over time, de Paul gathered a core of four or five clerics, who were so charmed by their experiences that they decided to commit to missionary work permanently. Féron was amongst these, as was a young

[5] Paul enlisted the help of several local religious for this work, prescribing that two should preach and administer the sacraments on each galley: *CCD*, 13a: 58; Niclas, 'Gondi-Retz', 192–8.

[6] In June 1618, the archbishop of Paris issued a pastoral letter imploring his clergy to donate alms to this cause, and de Paul may have been able to use this to offer food and clothing to the men: Abelly, *Vie*, i, 58–60.

[7] Abelly also briefly mentioned that de Paul carried out a mission in *Petites-Maisons* hospital in Saint-Germain in Paris, which housed about 400 elderly and ill persons, along with some destitute families: *Vie*, ii, 20; *CCD*, 12: 179.

[8] Duchesne was a member of Bourdoise's community from 1612, and had a reputation for his preaching skill on missions. He later became archdeacon of Beauvais, and worked with the Lazarists there when Bishop Potier invited them to lead a two-week retreat for ordinands in September 1628. During this, de Paul, Duchesne, and Louis Messier, another of Bourdoise's companions and archdeacon of Beauvais, made presentations on spiritual topics, such as the Ten Commandments, to the assembled clerics. Similarly, in 1631, Duchesne led exercises for ordinands in Bons-Enfants: Bib. Maz., Ms 2453, 672; *CCD*, 1: 56–7, de Paul to François du Coudray, 15 September 1628; Abelly, *Vie*, i, 117–18. On Féron, see Darche, *Bourdoise*, i, 243.

man called Antoine Portail, whom de Paul had first met in Clichy, and who had taken some responsibility for teaching the Gondi boys and for ministering to galley convicts around 1619.[9] Belin, the Gondi's chaplain in Villepreux, may have joined de Paul for a few years too, having earned his stripes ministering to the galley convicts.[10] Included too by April 1626 were the Sorbonne doctor François du Coudray (1586–1649) and the recently ordained graduate Jean de La Salle (1598–1639).[11]

Initially, these mission units were created rather haphazardly, and their composition principally depended on which of de Paul's contacts was available to minister at short notice. Then, between 1624 and 1625, he abandoned this ad hoc approach in favour of a fixed congregational community, which was undergirded by the Gondi endowment. In hindsight, de Paul argued that he had never anticipated establishing it, and was humbled by the fact that God 'looked to this little Company to serve his Church—if we can call a Company a fistful of men of lowly birth, learning, virtue, the dregs, the sweepings, and the rejects of the world'.[12] Perhaps this was true for a period in the early 1620s. Yet once de Paul had assembled the right combination of resources, experience, and objectives he was ready to grasp the opportunity when the Gondis presented it. Indeed, at this point of formation, he was far more clear-sighted than, say, Ignatius of Loyola and his fellows had been during the 1530s. Although the Society of Jesus was the largest missionary association in the Catholic church by the 1620s, its seven original members maintained that they had had no intention of founding a religious order or congregation, and their company, as Ignatius termed it, remained bound together simply by his leadership and their common search for a spiritual identity, until its formal approval by Pope Paul III in 1540.[13] Nearly a century later, de Paul's search for papal approval for his community took approximately the same length of time, and was achieved in 1633. In contrast to Ignatius, however, he had decided on its structure and purpose at least six years earlier, and it enjoyed financial security from this first stage of its existence.

At the same time, the circumstances of the Congregation's foundation were to some extent similar to those of other religious communities that emerged over the course of the Catholic Reformation. The majority incubated as confraternities, and only gradually picked up more clerical features.[14] Thus, from the moment of its

[9] According to Louis Robineau, one of the Lazarists who served as de Paul's secretary, Portail told him that he lived with de Paul in Clichy, when he was 'about nineteen or twenty'. (Portail was born in 1590 so he was actually 22 or 23). He probably learned the skills of pastoral and liturgical ministry from the older priest, a common form of priestly training for young men in France before the development of diocesan seminaries: ACMP, Robineau, 'Remarques', 158; *Notices sur les prêtres, clercs et frères*, i, 2–3. A printed edition of Robineau's manuscript is also available: Robineau, *Remarques*, ed. Dodin.

[10] At some stage between 1618 and 1624, Portail and Belin lived in rooms at the convicts' lodging: Abelly, *Vie*, i, 58–60.

[11] La Salle was ordained in 1622: *Notices sur les prêtres, clercs et frères*, i, 118.

[12] *CCD*, 11: 2. [13] O'Malley, *First Jesuits*, 33.

[14] Terpstra, 'Ignatius, Confratello'. See also the essays on individual orders such as the Theatines and Barnabites in Demolen (ed.), *Religious Orders*.

foundation, de Paul liked to describe the Congregation as a company and confraternity, affirming that its confreres were united by their sense of spiritual solidarity and fraternity, and motivated by a common sense of spiritual service. Very quickly, however, and more rapidly than many confraternities that subsequently matured into religious orders, de Paul's group also assumed the characteristics of a particular type of clerical association, which was both secular and congregational. It provided a readymade, though flexible, formula for community living, and a stable framework within which de Paul could implement his missionary vision. At no point, however, did de Paul intend that it should comprise a religious order.

The first sure sign that de Paul was ready to establish a formal grouping of missionaries appeared in March 1624 when he accepted the offices of chaplain and principal of the College of Bons-Enfants in Paris from Archbishop Jean-François de Gondi, as a means of finding a residence suitable for a community.[15] However enthusiastic de Paul may have been to accept responsibility for the college, he could not have done so without the support of his employer's brother, and it is clear that the transfer of the college was simply the first step in a newly agreed series; subsequent events were to demonstrate that the trio of husband, wife, and archbishop had resolved to pool their resources to enable de Paul to fulfil what they now knew to be his desire to lead a missionary community. Dynastic ties aside, the archbishop was customarily an advocate of such initiatives amongst his clergy. Around the same time that he sought to promote de Paul's proposal, he also approved the establishment of the Fathers of Christian Doctrine in the capital after one of them, Antoine Vigier, became his spiritual director.[16] The 300-year-old institution that Gondi offered to de Paul was a college of the University of Paris, centrally situated on 16 acres along the rue Saint-Victor, and beside the College of Cardinal Lemoine. It also neighboured Adrien Bourdoise's community. As a report that de Paul commissioned in 1625 records, the college was in shabby but habitable condition, and was only used to provide lodgings for seven or eight students, and perhaps a few Irish Franciscans.[17]

Significantly, it was not primarily from Bérulle that de Paul sought advice on this acquisition, but other trusted confidants. One was André Duval, to whom de Paul described the spiritual hunger of the people that he met in rural France during their

[15] As chaplain, de Paul claimed an annual emolument of 18 *livres* from the city of Paris. The Bibliothèque Municipale de Laon (carton 12, no. 126), holds a receipt acknowledging the payment of 18 *livres* 5 *sols*; this was signed by de Paul and dated 2 September 1646.

[16] The *Pères de la Doctrine Chrétienne* or *Doctrinaires* was founded by César de Bus in 1592: Viguerie, *Œuvre d'éducation*, 72; Niclas, 'Gondi-Retz', 287–8.

[17] The report specified that the college chapel required substantial refurbishment and that several sections of its living quarters were uninhabitable, so much so that the visiting masons recommended that they be knocked down and rebuilt! AN S6373a, H5 3288; AN, Minutier Central, Registre 184, fo. 163; *CCD*, 1: 22–3, de Paul to Nicolas de Bailleul, 25 July 1625. Amongst the students were two descendants of a former principal, Jean Pluyette, who had endowed two bursaries in 1469. These continued to be awarded until 1789, but the Congregation only provided accommodation until 1639: AN, M105 and H[3]2554; Pluyette, *Recteur de l'Université*. See *CCD*, 1, for letters from Gilles Pluyette to de Paul on this arrangement.

conversations about the college. He may also have gained conviction from his talks with another individual who was very experienced in pastoral work and had also become a friend, Adrien Bourdoise.[18] They had initially became acquainted when they met through Bérulle around 1611, but Bourdoise had progressed much more rapidly than de Paul in establishing a community of clerics in Saint-Nicolas-du-Chardonnet parish. From 1615, he had begun to arrange missions of thirty or more missionaries in dioceses surrounding Paris, particularly Chartres where he had been born.[19] In the early 1620s, de Paul began to collaborate on missions with some of his priests, which was a sensible choice given their numbers and specialist skills.[20] It was also symptomatic of de Paul's broadening horizons, as he became less reliant on Bérulle and the Oratorians for support and example, and looked towards other expressions of clerical life to design his own. For example, it is possible that he borrowed his policy that the Lazarists should not charge parishes for their services from Bourdoise, who had since the 1610s been adamant that missions should not become a burden to parishioners.[21]

De Paul vacillated for a time over the implications of accepting the archbishop's offer, partly because he could not yet be sure that he could gather a sufficient number of companions to establish a permanent community. Portail and Féron soon moved into the college, however, and de Paul joined them there full-time in June 1625.[22] Following its acquisition, the next stage in the Congregation's gestation was the provision of a legal framework and financial underpinning for its activities.[23] Two contracts, signed on 17 April 1625 and 17 April 1627, laid out the terms.[24] Almost concurrently, the archbishop and king bestowed their approval of these and, as a further mark of appreciation, the archbishop gave leave to the new association to complete missions in his diocese.[25] Time was pressing: by the time that the parties signed the first contract, Madame de Gondi's health was deteriorating rapidly. In the preceding months, it had become her urgent wish to ensure that de Paul was provided with a permanent means of pursuing this work after her death;[26] equally, within two years of his wife's death, Monsieur entered the

18 Archives des Carmélites de Clamart, Duval, 'Vie de Mre André Duval', 43–5.

19 Bourdoise's mission in Brou in 1615 counted ninety missionaries, making it an imposing affair: Sauzet, 'Prédication et missions'.

20 See *CCD*, 1: 176–80, de Paul to Antoine Portail, 28 November 1632, for an example of the teamwork of the Congregation and the priests of Saint-Nicolas-du-Chardonnet during a mission in Joigny.

21 Sauzet, 'Prédication et missions'.

22 Coste wrongly guesses that the second priest was Belin, but it was Blaise Féron: both Portail and Blaise Féron were given power of attorney to take possession of the college on 2 March 1624, and on 25 April 1625 Féron certified that he celebrated mass every week in the college chapel, which was a requirement of the group's residence: *CCD*, 13a: 70–2, 75n.; AN, S6373a; Abelly, *Vie*, i, 85.

23 Also influential on de Paul's tardiness was his desire to curtail his eagerness, in case it stemmed from 'nature or from the malign spirit'. In later years, he recalled that he completed a retreat in Soissons 'in the early stages of the plan of the Mission', so that God allowed that he fall 'in the opposite dispositions', and used this to justify why important decisions should not be taken while one was caught up 'in these ardent hopes at the prospect of great benefits': the spirit of God, de Paul ruminated, 'goes softly and always humbly': *CCD*, 2: 277–8, de Paul to Bernard Codoing, 1 April 1642.

24 *CCD*, 13a: 213–17, 224–5.

25 *CCD*, 13a: 218, 226–7.

26 *CCD*, 13a: 224.

Oratory, and his plan to do so was probably known to both his wife and de Paul at the time that they negotiated the contract. It certainly explains why Monsieur in particular wished to 'fulfil what he feels obliged to do' in institutionalizing the care that de Paul provided to galley convicts.[27]

In the first contract, the financial basis for the new 'congregation' was set out. The Gondi couple pledged de Paul's community a capital sum of 45,000 *livres*, comparable in size to the 50,000 *livres* with which Monsieur's sister, the marchioness of Maignelay, had founded Bérulle's Oratory in 1611, or indeed to the 64,000 *livres* that he presented to it in 1629.[28] To do so, they capitalized on their formidable access to an array of ecclesiastical resources, drawing money from two abbeys that their youngest son held *in commendam*: Buzay in Nantes, which had an annual revenue of 8,000 *livres*, and Sainte-Croix-de-Quimperlé, which enjoyed one of 15,000 *livres*.[29] The couple attached particular conditions to their gift, for the contract terms decreed that de Paul should spend it 'on land investments or other established revenues', the income from which should be dedicated to maintaining at least six priests who would perform missions every five years on the rural Gondi lands and amongst galley convicts, and 'in places they judge most suitable'. In turn, de Paul invested the lump sum quickly; although it is not possible to account for every *sou*, it can be deduced that until 1654 his Congregation earned a respectable 2,000 *livres* annually from a principle of 32,000 *livres* assigned to the *ferme des gabelles* on 3 June 1625.[30] If de Paul felt any qualms at this time or subsequently about accepting the revenue of an abbey held by an absentee and under-age incumbent, he rationalized it by arguing that he had accepted a temporal good of the church which was part of the patrimony of Jesus and the poor, but that he had used it to their advantage, that is, for a good and Christian cause, the care of the rural poor.[31]

In addition to the substantial funding provided, the most important implication for the structure and functioning of the new community lay in the extensive control that the Gondi were permitted to exert over its use of the income and its 'manner of

[27] *CCD*, 13a: 216.

[28] AN, MM623, 'Annales de la maison de l'Oratoire', 9. De Paul received 37,000 *livres* on 17 April 1625, and the remainder one year later: *CCD*, 13a: 214. Philippe-Emmanuel de Gondi's donation to the Oratory (22 August 1629) produced 4,000 *livres* annually which was assigned to the maintenance of twelve confreres and their director: AN, MM623, 'Annales de la maison de l'Oratoire', 140.

[29] The abbeys were transferred to the youngest son of the Gondi, who was tonsured in 1623, after his brother Henri died in 1622: Beaunier, *Recueil historique*, ii, 940; ACMP, Robineau, 'Remarques', 24–7. See Battiffol, *Retz*, 10–11.

[30] This income is mentioned in the contract transferring the priory of Saint-Lazare to the Congregation on 7 January 1632, but already, on 26 August 1631, in partnership with Louise de Marillac, de Paul had sold a small portion of the income to Gilles Guérin, husband of a woman who later became a member of the confraternity of charity at the Paris *Hôtel-Dieu*, for the sum of 2,700 *livres*. In 1654, the crown reduced the return on the remainder to 1,250 *livres* yearly: AN, M213, 'Mémoires sur la fondation de Monsieur de Gondy comte de Joigny et de la dame son épouse'; *CCD*, 13a: 259–62, 266.

[31] ACMP, Robineau, 'Remarques', 26–7. This was a maxim common to reformers. For an analysis in relation to the episcopate's use of ecclesiastical patrimony for personal or secular benefits, see Forrestal, *Fathers*, 186.

life': the contract outlined a strict calendar for the missions between October and June, and required that the priests catechize in the villages on Sundays for the remainder of the year. Given their commitment to fund the enterprise, it was natural that the Gondi wished to prioritize the delivery of missions and routine instruction on their estates and the galleys, for their *dévot* sentiments went hand in hand with a sense of social responsibility to the spiritual and material wellbeing of their tenants and the convicts that manned the ships. But they also required that de Paul continue to live in their household, rather than at Bons-Enfants, a pronounced inconvenience for the head of a community. It was certainly not what de Paul wished to do for any longer than necessary to placate his employers. However, his years with the Gondi had taught him a valuable and lifelong lesson: first, his own religious objectives would not always be identical to those of his patrons, and, on this occasion, they were reluctant to release him entirely even to the most laudable of activities; second, he knew that, although it was essential to fix common goals with patrons for the promotion of piety, the meeting of those objectives required flexibility and compromise on his part, as well as the skill to prioritize immediate necessities over those that could wait for the future. In this case, de Paul apparently conceded that it was more important to secure funding and to preserve good relations with his patrons through obeying the criteria that they set for their donation than to reside with his companions immediately.

After Madame died and her widower joined the Oratorians, he was amenable to modifications to the original terms. With his eyes trained on the future, de Paul was keen to take this opportunity to ensure that his group was not saddled with restrictions that would hinder its growth and freedom of action. In addition, over the previous two years, he had perhaps recognized that it was extremely difficult for his tiny cohort to meet the stringent pastoral obligations that their patrons had placed on them. Indeed, their inability to do so probably inspired Gondi to request special faculties from Rome in early 1627 for the Capuchins to hear confessions in Joigny, because the inhabitants were 'badly instructed'. He had also depended on them to instruct and confess galley crews since 1625, presumably under de Paul's oversight, and in an effort to supplement the meagre results that the Congregation could achieve.[32] Now, Gondi conceded full liberty in determining the Congregation's structure, government, and rules of living to de Paul, by confirming that he and his family entirely waived their influence over the members' 'manner of life, retreat and personal conduct'. Further, he forfeited all contractual clauses that had ascribed control of the missions to him or his family, leaving the timing and duration of these entirely in de Paul's hands.[33]

[32] De Paul led his priests in a mission in Joigny in January 1628: *CCD*, 1: 34–5, de Paul to Louise de Marillac, 17 January 1628. For the Capuchins, see SCPF, 387, fos 142r and 148v, and ACTA 4, fo. 208r (Joigny). The cardinals rejected Gondi's request that the Capuchins be granted leave to continue their work on 5 June 1627: SCPF, SOCG 129, fos 140r–141r, and ACTA 4, fo. 237r.

[33] *CCD*, 13a: 224–5.

III

Before the ink was dry on the second contract, de Paul took the next logical step of seeking a papal mandate for his group's work, and approval of the foundation itself. Without these, the company could never enjoy full status within the Catholic church; papal recognition would provide it with the definitive badges of favour and legitimacy, thus inserting it securely into the church's universal mission of evangelization and the history of salvation. In this final stage of formation, de Paul endured the most troublesome period of his campaign to secure the future of his association of missionaries, but it culminated successfully in the papal bull *Salvatoris Nostri* in January 1633. The history of the negotiations reveals that he struggled to explain his ambitions to the Roman hierarchy, and that his efforts to ensure that it recognize his incipient association were beset by resistance and misunderstanding. Yet de Paul's elaboration of its structure and remit provide remarkable insights into what he thought the character and purpose of his congregation to be. Just as valuably, the converse is also true: the variations between them demonstrate his ability to interpret, and occasionally anticipate, what the pope and cardinals expected them to be, and to expound and adjust his appeals accordingly. Ultimately, de Paul's challenge was not only to secure approbation, but to do so without abandoning the core principles that he thought should govern the association's functions.

Although de Paul's difficulties were partly due to the unfamiliar character of his association in the Catholic church, he was not the first to seek to establish a congregation of secular priests in France or elsewhere; as long ago as 1575, Pope Gregory XIII had approved the Congregation of the Oratory established by Philip Neri in Rome in 1566, and the French Congregation of the Oratory had recently received papal sanction in 1613. But, unlike de Paul, Bérulle did not have to tackle the Roman congregations when he sought papal confirmation for the Oratory; his elevated position within French clerical and noble circles meant that he was able to rely on high-ranking clerics, especially Denis de Marquemont, the Auditor of the Rota, and agent of French interests in Rome, and the Cardinal Protector of France, François de Joyeuse, with both of whom he was closely acquainted, to usher his proposal directly to Paul V for easy approval two years after he established the Oratory. Indeed, Bérulle assumed that supplications to the congregations of cardinals should be avoided at all cost because they would be subject to 'long and difficult' examinations.[34] He was correct, as de Paul found out to his chagrin when he presented three petitions for approval to two different Roman congregations before achieving the result he desired: two near identical in 1628, and a final one in 1632. De Paul also could not rely on consistent representation in Rome, so he deputed Féron and du Coudray to represent the Congregation periodically in the Eternal City.

[34] Dagens (ed.), *Correspondance*, i, 130, Pierre de Bérulle to Nicolas de Soulfour, 16 August 1611. This volume of letters contains multiple references to the process.

A second complicating factor lay in the difference between the objectives of the groups. De Paul borrowed his model of congregational organization from Bérulle's Oratory, which already enjoyed universal recognition as an institute of clerics which was exempt from episcopal jurisdiction for its internal affairs, even though its members were secular clerics. If de Paul's group was approved, therefore, it would not be unique in canonical status (though it is sometimes erroneously presented as such).[35] Even so, it was an innovative type of mission association in the 1620s, which did not fit the conventional categories of clerical organization or missionary venture. The Oratorians' main purpose was the sanctification of the priestly body of France, principally through reformed community life and the foundation of colleges and seminaries to train clergy.[36] Missions were a worthy but secondary occupation.[37] De Paul's association, on the other hand, placed equal emphasis on both sanctification and missions, because he conceived it as a community of clerics who were made holy through their evangelizing missions to rural people. His vision can also be distinguished from the other form of congregational life implemented by reform groups such as the Oblates of Saint Ambrose, originally founded by Charles Borromeo in 1578 to perform missions and direct colleges in Milan diocese under his exclusive command.[38] These were restricted to a particular diocese or formed independent communities in individual sees under episcopal control. In contrast, de Paul planned that his group would transcend diocesan perimeters and remain united under the leadership of a single superior general, rather than become a series of autonomous communities defined by the geography of diocesan boundaries. Moreover, de Paul knew that the term 'congregation' itself had very exact implications: his fraternal company would remain a society of secular priests, living in common and under the obedience of a superior general, without personal benefices, but also without a novitiate, religious dress, or the other essential elements of religious life, such as solemnly professed vows.[39] In every action that he took to gain papal confirmation for his association over the next seven years he stuck firmly to this vision of community life, and yoked it to the missionary agenda that he evoked for its members.[40]

De Paul first presented his case to the Roman Congregation of Propaganda Fide, because it, under the stewardship of Cardinal Ludovico Ludovisio, oversaw the missions of the Catholic church worldwide, and appeared to be the obvious authority to which to direct the petitions of a community of clerics who specialized

[35] Mezzadri and Román, *Vincentians*, 1: 31.

[36] By 1630, the Oratorians had 73 houses of varying sizes, of which 25 were colleges, seminaries, or houses of retreat for other clergy: Julia and Frijhoff, 'Oratoriens de France'.

[37] Dupuy, *Bérulle*, 211.

[38] Hélyot, *Histoire*, iv, cols 56–68; Deroo, *Borromée*, 345–6.

[39] Eventually, the Lazarists agreed that members would take simple vows of poverty, chastity, and obedience, as well as a fourth vow of stability, mainly to preserve a sense of community life, but these were not solemn religious vows. Román efficiently summarizes their introduction: Román, *Vincent de Paul*, 317–38.

[40] For these reasons, it is misleading, as Román does, to intimate that de Paul's understanding of the term 'congregation' at this stage was imprecise, because he was not yet certain of the direction in which he wished to take his 'child': Román, *Vincent de Paul*, 175. Perez-Flores offers more perceptive comments in 'De l'Équipe missionnaire'.

in these. Moreover, amongst its members was Cardinal Guido Bentivoglio, who had since 1621 acted as the protector of French interests in Rome, and could be expected to support the cause after he learned that it had royal favour in September 1628. In June 1627, de Paul initially submitted a simple request that he and his companions be granted 'the customary faculties granted to missionaries'.[41] This was a preliminary step, a testing of the reception that more ambitious requests might meet; once it received a positive answer, de Paul followed it up with the far more demanding appeal that the pope approve and confirm the community and its work in perpetuity, so that its members could strive 'for their own perfection and to devote themselves entirely to the country people' through their communal life and shared ministry. In two near identical petitions, he provided what should have been a welcome account of his group's origins and contribution to missionary evangelization in order to dispose the cardinals positively to it.[42] Further signalling the intensification of the campaign, his petitions were accompanied by supporting letters from powerful advocates in France, including Louis XIII, his wife Anne of Austria, and papal nuncio Giovanni di Bagno, solicited by the Gondi brothers on de Paul's behalf.[43] Despite this, his petitions were roundly rejected in August and September, and de Paul was forced to begin anew.

At first glance, there appeared little in the petitions that should displease the cardinals, for de Paul characterized the missionaries as ministers to rural Catholics who were 'oppressed by ignorance and poverty', and as moving 'from town to town . . . preaching sermons', 'teaching catechism and the mysteries of faith . . . of which most of the people are completely ignorant'. The petitions noted that they established confraternities of charity for 'the corporal and spiritual relief of the sick poor', and carried out all of their activities free of charge. They then went on to ask that the group's superior general be ascribed power to found new houses in 'places to where the local Bishops might call' for them, as well as authority over the reception of new members and community regulations.[44] Because de Paul insisted that the missionaries did not charge for their services, the petitions confirmed that they would not be a burden on local communities; nor would they antagonize local *curés*, or indeed religious, by competing against them for a share in the limited financial resources of parishes. There should therefore be no reason for the pope to deny faculties for the missionaries' pastoral functions (including the right to absolve reserved sins) and no reason for any *curé* to oppose their work.

Though a precise synopsis of the association's purpose and practice, this did not convince those to whom it was directed. To pinpoint why, it is vital to focus on de

[41] SOCG 198, fos 116r–121v, and SOCG 387, fo. 370r; *CCD*, 13a: 228–30.

[42] *CCD*, 1: 39–45, 47–53. The second petition differed from the first by referring additionally to the superior general's right to transfer Congregation members between houses.

[43] The king also instructed the French ambassador to the papacy, the count of Béthune, to make every possible effort to ensure success: *CCD*, 13a: 242, Giovanni di Bagno to Ludovico Ludovisio, 21 June 1628; *CCD*, 13a: 243, Louis XIII to Urban VIII, 24 June 1628; *CCD*, 13a: 244, Louis XIII to count of Béthune, 24 June 1628; *CCD*, 13a: 244, Giovanni di Bagno to Francesco Ingoli, 23 July 1628.

[44] *CCD*, 1: 42.

Paul's decision to adopt the term 'congregation' in the documents to describe the special nature of the community and its common life. This was the first time that he allowed it to appear in official paperwork relating to it; in his earlier request for faculties, he had neither described the community nor explicitly recognized the special nature of its common life. Now, in contrast, he deliberately chose to use the term, with the objective of persuading Rome to recognize the association's intermediary status, as neither a religious order nor a simple group of secular priests, but still a valid, purposeful, and perennial expression of the clerical vocation. This was a gamble that did not pay off. In adjudicating the supplication, Propaganda rejected it precisely because it concluded that, in spite of de Paul's protestations to the contrary, his group was a religious order in all but name.[45]

Since Propaganda had been established by Pope Gregory XV in 1622, its members had generally viewed propositions to establish new religious orders for missions negatively, and tended to favour simple requests for faculties or mobile groupings of missionaries rather than permanent institutes, especially of religious clergy.[46] On this occasion, it based its decision specifically on the report of one of its number, the cardinal secretary, Francesco Ingoli, who had been sufficiently disturbed by the version of the petition that he read (the second) to compose a lengthy critique of it between 23 July and mid-August.[47] Not present at the meeting on 22 August, he charged his fellow cardinal Guido Bentivoglio to present a summary of its main points, which proved overwhelmingly negative. This placed Bentivoglio in an awkward position as the protector of French interests.[48] But his voice mattered little on this occasion anyway, because the meeting as a whole was won over by Ingoli's criticisms of the project, chief of which was the proposition that the proposed congregation was, to all intents and purposes, a religious order. He expressed further pertinent points: if approved, the group would have a detrimental effect on relations between the different ranks of clergy, particularly bishops and regulars, because it would undermine episcopal authority:

> The obstacle for this Congregation is that introducing a new religious Community with exemption from the Ordinaries is very prejudicial to them because many priests will join this Congregation to escape that, and in this way the secular clergy will be weakened and reduced.

[45] *CCD*, 13a: 250–1, cardinals of Propaganda Fide to Giovanni di Bagno, 1 September 1628.

[46] Dompnier, 'Congrégation Romaine "de Propaganda Fide"'.

[47] It was Ingoli's assessment that swayed his companions in Propaganda Fide, contrary to what *CCD*, 1: 38n. concludes. Equally, his report was written before 22 August, and not on it, as *CCD*, 13a: 245 suggests: SOCG 130, fos 47r–48v; Coppo, 'Documenti inediti . . . I'; Coppo, 'Documenti inediti . . . II'.

[48] Moreover, Bentivoglio was handicapped by the fact the meeting of cardinals did not discuss the royal letters of support on 22 August; having been sent from La Rochelle on 28 July, they probably had not yet arrived in Rome. If they had, perhaps Bentivoglio would have blanched at the prospect of rejecting the French monarch's wishes. But the letters would not have changed the cardinals' minds anyway, for they still refused to overturn their decision after they studied them on 25 September: *CCD*, 13a: 250–1; SCPF, ACTA 6, fos 110v–111r; SOCG 130, fos 54r and 57v; Coppo, 'Documenti inediti . . . II'.

Furthermore, the cardinal noted that, as the group was de facto a religious order, it would be impossible to allow it the right to hold benefices, always the exclusive entitlement of secular clerics. The maximum concession that the pope should permit, therefore, Ingoli advised, was that the missionaries should be awarded faculties for their missions but be forbidden to increase their number to more than twenty or twenty-five priests. This should be perfectly satisfactory; the nature of mission was temporary and mutable as the church's ministerial and evangelistic needs changed and as conversions were won, so that an organization established to pursue it should be equally flexible, responsive, and finite. New religious orders were, most definitely, not what the church required to pursue evangelization.

For de Paul, the decision was deeply disappointing. He desperately desired that his association acquire the security of permanency and the ability to expand so that its members could meet the responsibilities that he believed God was placing on them. In that sense, the vision of mission that de Paul expressed in the 1628 petitions primarily comprised the traditional theological characteristic of *propagatio Christianae fidei*, or 'sending out' of missionaries to preach the gospel. Their target, rural people, mattered more than the specific locations of these people, for rural dwellers in need of instruction existed virtually everywhere in France. His approach corresponded to a then prevalent sense of mission that designated forays to Protestant, heathen, and Catholic lands as missions, but existed alongside the formal definition of a mission as a collection of missionaries in a designated political unit, such as the Jesuit *missio hollandica*.[49] However, because de Paul ascribed precedence to the need for widespread rural evangelization, he only exceptionally reconciled the work of his association with the geography of dioceses and the disciplinary power of local bishops. He advocated that the group should be exempt from episcopal jurisdiction in all matters excepting missions, and remain instead dependent on the Holy See. When compared to the course that Bérulle adopted to gain official status for the Oratorians in the early 1610s, de Paul's mistake becomes starkly apparent. While de Paul may not have intended to challenge episcopal authority, his choice of emphasis appeared to do exactly that. In contrast, when Bérulle described the remit of his proposed new congregation, he professed customary obedience to diocesan bishops in all but internal affairs, rather than customary exemption. Most diplomatically, he affirmed that the Oratorians continually renewed the vow of obedience that they made at their ordination in submitting to episcopal jurisdiction over 'the exercise and employment of ecclesiastical functions', and would never 'seek any employment from prelates, or anticipate . . . their command'.[50]

For de Paul, the right of his association to autonomy in its internal affairs was unassailable, but he eventually realized that if he was to win a future for it at all, he would need to adjust his tactics. After seeking counsel from Duval, he abandoned

[49] Clossey, *Salvation and Globalization*, 15.

[50] Bérulle, 'Projet de l'érection de la Congrégation de l'Oratoire de Jésus', Dagens (ed.), *Correspondance*, i, 118: '. . . à l'exercice et employ des fonctions ecclésiastiques . . . et ne pourraient rechercher des prélats aucun employ, ni prévenir en rien leur commandement.'

his hopes of convincing the cardinals of Propaganda Fide of the justice of his case, and switched his focus to those of the Congregation of Bishops and Regulars, where he hoped to gain a fresh and more sympathetic hearing. This was a radical shift, especially given that this Congregation, under the stewardship of Antonio Barberini, dealt with the jurisdictional relations between bishops and religious orders, the latter of which de Paul insistently professed his association was not. Furthermore, the cardinals who served on it were far more concerned about jurisdictional hierarchy in dioceses, particularly in relation to the smooth operation of clerical discipline, and were likely to read hawkishly and judge critically any proposal that a secular association of clerics should be exempt from episcopal oversight in any way. However, having made little headway in the chambers of Propaganda Fide over the course of two years, de Paul had little to lose in striking out for new ground. It is tempting to conclude, although available evidence cannot confirm it, that he may have done so on the advice of Bentivoglio as well as Duval; Bentivoglio was a seasoned papal servant who understood the conventions of government in Rome and the dispositions, nay prejudices, of its cardinal assessors. Indeed, he attended the meeting during which the petition was assessed on 30 April, and without Ingoli's views to impede him on this occasion, he spoke firmly in favour of the petition. He also sought letters from the nuncio and Archbishop Gondi to bolster his endorsement.[51]

De Paul also took care to ensure that the petition's arguments were tailored to accord with the concerns of its new assessors. For instance, in its earlier drafts, the conversion of heretics had been listed as one of the missionaries' functions, because this objective was a primary interest of Propaganda Fide, but this version simply referred at length to their efforts to minister to the rural poor in France, which was a far more accurate representation. De Paul's decision to drop the reference to heretics reflected the new readership he was targeting; while their conversion was an issue of some concern to the cardinals of the Congregation of Bishops and Regulars, as it was to any member of the curia with an interest in the church's spiritual health, it did not possess the same resonance there as it did in the meetings of Propaganda Fide.[52] In contrast, for governmental structures and procedures de Paul insisted vehemently that the application should reiterate the same principles as previously, that is, that it should posit that bishops would choose where the missionaries worked in their dioceses, that the missionaries would submit to *curés* whose parishes they visited, and that they would live at their own expense, but that, outside missions, the superior general would retain control of the association.[53]

[51] *CCD*, 1: 140n.; *CCD*, 1: 164, de Paul to François du Coudray, 12 July 1632.

[52] De Paul's logic in emphasizing the conversion of heretics in his petitions to Propaganda is evident when it is compared to the Oratorians' experience some years later. When these asked that the papacy recognize their congregation as one of 'mission' in 1644, Nuncio Grimaldi advised Propaganda's cardinals that this was unnecessary because their function, by their own admission, was to instruct the ignorant rather than to convert heretics. He also concluded that this request did not fit the remit of Propaganda's interests: SOCG 89, fos 292r–v, 293v, Girolamo Grimaldi to Propaganda Fide (probably Ingoli), 2 March 1644.

[53] The petition also noted that the group would minister in archiepiscopal or episcopal towns or in towns with presidial courts only when instructing ordinands or retreatants, an additional principle

Crucially, however, he also ensured that the petition concentrated on the obedience that the group would ordinarily demonstrate to bishops, presenting submission to episcopal jurisdiction, rather than congregational autonomy, as the norm rather than the exception. It celebrated that the priests were 'sent by the local Ordinaries' on missions, and professed 'perfect obedience to them'; it begged that the sole deviation from this, that is, the independence that the association sought for its internal affairs, should be approved by the pope. This conciliatory approach was more likely to receive a receptive hearing from a set of assessors who were invariably sensitive to attempts by clerical communities to evade episcopal discipline in dioceses. To further ease their qualms, de Paul's petition expressly and repeatedly stressed that he proposed a congregation of secular missionaries, and he avoided using the terms 'Congregation of the Mission' or 'Priests of the Mission' in order to avoid implanting the idea that his was an order of religious missionaries likely to cause dissension in dioceses.

Finally, de Paul also integrated a more overt and specific theological thread into his application, which was designed to explain explicitly and precisely the reasons for the association's existence, and to persuade doubtful cardinals of its service to souls and to the church as a whole. While the earlier petitions had simply presented the organization's purpose as the perfection of its members and the salvation of the souls of rural dwellers, their successor expressly articulated the dual purpose of their mission as a never-ending and perennially necessary activity that saved the souls of both the missionary and the evangelized. From the opening sentence, it stressed the overwhelming need in France for a congregation such as de Paul envisaged. In volunteering to meet the needs of rural dwellers 'deprived of spiritual consolation', the missionaries were said to be guided by their principal purpose, veneration 'of the Most Holy Trinity and the sacred mystery of the Incarnation', through which they and the laity could hope to gain salvation. The sanctification of the community of clerics who performed the missions hinged on their dedication to this work, specifically on the evangelizing process that it involved, and on the discipline with which they pursued it; therefore, the community and its pastoral activities needed the protection that official papal recognition would provide if their reciprocal relationship of sanctification and evangelization were to prosper.

While de Paul awaited the outcome of the cardinals' review, he fretted that precious time was being lost and that the souls of missionaries and potential converts damned while Rome continued to refuse to acknowledge his community's 'happy beginnings'.[54] Indeed, without the key adjustments described above, the final petition would have died precisely the same death as its predecessors. When de Paul finally received the news that Urban VIII was to issue *Salvatoris Nostri*, he

which reflected the expansion of the Congregation's activities since 1628: *CCD*, 1: 113, de Paul to François du Coudray, 1631.

[54] *CCD*, 1: 119, de Paul to François du Coudray, 4 September 1631: 'He who is ignorant of the mysteries of the Trinity and the Incarnation, and dies in that state, dies in a state of damnation . . . That touched me so strongly and still touches me, that I am afraid of being damned myself for not being incessantly occupied with the instruction of the poor people.'

must, therefore, have greeted it with unbridled joy and relief, and read each line with eagerness and growing satisfaction. In it, the pope 'embrac[ed] with fatherly affection' the 'devout priests who give themselves to the service of God and the salvation of souls', and approved the establishment of the Congregation of the Mission as a secular institution of mission exempt from episcopal jurisdiction in its internal affairs.[55] Although the bull did not include the term secular priests, the pope acquiesced to every one of the petition's appeals, while, crucially for the future, professing greater optimism for the Congregation's expansion and contribution to the church than any of the petitions had dared to hope; it permitted, indeed assumed, that the association would and should expand beyond the borders of France, so that the dimensions of its ministry were not simply local or even regional, but universal and of service to the entire church. Fulsome in their praise, Urban VIII's words confirmed that he had finally accepted the viability and validity of the Congregation of the Mission as a missionary enterprise.

IV

If the establishment of de Paul's new community was initially greeted with misgiving in the Roman curia, its potential to cause upset amongst clergy at home was no less likely. For dubious observers in Paris, it was not the association's novelty which unsettled them, but its arrival in an environment where competition amongst the clergy was already fierce. Not only did the inauguration and early growth of the Congregation alter the ecclesiastical map of Paris, it stoked the type of rivalries which customarily pitted secular against regular clerics, or turned religious orders against one another in bids to guard their interests and possessions. Thus, the criticisms meted out to de Paul's initiative by Parisian clergy were inspired by competition for limited material resources as well as by more rarefied goals of reform.

As early as 1630, a group of *curés* in Paris lodged a supplication against the Congregation with the Paris *parlement* in order to dissuade it from registering the royal letters of approval. Their objections indicated that they were not convinced by the distinction that de Paul made between a congregation and a religious order, and that they assumed, as a result, that his community would produce the same set of troubles as religious. The complaint captured the generally antagonistic attitude of many *curés* towards religious orders, particularly those who specialized in 'extraordinary' missions in parishes. Its authors were particularly perturbed by the possibility that the community's members would not seek leave from parish priests before they began to minister in their parishes. They avowed fear that 'ambition and avarice' would govern the missionaries, and that, before long, they would encroach 'on parishes in the small towns and country villages', resulting in 'daily fights and quarrels'. Indeed, the *curés* even dared to issue a thinly veiled criticism of

[55] *CCD*, 13a: 296–304. The crown issued letters patent for the bull in May 1642, and the Paris *parlement* registered these on 3 September 1642: Félibien, *Histoire*, v, 133.

their own bishop, who had approved de Paul's association, in sharply denying that there would be any need for these kind of missions at all if prelates simply appointed 'persons of recognised piety and ability' to parishes, rather than relying on 'extraordinary' missionaries to compensate for poor pastoral care. Lurking behind this comment may also have been frustration at and jealousy of the protection that the Congregation enjoyed from its patrons of high stature.[56]

Despite their dismal forecast, the *curés'* plea came to nothing, because the *parlement* simply registered the royal letters patent in April 1631.[57] But they were not alone in their attitude. Around the same time, a number of Oratorians fostered a competitive attitude towards de Paul's community, which was borne of their sense that they held prior and superior claim to the work of mission in France. The roots of their displeasure lay some years earlier, when their late superior, Bérulle, had gently expressed some resentment towards de Paul's new community, because he judged that de Paul implied in his petitions, 'by diverse and, in my opinion, oblique ways', that his was the only community striving to meet the spiritual needs of rural people in France. Such a claim about the Congregation's specialization in mission work, however subtly expressed, was made at the expense of the Oratory, and was bound to raise the ire of its founder. Although the Oratory's primary objective was to sanctify the clergy, its members did perform missions, as Bérulle recalled in his letter, but 'without glamour and noise'. He indignantly asked the Oratorian agent in Rome, Claude Bertin, to inform the French ambassador of this fact, so that he could not be in any doubt that the Oratorians were endeavouring to meet the spiritual needs of the French church. Some authors misconstrue this, and conclude that the old priest was turning on his former *protégé* to thwart his ambition, because he resented his growing independence and rising status.[58] But Bérulle wrote this missive two months after de Paul's supplication for approval had been rejected for the second time, and there is no indication that he had done anything at all to derail it.[59] However, Bertin certainly had shared his view, and he resurrected his discontent in 1631 by trying to orchestrate a whispering campaign of sabotage with other aggrieved Oratorians in Paris; according to de Paul, these spied on the Congregation's missions and complained to the archbishop and nuncio about them. He was sufficiently provoked by their subterfuge to visit their superior, Charles de Condren, to remonstrate. According to de Paul, Condren denied any knowledge of the 'deceit', and promised to write to the nuncio and ambassador.[60]

56 AN, M210; *CCD*, 13a: 253–7.

57 The crown reiterated its command to the *parlement* to ratify its approval in February 1630: *CCD*, 13a: 252–3, 258–9.

58 See, for instance, Coste, *Saint*, i, 185; Pujo, *Vincent de Paul*, 89; Román, *Vincent de Paul*, 213.

59 Dagens (ed.), *Correspondance*, i, 434–5, Pierre de Bérulle to Claude Bertin, November–December 1628. Bérulle noted that 'prudence and moderation' meant that he had not revealed his anxiety to Philippe-Emmanuel de Gondi, in case others twisted it to give him 'different thoughts of our intentions'.

60 Condren also offered to write to a senior Oratorian, René Barrème, perhaps to ask him to reprimand the troublemakers involved. De Paul appeared disappointed that Philippe-Emmanuel de Gondi, now an Oratorian, might have indulged them: *CCD*, 1: 164–6, de Paul to François du Coudray, 12 July 1632.

The most vociferous and penetrating criticism of the new association, however, should be examined in conjunction with de Paul's final achievement in its early years, that is, the acquisition of the priory of Saint-Lazare in 1632. Two parties emerged in opposition in this instance, both of whom believed that they held prior claim to this venerable establishment: the abbey of Saint-Victor-de-Senlis, and the Congregation of France/Sainte-Geneviève. The contest for possession that ensued challenged the claim that de Paul made for Saint-Lazare, but the arguments used by the attackers were about more than material gain; they undermined the fledgling group's claim to vocational integrity and to the identity that it sought to carve out as a clerical congregation. This combination of issues rendered the dispute especially dangerous, raising it well above the level of the petty clerical squabbles that were commonplace at the time over, for instance, the timing of masses in neighbouring churches on feast days.

The material advantages of the large site of Saint-Lazare, from which missionary initiatives could be centrally organized, were especially propitious at this time, because the dilapidated state of Bons-Enfants was proving an ongoing problem. With the Gondi endowment earmarked for missions, the moderate income for the college came mainly from nine houses on rue Saint-Victor. Total revenue averaged 450 *livres* 15 *sous* during the first three years.[61] De Paul took steps to increase it in 1629, when he contracted new rental agreements which in theory ensured an annual income of 732 *livres* 5 *sous*. However, the college still consistently ran up losses, for its expenses averaged 1,200 *livres* annually between 1632 and 1635.[62] De Paul was forced to order financially draining repairs as soon as he acquired it, and repairs to fabric continued to make the greatest inroads into income in the succeeding decade: for instance, in 1625, urgent renovation of the living quarters, especially its roof, cost 2,522 *livres* 15 *sous*, a sum that was paid mainly through a loan of 2,400 *livres* given by de Paul's friend, Charles du Fresne. In the seemingly endless efforts to renovate the property, de Paul borrowed 3,000 *livres* to pay for repairs there and at the newly acquired priory of Saint-Lazare around 1633.[63]

Simultaneously, the community's expansion meant that it would need larger or additional premises. By the close of 1627, numbers had swelled promisingly to twelve, then to twenty-five by December 1630, and were to stand at thirty-five by 1634.[64] These could be easily accommodated at Saint-Lazare, which then covered 80 *arpents* (32 hectares) in Saint-Laurent parish. With a frontage on the rue du faubourg Saint-Denis, it was composed of a large house of residence and a Gothic chapel. Unlike Bons-Enfants, it also included extensive agricultural land, which

[61] The college also had a small house and garden on the nearby rue des Fossés-de-Saint-Victor, and the right to four *setiers* of *bled froment* annually in Mesnil-Aubry: AN, S6373a, S6373b, and $H^3$2554.

[62] Included in these costs was a 200*livre* pension payable annually to Louis de Guyard, de Paul's predecessor as chaplain and principal from 28 December 1624. Guyard subsequently became vicar general of Paris: *CCD*, 1: 72, de Paul to Louise de Marillac, 1630.

[63] For accounts and contracts, see AN, S6373a, S6850, and H5 3288. The loan of 3,000 *livres* came from Pierre de Glanderon: AN, Y 174, 23 January 1634.

[64] *Notices sur les prêtres, clercs et frères*, i, 373–5, appendices i and ii.

produced wheat, barley, and alfalfa for sale and consumption. It garnered more revenue from the rental of houses and a windmill, and was entitled to seigneurial income, such as that from the annual fair of Saint-Laurent. Historically, as an ecclesiastical *seigneurie*, it had a court and prison. It also traditionally housed lepers, although this practice had been virtually abandoned by 1630.[65]

Saint-Lazare was a historical landmark of the archdiocese, and de Paul was probably aware of its size and situation even before it was proposed that his community should move into it. This suggestion came from its prior, Adrien Le Bon, who finally, with the aid of the *curé* of Saint-Laurent, managed to convince de Paul to accept it after a succession of discussions in 1630 and 1631 which also involved Duval. Duval was by this stage an automatic source of guidance for de Paul in practical matters relating to the Congregation's structure and operation, and on this occasion his experience as an adviser on the reform of a number of abbeys in Paris and the proposed Benedictine reform of the Congregation of St Vanne of Verdun (known as the Congregation of St Maur from 1618), rendered his viewpoint indispensable.[66] Finally, by the end of 1631, de Paul was ready to sign a contract to take Saint-Lazare. He duly did this on 7 January 1632, and his Congregation took formal possession of it the following day. Directly afterwards, the crown and archbishop, supportive as usual, confirmed the union of the former priory with de Paul's Congregation.[67] And the archbishop's brother generously agreed to guarantee the hefty pensions totalling 5,600 *livres* that de Paul bound the new 'Lazarists' to pay annually to the religious who remained in residence at Saint-Lazare.[68]

These seemingly cast-iron protections did not forestall opponents to the union from disputing both its desirability and legality, however. The first concerted effort to reverse it emanated from the Augustinian abbey of Saint-Victor-de-Senlis, which

[65] There were no lepers at Saint-Lazare in January 1632, and the last reference to a leper in residence was made by de Paul in 1635. In this letter, de Paul also refers to an individual who had escaped through a side door of Saint-Lazare. This was Jean de Montholon, the brother of Guy-François de Montholon, one of a number of individuals periodically detained at Saint-Lazare; in Montholon's case, he was held there on his family's request after he had engaged in a clandestine marriage. According to Abelly, there were three or four detainees, those 'alienated of spirit', at Saint-Lazare around 1632: *CCD*, 1: 273, de Paul to Guy-François de Montholon, 1635; *CCD*, 13a: 264; Abelly, *Vie*, i, 101. One of them was probably the boy who de Paul wished to return to his parents in 1633 because he did not consider it 'expedient to keep him confined for so long' (a month), as even 'the strongest spirits' were weakened in such circumstances: BSG, Ms 3278, fo. 364r, de Paul to François Boulart, 1633.

[66] Abelly, *Vie*, i, 97–8; Archives des Carmélites de Clamart, Duval, 'La Vie de Mre André Duval', 35–42. On the development of the Congregation of St Maur, see Martène, *Histoire*.

[67] *CCD*, 13a: 263–71, 275–83.

[68] Le Bon negotiated an annual pension of 2,100 *livres*. He also reserved the rural property of Rougemont, which was a possession of the priory, and the priory of Sainte-Marie-Madeleine-de-Limouron in Chartres diocese, which it leased, for his usage. In 1645, Le Bon bequeathed his personal possessions to the Lazarists, and passed Rougemont to them. He lived at Saint-Lazare until his death in 1651: AN, S6698 and Y173 (12 January 1633); *CCD*, 1: 134–7, de Paul to Guillaume de Lestocq, 1631; *CCD*, 13a: 266, 285; Abelly, *Vie*, i, 189–91. The other religious received 500 *livres* annually, reduced to 300 *livres* if they took their meals with the Lazarists. Given that de Paul revealed that students at Bons-Enfants were paying 270 *livres* annually for their meals, this could hardly be considered a good deal for his party: *CCD*, 1: 135, de Paul to Guillaume Lestocq, 1631. See BSG, Ms 624, fo. 435r for a certified copy of Gondi's act of guarantee.

had exercised administrative power over Saint-Lazare until 1625. On this historical basis, the canons directed two appeals to the Paris *parlement*, arguing that Le Bon was not legally entitled to resign Saint-Lazare in favour of de Paul's association. Furthermore, they took advantage of an error in the contract, which stated that Le Bon would yield his position to the pope, rather than to the archbishop of Paris.[69] However, after Le Bon made a declaration that he resigned Saint-Lazare into the hands of the archbishop so that he might entrust it to the Congregation of the Mission, the *parlementaires* formally registered the letters patent in early 1633.[70]

While he awaited the outcome of the appeals, de Paul professed that he was tempted to abandon Saint-Lazare, but was convinced by André Duval and members of his own community that his stance was irreproachable.[71] Even so, he decided to do all he could to ensure that a papal bull expediting the union was issued as soon as possible, for it was 'absolutely necessary to us, because of the opposition we are getting'.[72] The context for Saint-Victor's claim stretched back as far as 1513, but was also contemporary to reform initiatives of the 1620s, and to the entrance of the Congregation of France to the dispute. Saint-Lazare had been founded in the twelfth century, and the bishop of Paris had passed its administration to the abbey of Saint-Victor in 1513–14. In 1625, the Saint-Lazare religious voted to dissolve this connection, and to place their priory under the jurisdiction of the archbishop of Paris.[73] By 1630, the fortunes of the institution had waned, for despite its revenues its numbers had dwindled to nine canons regular, who still lived under the Augustinian rule but were split by disputes between the prior, Le Bon, and the rest of the community.[74] At this juncture, it caught the attention of reformers in the Congregation of France, who judged it to be an excellent candidate for reform under the aegis of their collective of monastic houses. In the negotiations that were pursued to this end, Saint-Lazare became a sought-after prize, but one that its prior sought to grant to a recipient whom he deemed worthy of his beneficence, and who was positively disposed towards his own wishes for its future. His personal future was naturally of concern too, given the tempestuous nature of his relations with the other residents. He hoped to make

[69] The archbishop clearly indicated his power of disposition in his approval of the contract on 8 January 1632: *CCD*, 13a: 277.

[70] AN, M212; BSG, Ms 624, fo. 801r; *CCD*, 13a: 283–95.

[71] *CCD*, 1: 151, de Paul to unnamed, 1632; *CCD*, 2: 382, de Paul to Pierre du Chesne, 1 January 1643. De Paul also felt the weight of his obligations towards the handful of detainees in the house of correction at Saint-Lazare, and professed his reluctance to abandon them to an uncertain future: *CCD*, 11: 17; Abelly, *Vie*, i, 101.

[72] Pope Urban VIII approved the union in 1635, although the bull was not published until 1655. At this point, the Saint-Victor canons sought to have Saint-Lazare returned to their possession, but did not make headway: ASV, Congregatio Vescovi e Regolari, Reg. Episcoporum, 79 (1635), fos 39r, 41r (the contract and judgement are contained in Positiones Vescovi (1635) (unpaginated)); *CCD*, 1: 242–4, de Paul to François du Coudray, 25 July 1634; *CCD*, 13a: 409–16; Félibien, *Histoire*, v, 190. For the quotation, see *CCD*, 1: 149, de Paul to François du Coudray, 2 March 1632.

[73] BSG, Ms 624, fos 429r, 801r; *CCD*, 13a: 264.

[74] AN, M212; *CCD*, 13a: 263. Coste mistakenly counted eleven canons, and Pujo ten: Coste, *Saint*, i, 193; Pujo, *Vincent de Paul*, 97.

his resignation conditional on the acquisition of a benefice or pension which would ensure a comfortable retirement.

Before Le Bon negotiated with de Paul, he had proved receptive to a suggestion that the Congregation of France might reform his priory. This grouping certainly supplied grounds to hope, for it appeared eminently qualified for the task. In 1622, Cardinal François de La Rochefoucauld had received a special papal commission to reform the older monastic orders of the French church, including the Benedictines, Cistercians, and Augustinian canons-regular. With the support of key figures amongst the Augustinian canons-regular, notably François Boulart and Charles Faure,[75] he had by 1628 successfully reformed five Augustinian houses and grouped them into a new congregation, the Congregation of France/Sainte-Geneviève. The trio subsequently brought negotiations for the reform of twenty-five houses 'to various stages of completion' between 1629 and 1634, with Saint-Lazare amongst them.[76] Their ambition to incorporate Saint-Lazare was partly spurred on by their hostility to the abbey of Saint-Victor. Since 1622, the religious of this abbey and its affiliates had distanced themselves from the reforming agenda that La Rochefoucauld and his collaborators promoted, and eventually in 1633 La Rochefoucauld dissolved the congregation centred on the abbey.[77] Boulart and Faure would certainly not have relished the return of Saint-Lazare to the control of Saint-Victor, which they considered hostile to reform, but, equally, they did not wish to lose the opportunity to restore pure Augustinian observance in this historical foundation. It came as an extremely disagreeable surprise to them when, after fruitless attempts to forge a peace with his fellows, Le Bon decided to resign his benefice in favour of the community of Vincent de Paul, for whose missionary work he professed to have great admiration. They objected vehemently to the transfer of the priory to a group of secular priests, who would not, indeed could not, maintain the discipline of a religious order.

The conditions that Le Bon sought to impose on de Paul's community indicate, however, that he had not surrendered his hope that the priory might be reformed, even if it were not to return completely to its original observance. From de Paul's perspective, these conditions threatened to irreparably damage the qualities that defined his association and governed its activities and purpose, and this, rather than a scrupulous humility, was the principal reason that he was so tardy in accepting Le Bon's offer. Le Bon anticipated that the example of a zealous group of clerics might in time excite the religious to revive traditional practices, and he consequently attempted to attach obligations to his donation which would have de Paul's community assume the appearance of a monastic order. He desired the two groups to live together routinely, sharing meals and sleeping quarters, that de Paul's men

[75] Boulart was the cardinal's secretary, and from 1632 acted as the prior of his abbey of Sainte-Geneviève. La Rochefoucauld appointed Faure to the office of vicar general of the Congregation of France in 1633: Bergin, *La Rochefoucauld*, 273–4.

[76] The Congregation had 12 houses by 1634, and 45 by 1645: Bergin, *La Rochefoucauld*, 161–92. On the Congregation's history to 1789, see Brian, *Messieurs de Sainte-Geneviève*.

[77] This was the cardinal's response to the religious' effort to revive their congregation, which they had dissolved in 1625: Bergin, *La Rochefoucauld*, 166–7, 173, 188–9.

submit to wearing the distinctive *domino* and *almuce* of canons, and that they chant divine office every day. De Paul riposted that these demands would lead to the *parlement*, amongst others, suspecting that his men were 'beginning to become canons' and, worse, were 'tacitly renouncing our plan to work unceasingly for the poor people of rural areas'. He was willing to compromise only in regard to the office; the community would normally recite it *media voce*, singing it only for high mass and vespers on Sundays and feasts.[78]

For reasons different to de Paul's, it was also the issue of monastic observance that Boulart and Faure found most contentious, and it was on this that they concentrated their firepower when they attacked the Lazarists' takeover of the priory. Their hostility was potentially a tougher trial for the union than that of the canons of Saint-Victor, since it gained credence from their impeccable reforming credentials and connections, and from their seemingly irreproachable agenda for the renewal of Saint-Lazare. The duo made their objections on the basis that true reform of the Augustinian monasteries could only be achieved through the retention of possessions and the revival of traditional observance. To pursue these objectives, they engaged in a two-pronged campaign, targeting the two churchmen in Paris who were the most likely to be able to halt the process of union. Faure initially approached the archbishop of Paris in 1631 to request that he should not approve the union, but was given short shrift by Gondi, who retorted that he was entitled to make the decision as he saw fit. Subsequently, once the Priests of the Mission moved into Saint-Lazare, Faure and Boulart still held hopes that the decision could be reversed, even though their installation had now granted the Lazarists the upper hand. Boulart first held meetings with de Paul and members of his community, but this was to no avail since they proved immovable either in mind or body. He and Faure then turned their attention to convincing La Rochefoucauld of the loss to the Congregation of France that the union implied. Unfortunately, they found that La Rochefoucauld himself had been won over to it, despite initial reservations. He had been persuaded to gaze more benignly on it when he met with de Paul before the contract of union was signed, and even Faure's disapproving presence at this meeting had been insufficient to prevent the shift in his perspective. Whether de Paul instigated the meeting in order to persuade the cardinal of his integrity and of the Congregation's pious intentions is not known. What is certain, however, is that, having been aware of the doubts about the union, he had succeeded in overturning those of the most senior advocate for Genovéfain monastic reform.[79]

In reaction, Boulart presented a detailed factum to La Rochefoucauld to counter the Lazarists' 'conservation' at Saint-Lazare, in which he depicted the union as a violation of ecclesiastical justice and an injury to the success of the monastic reforms

[78] *CCD*, 1: 134–7, de Paul to Guillaume Lestocq, 1631.

[79] BSG, Ms 611–14, Claude Molinet, 'Histoire des chanoines réguliers de l'Ordre de S. Augustin de la Congrégation de France', iii, 57. Without foundation, the story of La Rochefoucauld's change of heart has often been embellished to demonstrate de Paul's influence over members of the French hierarchy, with de Paul said to have argued with the cardinal before throwing himself at his feet to win him over. See, for example, Murnaghan, 'Simple Monsieur Vincent'.

that the cardinal had energetically pursued for over a decade.[80] He condemned the canons, who 'did a lot for themselves, very little for God', in allowing a secular community of 'incapables' to take over what was rightfully an Augustinian possession. But he heaped blame on the missionaries, writing bitterly that they trenchantly defended their acquisition of Saint-Lazare by claiming that they had been 'called to it by the consent of the religious'. If this was what de Paul had argued, then it was, of course, technically true, but it deliberately skirted around Boulart's principal grievance, which was that if the Congregation of the Mission claimed that it was not a religious order then it had no right to act as though it was by acceding to a monastic foundation. In laying out this argument, Boulart was careful not to infer that de Paul's men were not profitable to the church at all, for he admitted that they did 'a lot of good' in rural areas through their missions. But, he observed, a new community of clerics such as theirs should be more circumspect as it sought to secure its position, for in raising the hackles of other clergy by taking what was not their due, its members hindered any hope of establishing good relations with them, and disrupted the peace of the church. Boulart sourly lamented that headway could have been made in introducing Genovéfain reform to Saint-Lazare if more time had been given to this goal. With a final flourish, he endeavoured to stoke anxiety in La Rochefoucuald by pointing out the damaging precedent that the union had set for the future. The Congregation of France now risked losing the fruits of years of painstaking work, because the Lazarists could use their acquisition of Saint-Lazare to usurp other foundations such as Saint-Martin-de-Nevers, where the cardinal had recently succeeded in installing the Genovéfains.[81]

Though he injected both dismay and urgency into his warning about the future, Boulart gave the impression that he suspected that he would not succeed in preventing it coming to pass. He ruefully recognized that the Priests of the Mission had dismissed his concerns and were already bedded down in Saint-Lazare, and that their leader had convinced La Rochefoucauld not to question their possession. While his words encapsulate the confusion and rivalry that the novelty of the Lazarists engendered when they arrived on the clerical scene, therefore, they also point to de Paul's ability, as well as his need, to court high-level support in order to gain victory. Indeed, in acknowledging this, Boulart isolated what had been not just a decisive feature of this clash, but of the Congregation's process of foundation from 1624. In the decade that had since passed, de Paul had been assisted at every step by a powerful cross-section of the higher clergy in Paris, without whose endorsement his community would have struggled to develop in its early years.

De Paul spent much of the late 1620s and early 1630s grappling with what at times appeared to be intractable obstacles as he sought to formalize his collective of missionaries in legal terms, to assure it a viable financial basis, and to provide a motherhouse from which its members could fan out to perform its eponymous missions. Only a combination of perseverance, adaptability, and recourse to the most advantageous sources of patronage ensured that he was able to achieve

[80] BSG, Ms 3250, fos 270r–271v.

[81] Bergin, *La Rochefoucauld*, 179.

his goals without abandoning core principles according to which the Congregation functioned. While he was sure of his youthful association's missionary purpose, its debut in the church was not greeted with universal applause. For some, the Priests of the Mission were simply an unnecessary addition to an already congested world of ecclesiastical ministry, while they troubled others because they could not be shoehorned into conventional categories of clerical organization or missionary venture. The Congregation was a unique form of clerical missionary association in the 1620s, and this fact lay at the heart of the scepticism and outright opposition that plagued it. In Rome, de Paul had to convince the authorities that his association was not a new religious order, in order to gain their seal of approval for the work that validated its community. In Paris, his protestations about the non-religious status of his group met disbelief in some quarters, because its missionary work and community life seemed to define it as a religious order or to infringe on the hopes and privileges of true monastic orders. Yet however much these critics questioned de Paul's intentions, railed against his refusal to operate within traditional and canonical boundaries, begrudged his Congregation a share in pastoral work, or coveted its newly acquired patrimony, they were eventually forced to acknowledge that the arrival of *Messieurs de Saint-Lazare* on the ecclesiastical landscape was not about to be reversed.

5

The Lazarist Missionary

Ethos and Praxis

I

When Philippe de Gondi freed the Priests of the Mission from the restrictive stipulations that had been set out in the original contract in 1627, he considerably enhanced their power of self-determination. For their superior general specifically, this meant that he could think realistically of expansion beyond original horizons, and accommodate desirable new opportunities as they arose. From Saint-Lazare, de Paul maintained a vigilant watch over the missionaries' work for nearly three decades, and as the years passed he fielded many invitations to expand it in France. Those that he accepted gradually dwarfed the obligations enshrined in the original Gondi endowment, while also causing the demands of his work as superior general to grow massively, to the point that his correspondence became a complex weave of instructions and counsel to missionaries on campaign in far-flung regions. Over time, he depended on the numerous summaries of the events, accomplishments, and difficulties of campaigns that his missionaries sent to him, at the centre of command in Paris, to stock his store of knowledge about mission sites and activities. This data was invaluable to decision-making and to the effort to perpetuate appropriate standards in pastoral care. Threaded through the letters too were de Paul's regular professions of delight and humility; as he confronted the challenges inherent in steering a true course for the Congregation, he recorded his confreres' achievements, or rather, as he put it, 'the blessings that the goodness of God . . . so kindly [lavished] on' their missions.[1]

Even more important for the growing association of missionaries was the cultivation of its members' common sense of purpose and practice. It was only in 1653 that de Paul sent a set of their Common Rules to the archbishop of Paris for his official approval. When he did so, however, he noted that they had 'lived by these' since the 1620s. After a few years of routine, de Paul had compiled a set for community life, in consultation with Portail, and one or two others who had lived longest with him. The content of these expanded by degrees as the number of Lazarists and their activities expanded, but they always echoed the words of the petitions that de Paul sent to Rome around the same time that he first set the Rules to paper, describing the Congregation's purpose precisely as the salvation of the

[1] *CCD*, 1: 183, de Paul to a Lazarist priest, 15 January 1633.

souls of the rural poor and the pursuit of perfection amongst those who worked for this goal.[2] As this chapter will confirm, de Paul himself exhibited remarkable consistency too in the pronouncements that he made about the methods that the missionaries should adopt to achieve their goal and the values by which they should operate to do so; those that he issued during the 1650s hark back substantially to the directives and counsel he offered during the preceding decades. For this reason, rather than providing a step-by-step narrative account of his pronouncements, this chapter offers a more telling distillation of de Paul's missionary thought over these years, which remains sensitive to the nuances of its evolution and to its application in the Lazarist Congregation as it expanded.

From the earliest years of operation, de Paul seized every opportunity in his communications with confreres to inculcate the requirement that they 'glorify God, to perfect [themselves], and to edify the neighbour . . . but by gentle means'.[3] He taught that the missionaries should sanctify themselves and others, both as individuals and as a collective, and that their success depended on their dedication to the work of evangelization, and on the discipline with which they pursued it. His views about their purpose, methods, and values formed what can be described as a congregational ethos, a kind of institutional code of fundamental qualities and practices that expressed the true nature of their vocation in the church. He expected that this mix would inspire and guide individuals to live out and live up to their obligations as Lazarists, and in doing so to contribute to the group's *esprit de corps*. If further incentive was needed to encourage de Paul to define an ethos for the Lazarists, it could be located in its potential to position them to the fore of clerical groups in France. The importance of this should not be underestimated: with the French church seemingly full to onlookers with groups that were fundamentally indistinguishable from his, to assert the Lazarists' character as a cohort of missionaries possessed of special vocational gifts would be to assert control over their public image. Ever in need of external support, this was a primary condition for the Congregation to thrive, indeed to survive, beyond the first flush of success in its foundation years.[4]

II

De Paul believed that the relationship between the missionary's attributes and the core acts of mission was symbiotic, for the ability to personify particular virtues would determine one's ability to carry out missionary activities successfully. But what was the precise nature of their interdependence? To best explore this issue, it is

[2] The Lazarists' Common Rules were formally approved by the archbishop of Paris in 1654, and by the pope in 1658. Bernard Koch provides a useful guide to the intermediary rules in his 'Drawing Up the Common Rules'. See particularly too, Rybolt, 'Primitive Rules', which compares the texts of the primitive and final rules. The 1658 Common Rules are printed in *CCD*, 13a: 430–71.

[3] *CCD*, 7: 606, de Paul to Pierre Cabel, 11 June 1659.

[4] For further discussion of the significance of this issue, see Ch. 12.

necessary first to inspect the features of the Lazarist mission programme itself, before moving on to de Paul's rationale for them.

In the first seven years of their operation, the Lazarist missionaries completed 140 missions, and their motherhouse was responsible for another 550 missions between 1632 and 1660.[5] Many more were added to the tally once satellite houses began to be established outside Paris from 1635.[6] Even before this date, however, the missionaries had travelled outside the confines of the dioceses in which the Gondi lands were situated (Paris, Chartres, Sens, and Amiens), to sees as distant as Montauban and Mende in the south, Bordeaux, Périgueux, Saintes, and Angoulême in the south-west, and the northern dioceses of Rouen, Saintes, Bayeux, and Coutances. Although his workload in Paris, and eventually his age and declining health, meant that de Paul participated in these campaigns less frequently as the years passed, he continued to apply himself personally at the coalface of mission whenever his commitments in Paris, his health, and his age allowed; in 1635, for instance, he moved between parishes in Mende for several weeks, and, remarkably, in his early seventies, he participated for over a week in a large mission held about 20 miles from Paris, and made 'several journeys to rural areas to announce three or four missions there, to continue one of them, and to visit others'.[7]

From the start, the Lazarists reported large crowds in attendance at their missions, which was a source simultaneously of both pleasure and alarm for their superior general. Such reports were a normal feature of missionary accounts across Europe in these years;[8] in France, other missionaries, the most active and widespread of whom were the Jesuits and Capuchins, attracted throngs to their missions, and were at times almost overwhelmed by the demand for their services.[9] But, for de Paul, it meant that from the outset he was obliged to take careful consideration of fluctuations in the number of missionaries available for deployment as well as the specific needs of the areas to which they were to travel. As soon as the growth in numbers allowed, he sent a minimum of two priests and a brother on each mission, with the priests assuming responsibility for the public work and the brothers carrying out private instruction and the mundane work of domestic chores. They generally moved from place to place between November to June, staying within a set of parishes in a specific area, such as Joigny in early 1628, Mende diocese in autumn 1635, and Nanterre in late 1637.[10] Normally, they spent between two and four weeks in each place, depending on the size of the local population,[11] but did not

[5] Abelly, *Vie*, ii, 20. [6] ACMP, 'Déposition du Frère Chollier' (unpaginated).

[7] *CCD*, 4: 576, de Paul to Marc Coglée, 11 June 1653.

[8] See, for instance, the report of Jean de La Salle and Joseph Brunet on their 1634 mission in Bordeaux: *CCD*, 1: 271, Jean de La Salle and Joseph Brunet to de Paul, 1634.

[9] The Dominicans in France did not undertake popular missions for most of the century, beginning them only in 1677: Mortier, *Histoire*, vii, 168.

[10] The mission in Nanterre took place at the time that the priory there was united to the Congregation of France, and a novitiate established, suggesting that good relations had been restored between de Paul's community and *Messieurs de Sainte-Geneviève*: Brian, *Messieurs de Sainte-Geneviève*, 281; Bergin, *La Rochefoucauld*, 195.

[11] *Cahiers* of missions are rare for this period of Lazarist history, but one surviving for the missions that the Lazarists carried out in Haute-Bretagne from 1646 uncovers a strenuous routine that saw them

receive any remuneration, despite the fact that, as de Paul reckoned in 1635, the cost of maintaining a mission team (or band) for a season could reach 1,000 *livres*.[12] To add to the burden of campaigns, the Lazarists provided the extensive cargo of materials needed, such as items of furniture, bibles, devotional books, altar vessels, and vestments, as well as an assortment of documents, including faculties for preaching and sacramental administration, indulgences, and the confraternal rule. For these, however, they were often able to depend on gifts from well-wishers anxious to assist their work; until her death around 1635, for instance, Isabelle du Fey kept de Paul supplied with large quantities of religious pictures and rosary beads for his men to distribute on missions.[13]

The design of the mission was both distinctive and consistent in application, with a choreography that was structured to bring about conversion and instil habits of piety.[14] Its key events evolved from de Paul's experiences in rural France during the 1610s, when he had first settled on catechesis, sacramental administration (particularly general confession), and confraternal charity as keystones of rural pastoral care. In format, the mission was therefore similar to those of other missionary groups. However, it differed from them in crucial aspects, a fact which did not go unnoticed by contemporaries.[15] In the early years, specific elements of the approach that de Paul and his companions took struck some eyewitnesses so acutely that they recorded their encounters with them. Depending on their perspective, they viewed the Lazarists' conduct and techniques differently; for some, they were intriguing and laudatory; for others, they were simply exasperating. All, however, drew attention to aspects of mission practice that seemed to set the Lazarists apart from other missionaries that they had encountered.

The first was their rejection of what de Paul dismissed as 'noise and fanfare', which the *parlementaire* Jean de Gaufreteau noted as one of the most striking marks of the missionaries' work when he encountered them in Bordeaux in 1635. The second feature, which he also noted approvingly, was that their interaction with parishioners was untouched by affectation, and marked instead by an 'absolutely naive and spiritual zeal'. Their direct and quiet approach aroused, Gaufreteau concluded, great admiration and enthusiasm amongst locals who participated in the missions (although he was wise enough to wonder whether their ardour would

recording forty-four missions before 1661: *CCD*, 2: 170, de Paul to Louis Lebreton, 3 February 1641; Lebrun, 'Missions des Lazaristes en Haute-Bretagne'.

12 *CCD*, 1: 298, de Paul to Clément de Bonzi, September–October 1635.

13 See AN, Z^2 4584, for a list of equipment carried in mission trunks. *CCD*, 1, contains a number of letters from de Paul to du Fey.

14 Whatever the situation in which they found themselves, Lazarists simply adapted the mission template that de Paul asked them to use in parishes. For example, around mid-1636, de Paul dispatched twenty-one missionaries to Luzarches and Senlis to care for French troops engaged in a campaign to repel the Spanish army from Picardy. To guide their pastorate, which lasted six weeks for the majority, he gave the missionaries a short rule that underlined the urgency of their responsibility to preach, catechize, and administer general confession and communion to the thousands who might die once they left the camps: *CCD*, 1: 307.

15 Dompnier, 'La Compagnie de Jésus'; Peyrous, 'Saint Vincent de Paul'; Sauzet, 'Prédication et missions'.

eventually deteriorate to languor after the missionaries departed). Similarly, in Mantes, west of Paris, where the Lazarists were invited to carry out a mission by Robert Guériteau in 1640, they were seen to operate with quiet fervour, rather than with 'roughness and severity'.[16] Not everyone was so complimentary, however. The famed Huguenot pastor, preacher, and controversialist Charles Drelincourt, who observed the Lazarists at work in the confessionally divided area of Sedan in the north-east a few years later, zoomed in on another of their traits, that is, their unwillingness to follow the conventions of controversial discourse to which he was accustomed. He was nonplussed to discover that, shying clear of direct altercations, the missionaries preferred to teach key doctrines repetitively to their audiences in catechetical sessions, and to concentrate on points and practices that he considered inconsequential for spiritual health, such as the Catholic sacraments, like 'flies' flying around in 'the same circle' again and again. Indeed, they refused to engage in disputations with Protestants at all, which greatly frustrated him. Far from admiring the Lazarists' catechetical speciality, Drelincourt found that it made their activity more difficult to combat than that of the Jesuits and Capuchins, both of whom were happy to engage in direct confrontation through their preaching and other public religious rituals.[17]

De Paul also did not permit the Lazarists to organize public penitential acts in which the faithful could emulate Christ's suffering and expiate guilt for their sins. Thus, the 'schools of mortification' described by scholars such as Jennifer Selwyn, in which penitential processions formed the focal point of a dramatic set of public acts of corporal mortification (such as a bonfire of the vanities, the wearing of crowns of thorns, and flagellation), did not figure at all in his approach to missionary work.[18] Instead of fanfare and controversy, he prioritized catechetical instruction, and to an extent that was unusual among contemporaries.[19] And although the observers did not refer to it, a further pronounced feature of the Lazarists' missions was their length. De Paul was adamant that his missionaries should not leave a parish until even the most obdurate souls had been instructed

[16] Gaufreteau, *Chronique Bordeloise*, ii, 173: 'zèle tout à fait naïf et spiritual.' The *Chronique* dates the mission on which Gaufreteau commented to 1632, but this is two years too early, since Archbishop Sourdis awarded faculties to the missionaries only on 24 October 1634: AD de la Gironde, G619. On Mantes, see Le Cousturier, *Guériteau*, 92.

[17] Drelincourt was a native of Sedan and a graduate of its academy. Although based in Charenton, he was a regular visitor to Sedan, and maintained close contact with kin and friends there. He was consequently well placed to comment on the new missionaries: Drelincourt, *Dialogues familiers*; Forrestal, 'Catholic Missionaries'; Luria, 'Rituals of Conversion'.

[18] Trevor Johnson states that secular rulers did not permit the Jesuits to hold penitential processions in the Upper Palatinate and Bavaria, but they organized other penitential activities using props such as skulls and nooses: Johnson, 'Blood, Tears and Xavier-Water'; Selwyn, '"Schools of Mortification"'; Selwyn, *Paradise Inhabited by Devils*.

[19] Dompnier, 'La Compagnie de Jésus'; Peyrous, 'Saint Vincent de Paul'. Peyrous suggests that over the eighteenth century other missionaries adopted the Lazarist format, but the evidence of David Gentilcore and others confirms that this claim is too sweeping. Even Alphonse de Liguori's Redemptorists combined elements of the Jesuit and Lazarist approaches, while the Lazarists incorporated dramas such as the planting of the cross into their missions in the decades that followed de Paul's death: Gentilcore, '"Adapt yourselves to the people's capabilities"'; Mezzadri and Román, *Vincentians*, 1: 164.

and absolved from sins, and therefore insisted that the missionaries spend two to four weeks in one place.[20] Obviously, since their missions were longer than those of other groups, they devoted more hours to catechism. However, this fact also holds true in proportional terms, which is more telling. Moreover, although, like all missionaries, the Lazarists preached sermons, these were far fewer in number and shorter in duration overall. One confrere travelled to announce the forthcoming mission in a sermon in the parish church a few weeks before it began; the opening sermon of the mission set the scene by outlining the purpose of the event (the expression of sorrow for sins, the obtaining of divine mercy, and reconciliation with God).[21] The missionaries also delivered a sermon each morning before the adults set out to work. For this, de Paul insisted from an early stage that they adopt a style that he called the 'little method', which he argued was the best means to explain the essential elements of virtues lucidly and rationally.

Normally, missionary groups such as the Jesuits gathered parishioners again in the evening for the major sermon of the day.[22] Instead of this classic technique, however, the Lazarists held their 'grand catéchisme'. Although orchestrated from the pulpit, it allowed the audience to interact with the catechist through answering questions that he put to them and repeating pious phrases by rote, the exchange lasting about forty-five minutes. The catechist concentrated on teaching the creed, the commandments, the Our Father and Hail Mary, and major mysteries of faith such as the eucharist.[23] Sensitive to the limits of human concentration, de Paul instructed that they should not retain the people any longer, because 'wordiness [tries] the patience of the listeners'.[24] Before this event, which capped off each day's proceedings, other sessions of catechesis were organized, beginning at 2 p.m. and lasting for approximately ninety minutes. These were tailored to groups of adults and children in need of instruction, and followed a simple and low-key format: generally, the missionaries were directed to shape their session around two or three questions that they posed on topics such as 'the mystery of the Trinity, the Incarnation and the Holy Sacrament of the altar, sin, confession and the five conditions that are required', when the participants gathered around their seats. They explained the basic meaning of the Our Father, Hail Mary, Creed, and Commandments, and invited the faithful to recite them verbatim over and over again. Finally, they pricked their consciences about the nature of their Christian

[20] *CCD*, 1: 555, de Paul to Jeanne de Chantal, 14 July 1639; *CCD*, 2: 170, de Paul to Louis Lebreton, 3 February 1641; *CCD*, 7: 71, de Paul to Jacques Tholard, 18 January 1658: 'Only about 150 of the five or six hundred communicants have made their duty . . . I think it advisable . . . to postpone leaving . . . until those good people have benefited.'

[21] Abelly, *Vie*, ii, 11.

[22] The Jesuits usually delivered two sermons daily, in the morning and evening: Dompnier, 'La Compagnie de Jésus'.

[23] *CCD*, 1: 178, de Paul to Antoine Portail, 28 November 1632; *CCD*, 1: 554, de Paul to Jeanne de Chantal, 14 July 1639; Abelly, *Vie*, ii, 11–17; Chalumeau, 'Saint Vincent de Paul'; Mezzadri and Román, *Vincentians*, 1: 150–60.

[24] *CCD*, 6: 623, de Paul to Pierre Cabel, 17 November 1657. In 1651, de Paul and other senior Lazarists had already reiterated this long-standing rule, and reminded superiors to ensure that it was observed: *CCD*, 13a: 370–1.

duties through conversation about the importance of daily prayer, regular attendance at mass, and confession.[25]

After a number of catechetical sessions, the next exercise was the administration of general confessions to penitents. Sacramental observance then culminated in the reception of communion during mass. By the 1640s, de Paul permitted this to be accompanied sometimes by the newly popular ceremony of 'first communion' for children, initially pioneered by Adrien Bourdoise. It acted effectively to celebrate the admittance of God's children to participation in the most supreme of sacraments, and, de Paul hoped, to win over the obdurate hearts of older people who witnessed 'the devotion of the children and the care that is taken with them'.[26] Afterwards, the foundation of a confraternity of charity formed the final major element of the mission. Before the missionaries left, they normally visited the sick of the community and instituted a confraternity, while in localities where they had already done so they held a meeting with members to ensure that its rule was being maintained. De Paul intended that the confraternities should be permanent fixtures that would continually prompt the faithful to remember and implement the virtuous rules of Christian living once the intensity of the mission period abated. However, he ruled out the symbolic and flamboyant gestures that other missionary groups used to achieve the same objective, such as the planting of the cross at parish limits. Proponents of these kind of public displays and rituals assumed that it helped to interiorize the message of contrition, and offered proof that it had been successfully transmitted to penitents. De Paul's doubts about their ability either to bring about or demonstrate true conversion was one reason why he did not approve of them. However, more fundamentally, his reason for rejecting them was his ability to put forward what he judged to be a superior alternative, one in which he was so confident that he could persist in stating that 'noise and fanfare' were contrary to the Congregation's manner of evangelization.[27] The Lazarists, like all missionaries, were to endeavour to convert their subjects, but their special manner of proceeding was to be determined by their articulation of particular virtues or values characteristic of the vocational model that de Paul devised for them.

III

From the early years of the Lazarists' history, de Paul sought to carve out a specific identity for its members and their work in the church; his petitions to the papacy for the association's approval emphasized the specialized service that they provided as rural missionaries, and thereafter de Paul continued to aver that their duty to undertake missions for the rural poor was the guiding light of their vocation.

25 A summary of the format and content of the *petite catéchisme* is included in the rule of the internal seminary, dating from 1652 but including practices which were long customary: ACMP, 'Règles du Séminaire', fos 104r–105r.

26 *CCD*, 3: 129, de Paul to a Lazarist priest, 27 November 1646. See also Delumeau (ed.), *Première communion*.

27 *CCD*, 1: 277, de Paul to Antoine Portail, 1 May 1635.

But every clerical order or congregation, he realized, had a special goal in serving God. Furthermore, each possessed a special means of achieving it: 'All [orders] aim to love [God] in different ways: the Carthusians by solitude, the Capuchins by poverty, others by chanting his praises.' What, therefore, rendered his own Congregation special? To this question, he answered that it was not only that it was uniquely dedicated to the evangelization of the rural poor, but that those in it were in 'a state of love' which was not exactly replicated in any other clerical association, religious or secular: its members had been 'chosen by God as instruments of his immense, paternal charity, which is intended to be established and to expand in souls'.[28] To love God, as they should, was to make his name known, so that his will would 'be done on earth as it is in Heaven'; this was a 'heartfelt act of charity', or of charitable love, and the chief duty of a Lazarist on mission.[29] Charity, therefore, was the overarching value of the Lazarists' ethos, and the guiding force of their missionary work. It topped a set of hierarchical virtues, which de Paul termed 'the faculties of the soul of the Congregation': he supposed that humility, simplicity, gentleness, zeal, and mortification were the core virtues which united the confreres in their shared ministry of rural mission, and determined their approach to it, individually and collectively; even though de Paul could not argue that a Lazarist missionary held an exclusive right to any of them, he insisted that they had a special resonance when applied heroically to their evangelizing activities.[30]

Tracking the influences that carried de Paul to this conclusion is not a straightforward task. It is clear that he drew inspiration from a range of authorities and teachings in order to supply spiritual substance and justification to the tasks of mission, and that this was a cumulative process; the search is further complicated by the fact that although de Paul adopted the tactics of instruction, sacramental observance, and communal charity during the 1610s, he took longer to decide on their exact positions within his mission strategy, and the degree of emphasis that should be placed on each. But once he had a mission structure from 1625, he was able to elaborate a detailed vision of the good Lazarist missionary who would belong to it, as well as a mature rationale for mission exercises, in effect dovetailing theory and practice. In the years after his return to the Gondi, de Paul read avidly, nourishing himself with theological information and spiritual insights from a diversity of authors ranging from church fathers to medieval mystics such as Thomas à Kempis, preacher theologians like Louis of Granada, and near contemporary missionaries like Martin Bécan and François Xavier.[31] To add further sophistication to his learning, de Paul was blessed with the potential that existed in the Catholic reform movement in France, whereby particular strands of thought could coexist or braid into adapted forms. This accounts for the diversity of opinions amongst scholars about the impact of individuals such as Canfield,

[28] *CCD*, 12: 214. [29] *CCD*, 11: 35.

[30] *CCD*, 12: 70; *CCD*, 13a: 438.

[31] Becan's popular handbook for missionaries, aimed against Calvinist teaching, was published in France in 1625, and de Paul soon afterwards recommended it to his confreres. He also required that they read Xavier's letters, published by Louis Abelly in 1638: Abelly, *Lettres de S. François Xavier*; Bécan, *Manuale controversarium*: *CCD*, 1: 57, de Paul to François du Coudray, 15 September 1628.

Bérulle, and de Sales on de Paul's thought. Indeed, some simplistically conclude that he was merely a disciple of one or another of these, without any originality of thought or action.[32] When this assessment is applied specifically to de Paul's conception of the missionary, its errors become glaringly obvious. It was never his intention to innovate or speculate theologically, but his originality lay in his success in designing a composite missionary ideal to respond to what he identified as the most burning challenges of the Catholic church.

In prioritizing charity as the overarching value of the Lazarists' ethos, de Paul drew on a theology of what Thomas Aquinas termed the 'most excellent' of the three theological virtues. Citing Aquinas' precept that perfection consisted of loving God and neighbour, de Paul accepted that charity embraced and enlivened other virtues because it actively demonstrated love of God and neighbour. It was also the second 'great virtue' of Jesus Christ, the companion to his adoration of the Father, so that those who possessed it were clothed in Christ's spirit, but empty of self.[33] Amongst *dévots* in early seventeenth-century France, this requirement, that they should conform their thoughts and actions to God's will, was a constant preoccupation, and it was a concern that de Paul grew to share. As a foundational theme of *dévot* spirituality, it was particularly shaped by the mystical teaching contained in Benet of Canfield's *Rule of Perfection*, first published in 1609 but available in manuscript from at least 1592. The text was initially passed around members of the Acarie circle, one of whom, André Duval, was amongst the Sorbonne doctors who approved its publication in 1609 (Canfield had acted as Duval's confessor for a time in the later 1590s). It was reportedly Duval who recommended it to de Paul during the 1610s.

Canfield's *Rule* advocated a mystical spirituality that aimed to achieve Christ-like conformity to God's will, which was itself the rule of perfection. In describing the pure love that could be achieved through the cultivation of 'pure intentions' and self-abnegation, Canfield adopted a complex technical language to describe the human soul's ascent to union with God: the soul moved through active, contemplative, and 'supereminent' levels of spiritual intention and conformity, or from obedience to ecclesiastical rules revealed in Revelation (purgation), to illumination by the acceptance of grace, and finally to full acceptance of the grace that granted theological virtues which would govern the individual's memory, understanding, and will so that they imitated those of Jesus. He thought that few would reach the elevated delights of the final unitive stage, but that purgation of the senses, mind, and soul was a goal for which all could strive. This rendered the *Rule* particularly attractive for Catholics struggling to reconcile with God's will. A further reason for its appeal was its applicability to those who lived outside the cloistered walls of a Carthusian monastery or the like, as well as within: it was possible to live a secular life and still discover and follow God's will.[34]

[32] Notably, Henri Brémond in his monumental *Histoire*, iii, 246.

[33] *CCD*, 6: 413, de Paul to a Lazarist priest, undated; *CCD*, 11: 311.

[34] The first edition did not include the third section of the rule, but de Paul almost certainly read this when it was included in subsequent editions: Kent Emery Jr (trans.), *Benet of Canfield's Rule of Perfection*; Optat de Veghel, *Canfield*, 328–99.

The allure of Canfield's path of spiritual ascent to God-seeking Catholics is therefore obvious, but it is more taxing to assess the degree of direct influence that his work had on de Paul. At times, de Paul borrowed a phrase that he might have read in Canfield, but he never referred explicitly to him in his writings or conferences, and he did not use his technical terminology at all. Yet when he expressed his belief in the part that intentions played in spurring himself and others on towards Christian perfection and union with God, he most likely had Canfield's teaching in mind; for example, he confessed to a Lazarist priest that he found 'this morning . . . a great desire to want all that happens in the world, and good and bad, general and personal suffering, because God wants it, since he sends it . . . this practice seems to me to have marvellous circumstances, which are so necessary to missionaries'.[35] However, it is important not to overstate the extent of the direct impact that Canfield's thought had on de Paul in the long term. For instance, de Paul also read and recommended to his missionaries the teaching on conformity and denunciation that was promoted in the classic fifteenth-century text of the *Devotio Moderna*, Thomas à Kempis' *Imitation of Christ*, which was popular amongst *dévots* generally. Unlike de Paul, Kempis tended to urge readers to flee the world in favour of solitude where they could cleave to God, but his pronounced stress on the virtues of mortification and especially humility surely influenced de Paul's views of missionary virtue.[36] Moreover, de Paul was suspicious of the mystical tendencies of pure intention as Canfield presented them, since they ran the risk of freezing people in a state of excessive deliberation and indulgent interior absorption. Instead, he preferred to prioritize the translation of intentions into virtuous actions that fulfilled God's will, and he articulated rules of engagement that encouraged a balance between interior and exterior devotion: one could be confident of acting for the pleasure of God and in imitation of Jesus Christ if one followed divine rules as articulated by the church and ecclesiastical superiors, mortified natural instincts to choose unpalatable options over more attractive, and, when indifferent to the outcome of an affair, abandoned it to the decisions of providence.[37]

Furthermore, it is essential to acknowledge that Canfield also reached de Paul through the filter of another contemporary Parisian spiritual who had himself adopted the concepts of renunciation and union for his own purpose.[38] In his *Collationes*, composed when de Paul was under his wing, Pierre de Bérulle expressed his priestly spirituality using a powerful language of Christocentric conformity (including an emphasis on purity of intention) and sacrificial servitude, while incorporating personal emphases specific to his principal interest of clerical

[35] *CCD*, 6: 493, de Paul to a Lazarist priest, undated.

[36] *CCD*, 1: 373, de Paul to Louise de Marillac, 1636–9; *CCD*, 6: 146, de Paul to Pierre Leclerc, 12 November 1656; Thomas à Kempis, *Imitation of Christ*, 112–13, 176.

[37] *CCD*, 11: 283 and 360: 'Once a soul is sufficiently enlightened by considerations, what need is there to look for others and to strike and continue to strike our mind in order to multiply reasons and thoughts? . . . you must strive . . . to inflame your will and stir yourself up to affections . . .'; *CCD*, 12: 128–37, 189; *CCD*, 13a: 434.

[38] Most notably, Deffrennes, 'Vocation de Saint Vincent de Paul'.

renewal.[39] As the founding figure of the French school of priesthood, Bérulle based his conception of the sacerdotal order on its innate and magnificent dignity. To describe this, he adopted a modified Pseudo-Dionysian structure of heavenly and ecclesiastical hierarchy, in which the priest acted as a mediator of grace who drew those below him in rank, principally the laity, towards union with God by administering the sacraments, especially the eucharist. For Bérulle, the elevated dignity of the priestly vocation rested on its foundational link with the eternal priest, Jesus Christ, who delegated his authority to the ordained so that they could continue the salvific work that he had performed through his life, death, and resurrection. Simultaneously, the supreme dignity of priesthood conferred the obligation of sanctity upon its incumbents, requiring that the priest be utterly dedicated to his bond with Christ, consistently striving to live according to the status and holiness of his vocation by renouncing his own will. The priest was a servant of God, and as a mediator between God and man he was obliged to offer himself as victim for the sins of others, just as Jesus offered himself for the redemption of mankind.[40]

We search in vain for an extended explanation of de Paul's understanding of ordained priesthood at any point in his career, but elements of his former director and mentor's sacerdotal thought certainly proved invaluable to him when he articulated his view of the ideal Lazarist missionary. From the 1610s, his burgeoning commitment to rural pastoral care, itself facilitated by Bérulle, testified to a ripening understanding of his priestly vocation, and he was soon driven to criticize the imperfections in the practice of priestly duties that he witnessed around him. Over time, de Paul invariably included his own 'wretched . . . iniquities' in his condemnation of priestly mediocrity, and while he may have intended this to be a gesture of humility, it appears that the more his awareness of the 'sublime' status of the office grew the more he became conscious of his own failures as a priest.[41] The piecing together of his reflections on the topic leads to the conclusion that he became profoundly marked by his sense of the dignity of the office. De Paul agreed that all Christians belonged to the 'priesthood of the baptised', which implied that they were all missionaries of God, whatever their calling in life. Thus, he regularly reminded confreres that in the 'communion' of community every Lazarist, including brothers, should strive to support the missions in a manner suitable to their station, regardless of whether they were actually assigned to them.[42] Concurrently, he asserted that ordained priests 'received a very sacred and incomparable character, a power over the Body of Jesus Christ that the angels admire, and the authority to forgive people's sins'. Like his mentor Bérulle, de Paul concluded that this was a privileged sharing in one of the 'great virtues' of Jesus Christ, his adoring reverence

[39] Bérulle composed the *Collationes* between 1611 and 1615: Dupuy (ed.), *Œuvres complètes*, ii, 183, 232.

[40] Forrestal, *Fathers*, 52–5.

[41] *CCD*, 5: 569, de Paul to Canon de Saint-Martin, *c.*1656.

[42] Brothers contributed 'by their manual labour' and 'prayers, work, tears, mortifications, and good example' to 'the spiritual ministries of the priests and to the conversion of the world'. They would, de Paul admitted, 'compete with us at the gates of paradise' because they possessed such 'honourable qualities': *CCD*, 2: 363, de Paul to Pierre du Chesne, 1 January 1643; *CCD*, 12: 85; *CCD*, 13a: 432.

towards his Father.[43] When speaking to the brothers, de Paul admitted that they could love God just as much as a priest could by conforming to the 'hidden life' of household chores and manual labour that Jesus had led before his public ministry, but he simultaneously reminded them that they owed greater honour to priests than vice versa. They could expect that their priestly fathers would guide and support them, and would return the respect rendered to them with 'gracious condescension'.[44]

Like Bérulle, de Paul also proved anxious to convince the Lazarists that their ordination placed onerous obligations of personal sanctity on them. To articulate their gravity, he resorted to a language of missionary service and responsibility. He instructed his men that God held 'priests accountable for the [sins] of the people' if they did not carry out their duty to reconcile them with him. As well as doing so through the sacraments and teaching, they offered to the rural poor the example of their own lives, which ought to mirror 'the holiness of their specific character'.[45] He desired therefore that the Jesus of Luke's Gospel should speak out as compellingly to them as he did to him. Indeed, imitation is perhaps too restrictive a term to describe the relationship that de Paul posited between them; missionaries who 'preached totally to the poor' were, he taught, to identify with Christ who, as Luke's Gospel narrated, had become one of the poor, that is, had assumed the persona of a poor country carpenter, in order to evangelize the poor while on earth.[46]

'In order to die as Jesus Christ, we must live as Jesus Christ,' de Paul wrote memorably in 1635—offering a rallying call to his missionaries to embrace the selfless and humble service to the needy that the Son of God had carried out in the name of the Father.[47] Furthermore, he insisted Jesus could still be seen in the poor who were 'weighed down by corporal and spiritual sufferings', and were thus cast in his image and the object of his love. In reaching out to these people as Christ did, the missionary priest simultaneously offered himself to Christ. He even shouldered the burdens of his neighbours among the faithful, becoming 'afflicted in [his] own [heart]' by the extent of their suffering, and determining to free them from these by guiding them towards union with God.[48] This was a healthy advertisement for a vocation of active virtue, but de Paul further enriched and refined it with the 'faculties of the soul of the Congregation', the cultivation of which would enable him and his fellow missionaries to 'live as Jesus', the Lord of Charity.[49] In enacting God's 'good pleasure', they should, de Paul pleaded repeatedly, 'never meet a poor person without consoling him . . . or an ignorant man without teaching him in a few words the things he must believe and do for his salvation'.[50] In one of his final

[43] *CCD*, 1: 598–9, de Paul to Jean Duhamel, 15 December 1639; *CCD*, 6: 413, de Paul to a Lazarist priest, undated.

[44] *CCD*, 11: 83 and 99; *CCD*, 12: 89–90.

[45] *CCD*, 5: 570, de Paul to Canon de Saint-Martin, *c.*1656; *CCD*, 7:479, de Paul to Dupont-Fournier, 5 March 1659; *CCD*, 11: 194.

[46] See in particular Luke 4: 18, where Jesus informed listeners in Nazareth that he had been anointed to 'preach good news to the poor'.

[47] *CCD*, 1: 276, de Paul to Antoine Portail, 1635.

[48] *CCD*, 11: 69–70.

[49] *CCD*, 12: 126–37. See also *CCD*, 3: 207, de Paul to Jean Martin, 21 June 1647.

[50] *CCD*, 11: 309.

conferences on the subject (in May 1659), he referred explicitly to the authority of Aquinas, to remind his confreres that 'it is more meritorious to love the neighbour for the love of God than to love God without reference to the neighbour'.[51] Their charity, therefore, became effective when they reached out to their charges in humility, simplicity, gentleness, zeal, and a spirit of mortification.

IV

Although charity was a virtue with an ancient pedigree that stretched back to the New Testament, its prominence in de Paul's teaching was charged especially by the passionate affection that he developed from the late 1610s onwards for the person and teaching of François de Sales. Even before they met, de Paul had, like most of *dévot* Paris, become enamoured with the ideas and practices that the bishop promoted in his *Introduction to the Devout Life*, and had designated the text as required reading for the members of the confraternity of charity in Châtillon in 1617. When de Sales visited Paris for the second time between November 1618 and September 1619, de Paul was introduced to him, probably by Bérulle or Duval.[52] Although there is unfortunately no record of the exact nature and frequency of their conversations, it is clear that the relationship forged during them resulted in several benefits for de Paul. His interest in de Sales's teaching and his reverence for his sanctity helped to shape his own spiritual and pastoral thought; in 1628, he revealed that de Sales's second 'noble work', the *Treatise on the Love of God*, first published in 1616, was mandatory reading for members of his community as a 'universal remedy for all who are dispirited . . . an incentive to love, and a ladder for those striving for perfection'.[53] Their relations also provided a glue that would over time unite de Paul with others who were loyal to the bishop's memory, such as one of the Lazarists' principal patrons, Noel Brûlart de Sillery. And, in practical terms, their intimacy became publicly manifest when de Sales appointed de Paul ecclesiastical superior of the first convent of Visitation nuns established in Paris in 1622, effectively entrusting de Paul with a part in perpetuating his influence in the city.[54]

De Sales elucidated a form of 'spiritualized effectivity', meaning that he distinguished between affective and effective love, and it was perhaps he who led de Paul to concede that contemplative devotion served little purpose without conformity to God's will in holy indifference. De Sales was more optimistic than Bérulle or Canfield in his argument that the natural tendency of men was to turn towards and 'fasten onto' a loving, charitable, God and to contribute to his glory according to the grace of their vocation. As a result, he assumed that those who were in union

[51] *CCD*, 12: 214. [52] Trochu, *François de Sales*, i, 666; ii, 627, 436, 628.

[53] *CCD*, 13a: 84. André Dodin suggests that de Sales's influence may have helped de Paul to overcome a natural disposition towards melancholy: Dodin, *François de Sales*, 29. See also Abelly, *Vie*, iii, 173, for comments on this aspect of de Paul's personality.

[54] See Chs 7 and 9.

with God expressed their submission through 'complacency' (contentment and delight in God's perfection, and a compassionate sharing in the sorrowful pains that he endured for mankind's sin) and 'benevolence' (a desire to exalt God through actions and to bring oneself even closer to him). De Sales's teaching on union with God was less systematized than Bérulle's, but it offered more practical guidance on precisely how any Christian might serve God's will through sanctifying actions, some of it influenced by one of his favourite authors, the sixteenth-century Dominican Louis of Granada, who had pointed out forcefully in his devotional writings on the Christian pursuit of a charitable life that 'he who does one thing is as beneficial to the Church as he who does something entirely different'.[55] For instance, de Sales proposed a form of prayer, by which a Lazarist could, as de Paul put it, repeatedly dwell on making 'resolutions to work well in the future for the acquisition of virtue', identify the ways in which he might do so, and anticipate the pitfalls that might prevent him from advancing in holiness. De Paul incorporated this method of prayer into the regime that the Lazarists followed on a weekly basis.[56]

De Sales died in 1622, and such was his reputation for holiness that the process of gathering evidence for his assessment for beatification began almost immediately, in 1627. As someone who had been in direct contact with him for a time, de Paul was amongst the 500 witnesses asked to testify to his merits, which he did in Paris on 17 April 1628. Although his deposition was partially shaped by the leading and formulaic nature of the questions that he was asked to answer and his desire to ensure that he did not unwittingly hinder de Sales's chances of beatification, the answers that he gave to his questioner still repay examination. His words contain highly revealing details and independent thoughts, which affirm that he had absorbed key elements of Salesian spirituality, both through 'private conversations' with the late bishop during their 'close friendship', and through familiarity with the teachings set out in his publications. Throughout, the respondent's admiration for de Sales was blatant: he 'was the man who best imitated the Son of God while he was here on earth', motivated by 'the great sorrow with which he was tormented by the loss of souls', and 'his ardent zeal for the salvation of souls'.[57]

The most arresting feature of de Paul's responses is their elaboration of an interpretation of charity that he associated and shared with de Sales. He was not asked specifically to comment on de Sales's charity, but the nature of the composition and occasion allowed him far more freedom to elaborate on his understanding of this virtue than the restrictive legalistic framework and language of the contracts and petitions that he produced in the same period. Turning to a striking phrase that he borrowed from de Sales, and which he was to repeat many times in later years, de Paul conceptualized charity as a fire of ardent love, which had burned so brightly in the late bishop that he had assisted everyone who needed spiritual or material help.[58] The admiring de Paul recalled that de Sales had worked to achieve

[55] Aumann (trans.), *Summa of the Christian Life*, ii, 410.

[56] *CCD*, 11: 358–60; de Sales, *Treatise*, 145–8, 193–5, 203–14, 220–2, 253; Lajeunie, *François de Sales*, ii, 232–5, 286–318; Rybolt, 'Saint Vincent's Daily Prayers'.

[57] *CCD*, 11: 191.

[58] See, for example, *CCD*, 11: 66.

conversions in numerous ways, but chief amongst those in his memory was de Sales's ability to enkindle 'a powerful flame of spiritual devotion' (another Salesian phrase) in those with whom he conversed or to whom he delivered sermons. Equally, de Paul adopted de Sales's teaching on the heart of Jesus to denote his purity and his unity with Christ who had been so 'humble of heart'. De Paul's portrait painted de Sales as magnanimous in adversity and tolerant of hardship, while blessed with such humility that he had been able to resist the honours that were offered to him as his fame grew. In mortifying his own will, de Paul observed, he had conformed to the image of the Son of God.[59]

Although de Sales had performed missions in Chablais in Savoy, de Paul did not make any effort in his deposition to present him as a missionary.[60] He did affirm, however, that the late bishop had exhibited the traditional virtues of mortification, zeal, gentleness, simplicity, and humility, and therefore showed himself quite aware that these qualities were not exclusive to any one vocation. Yet his exposition of his views elsewhere reveals that he was already in these years assigning them special priority for the Lazarists. Each of these core virtues stood in relation with its companions, and were cumulatively the means by which the missionary could become 'a charitable man', 'animated' into acts of charity.'[61] Thus, where zeal inspired the missionary in God's work, mortification stiffened his resolve to pursue it. To be mortified could mean bearing poor working conditions, threats and adversity, or particular forms of penitential discipline such as fasting, but, for de Paul, it primarily involved the nurturing of interior strength to endure aggravation, suffering, and temptation, so that God's will could be done.

Naturally, some mission locations were more likely than others to produce challenges to mortification, as were the tendencies of some missionaries to seek a passage of ease in them. In 1632, de Paul asked Antoine Portail to lead a mission of six men in Joigny, and, when advising him on the best way to proceed, revealed that he had not been at all content with the previous mission held there. He felt that it had been hindered by two faults in the missionaries: 'sensuality, not to say intemperance, and an exaggerated love of self.' What would, de Paul fretted, become of a congregation of priests so 'immortified'?[62] This remained a perennial worry. Almost a decade after Duval died, de Paul remembered that he frequently said that an idle priest risked the onslaught of vice, 'for a spirit of laziness' and comfort-seeking could never inspire ardent zeal for God's glory and acceptance of troubles. A true missionary, in contrast, found 'everything good and indifferent; he accepts everything, he can do anything.' He simply wished that affairs be concluded as God wished, and not according to the selfish 'appeals' of human nature. If his work was not animated by the desire to follow God's will, then it was 'a dead work', a 'worthless currency'.[63]

[59] *CCD*, 13a: 80–96. [60] Secret, 'Saint François de Sales'. [61] *CCD*, 11: 66.

[62] *CCD*, 1: 179, de Paul to Antoine Portail, 28 November 1632.

[63] *CCD*, 11: 191. It was probably to Duval that de Paul referred when he spoke of a holy familiar who had reminded him on his deathbed that true love of God was characterized principally by good acts rather than ecstatic visions or advanced knowledge of theology. De Paul was likely to have attended Duval at his death, and his friend had made identical observations in his life of Acarie, in order to demonstrate the multidimensional nature of her sanctity. Dodin surmises that de Paul was referring to

It was humility, however, which de Paul set apart as the most significant of the quintet of missionary virtues. This had been, he remembered, 'especially engraved' on the heart of Jesus in preference to his other virtues; for the Lazarist missionary it was therefore, as their Common Rules eventually summarized, 'the basis of all holiness in the Gospels'.[64] What made humility especially suitable for primacy amongst the core virtues were the diverse applications to which it could be put to seemingly great effect, as well as its theological status as a universal virtue. These qualities meant that it related to all other virtues: both gentleness and simplicity, for instance, were inspired partly by self-abasement. First, therefore, de Paul confided on many occasions that he found the cultivation of humility to be hugely personally enriching, particularly since he feared that he tended to lurch towards its opposite, pride; the moderating quality of humility removed obstacles such as this which inhibited his faith, and helped him to become open to discerning and submitting to God's will, thus providing a sure 'route to heaven'.[65] De Paul was at pains to remind his missionaries habitually of the maxim that 'all the good done' through their work 'comes entirely from God', as he wrote to one of them in 1633.[66] From around this time, he also became partial to an analogy that was based on the mules of King David (Psalm 73), and provided a means to teach Lazarists that they should differentiate between their truly lowly status as instruments of God and the praise that was bestowed on them for their missionary works. 'Think about mules,' de Paul liked to suggest, 'are they proud because they are well harnessed, laden with gold and silver, and adorned with beautiful plumes?' Of course not, he answered! So too:

> In the same way, messieurs, if we are praised or held in esteem . . . let us pay no attention to that . . . Is it not God, messieurs, who does all that? Is it not to him that all the glory of it is due? My Saviour, please give us humility, holy humility.

De Paul went on to warn that in opposing situations, when missionaries were told that they were ignorant, they should simply bear it patiently and humbly.[67] When he endured 'tribulations' and admitted 'failings' while under obedience to God, he remarked, he found that he was rendered more sensitive to those of others, more inclined to share in their interests and suffering in a 'spirit of compassion', and to respond gently to their needs. Secondly, therefore, de Paul presented humility as the gift of an infinitely merciful God who 'gives us his graces according to our needs,' as he assured his confreres in 1641:

the Dominican Pierre Girardel, but the dating of the conversation and the lack of evidence for any contact between the two men makes this extremely unlikely: Abelly, *Vie*, i, 82; Duval, *Sœur Marie de l'Incarnation*, 491–2, 667–8, 673; Dodin, *François de Sales*, 58.

[64] *CCD*, 12: 165; 13a: 435. [65] *CCD*, 13a: 435.

[66] *CCD*, 1: 183, de Paul to a Lazarist priest, 15 January 1633.

[67] *CCD*, 11: 179; *CCD* 1: 227, de Paul to Jacques Perdu, February 1634. For a further instance in which de Paul used the mule to portray virtuous values, see *CCD*, 11: 87.

God is a fountain from which each of us draws water according to the need we have of it . . . a person who needs six buckets of water draws six, and someone who needs three draws three.

It is possible that de Paul borrowed this particular metaphor from Kempis. In the section of the *Imitation* where it was to be found, Kempis concentrated purely on the benefit that their adversities brought to those who were troubled, and suggested that they would lead them to realize that without God 'they can lay hold of nothing good'. De Paul concurred, but as he looked inwards to his relationship with God he also gazed outwards to the world, seeking to understand how suffering could benefit those whom he and his fellow Lazarists sought to convert.[68]

Thirdly, and equally importantly, de Paul allotted to humility a prime and intrinsic role in evangelization by turning it into the foremost tool of conversion among the virtues, as well as a core attribute of the missionary himself. His decision to do so rested partly on his belief that Christians cooperated in their salvation with a God who was generous and clement. This does not appear to be a conviction that he grasped late in his career, although it may have become more pronounced in his teaching as the years passed. It was certainly present in his early sermons during the 1610s, even though they betrayed some hesitancy as, caught between sober pessimism and more optimistic anticipation, he struggled to reconcile his fear of damnation with a hopeful belief in the mercy of God for those who chose to respond to his invitation to obey him. De Paul was never to be quite as optimistic as de Sales in assuming that the natural tendency of man was to turn towards God. Still, as he reminded his confreres during a conference on their rules in 1658, he had discovered in his encounters with peasants that there was nothing 'in the world more worthwhile than to teach' them what God's love had done for them, so that they could 'believe, hope, and love'.[69]

In the late 1620s, de Paul developed a new sermon style, with important implications for the Lazarists' work. In the sermons that survive from the 1610s, he had followed what is known as the 'modern method', first developed in the twelfth century; the sermons were therefore composed of four parts, first the theme and the *prothema*, then divisions which treated theological points and moral applications.[70] Then, in the late 1620s de Paul introduced the 'little method' to the Lazarists, which reflected his growing preoccupation with the need for simplicity in preaching. It should not be supposed, however, that he was a lone proponent of plain or unfussy preaching in the early seventeenth century, even though he is often presented as being so. Rather, his concentration on straightforward and unadorned delivery was foreshadowed, surrounded, and influenced by a host of clergy who had, since the Council of Trent, promoted an Augustinian style of sacred eloquence. Indeed, the Council recommended that clergy preach 'in proportion to their own and their people's mental capacity . . . and impressing

[68] *CCD*, 9: 207, 211; 11: 191, 102; 13a: 435; Aumann (trans.), *Summa of the Christian Life*, ii, 410; Thomas à Kempis, *Imitation of Christ*, 35, 40.

[69] *CCD*, 10: 11; 12: 72.

[70] Bayley, *French Pulpit Oratory*, 101–2; Taylor, *Soldiers of Christ*, 61–9.

upon them with briefness and plainness of speech the vices that they must avoid and the virtues that they must cultivate'.[71] In its wake, the influential Archbishop Charles Borromeo of Milan composed the *Pastorum concionatorumque instructiones*, published in the *Acta ecclesiae mediolanensis*, which advocated a familiar style of preaching, devoid of ornate and superfluous devices such as jokes and conjectures, and designed to instruct and move listeners to conversion.[72] In France, the principal individual responsible for Borromeo's reputation as a model preacher during the seventeenth century was the bishop of Belley, Jean-Pierre Camus. In 1623, he published eight panegyric homilies on the oratorical virtues of the newly canonized cardinal archbishop, in which he lauded Borromeo's success in overcoming his limited natural talents by relying on brevity, and adjustment of terms, style, and material according to the qualities of those to whom he spoke, as well as the simple and efficacious exposition of truth to move his audiences.[73]

Still, as Thomas Worcester confirms, the example that Camus followed most closely was not actually Borromeo but François de Sales, who was equally celebrated for his oratorical skills in France.[74] De Sales was a renowned preacher, who entranced crowds with his twice, even thrice, daily sermons from the pulpits of churches such as Saint-André-des-Arts and the Oratorian church of Saint-Martin (which was so thronged when he arrived that he had to climb in a window to reach the pulpit!) during his visit to Paris in 1618–19.[75] It is likely that de Paul was amongst the listeners at one or more of these, and on the basis of what he heard and saw there, as well as his personal exchanges with the bishop, he subsequently acknowledged that he owed him an irredeemable debt. De Sales explained on numerous occasions that his sermons were not based on what de Paul would later dismiss as 'pompous rhetoric'.[76] Instead, the bishop wished that his words should come from his heart, so that he could speak 'affectionately, devoutly, simply, candidly, and with confidence' to the hearts of his listeners.[77] For de Sales, the chief functions of a sermon were to teach and move, while he allowed that it could delight only if this encouraged the listener along 'the path of Heaven'.[78]

For the Lazarist sermon to be effective, de Paul believed that it needed to produce a permanent effect in its listeners. He too criticized the superficiality and insincerity of 'beautiful, set speeches', on the grounds that while they temporarily

71 Tanner (ed.), *Decrees*, ii, Sess. V, 669.

72 *Acta ecclesiae mediolanensis*, fos 212v–221r.

73 Camus, *Homélies*, 140–65.

74 Camus's own preaching was characterized by vivid representation of his subjects, in a bid to move his audience. Verbal images, in particular, played a crucial part in his communication, for he subscribed to the belief that they made spiritual matters more intelligible, disclosed the relations between the spiritual realm of heaven and the material realm of earth, and moved the emotions to elicit love. In short, he argued that the sensible and material images raised the mind to higher and celestial things, and inspired commitment to them: Worcester, *Seventeenth-Century Cultural Discourse*, 63–5.

75 Lajeunie, *François de Sales*, ii, 344–6.

76 *CCD*, 11: 238.

77 In this, de Sales was probably inspired by the interaction in Acts 2: 36–7, where listeners were 'cut to the heart' and began to ask what they ought to do after learning from Peter that the resurrected Jesus was their Lord and Messiah.

78 De Sales, 'À Monsieur André Frémyot', in *Œuvres de Saint François de Sales*, xii, 299–325.

aroused excitement or pleasure they did not alter the audience's understanding of their relationship with God permanently.[79] However, his own experience amongst rural peasants and with companion missionaries of widely varying oratorical talent (Portail, for instance, was a timid and nervous preacher) caused him to reject these for practical reasons too, and this set him on the road to structural innovation.

The arrangement of a sermon should, de Paul concluded, be determined by the education and ability of those who would hear it. It also dawned on him that whatever method the Lazarists used it needed to be fit to accommodate those naturally gifted in the art of preaching as well as to be a crutch for those less blessed amongst the diversity of missionaries and other priests who helped on their missions.[80] As a result, in the late 1620s, de Paul sought out the opinions of his companions before settling on the 'little method' as the form of eloquence in which the missionaries should be trained;[81] this had a pre-assembled skeleton which enabled the preacher to focus on a specific virtue necessary to living faith, to outline the reasons for seeking it (benefits), to identify its defining qualities (necessity), and to illustrate ways in which to attain it (means). In promoting this as best practice, de Paul characteristically led the way for his men, by exhibiting his acumen for delivering lessons that suited the knowledge and interests of his audiences. For example, in his 1655 conference on the little method, he employed the sermon on the beatitudes, one of his most beloved scriptural passages, to expose the blessings of poverty. But he also arranged his talk so that it offered an illuminating example of the way in which Jesus himself had used the little method to explain the benefits, necessity, and means of attaining this virtue: blessed were the poor, for a loving god had given them the kingdom of Heaven; true poverty was renunciation of all but God.[82] Furthermore, for both sermons and catechesis, he saw the pedagogical value of edifying, exemplary, and energizing stories and verbal imagery (rather than merely decorative), counselling his missionaries on the basis of his own experiences that these were 'a source of inspiration' to men, women, and children, because they applied abstract concepts to realistic situations and to people to whom they could relate.[83]

For sermons, de Paul placed a high degree of stress on humility as a rationale for the simplicity with which they were delivered. He emphasized principally that the

[79] *CCD*, 11: 239–41, 259.

[80] For instance, in 1655, de Paul was pleased to tell confreres that the bishops of Boulogne and Alet, François Perrochel and Nicolas Pavillon, had enthusiastically practised the method when they participated in missions during the 1630s: *CCD*, 11: 253, 255–6.

[81] On de Paul's order, Portail eventually gathered a set of instructions for the method in a large volume, which was condensed in 1666. The Lazarists also memorized prepared and approved sermons: *CCD*, 12: 238n., 241.

[82] *CCD*, 11: 243. Although de Paul is known to have been accomplished in the use of the little method because he taught it by example and spoke 'with strength', unwarranted assumptions are often made about the quality of preaching that other saintly clerics attained. The survival of only small numbers of sermons often makes judgement difficult; Pioger wrote an entire study of Jean Eudes's oratory without having access to even one verifiably authentic sermon by him: Pioger, *Orateur de l'école française*.

[83] *CCD*, 1: 275, de Paul to Antoine Portail, 1 May 1635; *CCD*, 1: 419–20, de Paul to Lambert aux Couteaux, 30 January 1638.

missionary should display his humility through the uncomplicated manner in which he delivered his words and in his avoidance of vainglory; the virtue of simplicity was as incompatible as humility with ostentation or diffusion in sermons. But, in fact, much of the time that the missionaries spent in teaching was actually organized in sessions of catechesis, and these, rather than the sermons, formed the didactic centrepiece of their programme. This meant that they were more likely to engage personally and for longer with individuals in these pedagogical sessions than they were when they delivered their morning sermons.

Of course, the missionaries were never really 'off duty' while on campaign, so de Paul instructed that humility should govern all forms of intercourse on the mission, from their application to the parish priest to perform on arrival in his parish, to their most casual conversations with individual parishioners. Even so, he assumed that the interaction that catechesis guaranteed offered the best opportunity for them to reach out via virtue, using straightforward language, quiet tones, and other gestures of humility, such as a willingness to accept rough seating or indulge naive queries; the missionaries' manner and bearing during their lessons had the potential to affect the choices that their small circles of listeners would make, so they should engage with them in ways that would inspire them to choose to commit to God themselves, seconded by the power of the Holy Spirit. The main 'fruit of the mission' should stem from the sustained inculcation of doctrine in the minds of the faithful, for knowledge of God's glory and the requirements of faith laid the base for their commitment to piety.[84] Yet if the missionary did not display true humility, the words that he spoke would lack their companion virtue; if they saw that he was good, then people would be prepared to listen, and would be placed in a state of readiness to turn freely to God and to learn of the redemptive sacrifice made by Christ on the cross. De Paul assumed, therefore, that their obedience to the wishes of the missionaries would be nurtured not through the use of artifices that manipulated people into submission, but through 'simplicity, uprightness, and firmness of mind', and through earnest 'requests rather than any language that might smack of authority or demands'.[85] The humble missionary would touch their listener to the point where they were ready to personalize the same virtues as he in making their submission to the divine will and removing the obstacles to faith. They would thus emulate the charitable love that he proffered. In doing so, both the evangelizer and the evangelized would become mutually dependent on each other for their heavenly reward, sharing the yields of charity.

As instruments of charity, who stirred the hearts of peasants to love their God, Lazarist missionaries were not the type, de Paul insisted, to thump pulpits, clap their hands, or cry out loud when they catechized or delivered a sermon.[86] This meant that they should also not be the type to engage in controversy, as Charles

[84] *CCD*, 1: 419, de Paul to Lambert aux Couteaux, 30 January 1638. See also *CCD*, 11: 360.

[85] *CCD*, 1: 276, de Paul to Antoine Portail, 1 May 1635; 6: 623, de Paul to Pierre Cabel, 17 November 1657.

[86] *CCD*, 11: 267.

Drelincourt discovered to his chagrin. De Paul granted little credence to controversy as a means of evangelization and conversion, and urged the missionaries that he sent to Sedan to exercise circumspection at all times.[87] This was not because he liked heretics or heresy, of course. He stood firm in the assessment that he made in 1616, which was common to most Catholic churchmen of the time, that the Huguenots were the 'enemies' of the Catholic church. Yet by 1628 he was willing to label them more compassionately—and more charitably—as 'poor misguided people' who should be treated, he observed to Portail, 'with meekness, humility, and patience'.[88] Coaching missionaries on the best stance to assume when they met Huguenots in Mende and Richelieu in the mid-1630s, he wrote that he had found controversy stemmed from a selfish and proud wish to earn applause and notoriety, that is, from an impure intention. Worse, it manifested a scornful attitude and an intemperate zeal which provoked unedifying disputes.[89] Subtlety, craftiness, and ambiguity robbed the missionary of his true spirit: 'People will never believe in us if we do not show love and compassion to those whom we wish to believe in us.'[90]

With such advice, de Paul schooled his missionaries to use the language, concepts, and conduct of the virtues to cross the boundaries between the faiths, as well as to connect with Catholics. They offered, he was sure, a unique vocational gift to the church, and he was invariably at pains to set out the qualities as well as the practices that defined their ability to present it. Core values were both idealistic and realistic, acting as bearings that mapped out their missionary model for individual Lazarists, while simultaneously informing the means by which they enacted it. In this framework of understanding, there should be no distinction between what the missionary should be and what the world saw when it gazed at him and at his actions. Simultaneously collective as well as individual values,

[87] De Paul and his men practised the art of controversy at Saint-Lazare, because he recognized that this would help them to become adept in separating true doctrines from falsehoods. However, the confines of the motherhouse formed a controlled environment, and he made a sharp distinction between the academic exercise of controversy and its practice in the mission field: *CCD*, 1: 289, de Paul to Antoine Portail, 10 August 1635; 1: 420, de Paul to Lambert aux Couteaux, 30 January 1638; 2: 442, de Paul to Guillaume Gallais, *c.*1643. De Paul was also a member of the Congregation for the Exaltation of the Cross, founded by the Capuchin *Père* Hyacinthe in 1632 'to aid the conversion of heretics and the subvention of the newly converted'. He attended at least one of the occasional exercises on controversy that it organized for its members, but in general he rarely went to its meetings, and was not a leading member: APF, SOGC, 199, fo. 85; BN, Ms Fr 2786, fos 12v and 71v–89r; Martin, *Compagnies de la propagation de la foi*, 142–3.

[88] De Paul converted several Huguenots in Châtillon and Marchais-en-Brie near Montmirail during his early career as a missionary, and his personal encounters may have softened the more abstract views he expressed beforehand. Abelly gave an account in the third person of a conference with a Lazarist audience, in which de Paul shared the details of the conversions in Marchais-en-Brie around 1620, but it is stylized to the point that it reveals little more than that de Paul engaged in catechetical instruction, and is designed to be a retrospective demonstration of his knowledge and defence of Catholic doctrines: Abelly, *Vie*, i, 57; *CCD*, 1: 40, de Paul to Urban VIII, June 1628; *CCD*, 1: 57–8, de Paul to Antoine Portail, 15 September 1628.

[89] *CCD*, 1: 276, de Paul to Antoine Portail, 1 May 1635; 1: 279, de Paul to Antoine Lucas, 28 June 1635.

[90] *CCD*, 1: 277, de Paul to Antoine Portail, 1 May 1635; 1: 420, de Paul to Lambert aux Couteaux, 30 January 1638; 1: 11, 55.

moreover, the critical importance of these specifications was not restricted to their actualization by particular persons; they should transcend any one man, de Paul included, to become collective marks that helped to define the ethos of the Lazarist Congregation, set it apart from other clerical groupings as a cohort of supremely humble and charitable clerics, and placed it at the heart of ecclesiastical renewal within the French church.

PART III

EXPANSION AND COLLABORATION

6

Saint-Lazare, Bons-Enfants, and Clerical Formation

I

In the late 1630s, de Paul adopted the arresting symbolism of the raising of Lazarus in the New Testament to describe community life in the former priory which bore his name and now housed the Congregation of the Mission. The message of spiritual conversion and healing that underlay Lazarus's miraculous restoration by Christ to life four days after his death provided the perfect analogy for the rebirth of the old priory and for those who now spent time there: Saint-Lazare had in the past, de Paul observed, 'served as a retreat for lepers', but had been injected with renewed purpose on the arrival of its new inhabitants:

> It is used to receive sinners, who are sick persons covered with spiritual leprosy, but who are cured, by the grace of God . . . these are dead people who come back to life . . . This saint, after remaining in the tomb for three days, left it fully alive; & Our Lord, who raised him, does the same favour for others . . . having remained here some days . . . [1]

De Paul's words referred first to the Lazarists themselves, who dedicated their lives to the pursuit of sanctity, and enjoyed welcome respite at the motherhouse when they returned from the exhausting demands of the mission fields in the provinces. But their author was also thinking of other ecclesiastics who had been entering Saint-Lazare in growing numbers from 1632; since then, the complex had become a hub of formation and rejuvenation for a range of clerics who sought retreat there at varying stages of their vocations. In 1636, de Paul decided to use Bons-Enfants for a similar purpose when he opened a seminary to train young boys, simultaneously to act as an incubator of possible Lazarist recruits and to answer the recommendation by the Council of Trent that dioceses should establish a college in which boys over 12 years old would be prepared for orders.[2] By the early 1640s, as a result, both the motherhouse and its subsidiary site had become not only bases from which the Lazarists reached out to the faithful through missions, but spaces where the community absorbed outsiders and invited them to experience a Pauline-like rebirth, and thus a new life in Christ.

[1] *CCD*, 11: 13. [2] Tanner (ed.), *Decrees*, ii, 750–1, Sess. XXIII.

The assignment of these sites to clerical formation was the first step in a long-term process of expansion, by the close of which the Lazarists had emerged as major providers of clerical training in France. That de Paul should have entertained the possibility that they turn their attention from their central purpose of rural mission toward the training of clergy is notable, since he had not initially included clerical formation within the vocational remit of his missionary association. Further, even after he made the decision to do so, he continued to wrestle with the nature and demands of the transition, only fully reconciling to it very late in his career, a struggle which Chapter 8 will explore in more detail. By the time that their founder died, however, the Lazarists had nineteen other houses in France, with eleven of these containing a seminary for diocesan clerics. Forty years later, they were managing twenty-seven seminaries, and by 1789, were responsible for more seminaries than any other congregation or order in the realm.[3] Indeed, for many, de Paul's choice to permit the Lazarists to enter this area of ministry was the root of both his and their greatness. One of those who knew at first hand the opportunities that they gave to clerics was Bishop Henri de Maupas du Tour, who delivered the oration in praise of de Paul on his death in 1660. To an assembly of admiring mourners, he alleged that his subject had 'virtually changed the face of the Church by Conferences, by instructions, by seminaries . . . it is he who re-established the Clergy's glory in its first splendour, by ordinands' exercises, by spiritual Retreats, by the opening of his heart and house.'[4] It has since become commonplace to credit de Paul with the lion's share of praise for the transformation of the French clergy during this period of Reformation.[5] Since many of the initiatives that he began experienced their greatest growth under his successors, this is hyperbolic. Yet, it remains undeniable that the origins of the large number of seminaries that the Lazarists held in the eighteenth century lay in the patterns of engagement with clerical education and formation that their founder devised during the first three decades of its existence.

II

By the early 1640s, Saint-Lazare and Bons-Enfants housed no fewer than four forums for clerical formation. Primary amongst these was the internal seminary on the grounds of Saint-Lazare, at which all new Congregation members spent

[3] The Lazarists ran forty-seven of the 160 *grands séminaires* in France (as well as two *petits* of the forty in total). It should be noted, however, that the Sulpicians had the greatest number of seminarians by then, and ran the most prestigious seminaries: Forrestal, *Fathers*, 59; Julia, 'L'Expansion de la Congrégation de la Mission'.

[4] Maupas du Tour, *Funeral Oration*, 96.

[5] While admitting that de Paul 'did not inaugurate a movement destined to end in the regeneration and organisation of the clergy', Coste concludes adamantly that 'he was, in the hands of God, the instrument that most powerfully contributed to its success'. Henry Kamen is reluctant to crown de Paul with this accolade, yet still acknowledges that his most effective contribution to Catholic reform in France was to change 'the Christian people by changing their ministers': Coste, *Saint*, i, 290–1; Kamen, *Iron Century*, 261–2.

two years after de Paul authorized its establishment around 1637. For external ecclesiastics, he had already instituted a formal programme of ten-day residential retreats at Saint-Lazare from 1631, while in 1636 he approved the foundation of a small or 'minor' seminary for boys at Bons-Enfants. In addition, from 1633, de Paul was also the director of a company of clerics, known as the Tuesday Conferences, based at Saint-Lazare. While the common objective that he pursued in organizing these various initiatives was the cultivation of disciplined clergy, each was tailored in structure and operation to meet what he assumed to be the particular requirements of the Lazarists, the diocese, or the wider church.

The centre of this set of operations was, of course, the Lazarists' own (internal) seminary, for it was here that the new Lazarist completed his initial programme of training in the missionary virtues and the duties that would enable him to live up to the demands of the Congregation's ethos. From its inception, the Congregation of the Mission had attracted entrants who were not ordained priests as well as some with prior experience in ecclesiastical office. When numbers were tiny, it was a relatively straightforward task to initiate them, because a secluded routine of prayer and reflection within the community could be readily combined with missionary fieldwork. But, by 1637, the Congregation had attracted at least thirty-eight entrants since foundation, and from this point onwards all entrants attended what de Paul optimistically termed the 'hope of the flock'.[6] He entrusted daily oversight of the institute initially to a long-standing and experienced missionary, Jean de La Salle, but he judged it so important to the Lazarists' growth that he always paid close attention to its regulation and functioning. Throughout his tenure as superior general it usually housed between thirty and forty seminarians.[7] The majority of the 611 individuals who entered the Lazarists during de Paul's superior generalship were mature candidates, aged at least 18 years and often ordained, although de Paul did made exceptions: at least three candidates were only 15 when they walked through the seminary's doors, even though it went against de Paul's instinct to accept such immature newcomers 'because very few of them give themselves to God with the right intention'.[8] He did his utmost to test the veracity of their intentions before accepting them, and the period in the seminary was itself a time of search and growth which only came to fruition when the candidates completed their programme, and were offered the opportunity to take simple vows.[9] Abelly reported that de Paul once wrote, paraphrasing Thomas à Kempis, that those who lived in community should become pilgrims on earth, whose seminary training fostered the dispositions of humility, obedience,

[6] De Paul regularly expressed concern that the seminary was filled to capacity, and in danger of overwhelming the Lazarists' ability to resource it. See, for instance, *CCD*, 6: 158, de Paul to Jean Martin, 1 December 1656; Abelly, *Vie*, i, 157–8.

[7] A small internal seminary was established at the Lazarists' house in Richelieu in 1653, but it produced only about twenty-five recruits while it functioned (to 1660): *CCD*, 4: 520, de Paul to Lambert aux Couteaux, 3 January 1653.

[8] *CCD*, 4: 164, de Paul to Étienne Blatiron, 4 March 1651. For figures on Lazarist numbers during the seventeenth and eighteenth centuries, see Mezzadri and Román, *Vincentians*, 1: 319–20.

[9] *CCD*, 6: 175, de Paul to Guillaume Delville, 6 January 1657.

and mortification that enabled them to serve God as missionaries of their congregation.[10]

De Paul did not design the seminary to be an academic institution, but to be a place in which the Lazarists developed their habits of missionary virtue, rooting them so deeply that they would hold fast when they were far from the routines and security that it provided. He did not permit many of them to proceed to formal studies in theology after their two-year training, though the readings that he approved for private reflection did of course contain a degree of theological teaching.[11] Mainly, however, he expected that these would provide the spiritual insights and the tools suitable for the cultivation of the Lazarist missionary virtues and pastoral competencies. Thus, in company with *The Imitation of Christ*, the New Testament was prominent in the Congregation's programme. Every morning, seminarians read a section, and learned ten or twelve lines 'by heart', while they also listened to passages read aloud from it at meals. Other works that de Paul permitted them to read, and to discuss with their designated superior, included the *Introduction* and *Entretiens* of François de Sales, as well as *The Spiritual Combat* of the Theatine Lorenzo Scupoli; the *Combat* was a favourite generally with *dévots* like Acarie, and de Sales had contributed to its stature when he recommended it as suitable reading for the pious Catholic in his *Introduction*.[12] The remaining texts formed an eclectic set of other well-thumbed spiritual classics of the period which mixed exemplary lives with instruction in virtue, notably Albertus Magnus' life of Christ, the *Confessions* of Augustine, the letters of Catherine of Siena and Francis Xavier, the Jesuit Alphonse Rodriguez's *Practice of Christian Perfection* (first published in 1609), and lives of Ignatius of Loyola and the blessed martyrs.[13]

The rule declared that the 'spirit of the Seminary' consisted of 'perfect interior and exterior mortification', obedience, love of poverty, perpetual silence, esteem for advice, and zeal for community practices, all aimed towards honouring 'the childhood of Our Lord', and practised in 'silence, solitude and recollection'. On entry, all Lazarists completed a retreat, and they repeated this exercise at six-monthly intervals thereafter in the hope of retaining the insights and habits gained in the seminary.[14] Ordinarily, they followed a rigorous daily routine to inculcate the missionary dispositions and

[10] Abelly, *Vie*, i, 162. The relevant passage is found in Kempis, *Imitation of Christ*, 40–1.

[11] A minority of academically capable students, such as René Alméras, went on to study scholastic theology for a time in the class of external clerics at Bons-Enfants. In adopting this policy, de Paul may have taken the advice of Bishop Barrault of Bazas: *CCD*, 1: 528–9, de Paul to Robert de Sergis, 3 February 1639; Sol (ed.), *Alain de Solminihac*, 96–7, Jean Jaubert de Barrault to Alain de Solminihac, 11 October 1630.

[12] The *Combat* was first published in French in 1594: Diefendorf, *Penitence*, 283n.

[13] ACMP, 'Règles du Séminaire', fos 4r–5r, 34r, 39r; ACMP, 'Règles du Directeur du Séminaire'. The seminary rule dates from 1652, and includes some material subsequent to that year, but it principally codified practices and customs developed from 1637 to 1652. The list of approved books also dates from 1652, but conformed 'to the intentions of Monsieur Vincent'. All of the works listed were available many years before 1652, and were probably staples of the seminary shelves from the 1630s. The rule for the director dates from the same period.

[14] ACMP, 'Règles du Directeur du Séminaire', fos 5r, 13r; *CCD*, 2: 374, de Paul to Pierre du Chesne, 1 January 1643.

values, consisting of mass, an hour-long *entretien* on a topic appropriate to their vocation, such as the little method or a virtue, moderate corporal mortification, examination of conscience, making of virtuous resolutions, practice of ecclesiastical functions, spiritual reading, and prayer. They were encouraged to carry out mundane household duties assigned to them, such as table service, in a spirit of humility, service, and charity, as Jesus had done when he assisted his parents at home or distributed the loaves and fish to a hungry audience; the aim was to foster a sense of constant imitation of Christ as they progressed towards a more mature sense of vocation.[15]

Interspersed in this routine de Paul allowed a series of responsibilities that related to the Lazarists' specific ministerial objectives. Each week, an advanced seminarian was assigned to deliver three catechism lessons to the local poor, following the format and topics used on missions, and mirroring the actions of Christ on earth. Twice weekly, the seminarians visited those interned at Saint-Lazare and a selection of the sick poor of the parish, in the assurance that they visited Christ in visiting them. In consoling these troubled people, they were to remind them that 'God loves them since he afflicts them', that their status was close to that which Jesus had held on earth, that they followed also in the footsteps of such saints as Peter, Paul, and Claire, and that they would ultimately be compensated with the 'glory of paradise'. In addition, they were directed to encourage them to confess and pray with them, and deliver some instruction if it was welcomed.[16] Advanced seminarians also developed their skills on missions, for it was common to send bands of them on campaigns, under the watchful eyes of the mission directors; those already ordained were permitted to confess the faithful, while the others spent their days teaching catechism.[17]

III

While the foundation of an internal seminary offered a framework for introducing recruits to the qualities and practices that expressed the Lazarist vocation, de Paul knew that the retreats and external seminary needed to serve the church in other ways if they were to succeed. His specific incentives to involve his men in both types of formation emerged from two quarters, both representing the growing desire of reforming church authorities to improve the quality of clergy in the Parisian diocese, and de Paul's ability to capitalize on the opportunities that this presented. One overture came in 1630 from Jean Coqueret, the principal of the College of Grassins. He and de Paul had first become acquainted around 1618 when they worked together on a mission, and Coqueret had subsequently

[15] ACMP, 'Règles du Séminaire', fos 23r, 37r, 89r–90r, and 94r–95r.

[16] The rule references Luke 4 and Matt. 25, in which Jesus began to evangelize publicly, and appealed to the Apostles to care for the poor, the sick, prisoners, and strangers as they would for him: ACMP, 'Règles du Séminaire', fos 104r–105r, 113r–117r, 119r.

[17] See, for instance, *CCD*, 2: 255, de Paul to Bernard Codoing, 9 February 1642, and *CCD*, 2: 395, same to same, 30 January 1643, for references to bands sent to Annecy and Champagne.

completed a short retreat at Bons-Enfants under de Paul's direction. As a college principal Coqueret was in a position to promote the Congregation's reputation as a provider of retreats, and it was no doubt his own positive experience on retreat that led him subsequently to send a number of his students to Bons-Enfants for the same.[18] De Paul was delighted, although he was too coy in expressing wonder that Coqueret's retreat should have led other individuals to follow suit.[19] This overlooked the fact that, in collaboration with the priests of Saint-Nicolas-du-Chardonnet, de Paul and his confreres had already begun to deliver retreats over two years earlier, albeit in Beauvais rather than Paris.[20] De Paul also skated over the fact that it was he who had initiated this service, by suggesting to the local bishop, Augustin Potier, when they met on a return coach journey to Paris, that a programme of retreats before ordination would tackle the ignorance of clerics at an earlier stage, and help to improve clerical standards in his diocese.[21]

The Lazarists' collaboration with Bourdoise's priests was significant, for these had taken the lead in offering this type of service for a number of years beforehand. However, though Bourdoise could not claim credit for its invention, it was still a rare type of enterprise. Years earlier in 1585, for instance, in an effort to improve clerical standards in his newly assigned diocese of Clermont, Cardinal de La Rochefoucauld had experimented with conferences for parish priests in which they were instructed on issues of moral theology that they might encounter in the confessional, and he had also asked the Jesuits of Montferrand to organize ten-day retreats for ordinands. Other reforming prelates, including Sourdis of Bordeaux and Richelieu, had subsequently resorted to similar methods.[22] In 1618, with greater ambition, Archbishop Henri de Gondi obtained letters patent for a diocesan seminary for Paris in the abbey of Saint-Magloire, and confided its direction to the Oratorians, but the pensions payable to the former religious of the abbey swallowed up the revenue that should have been used to keep students and it was twenty-four years before the seminary accepted its first students.[23]

Two years later, Gondi endured another false start when he commissioned Bourdoise's community to teach and examine newly ordained priests in the diocese in church ceremonies and rubrics; this time a lack of lodging for the candidates meant that this did not achieve the desired results.[24] Finally, Gondi turned to de Paul and his men, and during Lent 1631, they took on the duty of offering retreats to groups of clerics proceeding to ordination in the diocese of Paris. One year later,

[18] *CCD*, 11: 142–3. [19] *CCD*, 11: 143. [20] See Ch. 4.

[21] *CCD*, 1: 56–7, de Paul to François du Coudray, 15 September 1628; Abelly, *Vie*, i, 116–19. It is not clear when de Paul met Potier, although the bishop spent a significant amount of time in Paris after he became *grand aumônier* to Anne of Austria from 1624: Bergin, *French Episcopate*, 507.

[22] Bergin, *La Rochefoucauld*, 108; Bergin, *Rise of Richelieu*, 94; Broutin, *Réforme pastorale*, i, 42–3, 108–10; La Moriniere, *Les Vertus du vray prelat*, 396–9; Ravenez, *François de Sourdis*, 179.

[23] AN, L426; Ferté, *Vie religieuse*, 146–7.

[24] It is possible that Bourdoise may also have instituted conference-type meetings for clergy during the early 1620s, although this is based on Darché's contention that he rented a room at Bons-Enfants for this purpose. In the late 1620s, de Paul alluded to a meeting which may have been related to these gatherings: *CCD*, 1: 31, de Paul to Louise de Marillac, undated; Darché de Chevrières, *Bourdoise*, i, 488; Schoenher, *Séminaire de Saint-Nicolas-du-Chardonnet*, i, 97.

the archbishop made their continued adherence to this service a condition of his approval of the union of Saint-Lazare.[25] Thereafter, the Congregation directed five or six retreats annually, with Saint-Lazare in particular providing the spacious accommodation necessary.[26] Furthermore, de Paul assented to Gondi's request that its members should deliver these at no cost to the diocese of Paris, despite the fact that catering for the retreatants made considerable demands on them, in terms of providing lodging, meals, and personnel: to feed and house an ordinand on retreat in Paris normally cost twenty *sous* per day in the 1640s, while the number of ordinands averaged around eighty-five at any given conference.[27] To meet expenses, de Paul was forced to depend partially on donations.[28] However, he stuck fast to the no fee policy even when the Lazarists also began to accept candidates preparing for minor orders from 1647.[29] This was because the prestige that accrued from the retreats far outweighed the costs endured. As a further prize deriving from their founder's relations with the Gondi family, they publicly affirmed his and his association's good standing with the archbishop. In addition, the retreats boosted the reputations of Saint-Lazare and Bons-Enfants as centres of ecclesiastical vigour, demonstrating to others that de Paul and his associates could be depended on to deliver this type of service efficiently and expertly on a large scale.

To achieve this, de Paul selected a team of pastorally experienced and spiritually competent confreres such as La Salle, René Alméras, François Charles, and Nicolas de Monchy to conduct the different elements of the retreats for individuals and groups. He instructed those assigned to approach their retreatants in a blend of 'the three colours of modesty, cheerfulness, and gentleness', which indicated their submission and humility towards those whom they served. He deemed the adoption of a non-threatening demeanour essential to breaking down the defences of

[25] *CCD*, 13a: 278–9, 291.

[26] The number was reduced to five in 1643, although the number of clerics received remained high, particularly as clerics from outside Paris who were to be ordained in the diocese participated from 1638, as did candidates proceeding to minor orders from 1647. In the 1650s, de Paul had a new 'grand corps de logis' standing four storeys tall erected to accommodate the large number of retreatants staying at Saint-Lazare annually: Abelly, *Vie*, ii, 216–17; AN, M212, 'Procès-verbal d'une visite par Nicolas Porcher à Saint-Lazare' (27 June 1659).

[27] *CCD*, 2: 89, de Paul to Bernard Codoing, 26 July 1640; *CCD*, 4: 256, de Paul to Jean Martin, 15 September 1651; *CCD*, 4: 341, de Paul to Lambert aux Couteaux, 22 March 1652; *CCD*, 5: 588, de Paul to Charles Ozenne, 6 April 1656.

[28] Between 1638 and 1643, a Lady of Charity, Madame de Herse, paid 6,000 *livres* annually for the retreats, and Anne of Austria made a royal grant for the following two or three years. On her death in 1650, the marchioness of Maignelay bequeathed 18,000 *livres* to the Congregation, stipulating that its annual income of 1,000 *livres* should pay for maintaining ordinands on retreat. In 1651, de Paul redirected this legacy, exchanging it for 175 *arpents* of land at Plessis-Trappes, which he bought from the administrators of the *Incurables* hospital in Paris, but he specified in the contract that the farm's revenue was to be used to maintain the ordinands, thus ensuring that he acquiesced to the wishes of the now deceased benefactor. A few years later, Louis de Chandenier donated the priory of Saint-Pourçain-sur-Sioule (the Auvergne) to the Congregation, and de Paul used its income to pay for retreat expenses: BN, MS Clairambault 1136, 'Testament de la Marquise de Maignelay', 14; AN, M211, S6681A and S6712; Abelly, *Vie*, ii, 216; *CCD*, 6: 38, de Paul to Louis de Chandenier, 21 July 1656; *CCD*, 6: 401, de Paul to Edme Jolly, 3 August 1657; *CCD*, 7: 38, same to same, 21 December 1657.

[29] Abelly, *Vie*, i, 116–19; Schoenher, *Séminaire de Saint-Nicolas-du-Chardonnet* i, 55–61.

those who needed to learn to submit themselves to God, and would suffer feelings of isolation and vulnerability before any spiritual breakthrough. This he thought appropriate for the guidance of any retreatant, whether they sought assistance in the acquisition of a specific virtue, the abandonment of a tormenting vice, or enlightenment in their choice of vocation.[30] The goal was to provide the ordinands with at least an elementary understanding of the spiritual and pastoral essentials of their vocations, through teaching them 'all about mental prayer, practical and necessary theology, and the ceremonies of the Church'.[31] Over the ten-day schedule, a short programme of Salesian meditation guided by a Lazarist director led the retreatants to a general confession; they also learned how to perform ecclesiastical ceremonies, and attended *entretiens* on moral theology which specialized in problems that they might encounter when administering the sacraments.[32] De Paul hoped that the intense series of exercises would awaken them to the demands of their vocation, and stimulate a uniformity of sacerdotal thought and practice that was essential if the church was to preserve its cohesion and loyalty to God's wishes.[33]

Concurrently, however, de Paul was sufficiently realistic to recognize that the retreat exercises were not a panacea to the church's ills. Thus, he would have acquiesced with Bourdoise, that these were 'something', but paled 'in comparison with the benefits that one hopes of a good seminary . . . it will approach and resemble as closely as possible the first of all the seminaries which is that of Our Lord and the apostles.'[34] The admission confirms that both men were actors in a broader pre-existing campaign in the French church to identify the best means of systematizing clerical training. From 1567, when the Cardinal de Lorraine opened a seminary in Reims, successive bishops had attempted with limited success to establish seminaries according to the model proposed by the Council of Trent.[35] They had been impeded by financial and juridical obstacles, however, so that only about sixteen of the seminaries established between 1567 and 1620 survived into the mid-1600s; one failure was Richelieu's small establishment in Luçon diocese, which began to limp to final closure in 1625 as soon as he opened it in 1612 because the Oratorians could not provide sufficient personnel to staff it.[36] When, however, de Paul decided to open a seminary for boys in 1636, he took his immediate inspiration from closer to home. Bourdoise had eventually opened a seminary in Saint-Nicolas-du-Chardonnet in 1631, through which over 500 clerics and priests passed between 1631 and 1644.[37] From him de Paul received the

[30] *CCD*, 11: 147. [31] *CCD*, 12: 212.

[32] The composition of a book of *entretiens* helped to standardize the teaching on moral theology, on topics such as sin, the sacraments, and chastity: *CCD*, 1: 297, de Paul to Clement de Bonzi, September–October 1635; *CCD*, 1: 181, de Paul to unnamed, *c.*1633; *CCD*, 1: 553, de Paul to Jeanne de Chantal, 14 July 1639; Abelly, *Vie*, ii, 218–21; Delville, *Petit abrégé*, *passim.*

[33] *CCD*, 1: 516, de Paul to Antoine Lucas, 13 December 1638; *CCD*, 12: 201, 212.

[34] Adrien Bourdoise, 'Sentences chrétiennes et ecclésiastiques', cited by *Père* Courtin, Bib. Maz., Ms 2453, 'La Vie du venerable Serviteur de Dieu Messire Adrien Bourdoise', 1049: ' . . . quelque chose, mais ce n'est rien en comparaison des biens que l'on espère d'un bon seminaire . . . il approchera et ressemblera de plus près au premier de tous les seminaries qui est celui de N.S. et des apôtres.'

[35] Tanner (ed.), *Decrees*, ii, 750–1, Sess. XXIII. [36] Bergin, *Rise of Richelieu*, 94–6.

[37] Schoenher, *Séminaire de Saint-Nicolas-du-Chardonnet*, i, 123.

counsel that 'it was more important to instruct the clergy, since, if they are ignorant, the people they guide will, by necessity, be the same'. Throughout these years, the pair remained on close terms, their mutual appreciation for each other's values and work leading to Bourdoise completing a retreat at Saint-Lazare in 1639, and to de Paul's decision to send a Lazarist to do the same at Saint-Nicolas-du-Chardonnet.[38]

Bourdoise's seminary was for de Paul a beacon, which at times made the shadows over his own all the more gloomy. It was in an effort to lift these that he resolved to split it in two just nine years after it opened, though this was not because it had outgrown its premises. Similarly to the initiation of the retreats in 1631, the innovation was partly opportunistic, since Cardinal Richelieu, who retained an interest in the promotion of seminaries despite his own failed experiment in Luçon, offered 1,000 *écus* for the upkeep of twelve candidates.[39] But de Paul was also concerned with improving the models of vocational preparation that the Lazarists were providing. The seminary had originally admitted boys in their early teens, but he opened it to mature candidates as well in 1642, who normally stayed for a period of one year. Three years later, de Paul moved the younger residents to a new 'little seminary' of Saint-Charles at Saint-Lazare where they took courses in the Humanities, leaving the older clerics at Bons-Enfants.[40] This division reflected his misgivings about the original structure that he had established, and his desire to overcome its weaknesses. De Paul was usually canny enough to express his doubts privately, knowing that they implied criticism of a blueprint proposed by a Council whose 'ruling is to be respected as coming from the Holy Spirit'.[41] At the same time, his personal experience contradicted Trent's wish, for it demonstrated conclusively that there were impediments to success embedded within the regime it proposed. De Paul found that students who entered a seminary below the age of 20 were apt to change their minds as they progressed in their training, which was a waste of institutional resources as well as an upset to the student community generally. Thus, of the twenty-two boys in Bons-Enfants in 1644, he doubted that more than three or four would persevere to ordination. He pessimistically noted precisely the same pattern in seminaries in Reims, Bordeaux, Rouen, and Agen, for 'not one of these dioceses has received any benefit from them', and indeed the Rouen seminary only managed to produce about 2 per cent of the diocese's clergy during its first fifty years of existence.[42] What had still seemed like a good idea in 1636 was producing meagre returns in practice nearly a decade later.

[38] *CCD*, 1: 535, de Paul to the Saint-Nicolas community, 29 April 1639; *CCD*, 11: 185–6.

[39] *CCD*, 2: 256–7, de Paul to Bernard Codoing, 9 February 1642; Abelly, *Vie*, i, 147. For further discussion of Richelieu's patronage of the Lazarists, see Ch. 7, section IV.

[40] De Paul purchased four *arpents* of land, containing a house, yard, garden, and windmill, for this purpose from Nicolas Caron on the Congregation's behalf, for the price of 11,000 *livres*: AN, S6691 (20 July 1644).

[41] *CCD*, 2: 505–6, de Paul to Bernard Codoing, 13 May 1644.

[42] Reims, opened in 1567, Bordeaux in 1583, Rouen in 1613, and Agen in 1597. For further information on seminaries, see Degert, *Histoire des séminaires*.

De Paul's decision to split the seminary is often lauded as a major innovation in the development of the structures of seminary education in France. It enabled him to begin to tailor training especially to the needs of those preparing for or having taken major orders, and to pin his hopes for the future on these mature candidates.[43] Yet, it was actually the step that he had taken three years earlier, in 1642, to begin to train older clerics (often priests)—at all—which constituted the real advance. In this, however, he was not alone. It is important, therefore, to situate his personal insights alongside those of other contemporaries who followed in Bourdoise's wake, while recognizing simultaneously that de Paul was more successful than some of his contemporaries in doing so. On the advice of the Oratorian superior general, Condren, who was his spiritual director, Jean-Jacques Olier instituted a small seminary for adult clerics in Vaugirard one month before de Paul split his seminary, and he transferred it to his new parish of Saint-Sulpice shortly afterwards. Indeed, Condren had already expressed reservations to de Paul about housing youths in seminaries during the 1630s, and this may have influenced de Paul's thinking. Even so, the Oratorians struggled to respond to this concern themselves. Between 1640 and 1642 they opened a seminary at Saint-Magloire for fourteen adult students, but it closed in the 1650s before eventually reopening in 1660. Their other ventures in this decade also ended in failure.[44]

In contrast, through the 1640s and 1650s, Bons-Enfants hosted about forty students at any given time, and de Paul managed to keep it in operation even though it teetered permanently on a financial knife edge.[45] From 1642, the Lazarists also held a conference for clerics there each Thursday, which was publicly advertised in the calendar of ecclesiastical events published annually for Paris from 1646.[46] De Paul could therefore afford a degree of satisfaction in the vibrancy of the community, and the contribution that it made to ecclesiastical life in the city. Yet he continually fretted about the aptness of the service that it offered to its students and the church at large. He did not entirely share the optimistic view of Jean Dehorgny, the confrere he placed in charge on a daily basis, that the students

43 *CCD*, 2: 505–6, de Paul to Bernard Codoing, 13 May 1644.

44 The Oratorians opened seminaries in Rouen and Toulouse, but they lasted for only a short time: Faillon, *Olier*, i, 292; Ferté, *Vie religieuse*, 151, 153. Amongst these seminaries, only Bons-Enfants did not obtain letters of authorization from the archbishop soon after foundation. This appears to be because de Paul did not request them, though he had the archbishop's informal support for his seminary. Why he did not do so is unclear. He may have wished to ensure that it retain as much independence as possible, at least in its 'experimental' phase. The seminary finally received formal archiepiscopal approbation in 1707, when it was renamed Saint-Firmin: AN, S6849.

45 The students paid fees but these amounted to only one-third of their upkeep, and it normally cost the Lazarists about 21 *sous* per day to feed and lodge each one in the 1640s. Growing numbers meant that de Paul also had to approve major expenditure on the buildings that housed them. Between 1642 and 1645, soaring expenses overshot receipts by a yearly average of 718 *livres*, and jumped from 1,132 *livres* in 1641 to 2,100 *livres* in 1646: AN, H^5 3288 and S6850; Archives of the Congregation of the Mission, Krakow, 'Autographes de Saint Vincent et de ses premiers compagnons', no. 152, René Alméras to Lambert aux Couteaux, 8 May 1652 (I would like to thank John Rybolt, CM, for providing me with copies of letters in this collection); *CCD*, 3: 235, de Paul to Jean-François de Gondi, 3 September 1647.

46 Several volumes of the calendar are held in the BN; see, for example, du Mans, *Almanach*.

were 'innocent' in behaviour, or that their time in study and reflection led them to renewed dedication to their sacerdotal calling.[47] More compellingly, over time he grew disenchanted with aspects of seminary life, yet found no route to overcoming its deficiencies. This was all the more troubling to him since Bons-Enfants was the Lazarists' flagship institution for the formation of non-Lazarist diocesan clergy, and therefore in theory the model for any other seminary that the Lazarists managed.

De Paul's apprehension focused on the preparation that the students received for the parishes in which they would spend their time once they left Bons-Enfants. It probably took root as early as 1643, when the Lazarists began to organize a seminary that was attached to a parish in Cahors. There, the students lived under the rule of Bons-Enfants within the seminary, but, crucially, were permitted to practise their newly formed pastoral skills in the parish, an outlet not open to them in Paris. Thereafter, de Paul ensured that the same relationship normally pertained wherever the Lazarists managed a seminary for diocesan clergy.[48] In the later 1650s, he contrasted these arrangements with that still pertaining at Bons-Enfants, when he baldly exposed the structural flaws that he had noticed there over the years:

> Experience has taught us that wherever there is a seminary, it is good for us to have a parish to train the seminarians, who learn parish functions better by practice than by theory. We have the example of this in Saint-Nicolas-du-Chardonnet . . . For lack of similar experience, those at the Bons-Enfants seminary are not so ready, although we have tried to train them for this.[49]

De Paul here described the permeability that he believed should exist between the seminary and the parish, as well as the fortifying reciprocity that should characterize the bond between training and parochial service. The Lazarists' own internal seminary incorporated a version of these features—theoretical instruction and practical mission work—which de Paul considered indispensable for their formation. Ideally, he would have wished to implement a similar blend of formation in the seminary at Bons-Enfants, but was handicapped by the fact that there was no parish available as a training ground. Perhaps he might have sought to compensate for this by allowing the students to share in some of the duties undertaken by the Congregation's own trainees, or to assist in the parish of Saint-Nicolas, where the seminary was located.[50] Instead, its residents remained completely enclosed, both physically and mentally, and isolated from the types of communities that they were training to serve. Their rule prohibited them from participating in any mission until after they

[47] Dehorgny was principal of Bons-Enfants on three occasions, 1632–5, 1638–43, and 1654–9, the second of which saw the opening of the seminary for major orders. One of his reports to de Paul is printed in Maynard, *Vincent de Paul*, 198–200.

[48] Solminihac's first biographer, Chastenet, stated that the Lazarists used their own rule in the seminary, rather than one devised by the bishop, and a copy of this is found in both ACMP and the diocesan archives. Following Foissac, however, Coste mistakes a later rule from Cahors for the original used in its seminary and in other Lazarist seminaries at the time: ACMP, Dossier 'Cahors'; Chastenet, *Solminihac*, 224; Coste, *Saint*, ii, 376–8; Foissac, *Séminaire de Cahors*, 15–17.

[49] *CCD*, 7: 268, de Paul to Edme Jolly, 6 September 1658.

[50] Ferté wrongly assumes that the Bons-Enfants seminarians participated in the Congregation's missions: Ferté, *Vie religieuse*, 159.

left the seminary, and bluntly stated that their first thought at this time should be to return to their native diocese to offer their service to their bishop anyway.[51]

It was nevertheless desirable that the seminarians be afforded sanctuary, since one of the main functions of the seminary was to incite them to reflect on the nature of their office, and to cultivate 'the virtue and knowledge that their order and vocation asks of them'. The seminary rule indicated that the establishment was 'instituted to honour the priesthood of Our Lord', and advised the students to repeat frequently a spiritual mantra that summarized de Paul's theology of priestly sanctity: 'He is in me and me in him. Oh God what restraint, what devotion and what sanctity must I not have therefore throughout the day?' It encouraged the seminarians to concentrate their devotion on the eucharistic sacrament: for those who were already ordained, this was their route to sharing in the eternal priesthood of Christ; for those who were not, it permitted them to testify to the reverence in which they held him.[52] In this emphasis, the rule differed from that of the internal seminary; the latter's regime was specific to the Congregation's needs and character, and its rule emphasized practices that were designed to gradually embed the missionary virtues in the recruits while they honoured the childhood of Christ. The alternative stress at Bon-Enfants on Christ's public ministry cannot be explained by the fact that some of its students were mature in age and perhaps even ordained, for so were some of the new Lazarists. Rather, it reflected the fact that the students were not members of a formal institutional grouping whose members were to unify around a set of keystone values and practices. It also signalled that de Paul acknowledged the limits of a condensed and intense spell of formation for ministry; he knew that a year's residence did not allow for the slow nurturing of spiritual maturity. His best hope lay in installing a regime that imparted essential tenets of sacerdotal spirituality, so that the vocational efforts of residents would be grounded on healthy principles of piety once they left the supportive and isolated environment of the seminary.

At the same time, de Paul permitted the students to engage in theological study only to the extent that it would assist them in parish praxis, and they were not encouraged to drift into the more rarefied heights of mystical or abstract theology. As a result, he introduced a curriculum consisting of scholastic doctrinal theology, philosophy, and moral theology, as well as instruction in ecclesiastical ceremonies, chant, and the little method. He insisted that these were taught in a style suited to the diverse capabilities of the students, and that intellectual endeavour did not assume more importance than the inculcation of piety.[53] For this reason, he

[51] The students said occasional masses in Notre-Dame de Paris to earn money to pay for their room and board, but this was a specific and restricted form of interaction with churchgoers: ACMP, 'Règlement de Bons-Enfants 1645' (unpaginated); *CCD*, 2: 585, de Paul to Jean Dehorgny, 6 July 1645.

[52] ACMP, 'Règlement de Bons-Enfants 1645' (unpaginated): 'Ce Séminaire est institué pour honorer le sacerdoce de Notre Seigneur et former Messieurs les Ecclésiastiques en la vertu et science que leur ordre et vocation demande d'eux... Il est dans moi et moi en lui. O Dieu quelle retenue, quelle devotion et quelle sainteté ne dois-je donc poin avoir toute cette journée?'; Roche, *Vincent de Paul*, 164–84.

[53] There is no complete record of the syllabus or reading materials, but typical of the type of manuals adopted were Bécan's *Manuale controversarium* and one of the works of Pierre Binsfeld,

did not find any profitable comparison between the practices at Bons-Enfants and those that Olier adopted in Saint-Sulpice, even though the Sulpicians' seminarians taught catechism to groups of parishioners on feast days and Sundays. De Paul believed that the dominant feature of formation in their seminary was the cultivation of priests advanced in theology and spirituality, and occupied with 'elevated sentiments'.[54] This was not the objective that he wished the system at Bons-Enfants to meet.

To find a superior model of seminary formation against which to measure his venture, de Paul once again looked to the groundbreaking example that Bourdoise provided: 'We have the example of this in Saint-Nicolas-du-Chardonnet . . . ' Bourdoise envisaged his clerical community as a 'parish family', with each member actively contributing to its pastoral life.[55] As such, its routine was based on a symbiotic relationship between the seminarians and the faithful, which was designed to enable the students to practise their ministerial skills as they learned how to do them. De Paul knew that they practised their duties through role play before carrying them out in the parish; he even seems to have possessed a copy of the rules that prescribed this tactic, for he described the relevant regulation in them approvingly to his confreres in 1659.[56] Over time, he reached the conclusion that it was the crucial strategic relationship between theory, rehearsal, and actual practice that rendered the regimen at Saint-Nicolas superior to that at Bons-Enfants, and left students of the latter less than fully prepared for their ministries once they departed its confines.

IV

With his bird's eye view, de Paul was uniquely positioned to identify the strengths and weaknesses of the institutes of clerical formation at Saint-Lazare and Bons-Enfants, and, characteristically for one accustomed to exacting spiritual and moral self-assessment, he was a tough critic. Yet he must have accepted that they were successful in measurable terms, for they dramatically augmented the number of clerics who passed through the doors of Saint-Lazare and Bons-Enfants for short or medium periods of training. Simultaneously, however, this meant that de Paul's direct interaction with the majority of retreatants and seminarians reduced over time; busy as he was on a daily basis with letter-writing, meetings, prayers, and so

probably his *Enchiridion theologiae pastoralis*, which had undergone multiple editions since first published in 1591. The most recent edition had been published in 1630, with notes by Francis Sylvius, the noted Douai theologian: Binsfeld, *Enchiridion*.

De Paul did not permit the teachers to use the time-consuming *dictée* method to instruct; instead, he ordered that they concentrate on one approved author, and ask the students to learn the extracts from his text by heart. He considered this the most efficacious means of teaching a class of mixed knowledge and ability, whose end goal was parish pastoral work, since it conveniently taught seminarians what they needed to know for their future duties: *CCD*, 2: 240–1, de Paul to Bernard Codoing, December 1641; *CCD*, 2: 268–73, same to same, 18 March 1642. On the *dictée*, see Brockliss, *Higher Education*, 234–5.

54 *CCD*, 13a: 201.

55 Schoenher, *Séminaire de Saint-Nicolas-du-Chardonnet*, i, 84.

56 *CCD*, 10: 502. For the Saint-Nicolas rule, see AN, MM 475.

on, he would have encountered most of them only in brief conversations or when they attended conferences that he gave, and he relied heavily on reports on their conduct from those assigned to their care. The solution that he applied to this distance lay in the inauguration of the confraternity or company known as the Tuesday Conferences in 1633, for which he cherry-picked members from those who had come to his attention by manifesting spiritual and pastoral promise on retreat or in the seminary.[57] In July 1633, eleven clerics banded together under de Paul's direction, to form this apostolic-type grouping, in which they could further pursue their religious interests in formal association with him.[58] Until his death, de Paul held the position of director within this company, whose Paris-based members met on a weekly basis at Saint-Lazare.

The company was actually the brainchild of one of the original recruits rather than de Paul, which demonstrates the appetite for this type of organization amongst devout young clerics in Paris at this time. Most of the set had by then completed or were completing their university education, while all were also either already ordained or soon to be so (seven were ordained within three years of the group's inauguration), and therefore on the cusp of their careers. They were intellectually able and socially privileged, and the company's structure provided an excellent opportunity to encourage them to ascribe to what de Paul termed its priestly 'uniformity of spirit', even after they graduated to benefices in parishes or to posts in spiritual direction and diocesan administration. The Tuesday Conferences were, therefore, far more than simply weekly classes that supplied clerics with basic instruction on, for example, moral dilemmas that they might encounter in the confessional. They bore some similarity to congregations for priests that the Jesuits had organized at the *Gesù* in Rome in the early part of the century around common devotion to doctrines such as the Immaculate Conception.[59] However, the purpose of this company was not to promote a specific belief or dogma, but to encourage reverence for the priesthood itself. To perpetuate spiritual fellowship amongst those who joined—and to retain it whatever their distance from Paris—de Paul assigned a daily rule of life, which incorporated a regime of meditation, mass, reading of New Testament passages and other spiritual texts, as well as three examinations of conscience that enabled them to scrutinize themselves for faults and to identify the virtues that they needed to prioritize in the future. All of this was based on their pledge, recited in unison at the beginning of each meeting, to take Jesus as the model for their life, to observe the company's regulations, and 'to live and die in it', with the help of grace.[60] These meetings were the bedrock of the company, but the

[57] The individual who suggested the group is often wrongly thought to have been Jean-Jacques Olier; although certainly not him, it could have been any one of the other founding members: Forrestal, 'Venues for Clerical Formation'.

[58] Besides de Paul, the group was composed of Nicolas Barreau, Balthazar Brandon (*abbé de* Bassancourt), Étienne Caulet, François Fouquet, Adrien Gambart, Jean-Jacques Olier, Nicolas Pavillon, François Perrochel, and François Renar. The final two slots cannot be filled without considerable guesswork: *CCD*, 12: 236; Forrestal, 'Venues for Clerical Formation'.

[59] Maher, 'How the Jesuits Used their Congregations'.

[60] ACMP, Ms 'De la Compagnie de M[ss] de la Conférence . . . '. For a shorter version of the rules, see *CCD*, 13a: 140–3. Evidence suggests that, at the very least, the more dedicated members preserved

obligations to the attendees travelled far beyond a minimal duty to enjoy pious conversations, and extended to the practice of pastoral works, partly as an expression of piety and partly to master the skills required of good priests. On occasion, they lent manpower to Lazarist missions, and those in Paris carried out sixteen special missions for a variety of audiences to 1660, including, for instance, one in January 1657 at the Paris *Réfuge*, which had been recently established for women 'led astray' through prostitution.[61]

The group was by definition a select and exclusive body, and the air of privilege surrounding it was probably one of the reasons why it proved attractive: almost a decade into its existence, de Paul displayed open satisfaction for the renown that it enjoyed when he claimed that 'Our Lord so permits that everyone wants to be a member.'[62] In addition, over time, contemporaries also seemed to conclude that membership was a sure sign of enjoying de Paul's favour and a step along the road to ecclesiastical promotion; famously, Cardinal de Retz joined after completing a retreat before his ordination in 1643, mainly in the hope that its reputation for piety would recolour his own rather scarlet one in a paler hue. In his case, de Paul's judgement in permitting him entry to the Conferences may have been clouded by the obligation that he felt to the Lazarist founders, but other recruits to the company proved more dedicated to the values he sought to perpetuate through it.[63]

Since the production of devout priests was the goal of the company, de Paul's ability to influence its functions was critical. As its director, the formal hierarchy of decision-making afforded him plenty of opportunity to grant rewards of favour and promotion to those were malleable, who pleased him, and who showed themselves sympathetic to his wishes and views. He exercised tight control over recruitment to the company, for although any member could propose potential 'postulants', only de Paul gave them leave to join and to pledge obedience to 'the Company' during a ceremony over which he presided after he had interviewed them at length. It was he who selected individuals to partake in missions, and met with them to discuss their priorities before they began them. He also headed an inner grouping of officers, the small assembly, comprising a prefect, two assistants, and a secretary, which met monthly to make major decisions, and to review the conduct of individual members. The rules enabled de Paul to exercise considerable control over their selection on a six-monthly basis: he suggested candidates for the offices, justified his

the routine once they moved to new pastures; for example, the bishop of Alet, Nicolas Pavillon, quoted the Tuesday Conferences' rule directly in expropriating its practices for his episcopal rule of life: *CCD*, 13: 141–2; BN, Ms 14428(i), fo. 138r–v.

[61] A band of seven completed this mission: Laurent Bouchet, Adrien Gambart, Pierre de Poussemothe, Le Prêtre, Courtin, Le Gouteux, and Abraham Ribier. The *Réfuge*, located adjacent to the *Hôpital de la Pitié*, was founded by Marie Bonneau (Madame de Miramion), who donated 10,000 *livres* for this purpose. By this time, she was closely associated with de Paul and Louise de Marillac, having completed a retreat in the motherhouse of the Daughters of Charity in 1649, and afterwards joining the Ladies of Charity of the *Hôtel-Dieu*. The *Réfuge* was subsequently absorbed into the General Hospital of Paris in 1662: Bibliothèque de Chartres, Ms 453, t. viii, fo. 384r; Bonneau, *Miramion*, 176–8.

[62] *CCD*, 2: 265, de Paul to Bernard Codoing, 17 March 1642.

[63] Gondi, 'Mémoires', in Feillet et al. (eds), *Œuvres du Cardinal de Retz*, i, 167, 216.

selection, and asked the sitting officers to confirm it. It was then his responsibility to inform the remaining members of the results 'as if', as the rule delicately put it, 'he wanted to take [their] approbation regarding the election'.[64]

In the meetings themselves, de Paul's constitutional dominance was not exactly replicated for the participants spoke freely, and nobody, not even the director, was permitted to speak for more than fifteen minutes throughout. De Paul spoke only at the conclusion in order to summarize the points made by those who had volunteered their thoughts to the group. However, collegial though the format was, it was de Paul who determined what the topics for discussion were each week. Subjects such as sanctity, avarice, spiritual alms, and the functions of the spiritual director represented the basic themes of virtues, works and obligations of ecclesiastics, and ecclesiastical charges and dignities, and reveal that de Paul's pressing aim was to prepare these men for positions of leadership in which they could humbly serve the church's needs.[65] 'The spirit of Our Lord', he drily observed, was a spirit of doing things, but it was not a spirit of doing things 'to be esteemed'. Consequently, he insisted that the group made a 'profession of treating subjects very simply', and the rule laid out a procedure for discussion which was taken from his formula for the 'little method' of preaching.[66]

Collectively, the confreres were hardly typical of the clerics who sojourned at Saint-Lazare and Bons-Enfants, and the spiritually elevated and extended formation that they enjoyed in their association was not representative of what the Lazarists generally offered in Paris. The diversity in the types of training that de Paul devised for them to implement was fundamental to their early surge to the fore of clerical training in the capital, but his ability to organize structured programmes for clerics with differing needs and probable career paths on such a grand scale, despite the relatively small size of his own association, also testifies to the exceptional nature of this achievement in the 1630s and early 1640s. He was therefore free to assume that the Tuesday Conferences filled an important niche in Parisian church life, maintaining that 'when I came to Paris, I had never seen anything like these conferences, at least on the virtue proper to their particular state and how to live their vocation well'.[67]

Two further significant questions therefore arise from the analysis of the objectives that de Paul set for the company and the manner in which it functioned. Though both are applicable to the entire system of institutional formation that he debuted in Paris, they are particularly pertinent to the Tuesday Conferences. The first concerns the extent to which de Paul was able to sustain his links with confreres once they moved on

[64] ACMP, 'De la Compagnie de M^ss de la Conférence . . . ' (unpaginated): 'comme s'il voulait prendre son approbation touchant l'élection'.

[65] Abelly, *Vie*, ii, 249 and 252; ACMP, 'De la Compagnie de M^ss de la Conférence . . . '; Bibliothèque de Chartres, Ms 453, t. viii, fo. 378r; CCD, 7: 405, de Paul to Louis de Chandenier, 6 December 1658; Bibliothèque de Chartres (Mss 453, t. viii, and 457); Guichard, 'Laurent Bouchet . . . Appendice'.

[66] ACMP, 'De la Compagnie de M^ss de la Conférence . . . '; *CCD*, 2: 264–5, de Paul to Bernard Codoing, 17 March 1642; *CCD*, 12: 247.

[67] *CCD*, 11: 11.

to new pastoral pastures far from Saint-Lazare, and the second is the degree to which he was capable of positioning them in posts where they could promote the interests with which he was concerned. Together, these address de Paul's ability to construct a network of associates for his missionary work, and to act as a patron of reform within the church. For now, it is appropriate, therefore, that the conclusion to this chapter should simultaneously form a partial prelude for those which will succeed it, by identifying as far as possible the type of individual that made up the company's membership. An exhaustive list of recruits does not survive, but cautious conclusions can be drawn about the general character of the grouping from the careers of the sixty-two persons definitely known to have joined. Like the original cohort, the majority of these were recruited at an early stage of their clerical formation, and had already advanced through a university education. Most never proceeded to a parish cure (only seven did so), but there was considerable variety in the type of post that they occupied, and in the learning and experiences that they were able to bring to conference discussions as time passed. Nicolas Gedouin was typical; he joined the group in 1650 when he was ordained after his retreat at Saint-Lazare, and then spent a period delivering pastoral care in Saint-Eustache parish (he was apparently a preacher of such zeal that he became 'soaked to his soutane and surplice' in the pulpit). After this, he held almonerships in the *Hôtel-Dieu* and General Hospital of Paris during the later 1650s, while he also worked at court as a chaplain for Gaston of Orléans.[68]

Once ordained, a great number of the confreres also proceeded to posts in diocesan administration. For example, Hippolyte Féret became *grande vicaire* for Nicolas Pavillon, bishop of Alet, in 1642, after the two spent some years together in the company. Unusually, he went on to hold a cure, at Saint-Nicolas-du-Chardonnet in 1646, before returning to diocesan administration when he became *grande vicaire* of Paris in 1656.[69] More generally, eight of the sixty-two served as diocesan officials, and no fewer than sixteen more were appointed as bishops. At 39 per cent of the grouping, this is a very significant proportion. It suggests a co-relation between membership and preferment to diocesan administration, which de Paul implied; at the very least, he certainly associated the Conferences with the production of candidates for high office, and in 1638 noted with satisfaction that 'three bishops have just been drawn from among' its members.[70] Chapter 11 will assess if this was a straightforward relationship of cause and effect, and the result of de Paul's ability to ensure the promotion of his favourites. Equally, at a minimum, such connections had the potential to facilitate the Lazarists' expansion in dioceses around the realm. The debt that de Paul owed to them in advancing this process of institutional growth is a question of immediate relevance to Chapters 7 and 8.

[68] Gedouin was also the superior of the Ursulines of Saint-Cloud, and abbot of Saint-Mesmin-d'Orléans: *CCD*, 7: 315, de Paul to Louis d'Estaing, 18 October 1658; *CCD*, 7: 534–5, Nicolas Gedouin to de Paul, 16 September 1660; Bibliothèque de Chartres, Ms 596, fo. 106r: 'prêchant avec tant de zèle qu'il est trempé jusques à sa soutane et son surplis'.

[69] Péréfixe, *Hippolyte Feret*, *passim*.

[70] *CCD*, 1: 413, de Paul to Jean de Fonteneil, 8 January 1638. These were Antoine Godeau (Grasse), François Fouquet (Bayonne), and Nicolas Pavillon (Alet).

7

Patrons and Houses (1635–1643)

I

In the first few years of their activity, de Paul and his companions proved that the conducting of missions did not require the foundation of houses in the dioceses in which they operated. As long as they received formal permission for their work from the bishop and overnight lodging when they arrived in a village, the missionaries on tour could fulfil their end of the bargain. Even during these years, however, de Paul already envisaged that it might be advantageous to alter their *modus operandi*, and, at his request, the provisions of the 1633 papal bull of approval conceded the right to found new houses to the Congregation. Yet, although approved in principle, the Lazarists were few in number, and their leader still had little realistic reason to entertain the idea that they might be able to staff satellite mission houses outside Paris. As membership swelled from the mid-1630s, hope became expectation, and de Paul introduced a new era characterized by major expansions in activity and infrastructure. This was a critical juncture in the group's long-term development, and its demands led de Paul to alter his perception of the purpose and nature of the Lazarists' work indelibly. Once he approved the establishment of the first house in Toul in 1635 he quickly permitted others, so that, excluding Saint-Lazare and Bons-Enfants, the tally of Lazarist houses in France stood at nineteen on his death in 1660. As the number of houses expanded, so too did the pastoral work that the missionaries carried out in and from them: nine houses housed staff who delivered missions and managed a seminary for diocesan clergy, two were exclusively dedicated to a seminary, while eight were designated as houses of mission only (although some of these also offered retreats for ordinands). However, these numbers obscure the fact that there were two stages in provincial expansion, the second starkly differentiated from the first by the introduction of seminary work and the dominance of episcopal patronage from late 1643. Together, these phases offer the chronological basis for this chapter and Chapter 8.

II

The first requirement for any expansion in the provinces was patronage—of sufficient diversity, quality, and measure to allow the creation of a sturdy infrastructure. Until 1635, this was piecemeal, supplied by a small number of likeminded clerical associates who had worked on missions with de Paul and his confreres or were *curés* in parishes where they had carried out missions, as well as by a few individuals who approached de Paul for spiritual direction.[1] From 1629, the Lazarists carried out missions in new areas comprising dioceses in the north around Rouen, sees around Bordeaux in the south-west, and the outliers of Montauban and Mende. This pattern of operation depended on the wishes of those who paid for them, rather than on any deliberate geo-strategizing on the superior general's part, and this harsh truth placed de Paul and his companions in a position of dependency on benefactors. In addition, while the areas covered by these endowments could be quite tidy (for instance, when Elie Laisné, *sieur de la* Marguerie and La Dourville, donated 200 *livres* annually to the Lazarists for five yearly missions in Angoulême diocese, he specified that these should cover the four parishes in which his lands lay as well as the local town), they could also be so hopelessly vast that de Paul could only target specific localities within them:[2] in 1632, he agreed with Nicolas Vivian that his missionaries would carry out missions in the jurisdictions of the *parlements* of Toulouse, Bordeaux, and Aix-en-Provence (Bordeaux diocese alone had over 500 parishes), but had only two missionaries to send.[3] Lambert aux Couteaux and Robert de Sergis ministered in the diocese of Saintes in the Gironde, before travelling south-east to Périgueux. In the winter of 1634–5, the missionaries concentrated on parishes in the dioceses of Bordeaux and Saintes. They were to be found hard at work in Toulouse during the spring of 1638 and the following winter. The missions in Mende and Montauban probably also fell under the Vivian endowment, since they were respectively in the jurisdictions of the *parlements* of Toulouse and Aix-en-Provence.[4]

From 1635, de Paul introduced a new organizational model for missions, which would potentially allow for a more efficient use of personnel. Not only did this make strategic sense, it was already the model adopted by other groups including the Jesuits and Oratorians. Thus, with the support of a new set of patrons, he sought to place the meeting of pastoral ambitions in a distinctive structural setting, in which the motherhouse was surrounded by satellite houses which served the provinces permanently. This marked a crucial personal transition for de Paul as well as a decisive institutional progression for the Congregation; while the foundation of the houses was heavily dependent on the personal links that de Paul forged with key donors, he, and therefore the Congregation as a whole, gradually moved away from the orbit of the Gondi because of them. During this first phase of expansion,

[1] See Appendices 2 and 3.

[2] The four parishes were Ivrignas, Aubeuille, Champagne, and Plassas: AN, M211 (31 October 1633, 26 February 1637, 6 May 1642), and S6685; *CCD*, 1: 389, de Paul to Louise de Marillac, *c.* November 1637.

[3] AN, MM538, fos 292v–293v (20 January 1632), and Y 176, fo. 383v (5 July 1636).

[4] See AD de la Gironde, G619, for the faculties that Archbishop Henri de Sourdis awarded for the mission in Bordeaux on 21 October 1634. For the missions, see *CCD*, 1: 183–4, de Paul to a Lazarist priest, 15 January 1633; *CCD*, 1: 206–10, de Paul to Alain de Solminihac, 23 August 1633; *CCD*, 1: 268–9, de Paul to Jean de Fonteneil, 7 December 1634; *CCD*, 1: 271, Jean de La Salle and Jean Brunet to de Paul, 1634; *CCD*, 1: 429–31, de Paul to Robert de Sergis, *c.*21 February 1638; *CCD*, 1: 518–20, same to same, 17 December 1638; Abelly, *Vie*, ii, 26–7.

the Richelieu family stepped forward to offer patronage of enormous worth, and the cardinal's favourite niece, Marie de Vignerod de Pontcourlay (widow of the marquis of Combalet), commonly known as the duchess of Aiguillon, would remain one of the Lazarists' most generous benefactors thereafter. They were joined by eight others from the political and religious elite, and during the initial phase of development, de Paul was able to approve the opening of eight houses, beginning with Toul in 1635 and ending with Sedan in May 1643.

As the breadth of patronage grew, de Paul retained solid but more residual ties of loyalty with the children of the couple that he considered to be the Congregation's founders. Having been his and the Lazarists' primary patrons, the Gondi family was responsible for the establishment of only one new house, that of Montmirail in 1644. The involvement of both Philippe de Gondi and his son and heir, the duke of Retz, meant that the house's foundation bridged two generations, as the duke acknowledged.[5] However, it was Gondi senior who took the lead in making the deal, and he also played the role of intermediary with local townspeople.[6] Concurrently, however, the resourcing of the foundation reveals that de Paul's connection with the Gondi, both during and after his employment in their household, did extend over time to members of their household, and resulted in practical marks of attachment for his association: in this instance, the duke's secretary, Louis Toutblanc, bequeathed two farms to the Lazarists.[7]

The locations of houses could be influenced by the religious, political, and familial preferences of their patrons, but hagiographical tradition assumes that de Paul never solicited for the establishment of any of them, preferring to entrust such additions to the Lazarists' fortune to divine providence. There is, however, evidence to the contrary. For instance, de Paul's biographers often cite the fact that the saint never established a community in his native region to demonstrate the extent to which he distanced himself from his natural loyalty to his family and region of birth.[8] In doing so, they draw upon a historical tradition originating with Abelly, who recounted that de Paul examined his wish to establish a house in his native lands 'before God, and corrected himself... M. Vincent had mortified natural love of his region and his relatives'.[9] But if he did so, it must have been after he sent the frankly encouraging letter to the bishop of Dax in October 1647; in this, rather than politely raising objections to the plan, as Gayon-Molinié suggests, de Paul

[5] Retz did so in his formal request to Bishop Malier of Troyes to allow him to grant the *Hôtel de la Chaussée* to the Lazarists on 23 September 1643; Malier acquiesced on 20 June 1644: AN, S6708.

[6] The Lazarists had been carrying out missions in Montmirail since the 1620s, and the townspeople initially feared that they were about to abandon these: *CCD*, 2: 547–8, de Paul to Guillaume Delville, 20 November 1644.

[7] Both were located in the parish of Courbetost near Montmirail, and Toutblanc requested that the priests celebrate 100 low masses over ten years for the repose of his soul. In early 1646, the community began to reside in one of these properties, Fontaine-Essart. The other was known as Vieux-Moulins: AN, S6708 (29 September 1643, 20 June 1644). This dossier also contains a copy of Toutblanc's will, dated 12 May 1644.

[8] See, for example, Gayon-Molinié, 'Vincent de Paul'.

[9] Abelly, *Vie*, iii, 208: '... devant Dieu ce sentiment, et il se reprit... M. Vincent avait mortifié l'amour naturel de son pays et de ses parents.'

offered constructive advice on funding the enterprise.[10] Tellingly too, it was de Paul who instigated the deal with Vivian. He confided that his community needed a 'notable sum' to pay bills and to 'accommodate and conserve' his men in the former priory, and asked for his assistance. The donor duly supplied this when he stipulated that part of his donation should be directed towards expenses at Saint-Lazare.[11]

Abelly's narrative is indebted to, and entirely consistent with, the concerns that characterized seventeenth-century spiritual teaching. From the religious to the episcopal life, contemporary authors of spiritual manuals warned ominously of the need to detach oneself from family interests in order to serve God purely and simply. The greater the ecclesiastical office, the greater the need to achieve this, Antoine Godeau, the learned and devout bishop of Grasse and Vence, warned his abbot nephew in 1671: 'You must learn to smother all the considerations of your relatives, who dream rather of vanity than your consolation.'[12] It was also common for spiritual conversions to include a dramatic separation from the demands of family life, perhaps never more so than in the aftermath of the shocking psychological crisis of the Wars of Religion. De Paul's contemporary *Père* Joseph, the Capuchin friar who acted as diplomatic agent and political counsellor during the ministry of his long-time associate Cardinal Richelieu, underwent an overwhelming transformation in 1599 which involved his absolute renunciation of the familial responsibilities left to his care after his father's death in 1598 (including the recovery of the family fortune and his mother's carefully crafted plan for his marriage), in favour of the ascetic regime of a Capuchin friary.[13] His experience was far from unique in this climate of piety, where the spiritual values of the early reform movement seemed to demand a wholehearted surrender to the vocational call of a monastery or convent, despite parental pressure to remain in society.[14]

For those who chose to stay in society instead of heading to a monastery, communities such as de Paul's offered the perfect opportunity to use personal resources to indulge in religious acts of merit. This reveals another important fact traditionally ignored by biographers: in many cases de Paul did not even need to solicit patrons, because the earnest faith of *dévots* made them eager to initiate such praiseworthy foundations. They gravitated towards de Paul at Saint-Lazare in search of spiritual consolation, direction, or collaboration in acts of piety, finding outlets for their religious expression in the specialized works of the congregation in residence there. The early fruits of this were evident in the Vivian and Laisné endowments. By the 1630s, Vivian was already an enthusiastic patron of the

[10] *CCD*, 3: 244–5, de Paul to Jacques Desclaux, 2 October 1647; Gayon-Molinié, 'Vincent de Paul'. Probably on Bishop Desclaux's request, de Paul also used his influence at court to suggest that taxes in the *élection* of Les Lannes be diverted to fund the restoration of the cathedral in his native diocese around this time: *CCD*, 2: 566, de Paul to unnamed, 20 April 1645; Coste, 'Histoire des cathédrales de Dax'.

[11] AN, MM538, fos 292v–293v (20 January 1632), and Y 176, fo. 383v (5 July 1636).

[12] Godeau, *Lettres*, 427, Antoine Godeau to Abbé Thomassin, 23 October 1671: 'Vous doit apprendre à étouffer toutes les considérations de la parenté, qui songent plutôt à la vanité qu'à votre consolation.'

[13] Pierre, *Père Joseph*, 67–94.

[14] Diefendorf, 'Give us back our children'.

Discalced Carmelites in Paris and Toulouse, and Laisné was a member of the Company of the Holy Sacrament, founded in 1629 to promote religious discipline amongst the faithful. But their particular attachment to the Lazarists originated in their personal intimacy with de Paul, under whom they both completed retreats in the early 1630s. Laisné was to undertake several more of these before finally deciding to join the priesthood after his wife's death in 1640. It was likely the candour of the relations established during these soul-baring episodes that enabled de Paul to feel comfortable in instigating the deal with Vivian and subsequently negotiating with Laisné.[15]

The Lazarists' ability to provide specialized services was a key factor in their attraction of such patrons, but de Paul was indispensable in this, for he drew them towards the group in the first place, represented it, and nurtured the relations necessary to strike deals. With one possible exception, the foundation of the first eight satellite houses originated in three areas of his activity during the 1630s. Obviously, the first was that of the missions and clerical formation centred on Saint-Lazare, which provided the principal illustration of what the Lazarists offered to the church and society, and formed the command centre for their work. It was not, however, the sole focus of de Paul's attention. He had other outlets in which to expend his spiritual energy, and in which he could forge relationships and institute collaborations based on common spiritual sympathies and goals of evangelization. The principal of these were the Parisian convents of the Visitation order and the confraternities of charity. In devout individuals who frequented these, de Paul found the motivations which enabled him to marry the example of what he was implementing at Saint-Lazare with the material resources to do it elsewhere too. Furthermore, it was the associations and the achievements that arose from these three areas which led to de Paul's introduction to the royal court, and to preferment there in the early 1640s.

Lest this pattern appear too neat, a brief note of caution should be sounded. The exception may be Toul, though even here it is possible that Bishop de Gournay decided to invite the Lazarists to his diocese after he completed a retreat at Saint-Lazare before his consecration there in 1634.[16] Since this is not certain, however, it is more illuminating to consider the local context for the invitation, to identify the novice mistakes that de Paul made in accepting it, and to discern what he learned from the experiment, before proceeding to the remaining houses. Bishop de Gournay's approach to him in January 1635 appears to have been rather unforeseen, and did not allow him much time to evaluate what on paper at least appeared to be an excellent opportunity to embed the Lazarists in the east.[17] Officially, of

[15] On Vivian's support of the Carmelites in Paris, to whom he donated a house and grounds in 1611, see Guyot Desfontaines, du Castre d'Auvigny, and La Barre, *Histoire*, 8, and Dulaure, *Histoire*, v, 338. On his part in their introduction to Toulouse, see Morgain, 'L'Installation des Carmes Déchaux'.

[16] Calmet's suggestion that de Paul, with the duchess of Lorraine, recommended Gournay to the king for the see of Toul is difficult to credit. In 1634, de Paul had few contacts with the royal court, and certainly did not have the access required to influence episcopal nominations: Calmet, *Histoire*, col. 727.

[17] *CCD*, 1: 272, de Paul to Charles-Chrétien de Gournay, 19 January 1635; Collet, *Vie*, i, 355.

course, Toul was not in France, nor did the French king possess the right to nominate its bishop for, along with Metz and Verdun, it was one of the *trois-évêchés* that had not been genuinely incorporated into the French church since their seizure by Henri II in 1552.[18] However, in 1634 Louis XIII and Richelieu, as part of their effort to extend French influence in the region, nominated Gournay, then titular bishop of Scythia, to the see. He succeeded Nicolas-François de Lorraine in Toul, who had rejected an ecclesiastical career when he married his cousin in March 1634 and renounced a cardinal's hat and several benefices.

In early 1635, the bishop offered the residence and hospital of the Order of the Holy Spirit in Toul to de Paul for his men. Built in the twelfth century to provide care for the sick, the master (commander) of the Order of the Holy Spirit had petitioned the bishop to dispose of the buildings as he thought expedient because the remaining religious were unable to continue to carry out their duties, or to maintain a residence that had been constructed to accommodate over 100 people.[19] This was a godsend for the prelate, because he was under pressure to meet the terms of the will of his predecessor who had bequeathed 40,000 *livres* to the diocese for the foundation of a seminary in Toul.[20] As a result, a sense of urgency permeated the petition that he submitted to the crown in February; it successfully requested leave to use the goods of the Order of the Holy Spirit to found a seminary.[21]

The bishop offered the possessions to de Paul, envisaging that he would establish a seminary in them, so it is remarkable, as a result, not to find reference to a seminary in the contract that announced the arrival of the Lazarists in Toul. Around May, de Paul assigned two missionaries, Lambert aux Couteaux and Antoine Colée, to go there, and they signed an agreement on his behalf for the transfer of the church, house, and the extremely dilapidated hospital to the Congregation in June.[22] It may be inferred that de Paul had rebuffed the bishop's effort to contract the Congregation to establish a seminary, because he did not think that this kind of obligation was appropriate for it. But, even more remarkably, the contract did not make a single reference to the completion of missions, and implied that the community should concentrate on hospital management and pastoral care in two parishes assigned to it. In return, the Lazarists received a severely derelict set of buildings to house them as well as sick adults and children.[23]

Was this an oversight on de Paul's part? It is unlikely, but suggests that he was so eager to accept the opportunity to expand the Lazarists beyond Paris that he was

[18] Henri II had annexed Toul to France in 1552, and this was eventually recognized in the Peace of Westphalia in 1648. Ecclesiastically, Toul had remained a suffragan of the bishop of Trier in the Holy Roman Empire. When Gournay died unexpectedly in 1637, the king then nominated Henri Arnauld to succeed him, but was forced to backtrack in 1640 in the face of sustained papal resistance to this illegitimate incursion: Bergin, *French Episcopate*, 36–7; Bonnot, *Hérétique ou saint?*, 98–100; Calmet, *Histoire*, col. 727.

[19] AD de Meurthe-et-Moselle, G125 (3 March 1634).

[20] Martin, *Histoire*, ii, 208.

[21] AD de Meurthe-et-Moselle, G125 (6 March 1635).

[22] AD de Meurthe-et-Moselle, G125 (16 June 1635).

[23] AD de Meurthe-et-Moselle, G125 (16 June 1635). This dossier includes a report on the buildings completed by two canons of the cathedral chapter on 5 March 1635, which they described as being very poorly maintained.

willing to overlook certain undesirable obligations outlined in the contract. If so, this was a mistake, because they almost immediately gave rise to difficulties. Despite the absence of any stipulation about missions, de Paul's confreres assumed that these were precisely what should be occupying their time once they arrived in the area, and either had not been disabused of this mistake by their superior general or, much less likely, chose to ignore his instructions.[24] But the parishes were onerous burdens which reduced the time that they could spend on missions, and their successors struggled so much to carry them out that de Paul eventually suggested they should shift them onto salaried vicars.[25] Less than two years after de Paul acquiesced to the prelate's request to establish the Lazarists in Toul, he authorized Colée to surrender their responsibility for the hospital, by splitting its possessions from those of the former house of the Holy Spirit and returning two-thirds of them to the municipality.[26] After this, however, Bishop de Gournay's death created a power vacuum within the diocese that enabled opponents to mount a campaign against the incoming community.[27] The Besançon branch of the Order of the Holy Spirit, whose members claimed that the house in Toul was one of its dependants, launched a lawsuit against the transfer of the house and the division of its goods.[28] Sure of the legality of the Lazarists' position, de Paul reacted by obtaining approval of it from the general of the Order, as well as royal *arrêts* forbidding anyone to contest its possession. But the dispute still rumbled on for a number of years, and it was only in 1657 that the religious of the Holy Spirit finally gave up their case, and that Bishop du Saussay of Toul issued a decree formalizing the Lazarists' ownership of what they had held de facto since 1637.[29]

III

If the process of establishing a Congregation house in Toul was marred by tensions over its rights and responsibilities, the passage towards the foundation of other houses in succeeding years proved notably smoother. This was partly because de Paul was able to rely on committed patrons throughout. But, more importantly,

24 Abelly, *Vie*, ii, 41–2.

25 De Paul made this suggestion in 1654, but did not execute it, and the priests continued to serve in Saint-Amand thereafter, contrary to Coste's conclusion. In 1636, de Paul had also been forced to insist that Gournay did not add to his men's chores by ordering them to hear confessions at the local Dominican convent, which was anyway contrary to Lazarist policy. *CCD*, 1: 323, de Paul to Lambert aux Couteaux, 13 June 1636; *CCD*, 5: 236, de Paul to Nicolas Demonchy, 28 November 1654; Collet, *Vie*, i, 355; Coste, *Saint*, i, 531.

26 AD de Meurthe-et-Moselle, G155 (17 March 1637).

27 De Paul did receive some support for the Lazarists' position from Jean Midot, the capitular vicar of Toul, when Gournay died: *CCD*, 1: 417–18, de Paul to Lambert aux Couteaux, 30 January 1638; Collet, *Vie*, i, 291.

28 *CCD*, 1: 417–18, de Paul to Lambert aux Couteaux, 30 January 1638; *CCD*, 1: 544, de Paul to Robert de Sergis, 13 May 1639.

29 AD de Meurthe-et-Moselle, G125, contains copies of royal *arrêts* (29 December 1643, 26 June 1649, 13 June 1651), and the episcopal ordinance (1 September 1657); *CCD*, 2: 156, de Paul to Louise Lebreton, 14 November 1640.

in his eagerness to grasp the opportunity to create a permanent base for the Congregation in Toul, de Paul had made a novice error in accepting a set of responsibilities that his men could not fulfil. The failures of this experiment appear to have made him acutely conscious of the need to delineate appropriate ministerial obligations for them before they arrived in a locality, in order to reduce the likelihood that they would be forced to renege on their duties once they arrived, and to prevent discontentment within their ranks about the work asked of them. Only in one other case, that of Marseille, did de Paul repeat the error of acting in haste and without due consideration.[30]

The next houses that de Paul established were from the outset modelled on Saint-Lazare. In 1637, he again ventured east, this time to Troyes. The negotiations for the house founded there, and in Annecy in Savoy two years later, were rooted in de Paul's spiritual camaraderie with other devotees of François de Sales in Paris, the centre of which were the two convents of the Visitation order, instituted in the faubourg Saint-Antoine and faubourg Saint-Jacques in 1619 and 1626 respectively (a third convent was opened in 1660 in Saint-Denis). De Paul held an important position in the circle of Salesian disciples that lived in, visited, and provided resources for the convents, and it was their common affection for and reliance on the teaching of the late de Sales that brought him and the chief patron of Troyes and Annecy together. He owed his prominence to François de Sales, who had introduced him to the superioress general of the Visitation, Jeanne Françoise de Chantal, with whom de Sales had founded the order in 1607, and had then agreed with her that they should appoint de Paul as the second ecclesiastical superior of the convents in 1622.[31] In general, de Paul's duties as superior were those of a spiritual guardian, and he was obliged to attend the monthly chapters, carry out an annual visitation, attend professions and annual reviews of conscience, and so on.[32] His ascension to the office was a genuine mark of the esteem in which de Sales and Chantal had come to hold him, and their trust in his abilities certainly raised his profile amongst the devout of Paris.

In addition, this role extended the number and range of de Paul's contacts, one of whom was Noël Brûlart de Sillery, the impeccably connected former ambassador to Spain and the Holy See, and brother of the former keeper of the seals and chancellor, Nicolas Brûlart de Sillery. His attachment first to de Paul and then to the Lazarists more generally grew in proportion to his own spiritual transformation during the late 1620s and 1630s. Between 1637 and 1640, he made a series of lavish gifts to the Lazarists, which confirmed his stature as a principal patron during their early growth. These were mainly, but not exclusively, for the foundation of houses; in 1640, he assigned 80,000 *livres* in *rentes* from the *ferme des aides* of Angers to the Lazarists, leaving it to de Paul to decide the usage of its annual

[30] See Ch. 10, section III.

[31] De Paul was not the first superior of the Visitation, as commonly believed, since the role appears to have been given first to Charles de La Saussaye, *curé* of Saint-Jacques-de-la-Boucherie, who held it from 1619 until his death on 21 September 1621. De Sales and Jeanne de Chantal then asked de Paul to assume the vacancy left by his demise: Boulenger, *Abrégé de la vie*, 50; Villain, *Essai*, 232.

[32] See Ch. 9, section IV.

income, which grew exponentially from 10,000 *livres* annually in 1640 to nearly 19,000 *livres* during the 1650s.[33]

Although these kinds of donations fortified relations between them, the fundamental connection between de Paul and Brûlart was spiritual. After he discovered his works in the later 1620s, Brûlart had become a disciple of de Sales and he and de Paul had found common ground in their reverence for him and in their loyalty to his teaching. Their bond formalized when Brûlart placed himself under de Paul's spiritual direction in 1631, before deciding to enter the priesthood. He was ordained in 1634 after a retreat at Saint-Lazare. Brûlart also sought spiritual guidance from Jeanne de Chantal, with whom he maintained a frank correspondence from the late 1620s, and between 1635 and 1639 he and de Paul advised her on the introduction of an apostolic visitor to supervise discipline amongst the convents of the Visitation order, a source of considerable unease amongst the nuns.[34] Labelling himself the 'poor son' of de Paul, Brûlart consecrated the final decade of his life and his possessions to promoting pious causes, notably his director's association of missionaries and the Visitation. From 1631, he asked the Lazarists to perform missions in Brie, in Brie-Comte-Robert parish south-east of Paris, where he owned the *seigneurie* of Pamphou.[35] He also showered gifts on the Visitation convents in Paris, including a new chapel at the convent on rue Saint-Antoine in 1632, where he celebrated his first mass in 1634 after being ordained at his other favourite spiritual site. The ritualized combining of important influences continued on Brûlart's death in 1640, when he was interred in the same Visitation chapel after de Paul officiated at this funeral. Little of their spiritual exchanges remains, but, privately, de Paul expressed his high opinion of his directee when he observed that he had led a saintlike existence once he made the decision to withdraw from the 'cares of the world' in 1631.[36]

From 1637, Brûlart concentrated on helping de Paul to develop the Lazarists' presence in Troyes and Annecy, using his influence to mediate among the various parties involved, and providing the financial bedrock for the ventures. Firstly, he was commander of the Troyes temple of the Order of the Knights Hospitaller of St John of Jerusalem and Malta which had nine dependent parishes in Troyes diocese, from which he enjoyed an annual income of 13,979 *livres*. In Annecy, the Order held a number of parishes too, to which Brûlart also hoped to send Lazarists.[37]

33 De Paul may have applied some of the revenue to the costs of missions that Brûlart had requested in six parishes in Paris and Reims some months earlier. These included Sillery parish, where his nephew Pierre, son of the late chancellor, was marquis: AN, Minutier Central, ET/LI/505 and M209 (20 August 1640); *CCD*, 2: 144, de Paul to Louis Lebreton, 9 October 1640; Aubert de la Chesnaye-Desbois, *Dictionnaire*, ii, col. 363.

34 Devos, 'Le Testament spiritual'.

35 He sold it to his nephew in 1635: *CCD*, 1: 97–8, Noël Brûlart de Sillery to de Paul, *c.*1631.

36 De Paul to Louis Lebreton, 9 October 1640; Bois, *Noël Brûlart de Sillery*; Fosseyeux, 'Contribution à l'histoire du monastère Sainte-Marie'; *Le Chevalier Noël Brûlart de Sillery*, 31–3.

37 In late summer 1637, de Paul allowed a number of Lazarists to perform missions as they accompanied the commander on visitations of his parishes: *CCD*, 1: 380, Paul Lascaris to de Paul, 7 September 1637 (Lascaris was Grand Master of the Order of Malta); Abelly, *Vie*, i, 150–1. On the French history of this aristocratic crusading order, founded around 1113, see Petiet, *Le Roi et le Grand Maître*.

Secondly, his position in the order granted him invaluable local knowledge and put him in close contact with power holders in Troyes and Annecy such as Bishop René de Breslay of Troyes. Finally, Brûlart's links to the Visitation were useful in both areas. Jeanne de Chantal was living in Annecy, while he met the superioress of the local Carmelite convent in Troyes, Mother Marie de la Trinité (formerly Marie d'Hanivel), through her. The Carmelite had been a spiritual confidante of Jeanne de Chantal when they both resided in Dijon and still maintained a regular correspondence with the now ageing Visitation founder.[38] She also offered spiritual counsel to the commander in person and through letters, while the bishop of Troyes trusted her advice on even 'the most delicate of affairs.'[39] Either Brûlart or Jeanne de Chantal introduced de Paul to La Trinité.

De Paul relied on these figures to intercede with the bishops of Troyes and Annecy, since his own relationship with them was distant, even if positive.[40] In Troyes, Brûlart and La Trinité brought their suggestion that new missionaries should be housed in the diocese to Bishop de Breslay in late 1636, but then discovered that his first instinct was to invite the priests of Saint-Nicolas-du-Chardonnet![41] They had to work hard to convince him to change his mind, for which de Paul proved eternally grateful when he ascribed to La Trinité the highest accolade of spiritual motherhood, telling her that she had 'begotten in Our Lord' her Lazarist children in Troyes.[42] He had good reason, for he asked her to act as his spokesperson during the process of drafting and agreeing terms with Breslay between October 1637 and March 1638.[43] But he also travelled to Troyes to negotiate in person, and he personally signed the first contract in the Carmelite convent on 3 October. In addition, he made sure that the conditions of the Lazarists' presence in the area were made absolutely transparent from the outset in the foundation contracts. He took the same precautions when negotiating the foundation in Annecy, proving that he had taken the lessons of Toul to heart.

The terms reveal that the trio had managed to convince Breslay to join enthusiastically in the foundation of the new house, and that he had become keen to harness the talents of the Lazarists permanently. De Paul agreed that they would complete missions in his diocese and organize retreats for ordinands. To support the six priests and two brothers needed to fulfil these tasks, the bishop gave the sum

38 *Chroniques de l'ordre des Carmélites*, iii, 463–5; Sérouet, *Jean de Brétigny*, 212.

39 In 1639, Brûlart repaid Marie de La Trinité's friendship with a donation of 6000 *livres* to her convent. In the same week, he gave 15,000 *livres* to seven other Carmelite convents: *Chroniques de l'ordre des Carmélites*, iii, 428; Fosseyeux, 'Contribution à l'histoire du monastère Sainte-Marie'.

40 René de Breslay granted the Lazarists faculties for missions in his diocese in 1626, and again in 1634 (to allow them to fulfil the terms of the Lamy foundation), but this was the extent of their interaction. Juste Guérin was consecrated bishop of Geneva in June 1639, but only arrived in Annecy on 17 July, six weeks after the first contract was signed: AN, M211 (31 October 1633, 26 February 1637).

41 Prévost recounts an apocryphal tale by which the Carmelite nun and the bishop were jolted into action after independently receiving divine inspiration 'on the same day and at the same hour'. But there is no contemporary evidence for this rather fanciful notion: Prévost, *Vincent de Paul*, 6.

42 *CCD*, 1: 443, de Paul to Marie de La Trinité, 25 February 1638; *CCD*, 2: 132, same to same, 1 October 1640.

43 *CCD*, 1: 415–6, same to same, 22 January 1638.

of 6,000 *livres* to the Congregation, as well as the *Hôtel de Troyes* (rue d'Enfer) in Paris, which then had an annual rental income of 1,200 *livres*.[44] He supplemented his gift handsomely in his will in 1641, bequeathing 10,200 *livres* for the purchase of new lodgings and mission expenses. However, by this time, Brûlart's generosity had made this purchase unnecessary, and de Paul directed the superior to use the money for repairs to the existing accommodation.[45]

For his part, Brûlart expected the Lazarists to carry out missions every five years in his nine parishes, and exhibited his particular concern that they establish confraternities of charity within them with an intensity that was rather unusual in foundation contracts, and the fruit of his desire to participate in the 'prayers, sacrifices and good works' of the Congregation. He donated 3,000 *livres* to enable the Lazarists to purchase a residence in Troyes, though three years afterwards bought them a house anyway, leaving this money for missions. He also donated an annual sum of 1,000 *livres* from the *aides and huitième de vin* of two parishes near Angers.[46] The rights to this reverted entirely to the Lazarists on his death, by which time their income stood at 1,800 *livres* annually.[47]

In Brûlart de Paul found an extraordinarily generous patron who delighted in lavishing gifts on the Lazarists, and would have furbished their Troyes house in a style utterly unsuited to a 'poor Congregation', had not de Paul insisted that he allow his men to live amidst simple decor and furnishings.[48] They were preferred recipients of the enormous resources of this patron, but Troyes was just the first stage, and in Annecy Brûlart and de Paul found a special location replete with spiritual significance for admirers of de Sales. In addition to being the birthplace of Salesian spirituality and institutions, this 'diocese of saints', as de Paul termed it, was also the dwelling place of de Sales's closest living associate and guardian of his teaching, Jeanne de Chantal. He was delighted to place the Lazarists close to their 'worthy mother' in the heart of de Sales's terrain.[49]

De Paul and Brûlart agreed terms for the new house independently of episcopal input in June 1639.[50] This meant that when the new incumbent, Juste Gúerin, travelled to Annecy from Turin six weeks later, they depended on Jeanne de Chantal to represent them and to convince him to approve their scheme.

[44] Unfortunately, the premises did not provide a great return over the years, and after rising to a height of 1,900 *livres* in 1648, rent fell to 1,150 *livres* by 1656: AN, S6617.

[45] AN, S6617 (26 October 1641). Breslay also left 200 *livres* of *rentes* to the Lazarists in his will.

[46] AD l'Aube, 5G1 (3 October 1637 and 19 January 1638); AN, S6617 (12 March 1638).

[47] The revenues assigned provided a decent income for the house in theory, but de Paul lamented that the crown claimed 2,250 *livres* from them in 1642–3, and sought to encroach even more in succeeding years: AD l'Aube, 5G249 (16 February 1641); *CCD*, 2: 359, de Paul to Bernard Codoing, 25 December 1642.

[48] AN, Minutier Central, ET/LI/505 (26 August 1640); *CCD*, 2: 102, de Paul to Noël Brûlart de Sillery, 1640; Bois, *Noël Brûlart de Sillery*, 128.

[49] *CCD*, 1: 552–3, de Paul to Jeanne de Chantal, 14 July 1639. The author of Jeanne de Chantal's *vie*, Henri de Maupas du Tour, intimated that she originally suggested that Brûlart approach de Paul about establishing a house in Annecy, but the documentary evidence does not support this contention: Maupas du Tour, *Mère Jeanne Françoise Frémiot*, 255.

[50] AN, Minutier Central, ET/LI/505, M211, MM534 (3 June 1639); AN, MM534 (3 August 1639, 26 January 1640); *CCD*, 1: 275, de Paul to Antoine Portail, 1 May 1635.

De Paul wrote to thank her for her support for the endowment, and included a full description of the Lazarists' 'way of life' so that she could introduce them to the new bishop who had just arrived in the locality.[51] She was extremely encouraging of the proposal for missions, because, she confessed to de Paul, the region needed them urgently as there were many Protestant parishes bordering Catholic ones in Geneva diocese. On de Paul's instigation, the first two missionaries visited her when they arrived in Annecy in August, and she was reassured to find that they were 'faithful workers', whose mission was capable of bringing 'more souls to Paradise than any others'. Chantal gave this account of de Paul and his men when she met Gúerin, and duly reported to de Paul that he was well disposed to permitting them in his diocese.[52] Indeed, in the next few months, he decided to do more, and piggybacked on Brûlart's donation, as the bishop of Troyes had done three years earlier, to ask the Lazarists to organize ordinand retreats. Shortly afterwards, he undertook his diocesan visitation, and found the missionaries hard at work in the parishes. This personal encounter led the admiring Gúerin to pay for an additional priest to join the house while the success of the retreats inspired him to ask them to run a small seminary a year later.[53]

IV

The language of motherhood that de Paul adopted to describe the roles that Marie de La Trinité and Jeanne de Chantal played in the birth of the houses of Troyes and Annecy reflects the sense of spiritual kinship that he felt linked those who professed special devotion to François de Sales and to his legacy. This kinship extended beyond the first generation of Lazarist activity, so that he envisaged Jeanne de Chantal to be a mother to all Lazarists from the time of foundation, while Marie enabled them, through her 'begetting' of a new house in Troyes, to progress from the age of their birth to a new era of expansion. De Paul felt that de Sales's legacy bound him personally, and the Lazarists in general, to their advocates and benefactors in both locations; it united them in piety and compelled them to cooperate in the pursuit of objectives which manifested it.

De Paul did not describe his connections with the founders of the houses in the west in the same terms. Even so, these houses originated in a relationship that he cultivated through the confraternities of charity, on which Salesian teaching was an important influence. Indeed, Brûlart's special insistence on the foundation of

[51] *CCD*, 1: 552–7, de Paul to Jeanne de Chantal, 15 July 1639; *CCD*, 1: 566, same to same, 1639; *CCD*, 1: 568, same to same, 15 August 1639; *CCD*, 2: 57–8, same to same, 14 May 1640.

[52] 145 of the 600 parishes were, Jeanne counted, in Protestant hands: *CCD*, 2: 61, Jeanne de Chantal to de Paul, May 1640.

[53] De Paul expressed his reservations about accepting young boys in the institution but Guérin was not swayed. He wished the seminary's structure to follow loyally the directives of the Council of Trent, however contrary they were to the lessons that de Paul was then learning from the seminary of Bons-Enfants: Abelly, *Vie*, ii, 34–5; BN, Ms Fr 15721, fo. 755r–v; *CCD*, 2: 171–2, de Paul to Louis Lebreton, 3 February 1641; Juste Guérin, 'Notice sur l'institut de la Congrégation de la Mission', in *Notices sur les prètres, clercs et frères*, ii, 44–8 (see also 38–43).

confraternities in the contracts for Troyes and Annecy signals that he was conscious of this link, and knew that these were yet another initiative in which he and de Paul could join forces to express their spiritual imperatives as founder and sponsor. Around the same time as they did so, de Paul travelled to the west of the realm, his attention fixed on new schemes for houses in Richelieu, Notre-Dame de la Rose, and Luçon, all of which were located on lands belonging to the Richelieu family. Of the three, Richelieu was to act as a flagship house, to which de Paul sent a total of ninety priests and nineteen brothers to 1660, and in time dwarfing even Troyes, to which de Paul dispatched thirty-six priests and six brothers before 1660.

In the early 1630s, the duchess of Aiguillon joined the new confraternity of charity in the Parisian parish of Saint-Sulpice, and soon afterwards became a member of the Ladies of Charity at the *Hôtel-Dieu*.[54] The attraction of both groups for her lay in opportunities to cultivate her piety through acts of charity, a desire that she felt very keenly indeed. Always devout, once widowed Aiguillon had withdrawn to a Carmelite convent until, on her uncle's instigation, Pope Urban VIII ordered her to leave, and she had subsequently channelled her zeal into religious works, while also attending court. There, she became a close friend of Anne of Austria after she was appointed a lady of the bedchamber in 1625. Her frequent presence at court, and her attachment to both her uncle and the queen, ensured that Aiguillon was perfectly positioned to promote her favourite religious causes and those who pursued them there. Her intercessions meant that de Paul drew closer to the centre of the political establishment, bringing his congregation with him. Thus, although in the case of the houses in question here it is impossible to determine if it was Aiguillon or her uncle who made the initial offer to de Paul, it is most likely that she promoted de Paul and his interests to the cardinal. She also contributed significantly to solidifying the Congregation's bases in Richelieu and Luçon after her uncle died in 1642, her interest providing a level of continuity without which the future of the foundations might have been jeopardized.

As he grew to value de Paul's opinions on clerical standards and personnel and learned more about the ministerial services that the Lazarists could provide, the cardinal became willing to offer them opportunities for advancement that advantaged all of them. Historically, Richelieu had often exhibited interest in clerical training and discipline, and a man as well informed as he in the 1630s would certainly have been aware of the operation at Saint-Lazare before 1637. After he met its head on a number of occasions to discuss the terms of the Lazarists' presence in the *centre-ouest*, he asked him to suggest possible contenders for promotion to senior church benefices in the crown's control, and one of his final gestures in life was to fund twelve seminarians at Bons-Enfants. In the intervals between the meetings, de Paul communicated with the cardinal, on his order, through the bishop of Chartres, Léonor d'Étampes de Valençay, to sort out minor details of the foundation which did not merit Richelieu's personal attention (such as the

[54] De Paul first mentioned Aiguillon in his surviving correspondence in 1636, but it is clear from the content of the letter that he had already known her for some time: *CCD*, 1: 321–2, de Paul to Louise de Marillac, 27 May 1636.

decoration of the Lazarists' house).[55] 'The goodness and gentleness with which [Étampes] . . . negotiated' earned him de Paul's gratitude, and encouraged an acquaintance that would prove valuable to him a few years later in Sedan.[56]

The speed with which the three houses here in question were set up suggests that uncle and niece devised a concerted strategy to fulfil their religious responsibilities to the local populations by means of de Paul's organization. In 1631, the king had permitted Richelieu to combine three baronies to form the duchy of Richelieu in Poitou, and he followed this in March 1637 by combining the former parishes of Braye and Sablon into one large parish centred around the town and *château* of Richelieu, his family seat. Close to the *château*, the cardinal minister constructed a handsome parish church 40 metres in length, its three naves decorated with mottled marble pillars and sculpted cornicing.[57] In August, his niece purchased the duchy of Aiguillon further south in the diocese of Agen, and promptly installed the Lazarists there, first in Aiguillon town itself and subsequently in Notre-Dame de la Rose in nearby Sainte-Livrade parish.[58] De Paul was pleased to update her on the missions that Robert de Sergis was leading in the duchy by December.[59] Meanwhile, on 4 January 1638, he met her uncle at his *château* in Rueil to sign a contract to send confreres to Richelieu. Finally, in 1641, the Lazarists moved into a house in Luçon that de Paul purchased using funds that the cardinal supplied.[60]

In addition to Richelieu's concerns to develop his family's patrimony and powerbases, there were also broader political considerations at play in the expansion of Lazarist interests in this region. Of the areas in which all of the new houses were located, only Luçon contained a sizeable Huguenot population, and it was prey to periodic disputes between the denominations over flashpoints such as sites of worship and community graveyards.[61] In general, however, all were situated in a region of considerable Huguenot strength, which had since 1628 become a major

[55] For example, Étampes also communicated de Paul's request that the Lazarists be permitted to establish a confraternity of charity. Richelieu approved, and offered to maintain the confraternity until it could become self-supporting. The Lazarist Lambert aux Couteaux subsequently informed him that the members had collected a fund of 180 *livres*: *CCD*, 1: 448, de Paul to Lambert aux Couteaux, 3 March 1638; *CCD*, 1: 453, 15 March 1638; *CCD*, 1: 458, 22 March 1638; AAE, Mémoires et Documents, France, 830, fo. 105r, Lambert aux Couteaux to Armand de Richelieu, 16 April 1638.

[56] Avenel (ed.), *Lettres, instructions diplomatiques et papiers d'état*, vi, 4–5, Armand de Richelieu to Léonor d'Étampes de Valençay, 11 January 1638; *CCD*, 1: 438–9, de Paul to Lambert aux Couteaux, 20 February 1638.

[57] Bosseboeuf, *Richelieu*, 291–2.

[58] In 1639, Aiguillon extended her holdings in the region by buying the *comtes* of Agen and Condom. For relevant documentation see AD de la Gironde, C3831. On the foundation of the duchy and parish of Richelieu, see Bosseboeuf, *Richelieu*, 298–9.

[59] AN, MM534 (18 August 1637); *CCD*, 1: 431, de Paul to Robert de Sergis, *c.*21 February 1638; *CCD*, 1: 442, de Paul to Antoine Lucas, 21 February 1638.

[60] Luçon might justifiably be called an outpost for Richelieu; de Paul did not sign a separate foundation contract for it, and purchased the residence (costing 4,850 *livres*) merely for convenience: AN, S6706 (7 December 1641); AD d'Indre et Loire, H699; *CCD*, 13a: 317–21; Fillon, *Fondation de Saint Vincent de Paul*, 4–8.

[61] The Edict of Nantes had provided for the separation of burial grounds for the two denominations, but interpretation of its terms regularly provoked disputes between the denominations: Luria, *Sacred Boundaries*, 29, 131–2.

focus of crown intervention.[62] After the siege of La Rochelle, Poitiers town in particular became a key base in the drive to reinforce crown authority and Catholic hegemony in the *centre-ouest*, with secular and ecclesiastical officials combining to ensure that the area, hitherto dominated by Huguenot nobles, subsequently remained quiescent and obedient. In 1634, Jean Filleau, a member of the newly formed Company of the Holy Sacrament in Poitiers, led an inspection of Poitiers' parishes on the order of the *Grands Jours de Poitiers*, which found the standard of Catholic clergy in the area to be very poor, with lack of residence a particular blemish. Half of the members of this commission were appointed by Bishop La Rocheposay, who had led the ecclesiastical charge against heresy in Poitiers from 1612. Since then, he had attempted to target non-resident clergy, presided over the establishment of sixty colleges, and welcomed numerous religious communities to the diocese, most notably his favoured missionaries, the Capuchins, in 1613.[63]

Richelieu did not invite the Lazarists to the region to evangelize Huguenots but to meet the 'spiritual needs' of Catholics who were vulnerable in the 'great empire' that Satan had established there.[64] These were the words that de Paul adopted in giving instructions to one of the ten priest missionaries that he initially sent to Richelieu, and all of their assigned duties, which included the cure of Richelieu parish itself, were designed to bolster the faith of besieged Catholics.[65] But he knew that he needed secure resources in order to fulfil such a demanding set of responsibilities, the extent of which, he confessed, frightened him.[66] For this, Richelieu assigned the rent from four town properties (amounting to 300 *livres* annually) and the revenues from one of his benefices, the priory of Saint-Nicolas-de-Champvant.[67] He also sold his rights to the *greffes* of Loudun to buy land which the Lazarists could lease out, and for some months de Paul searched fruitlessly for suitable holdings to purchase.[68] Eventually, the cardinal decided simply to make a splendid gift of 60,000 *livres* on his deathbed in December 1642, and asked in return that the Lazarists double the number of priests in their house.[69]

The terms of Richelieu's endowment were therefore unambiguously set out at the time of foundation. However, his death delayed the transfer of resources,

[62] Hanlon, *Confession and Community*, 38; Luria, *Sacred Boundaries*, pp. xl, 29.

[63] Favreau et al. (eds), *Diocèse de Poitiers*, 136–55; Forman, 'Henri Louis Chasteigner de la Rocheposay'; Hickey, 'Le Rôle de l'état dans la réforme catholique'; Luria, *Sacred Boundaries*; Perouas, 'La "Mission de Poitou"'.

[64] *CCD*, 1: 404–5, de Paul to Bernard Codoing, 27 December 1637.

[65] The initial number of priests was seven, but the contract stipulated that three more should be added over the next two years. De Paul agreed that they would also hold conferences for ordained priests of the diocese: AN, MM534; AD d'Indre et Loire, G1291 (4 January 1638).

[66] *CCD*, 1: 418, de Paul to Lambert aux Couteaux, 30 January 1638. In particular, de Paul found the size of the parish intimidating.

[67] The Lazarists took formal possession of the priory in 1646. Richelieu's secretary, Michel Lemasle also donated a house and four *arpents* of land in the area to them at this time: AD d'Indre et Loire, H702 (8 January 1638), H706 and H708; Bosseboeuf, *Richelieu*, 298–9.

[68] Worth 4,550 *livres* annually, these sold for 87,726 *livres* in March 1641: AN, MM534; AD d'Indre et Loire, G1291 (4 January 1638) and H705, fos 4r–v (27 March 1641).

[69] See AAE, France, vol. 84, fo. 162r, Le Rivoui to Armand de Richelieu, 6 August 1642, for de Paul's proposal to buy a land holding offering 1,750 *livres* in rent annually; *Testament de Monsieur le Cardinal Duc de Richelieu*, 10; BN, Dupuy 835, fos 247r–257v.

and from this time de Paul engaged with Aiguillon to ensure that the Lazarists received their due. The matter was pressing; in August 1643, he reminded the commissioners responsible for the liquidation of the cardinal's estate that his association had already incurred large debts in establishing the house in Richelieu. Soon after, he complained privately to his colleague Codoing that the 'Richelieu affair' had come to a standstill, and that he had been forced to give up 'a lot, because of the heavy debts of this succession and the mood of those with whom we had to deal'.[70] But, if, as these words suggest, de Paul was disappointed, he did not really have any right to be, because Aiguillon had proved extremely fair in executing her late uncle's wishes. His regret may have stemmed from the fact that the original lump sum was reduced to 46,400 *livres*, but the Lazarists still gained a yearly income of 5,500 *livres* from the barony of Saint-Cassien in compensation.[71] They also retained the cure of Richelieu, and therefore the buildings attached to it, and amassed properties in the town, comprising four shops, ten houses, and twelve other houses with shops, all rented to a variety of local individuals and businesses. In total, the rental income reached approximately 3,000 *livres* annually.[72] Within weeks, de Paul added to this portfolio when he authorized Lambert to purchase a house adjacent to the community's residence in Richelieu for 1,500 *livres*. When he subsequently visited the community in October 1644, he signed a contract to buy the *seigneurie* of Boisbouchard from Marie Lestoile, the widow of Vincent Langlois de Blasque, a former counsellor of Marie de Medici, for 25,350 *livres*. This offered the community an annual rental return of 195 *livres* during the next decade.[73]

Aiguillon also took the opportunity at this time to expand the Lazarist presence in Notre-Dame de la Rose, in honour of her uncle, and in thanksgiving for the graces with which God blessed him in his final illness.[74] For the first time, she was joined by Bishop Delbène of Agen in her patronage, when he offered a new house to the Lazarists.[75] Slowly, a closer relationship evolved between the missionaries and the prelate, culminating in de Paul's agreement with him that they would manage a seminary in Agen town in 1650.[76] It is notable, once again, that the

[70] *CCD*, 2: 462, de Paul to Bernard Codoing, 11 September 1643.

[71] This revenue came from the rent of land totalling 91.5 *arpents*; the Lazarists initially owned half the mill on the property, and purchased the remainder in 1647 before renting out the mill for 72 *livres* annually: AD de la Vienne, 1H18 103; AN, MM534 (2 September 1643).

[72] AD d'Indre et Loire, H701 (2 September 1643) and H705.

[73] AD d'Indre et Loire, H702 (5 October 1643), H705 (11 October 1644), and H700; *CCD*, 2: 528–30, de Paul to Antoine Portail, 5 October 1644. In 1654, the duke of Richelieu granted the Congregation a small piece of land (measuring 900 *toises* in area) in the town to erect further buildings: AD d'Indre et Loire, H702 (7 November 1654).

[74] AN, MM534 (4 July 1642); *CCD*, 2: 318, de Paul to Bernard Codoing, 19 August 1642. See also Appendix 1.

[75] The Lazarists also maintained an ancient sanctuary dedicated to Our Lady, which had been restored in the 1620s after falling into disuse by the close of the sixteenth century: ACMP, Dossier 'La Rose' (14 June 1640, 21 April 1641); *CCD*, 1: 589, de Paul to Benôit Bécu, 28 October 1639; Marboutin, *Sainte-Livrade*, 35–6.

[76] Delbène united the priories of Sainte-Foy and Saint-Pierre de Montmagnerie to the seminary, and assigned lands producing 900 *livres* in rent annually to run it. De Paul provided a staff of three priests and two brothers: ACMP, Dossier 'Agen' (1 March 1650). The priories had been in the hands of Nicolas Pignay, a diocesan official in Luçon from 1654 who subsequently stayed in the Lazarists'

bishop emerged very slowly as a patron of the community. Yet even his degree of involvement was greater than that of the bishop of Poitiers, Henri Chasteigner de La Rocheposay. Richelieu only included the bishop cursorily in his summoning of the Lazarists to Richelieu, by asking him to assent to his plans when they reached maturity in December 1637.[77] After they arrived in La Rocheposay's territory in the same month, the bishop continued to concentrate his support on the Capuchins. He remained detached from the Lazarists' work, and neither they nor de Paul had much communication with him.[78] Likewise, in Luçon, the missionaries must have acquired faculties to minister from Bishop Nivelle, but there is no evidence to suggest that he assisted them in any other way to settle there. It was only when de Paul nearly closed the tiny house a few years later that the bishop sprang into action to provide a small building and funds to buy rentable land. This injected new life into the struggling community, but Luçon remained a small house, with only a total of fifteen priests and two brothers serving there before 1660.[79]

V

The bestowal by Richelieu and Aiguillon of their seal of approval was of enormous advantage to de Paul and the Lazarists. In a society obsessed with rank, the elevated status of their new patrons was such that it was likely that others would emulate their actions and associate themselves with those that they had judged suitable recipients of their patronage. More practically, uncle and niece provided access to the royal court, and their preferment ushered de Paul and his men towards a wealth of potential resources in the hands of courtiers and at the heart of the royal family itself. Two new foundations resulted from de Paul's representation of his association's interests at court in the early 1640s, in Crécy-en-Brie in Meaux diocese, and Sedan on the north-eastern border of France. The two experienced markedly different outcomes during his lifetime, because de Paul had to close the Crécy

house there for a few years. By 1671, he had retired to Bons-Enfants (AN M213 (10 August 1671)). In 1658, he donated twenty-five *boiselées de terre* and over 3,000 *livres* to the house in Luçon: AD d'Indre et Loire, H702 (8 March 1658).

For units of measurement in the *Centre-Ouest*, see Charbonnier and Poitrineau, *Anciennes Mesures*. A *boiselée* was equivalent to one-eighth of an *arpent* in the region.

77 La Rocheposay issued a decree to create the new cure of Richelieu on 27 May 1638, and the pope issued a bull to the same effect on 7 January 1639: AN, MM534; Avenel (ed.), *Lettres, instructions diplomatiques et papiers d'état*, vi, 4–5, Armand de Richelieu to Léonor d'Étampes de Valençay, 11 January 1638.

78 See APF, SOCG 83, fos 328r–v, 331v, Henri-Louis Chasteigner de La Rocheposay to Urban VIII, 2 May 1641, for La Rocheposay's request that the pope should approve an increase in the number of Capuchins in Poitiers from twenty to thirty or forty, and that new fixed missions should be established for the order; Favreau et al. (eds), *Diocèse de Poitiers*, 144; Pérouas, 'La "Mission de Poitou"'.

79 De Paul approved the purchase of three houses and agricultural land using Nivelle's donation. A number of parcels of land and small sums of cash for missions were donated by Claude Thouvant, a canon of Luçon cathedral and archdeacon of Aizenay, and Nicolas Pignay, between 1647 and 1658, amounting to 6,000 *livres* and 25 *boiselées de terre*. These contracts can be found in AD d'Indre et Loire, H702 and AN, S6706.

house temporarily in 1654 and it did not reopen until 1660.[80] In contrast, the success of the house that he established in Sedan, more than any other similar initiative that he undertook during his superior generalship, manifestly tied the Congregation's spiritual task of evangelization to the territorial and political ambitions of the French monarchy. Here the alliance that he forged between the crown and the Lazarists proved very advantageous and enduring.

At the time of its making the king and queen's opinion of de Paul had reached so high that he was invited to assist at the king's deathbed on 23 April 1643, a privilege offered only to trusted ecclesiastics or those in high office. Over the course of his eight-day presence there, de Paul struck a deal directly with the king about Sedan, although here, as in the *centre-ouest*, there was a political backdrop, originating with the late cardinal's strategy for the extension of royal influence along the north-eastern frontier. Given his history with the Lazarists, it is probable that Richelieu intended to ask de Paul to send missionaries to the region too, and his death in December did not derail this plan. Such a scheme must have been inserted into the crown's broader strategy during the winter, rather than to have been concocted by the king on his deathbed. Moreover, the rapidity with which de Paul put the monarch's instructions into practice implies that he had already been approached about the new foundation well before he stood before his bed. By then the crown had already identified the terms that it wanted for the Lazarists' establishment, and six days after de Paul left Louis, he wrote to Bernard Codoing to inform him of the king's wishes, and to let him know he had already sent five experienced missionaries to Sedan.[81]

The likelihood that the move originated with Richelieu becomes still more certain when the circumstances and conditions of the Lazarists' institution are studied. In Poitou, the cardinal had asked the Lazarists to concentrate on ministering to local Catholics, despite the presence of a large quantity of Protestants in apparent need of conversion, and their appointment to Sedan was made on a similar basis. Its population was overwhelmingly Protestant, with only 1,500 Catholics in a population of 4,000. Having emerged as a major centre of Protestant population between 1556 and 1574, when its Protestant convert prince, Henri-Robert de la Marck, had deprived the Catholic church of its independence, Sedan functioned as a refuge throughout the civil wars for Huguenots driven from their home places.[82] It retained its independence until taken over by the French crown when its ruler, Fréderick-Maurice de La Tour d'Auvergne, duke of Bouillon, became involved in the ill-fated Cinq-Mars conspiracy of 1642. Richelieu had long desired this annexation, and in September he asked Cardinal Mazarin to oversee the transition to French rule in this frontier area that was 'of such importance' because of its

[80] De Paul closed the house because a shortage of income meant that he could not even order essential repairs to the dilapidated residence (indeed, many of its rooms had been locked up for years): AN, MM534 (April 1641); *CCD*, 2: 359, de Paul to Bernard Codoing, 25 December 1652.

[81] *CCD*, 2: 431, de Paul to Bernard Codoing, 7 May 1643; Hersent, *Sacré Monument*, 47.

[82] Pregnon, *Histoire*, i, 304–60.

position cheek by jowl with Spanish territories, and its Protestant character.[83] At the same time, the king appointed Abraham de Fabert governor of the region, and he travelled to Sedan to represent the crown's interests shortly afterwards.[84]

The terms ensured that the Lazarists who worked there were representatives of both the church and the crown, and the returns for obedience were handsome. Louis XIII bequeathed 24,000 *livres*, which was to be used to establish a mission of six priests and two brothers in Sedan. He earmarked a further 40,000 *livres* for Lazarist missions in other as yet unspecified locations, but in June 1644 Anne of Austria directed that this too should be invested and the revenue placed at de Paul's disposal for use in Sedan.[85] At this point, she also drafted in the new archbishop of Reims, Léonor d'Étampes de Valençay, to assume episcopal jurisdiction of Sedan and to assist the Lazarists in their establishment there. News of the archbishop's late involvement in this 'so holy and so necessary work' probably pleased de Paul, because of his positive interaction with him some years earlier regarding the Richelieu house, but there is no evidence to suggest that he had contributed to the Sedan enterprise before this time.[86] In mid-August 1644, however, Étampes visited Sedan, and assigned substantial sums of revenue as well as the cure of Sedan and a small curacy to the Lazarists. They then became parish priests in the area as well as missionaries to it, dual functions which granted them extensive control over pastoral practices.[87]

All appeared settled, and Étampes acknowledged that he 'regarded [de Paul] and his company well'.[88] But the finalizing of the arrangement in the aftermath of his visit strained their relations irreparably, for the prelate grew exasperated at what he concluded were de Paul's attempts to stall progress until he gained better terms. In late September, de Paul wrote a letter of apology to him, excusing his procrastination by claiming that he had simply made 'modest representations' to the regent to reaffirm that the funds bequeathed by her husband 'should be used for the same end' as he had specified.[89] His deferential tone was insufficient to quell Étampes's displeasure, who issued revised terms, but penned a letter stiff with irritation to inform the secretary of state, the count of Brienne, that the matter was finally settled 'in the forms that Monsieur Vincent was able to desire it'; in his opinion, he concluded, no further adjustments should be necessary. For the second time, Étampes then asked

[83] Along with Raucourt and Saint-Menges, two small adjoining territories held by Fréderic-Maurice and also occupied by the French crown in 1642: Hodson, 'Sovereigns and Subjects', 329, 350–4.

[84] Avenel (ed.), *Lettres, instructions diplomatiques et papiers d'état*, vii, 144–6, Richelieu to Jules Mazarin, 26 September 1642; BN, Dupuy, 625, fos 150r–151v; Congar, 'Fabert à l'œuvres à Sedan'.

[85] The money paid for the construction of thirteen houses at the clos Saint-Laurent, just north of the Congregation's motherhouse in Paris (Saint-Lazare); these raised rent of 1,300 *livres* per year, to which de Paul added an additional 900 *livres* annually: BN, NAF, 22326, fo. 56v; AN, S6597 (22 August 1645); *CCD*, 13a: 337–8.

[86] Bib. Maz., Ms 2214, unpaginated, Jules Mazarin to Léonor d'Étampes de Valençay, 10 September 1644: '. . . une œuvre si saincte et si necessaire'.

[87] For further details, see Appendix 1, and Forrestal, 'Catholic Missionaries'.

[88] BN, NAF, 6210, fo. 86r, Léonor d'Étampes to the count of Brienne (Henri-Auguste de Loménie), 17 September 1644: '. . . le regardoit et sa compagnie bien'.

[89] *CCD*, 2: 524–5, de Paul to Léonor d'Étampes de Valençay, 21 September 1644.

that the letters patent be forwarded, and sent his ordinance to the council, presumably expecting the ratification by return of post. It had not arrived in Reims by 3 October, forcing the archbishop to complain yet again about the tardiness of the affair for what he hoped would be 'the last time', and to emphasize that it was imperative that the letters patent should be issued promptly in order for the 'disorders and differences' that were arising between the parties to be put to rest.[90] While conscious of his impatience, de Paul was not in a position to soothe it, for he was then in Richelieu, from where he asked Lambert aux Couteaux to write to Étampes to promise him that he would 'work on his affair when I get back'. The trail of letters runs out at this point, although de Paul must have approved the revised terms when he returned to Paris in mid-October because the letters patent were finally issued in November without changes other than those that Étampes had made on 24 September.[91]

De Paul did not procrastinate without reason, whatever Étampes chose to assume. Comparison of the first and final terms reveals that he was rightly worried that the use to which he had put the king's donation be recorded transparently in the legal documentation, presumably to avoid any suggestion that it had been illegitimately used, so the archbishop duly added the information that de Paul had invested it in housing to the final agreement. However, the terms also reveal that de Paul had concerns about the onerous duties that the archbishop expected of his men, no doubt arising from the reports that the superior (Guillaume Gallais) had sent to him on the demands that the parish and missions would engender. He thus succeeded in negotiating an increase of two in the number of missionaries that would reside in Sedan, as well as agricultural produce to maintain them.[92] Unfortunately, these hard-fought and worthwhile gains may have cooled Étampes's enthusiasm for the Lazarists, for a distant relationship developed between them thereafter, and he did not make any effort to promote or associate with de Paul or his missionaries. Unlike Annecy, for instance, where the bishop called on the Lazarists for visitations and missions, Étampes, like La Rochesposay of Poitiers, plumped consistently for the Capuchins in such endeavours.[93]

Why, then, the query begs, did the crown insist on de Paul's men for Sedan, when it could have chosen any one of the numerous clerical groups to which it regularly offered patronage? It is evident that the royal couple and their chief ministers judged this particular set to be especially well fitted to the political and religious landscape there, and selected it in the belief that its ethos and methods dovetailed neatly with the policy of conciliation that it wished to implement. With scarcely any Catholic clergy active in Sedan, it was imperative to ensure that

[90] BN, NAF 6210, fo. 109r, Léonor d'Étampes de Valençay to the count of Brienne, 23 September 1644; BN, NAF 6210, fo. 109r, same to same, 3 October 1644.

[91] *CCD*, 2: 529–30, de Paul to Antoine Portail, 5 October 1644; BN, NAF 22326, fo. 75r–v.

[92] BN, NAF 22326, fos 56v–57v.

[93] Thus, in 1647, Étampes deputed the Capuchin *Père* Hyacinthe to carry out visitations in the diocese, offering the opportunity for the friar to found confraternities of the rosary as he passed through each parish. Records for these visitations are preserved in AD de la Marne, 2G270, 2G275, and 2G278, but disappointingly there are none available for Sedan.

an adequate pastoral regime was provided. At the same time, the crown wished to avoid confrontation, in order to achieve the smooth reintegration of Sedan into the realm. Unfortunately, neither the principles nor the process of its occupation were universally agreed; historically, La Tour princes had not regarded themselves as subjects of the French king, and had insisted that they exercised sovereign authority over an independent principality, which they had freely placed under French protection. Through the 1640s and 1650s, Bouillon and his wife continued to assert their opposition to the French crown's 'domination' of Sedan through 'deprivation' of its rightful sovereigns.[94] Furthermore, the practice of Protestantism was associated closely with loyalty to the departed dynasty and could quickly be turned into a form of religious dissidence against the government of the French king. This was particularly likely should the crown's policy towards the Catholic minority infringe on traditional Protestant privileges. The crown therefore adopted a strategy of moderation and appeasement, but laced it with a firm show of authority. It was designed, as the queen mother emphasized to Fabert, to entice the Sedanese 'to love the domination of the king', and the Lazarists were to act as a stabilizing force in this seduction.[95] It was imperative, the chief minister Mazarin agreed, that the crown demonstrate through this approach that it had the best interests of the Sedanese at heart, that is, that its 'particular care of their interests' rested on a desire to 'protect them' in all encounters. While the king's paternal authority was absolute over this restored 'son', it would be expressed in as benign a manner as possible.[96] At the same time, Mazarin remained quite personally detached from the process of establishing de Paul's missionaries in Sedan, and simply engaged with it as a matter of official strategy. This set the tone for his relations with de Paul and his interests thereafter, for he was certainly never to replicate his predecessor, Cardinal Richelieu, in offering invaluable patronage to them.[97]

This strategy required a delicate balancing of rights and privileges. Following his orders from Paris, Fabert re-established 'the entire liberty and exercise of the catholic religion' in Sedan, oversaw restitution of Catholic church properties, and obliged shops to close on feast days, but mitigated the risk of alienating Protestants by providing two extra temples for worship, and separate cemeteries.[98] On his recommendation, the crown ordered a series of ceremonies in April and May 1644 in which the inhabitants swore an oath of fidelity to the French crown.[99] As custodians of Sedan parish, and the principal clergy in the locality, the Lazarists

[94] Eventually, in 1651, the crown agreed to recognize the formerly sovereign status of Sedan, but after the Paris *parlement* objected, it was 1657 before this was formalized: *Manifeste de Monsieur le duc de Bouillon*, 10; Hodson, 'Sovereigns and Subjects', 379–81.

[95] Arsenal, Paris, Ms 5416, fos 2016r–2017r, Anne of Austria to Abraham de Fabert, 24 July 1643: 'aymer la domination du Roy'.

[96] Bib. Maz., Ms 2214, fo. 11r, Jules Mazarin to the Protestant ministers of Sedan, 22 January, 1643; Bib. Maz., Ms 2214, fo. 183r–v, Jules Mazarin to Abraham Fabert.

[97] Chéruel (ed.), *Lettres du Cardinal Mazarin*. See also the cardinal's unpublished letters to Fabert and Étampes during 1643 and 1644 in Bib. Maz., Ms 2214.

[98] BN, Clairambault 1157, fos 106r–112r; BN, NAF 9787, fos 143r–147r.

[99] BSG, Ms 873, fos 4r–5r; BN, NAF 9787, fo. 123r.

took a leading role in these ceremonies. Indeed, they were the first to take the vow of fidelity before the governor and a 'great number of people' in their parish church, before celebrating mass and watching the procession wend its way to the town hall. They thereby set an example for other clergy, parishioners, and Protestants alike, and reiterated their loyalty and service to church and crown.[100]

De Paul was fully aware of the reasoning behind the crown's gift, and emphasized to his missionaries that the king had made it a 'condition' of their endowment that they stick rigidly to the pastoral methods characteristic to them, and avoid the temptation to challenge Protestants in dispute 'in the pulpit [or] in private', or to proselytize directly; in other words, they were not to adopt the confrontational tactics characteristic of other orders, such as the Capuchins or Jesuits.[101] Instead, they should concentrate their efforts on the Catholic population, and simply allow their exemplary living to give them the high moral ground over Protestants, inspire their admiration for living out the graceful virtues of humility and simplicity, and perhaps win them over.[102] Anything more prideful or vain would result in nothing but heightened antagonism towards the missionaries—who were the most obvious manifestation of the restoration of the Catholic church—and towards the crown which was sponsoring this. In the agreement for Sedan, therefore, *realpolitik* met idealism, and it was this conjunction which led to Charles Drelincourt's disquiet about the Lazarists' unusual pastoral conduct.[103]

By the 1640s, de Paul's message about the Lazarists' mission virtues and pastoral conduct had reached the highest and most influential quarters of the realm, with the result that the crown was prepared to draw his association fully into the reach of its patronage in order to meet its political objectives. The progress from the modest and troubled foundation in Toul to the parish and mission of Sedan may appear an organic one, for the gains en route were generally incremental in size. The social standing of the patrons who sponsored successive institutes proved ever greater, and the houses themselves tended to mirror the patron, for the larger the pool of resources on which they could call, the larger the endowment of the houses that they founded. Furthermore, as de Paul discovered, the aspirations of those who provided funding dictated their siting, for reasons of familial and political motivation as well as religious, and a key lesson of the testing apprenticeship that he served in these years was the importance of ensuring that the meeting of these did not prove detrimental to the Lazarist ministry. Of course, the contribution that patrons offered could not always be counted in coins, land, or buildings. It was often a gift of intercession made in return for de Paul's spiritual guidance, or on the basis of the spiritual camaraderie and common devotional loyalties that he cultivated using the structures of the confraternities and his official role in the Visitation's Salesian circle. These were, for the most part, areas of activity in which he met a variety of resource-laden lay and clerical sympathizers ready to engage in

[100] BN, NAF 9787, fos 125r–126r.

[101] *CCD*, 2: 442, de Paul to Guillaume Gallais, *c.*1643; *CCD*, 2: 495, same to same, 13 February 1644.

[102] *CCD*, 2:75, de Paul to Antoine Portail, 1 May 1635; *CCD*, 11: 55.

[103] See Ch. 5, sections II and IV.

the productive collaborations that he needed to expand the Lazarist infrastructure. Generally, they did not, however, facilitate the same with diocesan prelates, who played second fiddle to lay patrons and ecclesiastics such as Richelieu during this phase. When bishops did finally emerge as the dominant patrons of houses from later 1643, the terms that they set out as conditions for their benefaction were to set new tests for de Paul's understanding of the Lazarist mission.

8

New Houses, New Purposes, New Problems (1643–1660)

I

On 15 August, 1659, de Paul dispatched letters to a number of Lazarist house superiors. His objectives were the usual: to seek information or to respond to queries addressed to him in earlier letters, and to share snippets of news about colleagues, recent missions, and the general tenor of life at the motherhouse, on the presumption that the superior would share these lively, amusing, inspiring, salutary or sad items with his community. On this particular summer's day, de Paul was sufficiently excited about one piece of news to communicate it in three of the five letters that he sent to the post:

> We have begun a programme here aimed at making all of our missionaries equally qualified for assignments in seminaries and on the missions because we have had difficulty until now finding men capable of doing both.[1]

Behind this statement lie two seemingly dichotomous facts: first, the expansion of the Lazarists' works from missions to seminary management over two decades, and, secondly, de Paul's reticence in reconciling himself to this reality. By the time that he died, the Lazarists ran seminaries in eleven of the nineteen houses situated outside Paris (that is, in the French provinces), and the number gained post-1660 confirms that the administration of seminaries demanded even greater attention and resources thereafter. In the lifetime of their first superior general, however, the tipping point was 1643, the year in which the training of clerics in seminaries properly became a fixture in the calendar of duties that he devised for his confreres. In the second half of that year, he permitted them to assume responsibility for two seminaries in France (Troyes and Cahors) and, with the die cast, he approved their supervision of six more by the turn of the decade.[2] The onset of the Congregation's participation in seminary management was therefore most pronounced during the mid- to late 1640s. However, its pace outstripped the progress of de Paul's own views on the subject. It also outpaced his ability to devise training to prepare confreres for both elements of Lazarist labour. Until 1659, the internal

[1] *CCD*, 8: 91, de Paul to Firmin Get, 15 August 1659. For other letters of the same date, see 85–93.

[2] The Congregation's management of seminaries in Richelieu, Marseille, and Périgueux was short-lived, and none survived more than a year or two.

seminary's routine was directed entirely towards the formation of missionaries, and few Lazarists proceeded to further study in Theology. Herein lay the significance of de Paul's announcement to his confreres: the innovative programme was delivered through classes that provided instruction in topics such as moral theology, which the students could use as the basis for classes that they taught in seminaries. At last, they would receive formal training for a responsibility that they had already been carrying out on a rather ad hoc basis for many years.

Paul Broutin opines that de Paul never possessed any qualms about the wisdom or justification for this work at any stage in his career.[3] An ounce of scepticism is worth its weight here, however. Such certainty would have contrasted vastly with, for instance, the misgivings of his near contemporary Claudio Aquaviva, the fourth general of the Jesuits, under whom the Society multiplied its educational colleges during the late sixteenth and early seventeenth century. To Aquaviva, there was a genuine danger that the company's original and primary purpose, which obliged its men to go wherever they were needed as missionaries, would be destroyed if they were encouraged to favour a sedentary ministry over an itinerant one. To do so would mean an abandonment of their original spirit and animating identity, and he insisted that every province assign a proportion of its members to complete missions in order to guard against this.[4] On the other hand, de Paul's purported assurance about the place of clerical formation in the Lazarists' ministry would mirror that felt by his early associate Pierre de Bérulle, who confidently singled out the formation or 'institution' of priests, rather than missionary work, as the principal purpose of the Oratory at its foundation.[5]

A perusal of the first article of the Rules appears to corroborate Broutin's claim, for there the Lazarist's duty 'to help seminarians and priests to grow in knowledge and virtues, so they can be effective in their ministry' held parity with his commitment to seek his own perfection and to preach the gospel to the rural poor.[6] Yet, while this reflected the path that the Lazarists had taken in the preceding two decades, it hid their founder's years of personal turmoil. He had not initially included clerical formation within the vocational remit of his missionary association and, even after he made the decision to do so, he continued to wrestle with the nature and demands of the transition, only fully reconciling to it very late in his career. In the 1630s, he found it easier to accept the provision of retreats for ordinands, because he permitted himself to believe that it answered a command of divine providence. He concluded that it did not detract too much from missions, and would help to preserve their 'fruits' once the bands of Lazarists bid adieu to parishes.[7] De Paul still felt compelled, however, to remind his men that missions were the

[3] Broutin, *Réforme pastorale*, ii, 229.

[4] Bernard Dompnier concludes that, despite Aquaviva's efforts to protect the fundamental status of missions, they had become just one of many activities pursued by Jesuits by the mid-seventeenth century, and were considered to be of equal, but not greater, importance to their other works: Dompnier, 'La Compagnie de Jésus'.

[5] Pierre de Bérulle, 'Projet de l'érection de la Congrégation de l'Oratoire de Jésus', in Dupuy, *Bérulle*, 261.

[6] *CCD*, 13a: 432.

[7] *CCD*, 1: 553, de Paul to Jeanne de Chantal, 14 July 1639.

lifeblood of their company, because they enabled them to live authentically in Christ's likeness: 'For who lives better the way of life Jesus lived on earth than missionaries?'[8] He grew even more insistent as their obligations to seminaries grew from 1643, exposing his fear that the demands of education and administration would force him to curtail their mission campaigns, despite the 'blessings' they had thus far received. He continued to insist as late as 1650 that the Lazarists' 'service to the ecclesiastical state' was but an 'accessory' to their principal purpose of instructing the rural poor. Consequently, in total, de Paul permitted only two houses to concentrate exclusively on running a seminary, and admitted to regretting the pain that this caused their personnel who were prevented from attending 'to their principal work'. In telling contrast, he was quite happy to approve the foundation of houses in the provinces that were dedicated purely to the provision of missions, such as those of Montmirail, Crécy, and Luçon.[9]

Despite his nagging misgivings, de Paul did finally change heart, becoming convinced that the path along which he and his men were walking to the doors of seminaries was as spiritually valid as that of the missions. He concluded that a healthy reciprocity could exist between the duties of seminary management and missions, provided that the balance of labour was carefully struck, and that seminary administration did not undermine mission duties.[10] In a conference that he delivered to explain the Rule in 1658, he asserted that he and his first companions 'had been thinking only of ourselves and of the poor' in seeking their salvation during the first years of the Congregation's existence. In the fullness of time, God had called upon them to assist in the formation of 'good priests', so that de Paul had been led to it without choosing, and had in turn led his men to this 'lofty ministry'.[11] De Paul combined a comparison of his own life with that of Christ, who had first prayed, and then evangelized, before finally animating others 'not for themselves alone but for all the peoples of the earth', with a sense of his own instrumentality in God's divine plan. In this way, he legitimized the transition that the Lazarists had already navigated over four decades, while presenting his own doubts about the changes as a feature of being piloted through them by the unseen hand of the all-seeing God.

II

If de Paul was personally so conflicted about allowing the Lazarists to run seminaries, why did he permit them to extend their ministry at all? Beyond a providential reading, there are prosaic answers to this question, including de Paul's long-standing sense that somebody had to step into the breach to train a new generation of clergy. But why should it be he and other Lazarists in particular? The answer to this lies in the character of patronage to which he exposed the group from mid-1643, which changed radically from that on offer to that year. A number of

[8] *CCD*, 11: 121. [9] *CCD*, 4: 49, de Paul to Philibert de Brandon, 20 July 1650.
[10] *CCD*, 8: 524–6, de Paul to Luke Plunket, 19 April 1659. [11] *CCD*, 12: 74.

earlier benefactors had died by 1643, and were replaced by a new generation which was greater in number but less diverse in social composition. The first houses had been founded mainly by a string of distinguished lay patrons who were generally most interested in ensuring that the Lazarists carried out missions in their hinterlands. In the second phase of provincial expansion, only two of thirteen patrons were lay and only one was female (the duke of Retz and the duchess of Aiguillon), with the majority (ten) emerging from the episcopate. Neither of the houses (Montmirail and Marseille) endowed by Retz and Aiguillon included a seminary, but every one of those founded by the bishops did so. This indicated their conspicuous preference not only to improve standards of clerical performance in their dioceses by providing institutionalized training, but to call on de Paul's men to do so.

It is to the missions and clerical formation organized by and from Saint-Lazare that we should look in order to examine the collaborative relations that de Paul instituted with the bishops, rather than to the activities associated with the other outlets for his spiritual energy, the Visitation Salesian circle and confraternities of charity. With few exceptions, these prelates were representative of a new generation of bishops, buoyed up with obligations of duty set out in the decrees of Trent and by the admirable examples of pastoral government presented to them in the many *vitae* published on saintly bishops such as Charles Borromeo and François de Sales.[12] Having been blessed with patronage of the highest calibre, the Congregation was a rising star amongst clerical associations for bishops with pastoral ambitions; as its 'wise and pious ecclesiastics' answered their calls to deliver missions and retreats, they generally inspired hope amongst respected observers such as the former bishop of Belley that they could be counted on to repay the investments that patrons made in them.[13]

At Saint-Lazare, the Tuesday Conferences constituted a discrete structure of clerical formation from within which de Paul contributed to the nurturing of this kind of conscientious prelate. But further potential lay in the possibility that he might attract episcopal patronage for the Lazarists from within its ranks. After all, sixteen of the Company's known members were promoted to the episcopate during this period, and the bonds that de Paul formed with them were theoretically more likely than a short tailored course and several conversations to result in contracts for seminaries. Furthermore, many of the confreres undertook a retreat at Saint-Lazare, and some occasionally assisted the Lazarists on their missions before being raised to the episcopate. It was conceivable that their familiarity with the Lazarists' methods would mean that this group would be their obvious choice when they sought assistance for these activities in their dioceses, and indeed if they decided to establish seminaries. However, this process was not as straightforward as might be assumed. Some confreres, such as Pavillon and Vialart, did ask de Paul to send missionaries to their dioceses when elevated, but few of the relationships that de Paul cultivated in the Company actually led to invitations to manage seminaries. Indeed, only two episcopal members graced de Paul with this favour: Philibert de

12 For an extended exploration of this development, see Forrestal, *Fathers*, ch. 6.

13 Camus, *Noviciat cléricale*, 24.

Brandon invited the Lazarists to Périgueux in 1650, and François Fouquet asked de Paul to send them to Agde (1654) and latterly to Narbonne (1659); his younger brother Louis, also a confrere, continued the arrangement when he succeeded him in Agde in 1656. Others chose alternatively, even when the Lazarists were available, lending a competitive edge to the provision of institutes of clerical reform in dioceses: Maupas du Tour assigned the Sulpicians to his seminary in Le Puy in 1653,[14] and Felix Vialart successively confided his seminary in Châlons-sur-Marne to the priests of Saint Nicolas-du-Chardonnet (1640), the Doctrinaires (1652), and for a short time to the Oratorians (1679).[15] Manifestly, therefore, this paucity of support from Tuesday Conference bishops for new Lazarist foundations should not be blamed on their lack of commitment to the formation of diocesan clergy, quite the contrary. Yet while their discussions at the meetings may have encouraged such dedication in the long term, their connection to the Conferences and its director did not lead most of them to charge his association with care of their seminaries.

If not specifically or principally from Conference bishops then, where did the invitations for houses originate? Certainly, it was the perceived need for missionaries and retreat leaders to reform their dioceses that provoked these, but most patrons asked that de Paul demonstrate the competence of his missionaries in these domains before they risked offering them a permanent establishment there; therefore, de Paul used the services of missions and retreats to gain the trust necessary for this leap. In 1644, for instance, he signed terms with Bishop Jacques Raoul de La Guibourgère for a seminary and mission house in Saintes, but his missionaries had been active there since the winter of 1632, when Robert de Sergis and Lambert aux Couteaux progressed around this diocese and neighbouring Périgueux.[16] Nonetheless, the provision of retreats or missions did not automatically lead to an invitation to manage a seminary. Despite de Paul's close relationship with Augustin Potier, which resulted in the first retreats for ordinands in Beauvais diocese in 1628, there is no evidence to suggest that they ever negotiated to advance this arrangement to the level of a seminary there.[17] Nor did retreats or missions necessarily reap rapid results. When Balthazar Grangier de Liverdi was appointed to Tréguier in 1646, he was relatively inexperienced pastorally. Before he departed for his diocese, he took a short course in preaching the little method at Saint-Lazare, and accompanied Portail on a mission. Then, he asked de Paul to designate a Lazarist priest to assist him in beginning and sustaining 'visitations, exhortations, sermons, and catechetical instructions' in his see. In response, de Paul sent Bernard Codoing, then superior of a house in Saint-Méen in the nearby diocese of Saint-Malo, as a temporary adviser. But he was also a scout; in the course of their conversations, de Paul informed Codoing pointedly that the

[14] Maupas du Tour, *Funeral Oration*, 16.

[15] Nor did the Lazarists deliver ordinand retreats in the diocese. However, they did deliver missions in Vialart's diocese: Broutin, *Réforme pastorale*, i, 216–19; Degert, *Histoire des seminaries*, i, 219–20.

[16] AN, MM536 and S6710 (26 September 1644, 22 November 1644); *CCD*, 1: 206, de Paul to Alain de Solminihac, 23 August 1633; *CCD*, 1: 333, de Paul to Antoine Portail, 15 August 1636. See also Appendix 1.

[17] Or in Toulouse, where the Lazarists organized ordinand retreats from 1639: *CCD*, 1: 543, de Paul to Robert de Sergis, 13 May 1639.

bishop had confided to him that he hoped to establish a Lazarist house in his diocese, 'if he can find the means to do so'.[18]

As this case exhibits, the new foundations were not as dependent on de Paul's personal relationships with founders in this period as they had been in the decade or so preceding it. Instead, it became more common for him to trust experienced confreres like Portail or Codoing, who were by now long familiar with Lazarist customs, to coax initial expressions of interest towards practical commitment in the provinces when, as was increasingly the case, he was busy in Paris. In Tréguier, Codoing promoted awareness amongst inhabitants of the services available from de Paul's men through his own example and accounts of their manner of work. Then, following his departure from the area, de Paul allocated pairs of missionaries to perform missions intermittently from 1649, slowly establishing a reputation amongst locals, not least for having some ability to preach in Breton. He was duly rewarded five years later, when the bishop, in alliance with his *grand pénitencier*, erected a house for missions and a seminary. The contracts made explicit the impact that the missionaries had had on both clerics, for they cited the missions that they had completed 'with great success', as well as the example of the Lazarist seminary in Saint-Méen, as the reasons why they had decided to sponsor them. Confirming the depth of his attachment to de Paul's men, and his esteem for their pastoral judgement and competence, Grangier also directed that they should assist him on his annual diocesan visitations.[19]

III

When all of the houses established from mid-1643 are plotted on a map, the observer's gaze is immediately drawn to a single geographical region: the south-west.[20] There, de Paul approved the foundation of seven houses in as many dioceses between 1643 and 1659. The chronology of foundation was uneven—two houses were established in Cahors and Saintes in the early 1640s, with five more being founded during the 1650s, one of which (Périgueux) did not survive more than a year. By the late 1650s, the region had become a stronghold of the Congregation outside Paris, and one of its principal terrains of activity, in terms of both missions and seminary management. The presence of such a cluster in a region historically associated with Huguenot strength is noteworthy, and mirrored in magnified form the earlier development of houses in the *centre-ouest*. Although de Paul did not encourage his men to target heretics overtly for conversion, it was not unexpected that bishops in dioceses containing substantial Huguenot communities might wish to install them in their jurisdictions to augment the official church's

[18] *CCD*, 3: 195, de Paul to Bernard Codoing, 11 May 1647.

[19] *CCD*, 3: 447, de Paul to Michel Thepault de Rumelin, 7 June 1649; AN, S6713–6714 (16 March 1654, 28 June 1654); AN, S6718 (22 May 1660), and S6719 (September 1654). See also Appendix 1.

[20] See Map.

visibility as well as minister to Catholic inhabitants. For instance, de Paul sent three priests to Montauban in May 1652, on the request of Bishop Murviel, who had periodically welcomed the missionaries to his diocese since 1630 when he met de Paul in Paris.[21]

De Paul's personal ties to prelates also helped him to institutionalize the Lazarists' presence in the south-west, specifically in dioceses like Agde and Narbonne where the Fouquet brothers were bishops. However, personal intimacies between bishops in the region were crucial to this process too, even if not entirely profitable. In this type of interaction, Bishop Alain de Solminihac of Cahors proved a local asset for de Paul because of his close links to him and to other prelates in the south-west. Solminihac was not a disciple of Saint-Lazare and, unlike a number of other bishops, he did not choose to hold his episcopal consecration there in 1637.[22] But the strength of his friendship with de Paul should not be underestimated. They initially became well acquainted in the late 1620s, while Solminihac resided in Paris.[23] By the time that he travelled to take up his appointment to Cahors in 1636 the Lazarists had already been carrying out missions there for a number of years for his predecessor, Pierre Habert de Montfort, and he continued the arrangement for a few years before he and de Paul signed a contract allowing the Lazarists to manage the seminary that he had just begun.

The principal bond that glued Solminihac and de Paul together was not missions but their shared concern for improving the standard of clergy. Their missives, usually familiar and matter-of-fact in tone and language, are packed with exchanges on clerics and strategies for clerical reform which reveal that they valued each other's opinions, assumed that the frank information they offered would prove useful, and that their requests for help would be greeted with a wish to assist. There is little that can be defined openly as spiritual direction or exhortation in their communications, yet however practical in character these were, they produced and then sustained a relationship of mutual trust and admiration for piety. Moreover, even without explicitly exhorting or sharing spiritual revelations, the duo spurred each other on to further endeavour. For instance, in the 1630s, they improved their rapport by investigating the possibility that the abbeys of Foix and Pebrac might be united with that of Chancelade, where

[21] Abelly, *Vie*, ii, 49; AN, S6708 (3 September 1660) and MM 536 (5 September 1660); *CCD*, 4: 383, de Paul to Lambert aux Couteaux, 17 May 1652.

In Montpellier, another diocese with a large Huguenot population, de Paul explored the possibility of establishing a seminary with Bishop Bosquet, and dispatched a priest and brother as scouts there in mid-1659. Over the course of nine months, the proposed seminary failed to materialize, because the bishop (often absent from his diocese) did not provide financial support anywhere near to answering the needs of a seminary, and because it proved difficult to attract potential recruits. As a result, de Paul quietly pulled his men out of the diocese by July 1660, on the pretext that they were needed in Marseille and Narbonne, and the negotiations ended. Montpellier should not therefore be counted, as it often is, amongst the houses established during de Paul's superior generalship. See *CCD*, 8, for letters between de Paul and Firmin Get on this failed venture, and AN, S6707, for a short note on the matter, dated 1670.

[22] This was held instead at the abbatial church of Sainte-Geneviève-du-Mont in Paris. Solminihac undertook his preparatory retreat with the Cistercians nearby: Petot, *Solminihac*, i, 203–4.

[23] Sol (ed.), *Solminihac*, 90, Jean Jaubert de Barrault to Alain de Solminihac, 8 May 1630.

Solminihac was abbot. De Paul acted as an intermediary, recommending the young commendatory abbot of Pebrac, one Jean-Jacques Olier, and the commendatory abbot of Saint-Volusien-de-Foix, Étienne Caulet, to Solminihac. Both were anxious to place their abbeys under the reforming authority of Chancelade, although neither hope came to pass once members of the Congregation of France were alerted and raised their objections.[24] Solminihac then drew de Paul to his side in his fight to prevent the Congregation from swallowing Chancelade itself, inviting him to participate in a conference in October 1637 that persuaded *Genevévian* Charles Faure to declare that the monks of Chancelade would not be forced into such a 'union'. Subsequently, when the Congregation reneged on its promise, de Paul undermined its ambition by encouraging Solminihac in his hopes of establishing a congregation 'of Chancelade', and advising him to seek Roman approval for the initiative in order to ensure that it was confirmed at the highest ecclesiastical level. He even proposed a wording for the petition that would implore the pope to copperfasten the abbot's spiritual authority over the three houses, and over those who would join the congregation in the future.[25]

As Solminihac became an 'elder' figure of the episcopate during his two decades in Cahors, he acted as a mentor to less experienced bishops in the south-west, especially to his successor, Sévin, whilst he was bishop of adjoining Sarlat, and Brandon of nearby Périgueux. In this capacity, he was in a position to champion initiatives and organizations of which he approved. At times, he worked on individuals, for example, proposing to the incoming bishop of Clermont, Louis d'Estaing, that he invite de Paul's men to run the seminary that he planned to open, although there is no evidence that Estaing actually followed through on his advice.[26] But, amongst some, his influence was such that his own example in patronizing de Paul's association was a substantial incentive to them to do the same. Solminihac took the novice prelate Brandon under his wing after he arrived in Périgueux in 1648, and frequently counselled him on governmental decisions. When Brandon sought advice on the practicalities of establishing a seminary in 1650, Solminihac was in an excellent position to encourage him to choose the Lazarists, and was fulsome in his praise of 'the good that [de Paul's] men have accomplished in our seminary and which has spread throughout the province'.[27]

Solminihac was also efficacious in promoting de Paul's group in a collective setting, and particularly in helping Tuesday Conference prelates to maintain contact with each other and de Paul once they dispersed from Paris to distant sees in the south-west. In 1649, he invited four neighbours, Caulet, Pavillon,

[24] Petot, *Solminihac*, i, 178–83.

[25] The affair rumbled on for many years afterwards. From 1647, conflict focused on Rome, where Solminihac sent representatives of the monks to plead. During the 1650s, de Paul had little more to do with the quarrel, which was eventually resolved in 1670: *CCD*, 3: 225, de Paul to Alain de Solminihac, 30 July 1647; Petot, *Solminihac*, i, 207–12, 449–501.

[26] *CCD*, 4: 141, Alain de Solminihac to de Paul, 4 January 1651.

[27] *CCD*, 3: 340, Alain de Solminihac to de Paul, 15 July 1648; Sol (ed.), *Solminihac*, 428, Philibert de Brandon to Alain de Solminihac, 28 December 1650. Solminihac sent copies of the act of establishment and letters patent for his seminary to Brandon when requested around Christmas 1650, in order to help him to model his own on that of Cahors: *CCD*, 4: 141, Alain de Solminihac to de Paul, 4 January 1651.

Brandon, and Sévin (all members of the company), to a conference in Mercuès. Though the assembly was not an official micro-meeting of the Tuesday Conferences group it certainly gathered prelates who held a common interest in pursuing excellence in their vocations, and esteemed both Solminihac and de Paul. The reception of the latter's priorities in clerical formation was fully apparent in the conference proceedings. The participants made concentrated reflections on the character and purpose of their episcopal vocation, and the ways in which these could inform their behaviour most beneficially, as well as on a range of pastoral issues, including the provision of suitably trained parochial clergy for their dioceses.[28] Shortly after they dispersed, Solminihac wrote to inform de Paul that they had all concurred that, should they found diocesan seminaries, they would entrust them to his association. Solminihac confessed that he had prompted this, but all had proved receptive to the idea.[29]

Fulfilling it proved more difficult. Most of the bishops encountered financial obstacles that prevented them from doing so, and ultimately only Brandon was able to offer de Paul's men the promised opportunity.[30] Even so, the meeting forms an illuminating case study of the manner in which verbal recommendation from a respected figure within the episcopate could lead to new opportunities. Equally, however, de Paul's effort to respond to Brandon's invitation revealed that it took more than this to ensure the success of a venture. He sent two Lazarists to the diocese in autumn 1650, but teething problems over the number of priests needed and the difficulty of funding the institution in a diocese with quite a modest income of 18,000 *livres* annually emerged immediately. Then, a more damaging issue of principle loomed.[31] Shortly after the seminary opened, Brandon, prompted by his brother Balthasar who had moved to Périgueux to act as his *grand vicaire*, began to doubt the wisdom of allowing the Lazarists to manage it at all, with the result that he withdrew his support for them. Soon afterwards, he appointed a local society of priests to care for the seminary.[32]

Rather than question the bishop's decision, de Paul simply chose to accept it, although it is clear that his profession of submission masked his confusion about the reasons why Brandon had made it only six months after the first Lazarists arrived. De Paul possibly became more perplexed when Solminihac wrote to explain the change of heart after seeking in vain to convince Brandon to restore

[28] BN, Ms Fr 14428(i); Forrestal, *Fathers*, 175–6.

[29] *CCD*, 3: 517, Alain de Solminihac to de Paul, 15 December 1649.

[30] Pavillon had planned to open a small seminary run by Lazarists in Alet diocese in 1639. Coste assumes that the two missionaries that de Paul dispatched there established one, but there is no evidence to support this conjecture, and they seem to have just performed missions. In any case, de Paul withdrew them from Alet in October 1642, because Pavillon proved unable to furnish sufficient financial resources and housing for even a tiny community. Like Montauban, Alet should therefore not be counted amongst the Congregation's houses of this period: *CCD*, 2: 219–22, Nicolas Pavillon to de Paul, 20 October 1641; *CCD*, 2: 338–40, de Paul to Jean Brunet and Étienne Blatiron, 8 October 1642; *CCD*, 2: 340–1, Nicolas Pavillon to de Paul, October 1642; Coste, *Saint*, i, 550.

[31] Bergin, *French Episcopate*, 111.

[32] This group had gathered under the stewardship of Jean de La Cropte de Chantérac in 1646: Tamizey de Larroque (ed.), *Livre-Journal de Pierre de Bessot*, 105.

his men. The informant revealed that the bishop's brother had persuaded him that it would be better to install secular diocesan priests to administer the seminary, because they would accede more readily to his episcopal discipline. He noted ruefully that Balthaser de Brandon was primed with a copy of his close friend Olier's 'Projet de l'établissement d'un séminaire', which the Sulpician founder had recently presented to the Assembly of Clergy and which was now making its way into the sight of bishops throughout France.[33] Solminihac was summarily dismissive of the practicality of this blueprint for seminary management ('There is a vast difference between practice and theory'), and was disappointed that his colleague, less experienced and less discerning of the pitfalls involved in training clergy, had apparently fallen for it.[34]

Why had Brandon done so? It was most likely because Olier's vision represented the pinnacle of the French school of priesthood's promotion of episcopal status in the French church, and the 'Projet' offered a detailed and coherent description of this in microcosm. A seminary was, Olier proclaimed, 'filled with the spirit and grace of holy Prelates' who were their 'true and unique [superiors]'. This opinion was based on his positing of an intimate union between bishops and priests, which established the latter in a state of reliance on the former, their hierarchical superiors and the most godlike of any other members of the ecclesiastical hierarchy. Bishops nurtured the souls of their clergy as compassionate fathers, and led them as leaders and 'kings' through a plenitude of spirit, or a flowing of grace, which animated them with the virtues necessary to their state. As the possessor of a uniquely vivifying or perfecting spirit that he communicated to his priests, the bishop was distinguished from them both in terms of jurisdiction and order; he was thus the true superior of the seminary, the figure chosen by God to restore the priesthood to the perfection from which it had drifted in the contemporary church.[35]

This potent vision of episcopal supremacy was heady stuff for prelates exposed to it, and its impact was widely felt within the episcopate. De Paul was not equipped to compete with Olier's public and sophisticated reflection, which was as much a solicitation of episcopal patronage for the Sulpicians as an exercise in theological praxis. Having realized its benefit when presenting successive petitions to Rome for the approval of the Congregation of the Mission, de Paul could certainly never be accused of failing to stress his and his Congregation's obedience to episcopal authority and reverence for the elevated status of bishops whenever possible.[36] But he shied away from such ingratiation in print, partially on the grounds that good

[33] Brandon had been closely acquainted with Olier since they were ordained together in 1633, and was amongst his first companions in Vaugirard: Faillon, *Olier*, i, 358–9.

[34] *CCD*, 4: 137, de Paul to Alain de Solminihac, 31 December 1650; *CCD*, 4: 174, de Paul to Philibert de Brandon, 1 April 1651; *CCD*, 4: 175, same to same, 1 April 1651; *CCD*, 4: 189, Alain de Solminihac to de Paul, 26 April 1651.

[35] A copy of Olier's 'Projet' is printed in Faillon, *Olier*, iii, 551–78. See also Forrestal, *Fathers*, 59–65.

[36] See, for example, letters to Jeanne de Chantal and Bishop de Bonzi of Béziers, in which de Paul reiterated in even more categorical terms the sentiments that he expressed in the second and third petitions he sent to Rome: *CCD*, 1: 297, de Paul to Clément de Bonzi, September/October 1635; *CCD*, 1: 553, de Paul to Jeanne de Chantal, 14 July 1639.

works 'sooner or later speak a much more favourable language than anything done for one's own ostentation and show'.[37] Moreover, he assumed that competition with fellow churchmen over the spoils of clerical training was unseemly and undesirable, especially when the rival was such a close associate as Olier. Indeed, Olier and Balthasar de Brandon were founding members of the Tuesday Conferences, while Philibert de Brandon was also a member, thus making the company a common factor in the formation of their relationships with de Paul during the 1630s and 1640s.[38] But the unhappy outcome of this affair provided alarming testament that while spiritually gratifying relations might open doors into dioceses, they did not ensure that they remained ajar afterwards.

IV

De Paul's hasty recall of his men from Périgueux offered a salutary lesson in the troubles and sacrifices involved in preserving harmonious and communicative relationships with patron bishops. Even the firmest of relations founded on the intimate conversations of the Tuesday Company, and a common interest in cultivating the ecclesiastical 'spirit' it cherished, did not necessarily mitigate against these, for once a cleric of the Conferences attained high office, his relationship with his director altered. As a new bishop asserted his diocesan authority, de Paul became reliant on his favour if the Lazarists were to advance into his diocese. The power of patronage was not wholly tipped against de Paul as client, of course, for he could provide useful services for them. Yet, he had to tread extremely carefully in ensuring that he responded to the wishes, even whims, of bishops without prejudicing the Lazarists' core principles of ministry.

To do so, of course, de Paul had to do all he could to ensure that those he sent to speak for him were competent to do so. As a preliminary to investigating the interaction between the wishes of bishops and those of de Paul, it is useful to identify the type of man that de Paul felt would defend his vision of the Lazarist ethos and activities when he was not present. Typically, this man was a house superior, the choice of whom de Paul claimed as his exclusive right.[39] But he did not repeatedly choose superiors from a confined set of candidates who had years of experience on missions or retreats or who had already served as superior in a house. For instance, their lack of experience did not render the 'greenhorns' Guillaume Gallais and Louis Thibault unsuitable for promotion in de Paul's eyes, since he appointed both to supervise the new houses in Sedan and Saintes only two years after they were ordained.[40] Generally, however, most of the founding superiors that de Paul chose had a lot of 'in-house' experience under their belt before appointment,

[37] *CCD*, 2: 311, de Paul to Bernard Codoing, 11 July 1642.
[38] Joseph Bergin writes that Balthazar de Brandon was a Lazarist, but this is categorically not the case: Bergin, *French Episcopate*, 586.
[39] *CCD*, 2: 432–3, de Paul to Bernard Codoing, 15 March 1643.
[40] *Notices sur les prêtres, clercs et frères*, i, *passim*.

averaging eight years each (they also had an average age of 35 on promotion).[41] But few had gained equivalent pastoral or administrative skills before their recruitment, and only seven were ordained before they joined. Further, de Paul did not allow any of them to make a career of the office; he assigned only four to the position of founding superior in a second house, and none of these served a third term anywhere.[42]

It might be expected that de Paul would pick many of the first superiors of houses founded in the late 1630s and early 1640s from the men who joined the Congregation in its early years, trusting that the substantial knowledge that they had accumulated of Lazarist customs and rules would be of particular pertinence in a foundation that was finding its feet. But these were also men with whom he had lived and worked for years, so he knew the frailties as well as the strengths of their personalities. As a result, he decided that only two of the twenty men who joined the community between 1625 and 1630 were fitted to the post, François du Coudray and Lambert aux Couteaux. Of the two, the second proved so capable that de Paul subsequently asked him to manage other houses. He represented the 'type' of missionary that de Paul promoted to the role of superior, having spotted the potential to fill a position in which sensitivity to the demands of directing a resident community, diplomatic skills, and administrative proficiency were essential. Indeed, Lambert aux Couteaux was the man that de Paul entrusted with the onerous task of supervising the foundation of the Lazarists' first house outside Paris, as well as those of Richelieu and Sedan, houses of ministerial or royal origin. The pattern of his appointments reveals that de Paul identified his administrative and supervisory potential at an early stage of his career, and placed him in key positions where he could learn the ropes, gather information for his superior general, represent his wishes, and troubleshoot problems that threatened. Indeed, Lambert aux Couteaux specialized as a 'scout', sent to foray in new, risky, and complex environments, where diplomatic and administrative acumen were amongst the premium qualities required.[43]

When de Paul did not pick the right men, there were unfortunate repercussions, sometimes contained within the walls of a house but at other times spilling over. In disputes which involved outsiders, the superior's unwillingness or inability to balance submission to the authority of his superior general with proactive and

[41] There were a few extreme exceptions. Gerald Brin, for instance, did not become superior of Meaux until 1658. But he had previously developed a distinguished profile of service, having directed the seminary in Le Mans, travelled on mission to Ireland (1646–52) and for a short time to England (1656), carried out missions in south-west and east France, and acted as superior at Notre-Dame de La Rose and Troyes (1652–4, 1657–8): Forrestal, 'Irish Entrants'.

[42] Lambert aux Couteaux (superior in Toul and Richelieu), Pierre du Chesne (superior in Crécy and Agde), François Dufestel (superior in Cahors and Marseille), and Guillaume Gallais (superior in Sedan and Le Mans). This information is gathered from multiple documents, mainly contracts and correspondence, as well as *Notices sur les prêtres, clercs et frères*, i.

[43] Lambert aux Couteaux also acted as de Paul's assistant at Saint-Lazare in the 1640s and 1650s, visited a number of provincial houses, supervised Saint-Charles and Bons-Enfants seminaries, and headed the first community in Poland, where he died in 1653: *Notices sur les prêtres, clercs et frères*, i, *passim* and especially 109.

independent action caused disruption locally, but it also damaged the Congregation as a whole, since each house represented it. In such cases, de Paul's name could be associated with and even tarnished by them because he was ultimately responsible for the actions of his officers. Consequently, he emphasized the necessity of direct and regular consultation between superior general and house superiors, assuming that the deference that this paid to the hierarchy of oversight would ensure uniformity in Lazarist practices. Consultation acknowledged a line of management between centre and periphery, between superior general and superior, which would ensure that individual communities did not function as independent entities. Tactically too, it often functioned as a means to buy a superior time and to harness support from de Paul when pressurized by forces outside the Congregation itself, especially episcopal.[44]

One purported stain on de Paul's sanctity later caught the attention of papal officials during the investigative processes for his beatification and canonization during the early eighteenth century, and originated from this issue. This was the row over the Lazarists' acquisition of the former Benedictine abbey of Saint-Méen in Saint-Malo diocese in 1645. De Paul's fatal errors in this case were his disastrous choice of superior, and his inability to control him from distant Paris once he took up position. Superior Jean Bourdet lurched between a fear that he could not protect his men and a refusal to recognize that aggressive conduct exacerbated his community's problems, and he failed to heed de Paul's advice to avoid direct confrontation. He inflamed the Benedictines with his decision to refurbish the abbey because they classified it as a destruction of their sacred property; he also encouraged his confreres to barricade themselves into the seminary with ladders, carts, planks, benches, and anything else on which they could lay hands when confronted by the troop of hostile monks and parliamentary officers sent to expel them in July 1646.[45] In desperation, de Paul eventually replaced the impetuous Bourdet with the more diplomatic Bernard Codoing in 1647. But he had been unwise to ignore his own initial reservations about the shortcomings in Bourdet's spirit of obedience when he sent him to Saint-Méen.[46]

Eighty years later, the Roman investigators pored over de Paul's conduct, pitting the charge of sinful worldly ambition against veracity of virtue and integrity of conduct. That there might be justification for doing so lay in Abelly's conspicuous

[44] From the early 1640s, de Paul also had 'Visitors' travel to the houses in the provinces to identify problems and good practice, and to offer supportive recommendations to their colleagues for the future. He still did not, however, backtrack on his insistence that house superiors should consult with him regularly, and this remained the primary way in which he attempted to exert his influence over their decision-making. For further discussion of de Paul's relations with confreres, and his efforts to maintain authoritative oversight, see Forrestal, 'Vincent de Paul as Mentor', and Forrestal, 'Principles and Practices of Government'.

[45] De Paul, on the warning of Antoine Portail, who visited Saint-Méen in mid-1646, admonished Bourdet for his inability 'to curb the audacity of certain members of the community', and foresaw that his failure to control them, whether because he was unwilling or unable, would escalate unrest: *CCD*, 2: 668–9, de Paul to Antoine Portail, 22 July 1646; *CCD*, 2: 671, same to Jean Bourdet, 22 July 1646.

[46] *CCD*, 3: 41, de Paul to Jean Bourdet, 1 September 1646; *CCD*, 3: 115, de Paul to Antoine Portail, 10 December 1646; *CCD*, 3: 670, de Paul to Jean Bourdet, 22 July 1646.

silence about the sorry affair, the notoriety, indeed memory, of which he evidently hoped would fade. In addition, erudite Benedictines involved in it had publicized it through appeals to Rome in the later 1650s, and had left manuscript histories detailing their case against de Paul and the Lazarists. These placed a question mark over the purity of de Paul's intentions and actions in the affair, and sought to tar and feather him, and those under his authority, for the sin of ambition. To be fair, however, de Paul did not actively orchestrate the violent confrontations that broke out. Furthermore, he and his confreres were, unwittingly at first, caught in a contest that went far beyond the question of their rightful possession of the former abbey, in which they were treated as pawns by three parties engaged in a battle for supremacy. The dispute was typical in some ways of the many governmental fights between bishops and religious orders in French dioceses during this period, with a prelate determined to ensure that his authority was not undermined by independently minded monks who were supported by a *parlement* keen to assert its right to intervene in an ecclesiastical matter.

The bishop in question was Achille de Harlay de Sancy, an Oratorian whom de Paul had probably known for many years by the 1640s, and who was also commendatory abbot of Saint-Méen. There he decided to establish a diocesan seminary under the care of the Lazarists (after his own congregation refused it), and signed an agreement to this effect with de Paul in 1645. The Lazarists took responsibility for maintaining the popular shrine of the sixth-century St Méen, which was associated with the miraculous cure of psora (a skin disease known locally as the *mal de Saint-Méen*).[47] When news broke of the deal, there was a flurry of protests as the Benedictine Congregation of St Maur persuaded the *parlement* in Rennes to force the reinstalment of the monks in their former home. In turn, Harlay appealed to the superior authority of the royal council, banking on his nephew, Nicolas de Villeroy (recently appointed governor to Louis XIV), to achieve a favourable hearing there. The council duly issued an *arrêt*, to which the *parlement* and monks signified their resistance by expelling the Lazarists (even throwing one in prison for a few days), and installing a number of monks in July and August. The conflict became even more heated when the bishop asked the lieutenant-general of Brittany to eject the monks with a force of fifteen soldiers, and procured a second *arrêt* in January 1647. At this point, the *parlement* and monks finally conceded, and de Paul sought to prevent new opposition emerging from any quarter in the future by seeking papal confirmation of the union. After investigation, Alexander VII issued a bull to this effect in 1658.[48]

Throughout the dispute, the Benedictines painted the Congregation of the Mission as an outsider, an intruder, and an unknown new entity in local affairs, which brought 'scandal and disorder' to local ecclesiastical life. They fully implicated its superior general in this, by suggesting that he had sanctioned the actions

[47] ACMP, 'Dossier Saint-Méen' (14 July 1645). See also Appendix 1.

[48] The various stages of the conflict are evidenced in documents in: AN, S6711 and E1691, fo. 15r; BN, Ms Fr, 19831, fo. 135r; BSG, Ms 701, fos 24r–28r. For the bull of union, see *CCD*, 3: 111, de Paul to Jean Dehorgny, 8 November 1646; *CCD*, 13a: 423–9; AN, S6711 (3 April 1658).

that the Lazarists had taken in Saint-Méen. For instance, hoping to capitalize on the attachment of local people to a traditional place of devotion, the Benedictine Morel alleged that Bourdet, with de Paul's approval, had stripped the monastery of its treasures, thus desecrating the hallowed site for material ends, and placing in jeopardy the ability of future generations of Breton Catholics to access the blessings of pilgrimage. In their supplications, the Benedictines played on the traditional suspicions of Breton *parlementaires* regarding infringements on their legal prerogatives by external jurisdictional bodies, arguing that they should judge their claim to the abbey, and that they alone held the right to permit a new religious congregation to reside in the province.[49]

For his part, de Paul twice met with a delegation of monks at Saint-Lazare, insisting on both occasions that the transfer of the monastery was for the 'good and service of the church . . . and the greatest glory of God'. Such confidence, also expressed in letters to Bourdet and the chief justice of the *parlement*, Claude de Marbeuf, accorded neatly with his belief that his Congregation was the instrument that God had chosen to serve his people, and he was adamant that it would restore standards of piety which had collapsed in the area through pastoral neglect. Yet, as the affair intensified, de Paul appeared to realize that the Congregation was in danger of being trapped in an injurious dispute largely not of its own making, and he was wise enough to the rivalries involved to observe that the *parlementaires* hated the bishop because he had insulted them by having recourse to the royal council for approval of the abbey's transfer.[50] To avoid collateral damage, de Paul then sought to distance the Lazarists from the conflict, though without sacrificing his right to explain their stance, itself a form of secondary intervention. In a bid to deflect the shame associated with pursuing temporal possessions legally, he insisted to his opponents that the Lazarists would be glad to surrender the abbey if it were possible. Twinning the asset of obedience with that of detachment from worldly ambition, he placed all responsibility for the dispute on Harlay's shoulders: 'If the matter depended on us, we would recall our men, but it is the Bishop's affair.'[51]

In defending his position and the actions of the Lazarists in Saint-Méen in general, de Paul managed to anticipate the queries of the Roman investigators decades later, who accepted his contention that he had sent his men to Saint-Méen simply to restore discipline inside the monastery's walls, and practices of devotion amongst the faithful outside them. They were further convinced because he had legitimized his actions according to governmental and spiritual assumptions with which these early eighteenth-century churchmen could not find fault: deference to episcopal authority and detachment from worldly values.[52] De Paul's resort to these was not simply a ruse to manipulate public perception of his conduct; they

[49] BN, Ms Fr 19831. See also Ropartz, 'Dom Germain Morel'.

[50] *CCD*, 3: 52, de Paul to Boniface Nouelly, 7 September 1646.

[51] *CCD*, 3: 33, de Paul to Antoine Portail, 25 August 1646; *CCD*, 3: 41, de Paul to Jean Bourdet, September 1646; *CCD*, 3: 52, de Paul to Claude de Marbeuf, 8 September 1646; Guilloreau (ed.), *Mémoires de R. P. Dom Bernard Audebert*, 47.

[52] ACMP, 'Processus S. C. Rituum in causa beatificationis venerabilis servi Dei Vincentii a Paulo', ii, 69–72; *Sacra Rituum Congregatione Eminentissimo, & Reverendissimo D. Card de La Tremoille Parisien,*

were fundamental elements of his approach to missionary work. Moreover, he was technically correct in asserting that the bishop was the principal protagonist in the action against the religious and the *parlement*, for it was he who formally pursued the case. Even so, there is no doubt that de Paul abetted him by maintaining his community in the former abbey, defending their possession of it to all comers, and successfully enrooting his association in his diocese. As the bishop gained, so too did the Lazarists, of course, because de Paul safeguarded a new ministerial stronghold in the region and, as noted above, it acted as a point of entry to Tréguier a few years later.

V

In the Saint-Méen affair, the bishop, the superior general, and the superior were at least in agreement about the desired result of the conflict, if not the means to achieve it. This was not invariably the case; at times de Paul found himself in debates with bishops which not only tried his patience but jeopardized connections that he had nurtured over the years. These should not be dismissed as merely isolated or petty spats, for the issues at stake were fundamental to the definition of the Congregation's relations with prelates and to the shape of its government in the future. They centred on the terms on which de Paul's men operated in dioceses, and threatened precedents that would return to haunt the Lazarists if they were permitted to alter or destroy uniformity in governmental procedures or diminish the authority of the superior general. Although difficulties arose a number of times, they were most common during the years immediately subsequent to the foundation of a house, when the community was bedding down and the parameters of its existence in the diocese seemed either ill defined or open to reassessment. Outlining each instance individually would be a vast enterprise that would serve little purpose for a study of this nature, and would reach beyond its confines in any case. However, three significant case studies enable an illuminating analysis of the manner in which de Paul dealt with these tests of strength.

In principle, house superiors were answerable to de Paul on matters internal to the community, including financial affairs. But the success of their placement was subject to their ability to satisfy both their superior general and their bishop, without overstepping the line of jurisdiction that separated them. De Paul presciently warned the first superior that he dispatched to Cahors in 1643 that prelates were jealous of their authority and keen to ensure that the Lazarists remained dependent on them.[53] It is unlikely that any bishop tried to intervene in their internal affairs because he misunderstood their claim to autonomy. However, it was normally only religious orders that defended their liberty on this basis. In the eyes of some prelates, the Lazarists were secular clergy first and foremost, and members

109–14, 285–6, 338–40; *Sacra Rituum Congregation Eminentissimo, & Reverendissimo D. Card. Paulutio Parisien*, 206–18.

[53] *CCD*, 2: 462, de Paul to Bernard Codoing, 11 September 1643.

of a congregation second, so should therefore be subject to the same episcopal supervision as any other secular cleric in the diocese.

To safeguard both cordial relations and Lazarist liberty, de Paul implored his superiors to obey their bishops, but to express their discontent and even disagreement with him when necessary. When they did so, however, they did not always receive a warm reception, and, in instances that invoked a matter of principle, de Paul felt compelled to step in. In Agde and Narbonne, he came within a hair's breadth of undoing the good will that he had first forged with the bishop, François Fouquet, during the 1630s. Fouquet transferred to Agde in 1646 from Bayonne, before being promoted to Narbonne where he acted as coadjutor from 1656 and archbishop from 1659.[54] When he decided to establish seminaries, he gravitated to his old director's association, with the result that de Paul sent Pierre du Chesne to open a new establishment in Agde in February 1654, and Georges Des Jardins to Narbonne for the same purpose in September 1659.[55] In both locations, however, the superiors quickly ran into difficulties, some of which related to staff shortages caused by poor health amongst confreres. More acute headaches arose, however, over issues of principle, arising from the differing visions that their superior general and their bishop had for the structure of the seminaries. Shortly before he died, du Chesne delightedly informed his comrade Charles Ozenne that he had overseen the opening of a diocesan seminary, and was awaiting the arrival of masons to construct a new building to house its growing numbers.[56] But just over a year later, this expectation lay in tatters, as his successor, Jean-Jacques Mugnier, found himself in conflict with the bishop and diocesan officials. Inferring that relations between officials and the community had deteriorated drastically, de Paul ordered Mugnier to refrain from expressing any discontentment with the situation 'from the pulpit or elsewhere'. To smother the flames of disagreement, de Paul forbade his successor, Antoine Durand, to preach at all before local clergy, after they took his words to mean that the Congregation held 'a grudge against them'. At one point, de Paul even entertained the thought that he might withdraw his men permanently from the diocese.[57]

What specific issue prompted the deterioration in relations in Agde? Narbonne provides the explanation, for Fouquet brought to the negotiations there precisely the same issue that dogged his house in Agde. On promotion, he asked de Paul to establish a community, but the proposed terms of ministry were still not settled before de Paul's death.[58] Even so, two months before de Paul passed away, Fouquet issued an act of establishment for his seminary, and assigned its care and the parish

[54] Bergin, *French Episcopate*, 626.

[55] *CCD*, 5: 101, de Paul to Jacques Chiroye, 8 March 1654; *CCD*, 8: 144, same to François Fouquet, 12 September 1659.

[56] Archives of the Congregation of the Mission, Krakow, 'Autographes de Saint Vincent et de ses premiers compagnons', no. 156, Pierre du Chesne to Charles Ozenne, 8 June 1654.

[57] *CCD*, 5: 399, de Paul to Jean-Jacques Mugnier, 9 July 1655; *CCD*, 6: 344, de Paul to Antoine Durand, 15 June 1657.

[58] It was not until a year after de Paul's death that his successor René Alméras and Fouquet finally concurred on a revised act of establishment, which answered concerns that he had about proposed terms: AN, S6708 (10 September 1661).

of Maiour to the Lazarists.[59] Then, on 26 August, he wrote testily to de Paul about the sluggish pace of developments subsequently. He complained that he had purchased a house for the community at great expense, in the belief that de Paul was willing to establish a foundation that would endure after both their deaths. But de Paul's promise of two priests and a brother had not yet been met, and meant that the mission and visitation that the bishop had planned in anticipation of their assistance would now be thrown into confusion. Fouquet went on to identify a second and greater source of vexation, of sufficient significance, he asserted, to break their deal, and even ruin their friendship. He accused de Paul of dragging his feet in agreeing to his proposal to unite the seminary to the parish, leaving him to conclude that his partner was not as committed to the enterprise as he was.[60] De Paul's attitude was baffling to Fouquet because, as he reminded him, he had never raised a single objection to a similar union in Agde.[61]

In reply, de Paul apologized for testing the archbishop's forbearance, and blamed his tardiness on the restrictions of age that plagued 'a wretched old man', who '[blushed] with shame' as he offered assurances that he was making strenuous efforts to send men to Narbonne.[62] But he was just dissembling. Neither old age nor objection to the union was responsible for his slow-footedness in committing to Fouquet's scheme. Rather, de Paul was apprehensive about other organizational issues, which related to the balance of authority between superior general and prelate. He had already raised the first of these in Agde, and it was this which had caused the breach between the superiors and the bishop's officials there. Without fixity of tenure in its seminary, de Paul knew that the Lazarists would be at the mercy of episcopal whim. Consequently, in asking Durand to speak on his behalf to Fouquet about the seminary in 1656, he had underlined heavily that the act of establishment then being composed should specify that the Lazarists were given the perpetual direction of the seminary, because this had not been expressly set out in the initial contract that Durand's predecessor, du Chesne, had signed on his instruction in 1654. In what reads as an oblique reference to du Chesne's subsequent troubles, de Paul warned Durand not to undertake anything without informing him and seeking his advice, for those who had earlier acted independently had brought trouble and embarrassment to the Congregation. He also insisted that Durand should hold his tongue when he felt the urge to complain about the situation outside of official meetings.[63]

For Narbonne, de Paul had additional concerns, as he was unhappy with two provisions concerning financial management and personnel that the bishop had inserted into the draft act of establishment. These, he contended, contradicted Lazarist 'customs'. They were actually specific expressions of a crucial maxim that de Paul had defended since the foundation of the Lazarists thirty years before:

[59] AN, S6708 (6 July 1660).

[60] *CCD*, 8: 478, François Fouquet to de Paul, 26 August 1660.

[61] *CCD*, 8: 114, de Paul to Antoine Durand, 29 August 1659.

[62] *CCD*, 8: 383, de Paul to François Fouquet, 1660.

[63] *CCD*, 6: 78, de Paul to Antoine Durand, 1656; *CCD*, 6: 344, same to same, 15 June 1657; *CCD*, 11: 314.

the distinction of jurisdictions, which freed the Congregation from outside, meaning episcopal, interference.[64] Thus, he informed Fouquet that he had refused to accept the priory of Saint-Lazare in 1632 until the archbishop of Paris agreed to surrender his claim to oversight of the Lazarists' financial affairs. When other bishops claimed the right to scrutinize, he had refused, because the concession first gained for Paris was universally applicable. Now, confronted with the same demand yet again, de Paul made it quite plain that he was not about to abandon the habit of a lifetime. Secondly, de Paul told Fouquet that he could not claim 'the authority to dismiss from . . . [a] seminary any members of our Company' that he did not wish to employ, and no other bishop had ever been able to do so. This was because the power to move Lazarists lay exclusively in the hands of their superior general, and to allow a bishop to intervene would be a major 'infringement' on his rights of jurisdiction and the prerogatives of the Congregation.[65] It could concurrently allow a bishop to dominate a community by rooting out those who did not acquiesce to his every wish, even when they acted in obedience to the orders of their superior general. In this case, the house superiors would be caught between competing authorities, over issues to which they had historically answered to de Paul.

In an ecclesiastical environment increasingly characterized by the efforts of bishops like Fouquet to exercise jurisdictional power over all of the clergy in their dioceses, it was vital that de Paul do all he could to protect the Lazarists' institutional autonomy. To do so with a bishop such as Fouquet required considerable delicacy of argument, in which de Paul situated his intransigence on liberty in internal affairs alongside deferent promises of submission in all else. But, he mused, if he could not inspire the likes of Fouquet to accept his views when he elucidated them candidly and sincerely, they would not be won over either 'by trying to get them to adhere to our views and trying to get the better of them'.[66] As a result, in Narbonne, he and Fouquet reached an impasse in their negotiations, which remained in place until de Paul won his posthumous victory in late 1661.[67]

VI

Was de Paul steadfast in ensuring that the Lazarist rules of operation withstood alteration or wholesale overhaul by patron bishops? It may appear surprising that the answer to this query should be sought in one of his most enduring and productive relationships with a prelate, for their mutual respect and common zeal for clerical reform suggest that de Paul and Solminihac of Cahors diverged on very little. But while this was certainly true in regard to objectives, it was not so clear cut for means. As superior general of a congregation and bishop of a diocese

[64] *CCD*, 8: 538, de Paul to François Fouquet, 17 September 1660; *CCD*, 13a: 197–8. See also, *CCD*, 1: 51–2.

[65] *CCD*, 1: 51–2.

[66] De Paul recalled that he had learned this lesson from Pierre de Bérulle many years before: *CCD*, 8: 224, de Paul to Pierre Cabel, 17 December 1659.

[67] AN, S6708 (10 September 1661).

respectively, they viewed the issue of reform from distinct vantage points, and even when united on fundamental goals, their individual priorities and terms of engagement made it possible that they would differ in implementing them. In Cahors, de Paul struggled to reconcile Solminihac's ambitions and *modus operandi* with his own understanding of the structure and character of the services that the Lazarists offered. But, uniquely amongst his encounters with patron bishops, he made every effort to accommodate rather than dissatisfy him, despite their issues of dispute being similar in nature to those that cropped up elsewhere. It was not simply that de Paul bowed to Solminihac's episcopal stature, for he was not afraid to withstand autocratic behaviour from other bishops. However, his bond with Solminihac was firmer and more personal than with any other prelate. It was not founded merely on his acute awareness that the bishop provided a new ministerial vineyard for the Lazarists, since all patron bishops did so. He relished the fidelity to reform that they shared in their letters and their collaborations. He also appreciated intensely the holiness of a bishop whose soul he thought intimately linked to God. Just as importantly, Solminihac was his close friend, and de Paul was reluctant to deny him any service that might assist him in his quest to serve God in his see, even if this meant adapting, or compromising, his own and the Lazarists' interests.[68] First, as a result, de Paul allowed Soliminihac freedom in deciding the composition of the Lazarist community, which impinged on his rights as superior general, and broke the jurisdictional boundary preventing episcopal interference in internal Lazarist matters. Second, in response to Solminihac's wishes, and contravening his own opinion, de Paul set a precedent with long-term reach: Cahors was the first Lazarist house to function purely as a seminary, and an anticipation of the manner in which the Lazarists' specialities developed after 1660.

Solminihac and de Paul agreed terms for Cahors during the bishop's visit to Paris in autumn 1642, and these originally specified that the Lazarists would offer missions, as well as manage a seminary, run ordinand retreats, and administer Saint-Étienne/Saint-Barthélemy parish in Cahors town itself. After awarding revenue of 2,000 *livres* annually for the seminary's administration and pensions for six students, Solminihac offered other handsome graces which enabled the Lazarists to buy new premises in the town, and to purchase gardens and buildings on the outskirts of Cahors during the later 1650s as the numbers in the seminary grew.[69] But they paid a high price, for the bishop was an extremely demanding benefactor. His largesse was accompanied with a near obsessive desire to control even the most minute details of seminary life, and always to 'have his own way', as de Paul wryly warned one of the superiors.[70]

The unfortunate house superiors were not alone in finding Solminihac prickly to handle, for even his admirers pronounced him rigorous to the point of obsession.

[68] *CCD*, 2: 479–80, de Paul to an unnamed bishop, 1643–52. Sol (ed.), *Solminihac*, 277–8, for confirmation that Solminihac was the prelate in question.

[69] The bishop decided in 1646 to oblige all candidates for orders to study in the seminary for a year before they became subdeacons: *CCD*, 2: 631–2, de Paul to Guillaume Delattre, 7 April 1646; Foissac, *Premier séminaire*, 10; Petot, *Alain de Solminihac*, i, 286, 289, 291. See also Appendix 1.

[70] *CCD*, 2: 633, de Paul to Guillaume Delattre, 7 April 1646.

He was also obstinate to the point of outright intractability.[71] On installing de Paul's congregation of clerics, he deduced that the existence of two competing lines of hierarchical authority in one institution entailed a diminution of his power. His neighbour, Brandon, was to conclude that the best means of ensuring that his authority reigned supreme in the seminary was to install secular diocesan priests to manage it in his name. Solminihac, in contrast, simply did everything possible to guarantee his authority by reducing the house superiors' dependence on their superior general and getting rid of those who did not comply. Only months after he welcomed superiors Delattre and Testacy to Cahors, he took the extreme step of insisting that de Paul withdraw them altogether, placing their superior general in an extremely awkward position.

At the outset, Delattre and Testacy's appointments boded well, for de Paul selected them partially on the basis of their competence in administrative affairs.[72] Solminihac initially greeted both men positively, admiring Delattre's firmness and judging Testacy to be a fine priest after meeting him on his arrival in Cahors in late 1646.[73] However, he quickly revised his opinion. He was highly sensitive to the meeting of his ambition that the seminary should act as the principal recruiting ground for parish clergy, and was dismayed to discover that the superiors seemed to be viewing it as a means of recruiting new blood for the Lazarists.[74] In fact, there appears to be little truth in this, or if there was, few of those poached persisted in the long term: before de Paul's death, only two Lazarists originated from Cahors diocese. However, their entries in 1645 and 1648 were probably the source of Solminihac's apprehension, for he was even suspicious of his episcopal confreres, and accused them of stealing much needed clergy from his diocese.[75] Solminihac located further cause for irritation in Testacy's habit of reporting to de Paul on every issue that he thought significant, instead of yielding to his bishop's directions. He blamed Testacy's inexperience as a superior, lamenting that he wished he was as experienced as he was good, but ignored the fact that Testacy was simply following de Paul's instruction that he run proposed courses of action past him before acting. De Paul had also previously reminded Delattre that he should be kept up to date on events so that he could offer his opinions and give definitive orders. Indeed, de Paul had rebuked Delattre quite severely when he failed to do so in relation to financial transactions concerning the purchase of buildings and land in 1646, because it left de Paul completely in the dark about the individuals to whom he owed gratitude for seeing through the transfer of payments.[76]

[71] Forrestal, *Fathers, Pastors and Kings*, 203–4.

[72] While Testacy's occupation prior to his entry to the Lazarists in 1646 is not known, Delattre had served as a royal *avocat* in Amiens before his entry in 1642: *CCD*, 2: 322n.

[73] *CCD*, 2: 646, de Paul to Guillaume Delattre, 19 May 1646; *CCD*, 3: 81, de Paul to Antoine Portail, 6 October 1646.

[74] *CCD*, 3: 32, de Paul to Antoine Portail, 25 August 1646; *CCD*, 3: 84, same to same, 6 October 1646.

[75] The natives of Cahors were Étienne Biment and Jean Thiery: *Notices sur les prêtres, clercs et frères*, i, 471, 503; *CCD*, 3: 340, Alain de Solminihac to de Paul, 15 July 1648; *CCD*, 3: 340, same to same, 22 July 1648.

[76] *CCD*, 2: 632, de Paul to Guillaume Delattre, 7 April 1646.

Tensions came to a head when the unfortunate Testacy questioned Solminihac's opinions on the costs for maintaining boarders, and appealed to de Paul for guidance. If the superior had been less novice, the bishop snapped, he would have realized that he was correct in his assessments, and would not have worried his superior in faraway Paris. Not once did Solminihac acknowledge that the manner in which the Lazarists dealt with their finances was not up to him to decide.[77] Nor did de Paul make him face this fact. Instead, while he refrained from heaping blame on the superiors for Solminihac's inability to 'appreciate' them, he did not back them up or counsel them. He judged that it was better to agree to move them than to aggravate the prelate even more. In the end, Solminihac was finally satisfied with the arrival of Gilbert Cuissot in 1648, who accommodated enough of his questions and opinions to appease him. But the chopping and changing of superiors until one was found who could soothe the bishop was hardly a particularly attractive solution, since it came at a cost to the community's stability and to de Paul's authority.[78] Thus, de Paul was technically correct when he informed Fouquet some years later that he had never allowed any bishop the authority to dismiss Lazarists from houses, since it was he who had actually transferred the two superiors from Cahors. Yet the impetus for this had come solely from Solminihac, and since he could not move the superiors himself, de Paul acted for him. In doing so, he followed the letter of Lazarist law, though not its spirit.

Although injurious to de Paul and the Lazarists, the effects of the capitulation were confined to Cahors, since de Paul did not allow the precedent set there to be replicated elsewhere. On another issue, however, Solminihac's ascendancy over de Paul had a broader impact. In 1644, the bishop discovered that he could not afford to pay for all of the missionaries needed to staff a seminary, run a parish, and perform missions. Since the first was the closest of the trio to his heart, he decided to abandon the last to save it, and belatedly and abruptly resolved that the Lazarists should concentrate all their energies on clerical formation and parochial work.[79] In an extraordinary show of subjection, de Paul agreed to drop the mission obligations specified in the foundation contract, altering the course of Lazarist ministry in deference to the bishop's desire but in contradiction of his own judgement, and resigning his men to years of seminary teaching without any mission engagements. Throughout these years, de Paul was striving to safeguard the Lazarists' mooring to their missionary ethos, and averring vehemently to confreres and prelates alike that the training of clergy was simply an accessory to the Congregation's primary function of rural missions. Indeed, he admitted that he regretted surrendering to Solminihac, and in hindsight lamented how 'distressing' and 'painful' it was for the residents in Cahors who found it 'difficult' to 'be unable to attend to their principal work' of missions.[80] But once the barrier had been breached, it was difficult to

77 *CCD*, 3: 153, Alain de Solminihac to de Paul, 1647; *CCD*, 3: 163, same to same, 3 March 1647.

78 *CCD*, 3: 259, de Paul to Antoine Portail, 20 December 1647.

79 Solminihac enlisted the monks of Chancelade to carry out missions in his see, and the Lazarists completed only one, in 1652: Petot, *Solminihac*, i, 286–7, 331–8.

80 *CCD*, 4: 49, de Paul to Philibert de Brandon, 20 July 1650.

render it impregnable again, with the result that six years later the new house in Agen was also dedicated exclusively to a seminary.

Perhaps the survival of the establishments eventually offered de Paul some solace, persuading him that the reduction in functions had not been disastrous. But this does not detract from the fact that the sacrifice would not have happened on his watch if Solminihac had not pushed for it. Its significance lay not in the fact that the Lazarists were to manage a seminary since this step had already been taken elsewhere. Rather, it was the complete absence of the 'principal work' of missions amidst the community's duties that was innovative, and rebelled against de Paul's constant refrains about the primacy and necessity of this for individual confreres and the Congregation as a whole. Furthermore, the divorcing of a community from mission work did nothing at all to address his oft-voiced belief that his men should authentically emulate the virtues of Christ, and pursue their sanctification, through evangelizing the rural poor. Instead, it did everything to push the individual Lazarist and the Congregation towards greater engagement in seminary work, and an altered ethos. De Paul's efforts to please the friend for whom he held such high regard also signalled that the Lazarists might be prepared to prioritize seminary management over missions, if this was what a patron desired. In allowing the demand for labour to dictate the manner of its supply, de Paul set in train a process that would result in the Lazarists earning more fame for their seminaries and even their parishes than for their rural missions after his death.

PART IV

ENGAGING WITH LAY MISSION

9

The Confraternities of Charity

I

As missions, seminaries, and retreats became the mainstays of the Lazarists' work, their organization and practice became constant preoccupations of de Paul's daily life. According to church custom and law, these were male and clerical responsibilities, with the female role in them relegated to the provision of indirect support through financial and other donations, and prayers for successful conversions. Though absent from the foreground of these particular activities, however, women are known to have played a prominent and active part in de Paul's efforts to promote Catholic piety, particularly through works of charitable welfare. He sensibly realized early in his missionary life that confraternities offered a means to organize female religious expression; after his successful experiment in Châtillon, he established similar confraternities in parishes on the Gondi lands and latterly in other areas, before formally incorporating their foundation into the missions in which the Lazarists specialized.

The Daughters of Charity emerged from this pattern of evangelization, and de Paul remained their director and Louise de Marillac their superioress until they died within months of each other in 1660. In exploring the Daughters' early work, Susan Dinan unveils de Paul's contribution to their establishment as a confraternity of women who lived in community while providing assistance to the sick and poor, and she also provides a detailed exposition of the reasons why he insisted that they should remain a confraternal body whose members took renewable private vows, rather than become a traditional religious order.[1] Yet, however crucial they are, the Daughters are merely one product of the mission outreach that de Paul designed for the Lazarists and practised as their founder. To date, far less attention has been paid to the wider confraternal membership as a whole, and in particular to the significant personal opportunities that these vehicles of pastoral care offered to de Paul; individually and collectively, they comprised readymade networks of females, as well as granting access to labour and resources that would otherwise not have been available to him, and without which his mission of charity would have been much reduced in dimension and poorer in practice. Over time these confraternities became the principal means through which de Paul engaged with devout Catholic

[1] See particularly her *Women and Poor Relief*, 42–53.

women, who were excluded by their sex from expressing their faith through the functions of ordained ministry but aspired to find alternative means of doing so.

II

As a model, de Paul found Châtillon difficult to beat, not least because it offered an inspiring example of durability, and therefore appeared suited to the Lazarist missionary goals. His departure soon after its inauguration could have thrown the association into disarray, but the elected officers proved extremely committed to ensuring that the confraternity continued to be fit for purpose, and stretched the limited funds to meet the demand for services.[2] Tragically, most of the members died while nursing the victims of a plague which ravaged the area in 1630–1, but the confraternity survived this disaster, and was still operational in the 1650s.[3] During the epidemic, the community's needs certainly surpassed the confraternity's capability, for it was so severe that the town council was forced to isolate the contagious in a rundown *maladière* outside the town. Confraternity members dispensed food, medicine, bedding, and firewood for those in need from specially constructed cabins nearby.[4]

Their portable and adaptable nature was one of the great advantages of confraternities in general but was particularly applicable to those that shared a common devotional focus, such as charity. De Paul found that Châtillon's possessed these qualities in spades, and was therefore ideal for use when he returned to Gondi employment, and when he decided on the Lazarists' methods of evangelization. To 1625, he instigated up to thirty confraternities in parishes on the Gondi estates, and the model even proved suited to urban parishes after the first confraternity was founded in Saint-Sauveur parish in Paris in 1629.[5] He soon founded a number under the banner of missions, beginning with that in Villepreux in February 1618.[6] There and elsewhere, he invoked the assistance of Madame de Gondi, whose spiritual fervour and influence over her tenants rendered her an ideal figurehead for the new associations, and whose endorsement ensured that the confraternity gained the kind of prestige that had the wives of her tenants hurrying to enrol.[7]

[2] ACMP, 'Livre de la Charité des Pauvres de Chastillon'.

[3] Archives Communales de Châtillon-sur-Chalaronne, GG96 (10 November 1652); Collet, *Explication*, 72.

[4] Archives Communales de Châtillon-sur-Chalaronne, GG96, and GG105, 'Mémoire de ceux que la ville ne nourrissit pas'; Collet, *Vie*, i, 65–6.

[5] Abelly, *Vie*, i, 47. On page 45 of his *Chronologie historique*, Jean Bruté claimed that the first Parisian confraternity was established in Saint-Benoît parish on 11 January 1627 by the *curé*, Pierre de Hardivilliers, one of de Paul's early associates and future bishop of Bourges. Bruté claimed to have a printed copy of the confraternal rule before him when writing. However, de Paul wrote in 1630/1 that the confraternity had just been set up in the parish: *CCD*, 1: 95, de Paul to Louise de Marillac, 1630/1.

[6] While the rule for this confraternity has not survived, the association was still in existence in 1661, when Philippe-Emmanuel de Gondi bequeathed 500 *livres* to it under the terms of his will. He also left 300 *livres* to the poor of Villepreux: Corbinelli, *Histoire*, 609.

[7] In total, thirty-nine women inscribed as full members in Joigny, of whom twenty, or 51%, were unable to sign their names. This was a slightly lower percentage than that of Châtillon and Montmirail,

In Joigny, she agreed to act as the first prioress;[8] in Montmirail, she volunteered to act as first assistant (treasurer), and asked that the substitute she nominated to take her place should give her 'an account of whatever is entrusted to her' when she visited her estate;[9] in Paillart (Amiens diocese), Madame enrolled with sixteen other recruits as a 'servant of the poor'.[10] She attended the inaugural ceremonies for all of these groupings, joining the women who confessed and received communion, then processed through the church, lit candles in hand, to hear de Paul explain the aim and benefits of the work, before electing the confraternal officers.[11] Madame also played a crucial role in ensuring the survival of new confraternities. She applied to local bishops, on de Paul's behalf, to seek approbation for the associations, citing to the archbishop of Sens, for instance, the good she had witnessed from their 'establishment in several places of the kingdom'.[12] She also made material provision for the groups: in Joigny, she donated the fees collected from 'mariner merchants and others' whose vessels passed under the bridges of the town on Sundays and feast days to the confraternity; in Montmirail she transferred revenues from the local *maladière* to the new group for 'the nourishment and other necessities of the poor', and topped this up with a bequest of 800 *livres* on her death in 1625.[13]

The rules borrowed their essentials from Châtillon, while also gradually adopting a standard format that derived from other groups that de Paul founded up to 1620, and which he later had printed in booklet form for the Lazarists to distribute.[14] Generally, these were more practical in orientation than the original, which had lingered over the precise guidelines for interior and exterior exercises, but de Paul peppered them with a small set of words and phrases which aimed to sum up succinctly the spiritual motivation and outlook that the members should cultivate, without descending into trite or meaningless terms. Joigny's introduction, paraphrased or quoted verbatim by most of its successors, summarized:

> The Association of the Charity has been instituted to feed all the sick poor of the place where it will be established; to see that those who are going to die do so in a good state and those who will recover resolve never to offend God again; to honour Our Lord Jesus in the person of his poor members; and, lastly, to fulfil his ardent desire that we be charitable.[15]

where 69% and 65% respectively of the original members could not sign the acts of establishment, but it is indicative of the fact that the early confraternities drew their membership from across the social groups in these localities, with the exception of the indigent. Twenty-six women, including Madame de Gondi, joined the confraternity of Montmirail. For Joigny, Coste and Diefendorf err in stating that the members numbered forty-two, for even if the two nurses are included, the total was forty-one: ACMP, 'Acte de l'établissement de la Confrèrie de Montmirail' (copy); *CCD*, 13b: 28, 31–2; Coste, *Saint*, i, 123–4; Diefendorf, *Penitence*, 209.

[8] *CCD*, 13b: 27–8. [9] *CCD*, 13b: 30–3. [10] *CCD*, 13b: 48.

[11] *CCD*, 13b: 46 (the rule for Paillart, Folleville, and Sérévillers). [12] *CCD*, 13b: 25–7.

[13] For Joigny, see ACMP, 'Supplique de Marguerite de Silly, 25th September, 1618' (copy). The document of transfer for the *maladière* (18 June 1622) is printed in Mathieu, *Monsieur Vincent*, 24–6. See also *CCD*, 13a: 63.

[14] *CCD*, 2: 110, Charlotte-Marguerite de Gondi to de Paul, 21 August 1640.

[15] *CCD*, 13b: 23.

De Paul first introduced the term 'charity personified' in 1620 to describe Christ, to whom members were asked to pray five Our Fathers and Hail Marys in 'great honour and reverence' every day. The 'servant of the poor' was to 'strive throughout the day to perform [her] actions in union with those Our Lord practised when he was on earth', thereby expressing his charity in a consoling, 'humble and charitable manner'. In the introduction to Paillart's rule in 1620, de Paul adopted a formula that quickly became universal in the rules, in order to explain the means by which its members honoured 'Our Lord Jesus in the person of the poor', for it urged members to carry out 'his commandment that we love one another as he has loved us'.[16] Thus, to honour Jesus was to see him in the poor, serve him in the poor, and love him through loving the poor.

The rules also bore the imprint of local expectations and circumstances, however, and indulged idiosyncrasies of custom and practice. Most notably, the first associations were not all exclusively female in composition; indeed, in the early 1620s at least de Paul occasionally united men and women in them, although the rules of these foundations specified that the men should care for the able-bodied and the women for the sick.[17] In some cases, this was accompanied by a diminution of female responsibilities. De Paul later reacted to this by advising women to manage confraternal affairs themselves, without handing over governmental and financial decisions to men, and by reiterating their right to give instruction. The tensions engendered also led him to favour single-sex confraternities over mixed, and the majority of those founded from the later 1620s were for females.[18] He also inserted reminders in some rules that 'the men's and the women's associations . . . [have] the same patron and purpose and even the same spiritual practice . . . Our Lord receives as much glory from the women's ministry as from that of the men, and it even seems that the care of the sick is preferable to that of the healthy.' Indeed, so keen was de Paul to hammer home the point that charitable work was not gender specific that he actually prioritized the services that fell to the women, protesting that care of those disabled by illness was an offering of charity to those most at risk amongst the underprivileged. De Paul forged a reciprocal bond between two groups that he judged to be particularly vulnerable in their communities for different reasons; he sought to protect one by recognizing the validity of their charitable service, and the other by categorizing them as worthy recipients of assistance and the means through which others could win their salvation.[19]

The division of labour was also a product of the expanding remit of the confraternities, as they began to incorporate care for the physically hearty as well as the sick poor. In this, they followed a prevailing trend in the provision of welfare from the 1520s onwards. Numerous studies have illustrated a pronounced tendency to discriminate in alms in cities like Ypres and Lyon, whose authorities

[16] See *CCD*, 13b: 23 for copies of these early rules.

[17] For example, in Joigny in 1621, in Courboin in 1622, and perhaps in Montrueil in 1627: *CCD*, 13b: 54–67, 85–91. For the full rule of Courboin confraternity, see ACMP, 'Règlement de l'association de la Charité de Courboin'.

[18] *CCD*, 1: 70, de Paul to Louise de Marillac, 1630.

[19] *CCD*, 13b: 52, 62, 85–91.

directed that aid should not be distributed to the idle poor without obligations designed to guarantee that they learned to pay their way through life or strengthened their spiritual and moral fibre.[20] Some of the new rules directed that alms should be used to pay for placing youths who had reached puberty in a trade, and some insisted that the able poor should confess and attend mass in return for food.[21] The rule for Mâcon actually went further, threatening penalties on those who caused trouble by refusing to attend church.[22] Indeed, the context for its formulation is particularly instructive, because it exposes de Paul's ability to graft the association onto existing provisions for welfare if this was necessary for it to be accepted and successful.[23] The revised regime in Mâcon thus bore de Paul's hallmark, but confraternal piety formed just one element of it. It functioned through institutional cooperation between the cathedral chapter, the chapter of Saint Pierre church, and the town council, and was far more ambitious in scope than the confraternities that de Paul set up in other areas around this time .

De Paul visited the town in September 1621 to stay with the Oratorians, and it was probably they who introduced him to some urban notables who were impressed by his being the chaplain of the General of the Galleys and by his knowledge of the methods used in nearby towns to assist the poor.[24] As in many urban areas, mendicancy was reaching crisis point in Mâcon at this time, and the council had been forced to place guards at the city gates in order to prevent swarms of beggars entering. In the preceding months, the authorities had spent over 650 *livres* on food for the poor, but now concluded that the existing almonry could not provide for the 120 beggars, including 'young debauched and abandoned women', who swarmed the streets and might visit sickness on the townspeople through sexual contact or other contagions.[25] Although they were initially, according to de Paul, sceptical about the proposal that he made to deal with them, the authorities' anxiety overpowered their inhibition, and on his advice they first conducted a census to gain an accurate picture of the nature and extent of the problem, before initiating a Charity of Alms to replace the old almonry. This had been entirely subject to the cathedral chapter's oversight, but the new system of welfare was now to be managed by two laymen and two chapter canons. The council reserved the right to supervise its accounts, and all of these measures tend to suggest that the councillors may have opportunistically indulged de Paul's recommendations in

[20] The literature on this topic is extensive, but see in particular: Davis, 'Poor Relief, Humanism, and Heresy: The Case of Lyon'; Lindberg, *Beyond Charity*; Safley, *Reformation of Charity*; the collections of essays edited by Grell and Cunningham: *Health Care and Poor Relief in Protestant Europe* and *Health Care and Poor Relief in Counter-Reformation Europe*.

[21] AD de Saône-et-Loire, GG 253/19, 'Instruction'; *CCD*, 13b: 85–91.

[22] AD de Saône–et-Loire, GG 253/19, 'Instruction'.

[23] On occasion also, de Paul's confraternity replaced an existing devotional confraternity, for example, a confraternity of the rosary in Clichy in 1623, and a confraternity dedicated to the Holy Name of Jesus in Montreuil in 1627: *CCD* 13b: 94–5.

[24] AD de Saône-et-Loire, BB 84, fo. 97r.

[25] AD de Saône-et-Loire, G 207, fos 181r–187r: 'jeunes filles debauchées et abandonées'. I have favoured the original copy of the commission's report, as the version printed in *CCD*, 13b: 67–73, contains errors. I would like to thank Bernard Koch, CM, for pointing out the location of the original results of the census.

order to gain a decisive voice in welfare provision as well as to deal with a crisis of mendicancy.[26]

The system also depended on prescribed and voluntary support from local residents. The council accepted de Paul's proposal that a new confraternity of female volunteers would undertake visits to the sick poor, as well as coordinate the distribution of wood, linens, and food, and quest (collect alms) in the churches on Sundays and feasts.[27] It also stipulated that families above the poverty line were required to contribute a portion of agricultural produce to the Charity annually, while it placed alms boxes in churches, shops, and inns. A portion of their contents was designated for the maintenance of a granary and storeroom, and for the teaching of trades to young children 'in order to give them means to earn their living'. Those in receipt of alms were required to attend the catechism sessions and mass administered on a weekly basis by local clergy.[28]

III

De Paul and his missionaries never carried out missions in the French capital, but from 1629 the confraternities began to pop up in parishes there anyway. Beginning with Saint-Sauveur, Saint-Nicolas-du-Chardonnet, and Saint-Sulpice, they were soon set up in Saint-Benoît, Saint-Eustache, and Saint-Merri, and so on until at least twenty parishes contained one by the late 1640s. Their foundation signalled the transfer of the confraternal model from its mainly rural environment to an urban location. In this the enthusiasm of female supporters for them was critical at every stage. In the initial spread, the impetus came from noble women who moved regularly between family estates in the countryside and their residences in Paris, and saw little reason why the Lazarists could not establish confraternities to serve the poor in both. Among them was Catherine Lamy, the first president of the confraternity in Gentilly (founded on family lands in 1627), and an initial champion of the confraternity of Saint-Germain-l'Auxerrois parish where she resided in Paris (erected in 1632). Likewise, Isabelle du Fey was a stalwart member of the confraternity founded on her family's land in Villepreux, and when the number of confraternities in Paris began to grow she acted as the procurer general, sourcing dry

26 Not three canons, as *CCD*, 13b: 76 states. Coste read the original manuscript incorrectly: AD de Saône-et-Loire, BB 84, fos 99v, 100v–101r.

27 The group also paid two 'wise women' or *sage femmes* 2 *livres* each per month to serve the sick poor, a provision usually adopted in de Paul's confraternities. They probably acted as midwives, but may also have carried out other nursing duties: AD de Saône-et-Loire, GG 253/19, 'Instruction'. This rule is incomplete, but is considerably more trustworthy than Laplatte's eighteenth-century citation: AD de Saône-et-Loire, J562, 'Histoire de l'église et du diocèse de Mâcon', vol. ii, 349–51; Bibliothèque Municipale de Mâcon, Ms 294, J. Laplatte, 'Mémoire pour servir à l'histoire sacrée et profane de Mâcon', 322–3. The document printed in *CCD*, 13b: 79–84, may be a later version of this rule (a later hand added 'Mâcon' to the space for the location of the confraternity), but it is not the original.

28 AD de Saône-et-Loire, BB 84, fos 97v–98r: '. . . pour leur donner moyen de gaigner leur vye'.

goods for those in the Île de France. Like Lamy, both she and her mother also joined the confraternity established at the *Hôtel-Dieu* in Paris in 1634.[29]

In the city, the groups attracted and united women who already engaged informally or sporadically in caring for the sick or poor of their parishes, or desired to do so. The confraternities therefore found a hospitable environment, in which women had since the later years of the wars increasingly sought to express their beliefs not simply in prayer and penance but also in the good works of supporting convents and almsgiving.[30] Some of these, however, soon began to push for adaptations to the confraternal model, with important results for the inclusion of different segments of the female population in charitable provision. The first variation offered a framework for confraternal community living, and derived from the relations that de Paul established with du Fey's cousin, Louise de Marillac. He was fortunate to link with her in the mid-1620s, for this was precisely the point at which his promotion of the confraternities needed an individual with the potential for leadership and teamwork to develop them further. In the long term, Marillac's role in this domain was far more sustained and decisive than the late Françoise-Marguerite de Gondi's had been, for her widowed status offered her the freedom to use her talents in committing fully to the demands of caring for the poor. Confraternal piety provided the outlet to do so, and a much needed sense of spiritual camaraderie with those of like mind. Moreover, even though she was probably the illegitimate daughter of the disgraced Louis de Marillac, she was still entitled to a place at court; her contacts ranged throughout polite society, and included friendship with the queen.

After the death of her husband in 1625, Marillac returned for a time to her girlhood desire to enter a nunnery, but her spiritual director Jean-Pierre Camus persuaded her that she should place herself under the direction of de Paul, a fellow Salesian enthusiast, instead. Although it is probable that they had met some years before through the Hennequin family, they were not closely acquainted and it was some time before Marillac overcame her initial reluctance to open her conscience to her new director. However, Camus's instinct was proved right, for the first benefit of the new relationship lay in the fact that it enabled her to retain a Salesian sensitivity while accessing a specific structure in which to express it. Scruples of conscience about the merit of their thoughts and actions were common amongst acutely religious women of this era, and de Paul had encountered these before when in the employ of Madame de Gondi. Marillac now found a way, as she later reflected, to make her love of God effective, and revel in the goodness and power of his perfection:

> The person who does not love does not know God, for God is charity . . . The practice of charity is so powerful that it gives us the knowledge of God . . . we penetrate so deeply into the mystery of God and His greatness . . . our participation in this divine light . . . will inflame us with the fire of Holy Love.[31]

[29] AN, Y 180 (unpaginated), 30 December 1634; ACMP, 'Noms des premières Dames de la Charite, 1634–60' (unpaginated).

[30] Diefendorf, *Penitence*, 49–133.

[31] Sullivan (ed.), *Writings*, 710.

Vowing to 'practise the most holy virtues of humility, obedience, poverty, suffering and charity in order to honour these same virtues in Jesus Christ', Marillac, with de Paul's encouragement, began to visit confraternities, in order to provide supplies and funds, inspect their procedures, and advise and encourage their members in the accomplishment of their duties.[32] In 1630, a confraternity was inaugurated in her own parish of Saint-Nicolas-du-Chardonnet, probably on her instigation, and she subsequently opened her house to a small group of modestly born women who wished to live in community while serving the sick poor. These formed the nucleus of the Daughters of Charity. Although the 'little family' was already in being, Marillac waited, as convention expected, until her director approved it before founding it formally on 29 November 1633. For his part, he was not opposed to 'her plan', as he phrased it, but thought it his role to 'assist' her in seeking enlightenment through prayer.[33] Recruitment seemed to reinforce divine consent, and from 1638 Marillac was able to send Daughters, usually in pairs, to establish houses outside the capital. Forty-six of these were formed by the time that she died.[34]

The second variation was specifically suited to female aristocrats and other socially elevated women, but like the Daughters was not parish-bound. This time the instigator was Geneviève Goussault, the wealthy widow of a president of the *chambre des comptes*. Unlike Marillac, de Paul was not her director, but over the years she had found spiritual succour with a number of expert advisers who had encouraged her to direct her quest for holiness into prayer and good works. Amongst these were de Paul's friend Coqueret, and the bishop of Comminges, Barthélemy Donadieu de Griet, whose correspondence with Goussault is replete with references to the need to imitate Jesus Christ perfectly. Coqueret, in particular, was an enthusiastic supporter of her desire to evangelize and care for the poor; if she worked 'by [God] and for him', he advised, she could achieve marvels, and would be recompensed in Heaven for the 'innumerable number of souls' that she directed there.[35] Coqueret's words could just as easily have been written by de Paul, and it is quite possible that it was Coqueret who initially directed Goussault towards de Paul's confraternal enterprises around 1632. It is hardly coincidental that de Paul approved the foundation of a confraternity of charity in her parish of Saint-Gervais in the same year, of which she immediately became a member.

Goussault drew her spiritual nourishment from a well that affirmed the value of active professions of faith through spiritual and material care of the sick and poor, but the ways in which she expressed her piety were varied. After her husband left

[32] Sullivan (ed.), *Writings*, 693.

[33] *CCD*, 1: 200, de Paul to Louise de Marillac, May 1633; *CCD*, 1: 211, same to same, *c.*2 September 1633; *CCD*, 1: 212, same to same, undated.

[34] These included work at a number of hospitals, beginning with Angers in 1640: Dinan, *Women and Poor Relief*, 147–9.

[35] ACMP, Jean Coqueret to Geneviève Goussault, 8 June 1633, and Barthélemy Donadieu de Griet to Geneviève Goussault (undated). These are photocopies, the original documents are housed in the archives of the Daughters of Charity, Paris. The first was published in Koch, 'Lettre inédite d'un ami'.

her widowed in 1631, she had turned her attention to visiting the *Hôtel-Dieu* in Paris, and to the encouraging of devotion amongst the inhabitants of towns around Anjou, where her family held extensive lands. In April 1633, she wrote to de Paul to inform him of her activities and provided a lengthy assessment of the standards of religious practice and the provisions for care of the sick and poor there. Her trip was not made, as Barbara Diefendorf assumes, to inspect confraternities of charity, for she never mentioned them, but was an opportunity to evangelize in her own right through public talks, sessions of catechesis, and private conversations with locals. Of special concern was the condition of local hospitals. When she arrived in each town, she checked whether a *Hôtel-Dieu* existed, and visited the five that she found. Her concern for the supply of care was exacerbated by the poor facilities or complete absence of suitable accommodation in many towns. In Tours, she walked around the 'finest and most well-organised *Hôtel-Dieu* anywhere', but was less impressed with that in Blois, which she noted had 'many devotions' but was in disorder. She identified poor organization as the principal reason for this, and lamented that local women did not visit this or the other hospitals that she saw. Her experience in Paris was quite contrary; there, she commented, she and other 'women of rank' were in the habit of visiting the *Hôtel-Dieu* regularly.[36]

The reason for Goussault's interest in the hospitals was therefore extremely personal, and a natural extension of her religious observance in Paris. Indeed, what she saw in western France may have triggered her soon expressed opinion that the organization of even its *Hôtel-Dieu* could be improved. Shortly after her return, she proposed to de Paul that a confraternity of charity would be a suitable means of marshalling the female visitors, offering them invaluable guidance on their duties and a spiritual underpinning for them. He was rather slow to pledge support, and indeed Diefendorf amplifies his reluctance in order to emphasize Goussault's primacy in the foundation of the confraternity.[37] But while there is no doubt that Goussault was its initiator, de Paul's tardiness in supporting her proposal should be interpreted as a characteristic expression of his belief that the will should be held in 'holy indifference' until God's wishes became apparent.[38] Furthermore, the experimental nature of the proposal may have influenced his desire that he and Goussault reflect intensely before stepping into action. The confraternities that he had promoted to date were not institutionally based, and he could not be sure that the confraternal model would survive the complications of dealing with hospital administrators and full-time staff.[39] De Paul simply did not have any precedent to follow in acceding to Goussault's innovative proposition, and took time to acquiesce that it was both possible and godly. When, however, he attended the first meeting at Goussault's house around February 1634, he agreed to act as the group's director. Soon afterwards, the ten founding members began, in de Paul's words, 'to work wonders'; in turns, four visited the *Hôtel-Dieu* daily, bringing convalescent food such as jellies, soups, and preserves, and 'disposing those poor people to make

[36] *CCD*, 1: 191–6, Geneviève Goussault to de Paul, 16 April 1633.

[37] Diefendorf, *Penitence*, 226–30.

[38] *CCD*, 1: 212, de Paul to Louise de Marillac, undated.

[39] Abelly, *Vie*, i, 132, 134.

a general confession of their past life . . . and . . . take the resolution never to offend God again'. They quickly realized that the service was time-consuming, so decided to nominate fourteen women to perform it on a three-monthly rota, and asked Marillac to allow the Daughters to assist in preparing the dishes that they doled out.[40]

IV

The Ladies of Charity of the *Hôtel-Dieu* is the most celebrated of the Parisian confraternities of charity, having won its reputation partly via the status of those who belonged to it as well as its unusual nature. In total, the group numbered about 120 women 'of high rank' at the outset, and this number climbed to 300 in the first flush of activity during the mid- to late 1630s. Subsequently, as initial zeal gave way in the face of the commitment required, the association shrank to a hard core of fifty consoeurs. Within the group at large, however, were at least three princesses, seven duchesses and countesses, as well as marchionesses and baronesses, a large number of women from high-status families of the *robe* such as the Fouquet, Lamoignon, and Séguier, and the wives of prosperous merchants, such as Parnie Boulart.[41] It is important to emphasize that this association was one of a multitude founded in Paris, and that many of these women also participated in their parish confraternities, for example, the duchess of Aiguillon in Saint-Sulpice, and Goussault in Saint-Gervais.[42] The wider assembly of confraternities in the city's parishes counted up to 500 consoeurs.[43] For many of these, the Daughters distributed food and medicines, which lifted the burden of home visits from the shoulders of women who were of a social standing too elevated to go into poor areas or too occupied with the demands of a busy household to sacrifice time to it. But many functioned without their assistance, which puts paid to the widely held notion that their members did not do the menial and unpleasant tasks that visiting the sick often necessitated.[44]

[40] Abelly, *Vie*, i, 135; *CCD*, 1: 230, de Paul to Louise de Marillac, January–March 1634; *CCD*, 1: 246, de Paul to François du Coudray, 25 July 1634.

[41] Boulart was the widow of a merchant known as Vivant, and was one of the officers in 1645: AN, S6597 (22 October 1645).

[42] Goussault left legacies to both her parish confraternity (100 *livres*) and that of the *Hôtel-Dieu* (1,500 *livres*) in her will (1639): *CCD*, 13b: 390–6.

[43] Abelly, *Vie*, i, 135; *CCD*, 1: 230, de Paul to Louise de Marillac, January–March 1634; *CCD*, 1: 246, de Paul to François du Coudray, 25 July 1634; *CCD*, 13b: 430. See also ACMP, 'Noms des premières Dames de la Charite, 1634–60'. This list is not exhaustive even though its entries are not limited to the years announced in its title. Its accuracy is also questionable, as it contains some duplicate entries, and does not include a number of women whose membership of a Parisian confraternity of charity is verified by other documents. However, it is still an invaluable source of information if supplemented with other sources.

[44] This is often overlooked, as scholars assume that the women were freed of the burden of visits with the advent of the Daughters. While in more dangerous areas the Daughters did all of the visits, in others the consoeurs were still obliged to do them on days assigned to them in rota. See, for example, Marillac's description of the duties of the members of the confraternity of Saint-Étienne-du-Mont parish in December 1636: *CCD*, 1: 359, Louise de Marillac to de Paul, December 1636. De Paul's petition to the archbishop of Paris to approve the Daughters in 1646 emphasized that the women of

Similarly, specific works that were instigated and carried out by the parish associations are often erroneously attributed solely to the *Hôtel-Dieu* confraternity. The best example of this is the care of the city's numerous foundlings, begun in late 1637. Commonly thought to have been the responsibility of the *Hôtel-Dieu* confraternity from the outset, it was actually a dual project overseen by the confraternity of Saint-Nicholas-du-Chardonnet parish as well until 1640. Shocked by the huge number of babies that were abandoned, often in chapels or on the steps of Notre-Dame cathedral, and even more appalled by the 300 or 400 of these that died from lack of care afterwards at the institution known as *La Couche*, several members decided in late 1637 to ask the Daughters to care for a small number who were placed with nursing mothers or lodged in a small house on rue de Boulangers in their parish.[45] In response to the demand for the service, the Ladies of the *Hôtel-Dieu* then founded a home where the foundlings were housed in 1640 close to the Daughters' motherhouse in La Chapelle, in the hope that they could receive some education and training for the future. They established another north of Saint-Lazare in 1645.[46]

The initial impulsion for the project came from Marie de Lamoignon, who served several terms as president of the Saint-Nicolas confraternity, and was the third president of the *Hôtel-Dieu* confraternity (1643 to 1651), having joined it around 1636. Her daughter Madeleine was also a dedicated member of both, and she acted as the project's staunchest advocate amongst the Ladies from its inception. Madeleine regularly visited *La Couche* with her mother, and carried such a dreadful report of conditions there to other *Hôtel-Dieu* consoeurs that they were stirred into action. When they later proved reluctant to approve her proposal that they should supply milk to infants in their homes, Madeleine simply paid for it initially at her own expense, until a few other women joined her.[47] The Lamoignons remained deeply immersed in the venture thereafter, and Marie, in particular, was the main reason why the foundlings continued to be the concern of two confraternities for some time.

The above episode demonstrates that it was generally the members themselves who linked the individual groupings, since there were no formal connections between them. In turn, this signals the restrictions on de Paul's ability to work with them, for their enormous membership and independent functioning placed him at a distance from most consoeurs. Indeed, his direct contact with members of the parish confraternities was limited to an annual assembly which he chaired, and which brought them all together for uplifting instruction. This meant that he was remarkably dependent on cultivating relations with individuals in the groups in order to exercise influence on their activities, and in particular with those who

high social standing were unable to perform the most menial tasks. This was true for some, but the emphasis was also his and Marillac's means of demonstrating how essential the Daughters were to the provision of welfare in the archdiocese: *CCD*, 2: 600 de Paul to Jean-François de Gondi, August–September 1645.

[45] *CCD*, 1: 407, de Paul to Louise de Marillac, 1 January 1638.

[46] *CCD*, 13b: 400.

[47] BSG, Ms 4232, Marsolier, 'La Vie de Mademoiselle de Lamoignon', fos 96r–98r, 316r.

possessed the resources and contacts to ensure that these could proceed. Since the time that Madame de Gondi had lent her prestige, contacts, and material resources to the foundation of the first confraternities, de Paul had known that the participation of well-born women was highly desirable for these ventures. The founding members of the Ladies of the *Hôtel-Dieu* were the wives or widows of men who held upper positions within the Paris *parlement,* and the royal councils or households. Of these, the wife of Pierre Séguier, then *president à mortier* in the Paris *parlement* and later chancellor of France, was perhaps the most elevated in terms of direct access to a major political figure, although her position was rivalled over time by the prodigious achievements of Marie Fouquet's family. Her husband, François IV, was a councillor of state, while of their fifteen children, the second eldest, Nicolas, became superintendent of finances in 1653, and two others were appointed to the episcopate.[48] She herself was president of the confraternity for a time around 1652, sandwiched between Marie Lamoignon and the duchess of Aiguillon.

Louise de Marillac never presided over this group, but she was a dedicated member of it and a parish confraternity. She also headed the Daughters, and maintained relations with numerous consoeurs, both within and outside Paris. To de Paul, therefore, she offered an essential, indeed his best, means of communication with the wider community of female activists. Marillac was in a far better position than de Paul to understand the Daughters' work; as he noted, the Daughters wrote to her every week about their progress when away from Paris, but they were instructed to write to him only 'if needed', that is, if they had 'notable difficulties, as much for the spiritual as the temporal'.[49] Marillac also wrote the Daughters' first rule, in which she emphasized the unity of living habits and government that should define the group.[50] De Paul put forward only minor alterations to this, as he did to subsequent versions that she produced.[51] Her piercing critiques of these display a surety in spirituality and practice that built on the original vision of 1617. For example, in 1655, commenting on the use of the term 'the ungrateful' to describe the poor in the 1655 rule, she queried whether it seemed 'to presume that the poor owe gratitude to' the Daughters. 'This should not

[48] The husbands of two others held or had held senior positions in the Paris *parlement* (Traversay and Goussault), two had acted as royal councillors (those of Sainctor and Poulaillon), and two had been attached to the household of Marie de Medici (Le Gras (Marillac) and Villesabin). The final founding members were Élisabeth-Marie de Bailleul, married to Nicolas de Bailleul, *seigneur* of Vattetot-sur-Mer and Soisy-sur-Seine, and Madame Dumecq: ACMP, 'Noms des premières Dames de la Charite, 1634–60' (unpaginated); *CCD*, 1: 230, de Paul to Louise de Marillac, January–March 1634.

[49] *CCD*, 10: 183.

[50] For a thorough exposition of the Daughters' routines, see Dinan, *Women and Poor Relief,* 62–117.

[51] When the 1645 statutes were sent to the archbishop of Paris for his approval, they were presented as de Paul's work, and he wrote a letter of petition to accompany them. But these were formalities in line with the conventions of the period. Similarly, on Marillac's instigation, the Daughters took private, simple, and renewable vows of poverty, chastity, obedience, and service to the sick poor, their servants and masters. De Paul suggested that they might use these latter words, which he took verbatim from the vows taken by the Camillians, a society of priests founded by Camillus de Lellis in 1584: *CCD*, 2: 599, de Paul to Jean-François de Gondi, August–September 1645; *CCD*, 9: 22; *CCD*, 13b: 123–7; Rybolt, 'From Life to the Rules'; Brejon de Lavergnée, *Histoire*, 204–9.

be' because the Daughters 'are most obliged to serve the poor'.[52] Acknowledging her expertise, de Paul also took on board her proposals for appropriate conference topics because he accepted that she was best placed to identify subjects that would encourage the women to avoid the quarrels that tended to arise when they lived in close quarters, as well as the themes that were universal to their calling, such as indifference and love of the poor.[53]

Beyond the Daughters, Marillac's spiritual charisma enabled her to become a figure of considerable authority, not only through her exemplary piety and commitment to the work of charity, but also because of her ability to offer spiritual guidance directly through retreats. Just as Saint-Lazare became a respected place of retreat for males, Marillac welcomed their female counterparts to the Daughters' motherhouse, especially the most devoted of the *Hôtel-Dieu* confraternity who could afford to spend time in seclusion. De Paul marked out the spiritual framework that they should follow, by recommending readings particularly appropriate for lay women, principally the Gospels, de Sales's *Introduction*, Kempis's *Imitation of Christ*, and Louis of Granada's *Memorial of a Christian Life*, which he thought would 'excite [their] contrition'. He also devised a schedule and subjects for their meditations. But Marillac then took over, listening to and responding to their accounts of their reflections, and preparing them for their general confessions.[54] The retreatants also fitted into the Daughters' daily routine. Since this was geared fully towards service to the sick and poor, they received constant reminders that they should apply the lessons of their retreat to the schedules of their daily lives when they returned with a spiritual spring in their step to their own households.[55]

The newly widowed Marie de Miramion left an account of her experience of retreat in which she emphasized the decisive impact that it had on her future, and the manner in which de Paul and Marillac worked together to bring this about: widowed at 16, after less than a year of marriage to Jean-Jacques de Beauharnais, *seigneur* of Miramion and a counsellor in the Paris *parlement*, she underwent a period of intense grief and soul searching.[56] Her spiritual instinct directed her first to the Visitation convent of Sainte-Marie, where she lodged for a time before leaving her infant daughter to board there. Stressed almost beyond endurance, she

[52] Sullivan (ed.), *Writings*, 810.

[53] For another example, see de Paul's acquiescence to Marillac's plan to send Daughters to learn teaching methods from the Ursulines, despite his scepticism about its potential. Marillac afterwards composed a catechism for the Daughters to use: *CCD*, 1: 427, de Paul to Louise de Marillac, 1638; Sullivan (ed.), *Writings*, 766–7. The catechism is published in Charpy, *Compagnie des Filles de la Charité*, 958–70.

[54] See *CCD*, 1, in particular 372, de Paul to Louise de Marillac, 1636–9, for information on retreats by Madames Lamy, Goussault, and Le Roux under Marillac's direction. Although de Paul did not say so explicitly, he implied that other writings of Granada would also be beneficial, and probably meant *The Sinner's Guide*, first published in 1555.

[55] The order of their day is printed in Sullivan (ed.), *Writings*, 726–7.

[56] Miramion's account of her conversion is printed in Bonneau, *Miramion*, 365–70. This also contains other autobiographical fragments, as well as material drawn from the *vie* composed by her daughter after her death (Bib. Maz., Ms 2489, 'Mémoire pour servir à la vie de madame de Miramion . . . '), and that written by *Abbé* de Choisy, another relative, in 1706. I am grateful to Dr Jennifer Hillman for her generous insights into the origin and composition of the material.

suffered greatly as she struggled to withstand pressure from her family to remarry, and to decide how she could live the life of piety that she desired outside the protection of the convent walls. Finally, in desperation, she sought the sanctuary of the Daughters' motherhouse in 1649, where she completed a retreat under Marillac's guidance. After three days of seeking to know 'what God wanted of me', Miramion also received counsel from de Paul. She maintained that 'I never varied or doubted a moment' after these consultations. Soon after them, she made a vow of chastity, and devoted herself to prayer and works of charity, some of them through the confraternity of the *Hôtel-Dieu*:

> I occupied myself with . . . schools and charity for the sick poor . . . I learned to bleed, I distributed clothes to the poor . . . I had to have care of the spiritual and temporal [needs] of the poor.[57]

The fact that the troubled Miramion initially sought inspiration at the Visitation convent places her in the company of other high-born women whose affection for the legacy of de Sales led them into contact with de Paul, and kept them attached thereafter. These included Marillac herself, who had been sent to him by Camus, one of de Sales's closest associates in France and, as the author of a popular *vie* on the late bishop, the main promoter of his posthumous reputation.[58] As Chapter 7 showed, de Paul's position as ecclesiastical superior of the Visitation convents was a public mark of esteem that could be traced directly to de Sales himself. It also expanded the number of his associates, but the products of these relations were not confined to new Lazarist houses. In regard to the women with whom de Paul enjoyed closest relations, there was a significant degree of cross-pollination between two of the outlets in which he expended his spiritual energies, the confraternities of charity and the Visitation convents. The Visitation convents in Paris were amongst the most popular foci of devotion for wealthy women who donated to them, spent periods on retreat in them, and sent their daughters to them as boarders or nuns. Over half of the women who entered them in the seventeenth century came from noble families, a statistic of considerable import for the ties that de Paul formed with them and their relatives. Their attachment to the Visitation transferred to de Paul and his advocacy of charitable work, for these appeared to provide an authentic means of living out the Salesian message of vocation for lay women.

Leading families of the *robe*, the Luillier and Lamoignon, demonstrate these common loyalties distinctly. Once he became Visitation superior in early 1622, de Paul became closely connected with Hélène-Angelique Luillier, who entered the first Visitation convent in 1620 and filled the role of superior almost continually between 1622 and 1649.[59] Her sisters remained closely connected to her and to her convent; indeed, Marie, wife of Claude-Marcel, *seigneur* of Villeneuve and a master

[57] Bonneau, *Miramion*, 365–70: 'Je m'occupai . . . à établir des écoles etudes charités pour les pauvres maladies . . . j'appris àsaigner, je distribuai des habits aux pauvres . . . je devais avoir soin du spiritual et du temporal des pauvres.' Miramion's main legacies were an orphanage (*Sainte-Enfance*), a retreat house for lay women to stay in quiet recollection, and a community known as the *Filles de Sainte-Geneviève* who taught girls; she sought de Paul's advice when formulating rules for the *Filles*.

[58] Camus, *L'Esprit*.

[59] Bib. Maz., Ms 2430; Diefendorf, *Penitence*, 259.

of requests, enjoyed founder's privileges there in recognition of the enormous gift of 45,000 *livres* that her parents bestowed when Hélène-Angélique entered.[60] She presided over the confraternity established in Sartrouville, just north-west of Paris, in the 1620s, before joining the *Hôtel-Dieu* group with her sister Jeanne in 1634.[61] More intimately, de Paul sometimes offered Marie spiritual direction until her death in 1650, providing assistance, as she testified, 'just at the right moment in my corporal and spiritual extremities'. Turning confraternal membership into an even greater family speciality, Jeanne's mother-in-law, Élisabeth l'Aligre, was also a committed consoeur at the *Hôtel-Dieu*.[62]

Equally, almost every female member of the Lamoignon family was vigorously active in the confraternities, with the matriarch Marie as the core surrounded by two of her three daughters, Madeleine and Anne, duchess of Nesmond, as well as her daughter-in-law (also Madeleine née Potier).[63] The women were also closely linked to the Visitation. Marie de Lamoignon had received spiritual direction from François de Sales while he sojourned in Paris, and he prepared her daughter Madeleine for her first communion. Ties were maintained in the longer term when Marie's third daughter, Élisabeth, made her profession in the convent in the faubourg Saint-Jacques. After her father's death in 1636, her mother and sisters all retreated to the convent to mourn in seclusion for a time.[64] For these women, the bonds of maternal and sisterly kinship were instrumental in the construction of their long-lasting loyalty to religious causes and institutions. De Paul understood perfectly the potential that lay within them. He urged confraternal members to recruit their kin and to prepare them to accept the commitments their works of charity entailed. Mothers, he noted, who impassioned their daughters, nieces, and daughters-in-law through their words and example, rendered them all like 'burning coals that are united together'.[65]

V

As an ordained priest, de Paul had the type of functional assurance that would encourage a devout woman to attend to his words, but his unique position as the founder of the first confraternity and the head of the Congregation that perpetuated its message and practices multiplied the likelihood, even amongst consoeurs who were superior to him in social rank. Occupied with the wealth of tasks associated

60 Diefendorf, *Penitence*, 259–60.

61 *CCD*, 1: 130, de Paul to Louise de Marillac, 17 October 1631.

62 Jeanne was married to Étienne II l'Aligre, who enjoyed an illustrious career as ambassador to Venice, intendant of justice in Caen, superintendent of finance, head of the Council of the Marine, and chancellor: ACMP, 'Noms des premières Dames de la Charité 1634–1660' (unpaginated); Bleynie, *Villeneuve, passim*; Diefendorf, *Penitence*, 182, 218–22, 260; Salinis, *Villeneuve, passim*.

63 Nesmond was not Marie de Lamoignon's sister-in-law, as often stated. See BSG, Ms 4232, Marsolier, 'La Vie de Mademoiselle de Lamoignon', and Aubert de la Chenaye-Dubois, *Dictionnaire*, 6, col. 382.

64 BSG, Ms 4232, Marsolier, 'La Vie de Mademoiselle de Lamoignon', fo. 81r.

65 *CCD*, 13b: 439, 447.

with the Lazarists' works, however, he left decisions such as the rental or purchase of lodging, the sourcing and distribution of food, and the payment of suppliers, to the discretion of leading Ladies, and was kept abreast of developments by Marillac and the officers. These, and whatever women were assigned to performing the rota at the hospital at the time, attended a meeting every three months. They periodically attended extraordinary meetings too. At this kind of assembly, de Paul was always keen to ensure that the highest-ranking consoeurs were present, for he believed that their leadership in pledging resources was often decisive in transforming discussions into resolutions; for instance, in 1649 he was reluctant to hold an important assembly of the group without the presence of the duchess of Aiguillon, the countess of Brienne, and the princess of Condé.[66]

Although his meetings with the women were intermittent, de Paul was acutely conscious that they offered his best opportunities to act as both inspiration and counsel. He used the annual assembly of the Parisian parish groups to reiterate key lessons of charitable piety, and the more frequent meetings with the Ladies to couple his spiritual teaching with their current projects, such as their care of the foundlings or the aid that they organized for refugees who suffered from the depredations of soldiers and destruction of crops on the north-east front of the Thirty Years War during the 1640s and early 1650s. And the first lesson for those in attendance to absorb was one that de Paul had stressed from the founding period of the confraternities, that is, the variety and validity of the female vocation in its assortment of forms, and in its specific articulation in a life of charitable service to the sick and poor. There was no need, therefore, for women who were married, widowed, or single to be concerned about the purpose of their lives for, like the Daughters of Charity, their special contribution to the church was different from the professed nun who remained in her cloister. De Paul informed the Daughters that their Saviour had visited, healed, and instructed the sick while on earth, and that they left God 'for God' when they visited the 'cloister' of the street to tend to the sick poor. He reminded the assembly of consoeurs that in any task, whether it was visiting galley convicts, foundlings, or the sick poor, they venerated the Saviour's childhood, penances, and blessed death, honoured his 'states' in life, and replicated his mercies to those in need.[67]

Furthermore, de Paul likened these women to those who stood beneath the cross when Christ was most vulnerable and needy, remaining loyal to the one that they followed 'constantly on the narrow path of the practice of love of God and neighbour'. Amongst them, the mother of Christ was the supreme example: 'Glorified above the angels', she was the servant of her son through her holy motherhood. In this, de Paul followed contemporary theologians, including Bellarmine, Canisius, and indeed de Sales, who had judged that Mary's greatest dignity was not her bodily conception of Christ, but her spiritual motherhood, which she manifested above all in her obedience to God's will. Indeed, it was widely agreed that it was the ultimate reason for her glory and preferential treatment.

[66] *CCD*, 3: 404, de Paul to unnamed Ladies of Charity, 11 February 1649.

[67] *CCD*, 9: 14; *CCD*, 13b: 410.

Joining the consensus, de Paul cited the Gospel of Luke (1: 38) in advocating that the women learn to speak with God's voice in their works, as Mary had when she acquiesced to the angel Gabriel's announcement in the domestic surroundings of her home in Nazareth.[68] Simultaneously, however, he chose to plumb the experiences of natural motherhood that many consoeurs shared for inspiration, rather than to ignore it; notably, in 1640, a talk to the *Hôtel-Dieu* consoeurs was laden with references to their maternal duties to vulnerable infants, as de Paul bid to persuade them to increase the funds that they supplied to pay wet nurses and maintain older children. In this, he equated the concern that a mother felt for her natural progeny to that which the women should display for their spiritual children, who, in their suffering, were 'the image of Jesus Christ in a special way'. In adopting them, the women replaced the natural guardians who had abandoned or injured them, compensating for their neglect or abuse with the same kinds of corporal and spiritual acts of merciful charity that they lavished on their own offspring, that is, with food, shelter, instruction, and, most of all, comfort. 'Without your help', de Paul warned starkly, 'they will all die', spiritually and physically.[69] Just as de Sales had taught, this was how the consoeurs would 'pass through the narrow gate of salvation', for their middle state permitted them to live within the world, serving God according to their station in life. Teaching the Lazarist missionaries, de Paul had borrowed from de Sales to affirm that a heart on fire with charity would make its ardour felt, and he adopted this favourite trope to define the ideals of the women's behaviour. The hearts of those who cared for the needy sick and poor were 'touched' by God.[70] They should have 'no heart except for God', de Paul counselled; as their hearts overflowed with grace, every act would be infused with love for him.[71]

This kind of spiritual sustenance was sometimes all that stood between the survival and abandonment of the confraternal works. Within a decade of its foundation, the first flush of enthusiasm that many members of the *Hôtel-Dieu* group felt was receding rapidly, and de Paul was forced to hold several meetings with its members between 1645 and 1648, not only to revive their zeal, but to convince them not to disband altogether. Running short of funds and innovative ideas to increase income, the Ladies needed de Paul to point out the perils that would result from desertion: the death of children, the damnation of souls amongst consoeurs and the sick poor, the delighting 'of hell and the wicked of the world', and the utter ruination of God's work. In this climate of want, the appeals that de Paul issued to maternal compassion and charitable duty were vital to his striking a chord with his listeners, and inciting them to renewed action. Amongst the donations of the wealthy who attended the conferences in 1647 were those of Madames d'Aligre and de Bercy, who contributed 20,000 *livres* each to save 300 children who had been abandoned by their natural mothers.[72]

[68] *CCD*, 13b: 417–18; *Œuvres completes de Saint François de Sales*, pp. xi, 241; Spivey Ellington, *Sacred Body*, 179–81.

[69] *CCD*, 13b: 402–6.

[70] *CCD*, 13b: 417.

[71] *CCD*, 13b: 436–7. This teaching also opens the final rule of the confraternity of the *Hôtel-Dieu*, dating from 1660: *CCD*, 13b: 443.

[72] *CCD*, 13b: 411–20; Bonneau, *Miramion*, 109.

In this period of crisis, the women's work was challenged as much by their own lack of commitment or confidence as by social or ecclesiastical conventions about female piety, causing de Paul to draw to the fore additional elements of their vocational service. He did not do so purely in reaction to events, however; within his teaching on the charitable devotion of women there already lay a firm endorsement of their leadership capabilities, and of their legitimate right to assume what were customarily masculine rights to these, under obedience to God. For instance, de Paul considered the Daughters to be similar to the deaconesses of the early church who had taught the poor their faith, and he extended this to the other confraternal members. He did, however, specify that their predecessors had taught only the liturgical rubrics, and had not elevated their ambitions higher than basic teaching of doctrine and rules of ritual. Thus, he implied that this was the level of teaching that the women should master, leaving more complex pedagogy to those greater in learning and authority, that is, to the ordained male. Still, for de Paul, the precedent set by the early deaconesses contradicted the social and ecclesiastical customs that had denied the women of Joigny and a number of other localities their share in instructing the sick poor. More fundamentally, he expressly observed to the consoeurs that it trumped the teaching of St Paul, who had not only ordered women to remain silent in churches but refused to countenance that they should teach at all.[73]

De Paul also resorted to another category of female participation to convince the consoeurs that they were heirs to and restorers of public female leadership and service. When some tried to excuse themselves from their public duties of care for the foundlings by claiming that these were unsuitable for women, he countered that God had 'used persons of your sex to do the greatest things ever done in this world'. Reaching back through salvation history, he endeavoured to rally them by pointing out women who had surpassed men in their achievements, when they had taught others, fed others, and led others. He positioned the consoeurs in an unbroken line of God's female servants: the biblical Judith and Esther, who had saved the Jewish nation from massacre and destruction; the fifth-century patron of Paris, St Geneviève, who had rescued the city from the peril of the Huns by convincing its residents to pray, and had risked her life to feed its inhabitants; Joan, the divinely inspired maid of Orléans, who had saved France from English dominance during the Hundred Years War. In this hallowed company, the consoeurs, in their 'middle state', could not give up their responsibilities to God and man.[74]

These heroic women were not unproblematic, of course, for there were unsettling elements in all their stories. Judith, for instance, had enjoyed great popularity amongst preachers since the sixteenth century, but she had saved the city of Bethulia by beheading the Assyrian general Holofernes in his bedchamber![75]

[73] *CCD*, 12: 76–7; *CCD*, 13b: 381, 432; 1 Cor. 14: 34; 1 Tim. 2: 12.

[74] De Sales had mentioned Judith in a list of male and female figures who had lived devoutly outside the monastery in his *Introduction to the Devout Life*, but de Paul does not appear to have specifically drawn on this when choosing his examples: de Sales, *Introduction*, 45.

[75] Llewellyn, *Representing Judith*, 115–31.

Despite this, she could still offer an example to the consoeurs, even if she was not a model for their lives in every way, and de Paul therefore isolated her exemplary qualities of valour and devotion while ignoring more troubling aspects of her life. It was also true that the messages in the heroines' tales were perhaps especially tuned for the ears of women whose social privileges rendered it easier for them to cast their lives in the image of a queen like Esther. Yet de Paul chose the quartet—a widow, a queen, and two unlettered and virginal peasants—deliberately, knowing that despite their differences they all enabled him to declare that it was legitimate and realistic for the consoeurs to seek to emulate their particular virtues, if not in scale at least in type. He implied that their 'Christian militia' would save their fellow man; although militia was an overtly masculine term, de Paul used it in the sense of spiritual soldiery, to suggest that the women would not rescue their charges from invading soldiers, but from the effects of aggression—war, famine, and conquest—by virtuous acts, and from the wages of death, as represented by the horsemen of the apocalypse. Of course, none of these four servants of God had been members of the normal ecclesiastical hierarchy of the church, and de Paul acknowledged that for 800 years women had not had any public role within the church. Providence had deprived them of it, but the time was now ripe for the severed line of female achievements to be knotted. Divine providence called again for the new deaconesses to assume their mantle of leadership and assistance with 'zeal and firmness' as well as humility.[76]

Finally, de Paul's influence in the confraternities extended beyond the spiritual to the practical. For instance, funding for the foundlings often fluctuated unpredictably and alarmingly, while the demand for this service seemed to grow relentlessly. In 1642, on the request of the officers of the *Hôtel-Dieu*, led by Madame Souscarrière, Louis XIII approved an annual grant of 4,000 *livres* for the foundlings, although this fell far short of their requirements. However, the money did not materialize every year; by 1655, they were owed a staggering 28,960 *livres* in arrears, while the annual expenses for the foundlings stood at 17,221 *livres* two years later.[77] To assist, de Paul often joined with the officers in appealing to the council of state to seek the payment of the grant, but his allegiance to the cause meant that he was also not averse to using the assets of the Lazarists to help when it was most urgent. For example, between 1643 and 1645, he had thirteen houses constructed just north of Saint-Lazare, using a portion of the 64,000 *livres* that the crown had allocated for the Lazarist house in Sedan. He promptly rented them for a minimal 1,300 *livres* annually to the confraternal officers who were then desperately seeking more accommodation for foundlings. In doing so, he managed to kill two birds with one stone, for this generous arrangement not only solved the

[76] *CCD*, 13b: 420, 426, 432.

[77] For documents relating to the grant, see AN, S6160. Three thousand *livres* of this was to be deployed for the children's upkeep, and 1,000 *livres* for the maintenance of the Daughters who looked after them. A year later, Aiguillon gave 5,000 *livres* to the project: Archives de l'Assistance Publique, Paris, Ms 109, Foss 1, 77. For the 1657 expenses, see *CCD*, 13b: 426, 430.

confraternity's spatial problem but also initiated a new source of regular income for the mission in Sedan.[78]

VI

Many of the wealthiest confraternal members poured cash, precious goods, and labour into the causes of charity, as both Diefendorf and Dinan elucidate. The Daughters of Charity were prime beneficiaries of their largesse; of the forty-six houses established after they first moved outside the capital in 1638, ten were funded by women who belonged to the *Hôtel-Dieu* group (to 1660). Three more owed their foundation indirectly to consoeurs in the late 1650s.[79] The women principally supported the works of welfare because they were personally active in them, and therefore had a direct stake in their outcome. With de Paul so willing to offer both spiritual and practical assistance to the consoeurs, did their relations with him produce a similar sense of obligation towards the missions and seminaries in which they were not themselves actively engaged?

For a subset with whom de Paul worked regularly over the long term, it is apparent that personal proximity tended to lead them to diversify the destination of their resources to include these areas of male and clerical ministry. Indeed, they seemed to have been more willing and likely to do so than the Lazarists' male patrons who usually confined their generosity to areas in which their sex worked exclusively, and in which they often had a functional interest. These women should not be sought on the list of those who founded Lazarist houses, however, for it returns only one female name, the duchess of Aiguillon. Indeed, her choices were anomalous, for not only was she the only consoeur to expend her resources on a house, she was the sole woman to do so at all. As a result, she stands out conspicuously in the line-up of male patrons whose possessions underpinned the Lazarist residences. Aiguillon's companions, however, are represented in other forms of patronage. For some, it was the ongoing costs of missionary campaigns that captured their generosity, the kind that required modest outlays now and again. Prominent amongst these were Marillac and her cousin du Fey, who supplied gifts in kind, such as sacred pictures and rosary beads, which were essential to the Lazarists' pedagogy.[80] Yet others offered gifts far greater in both size and

[78] AN, S6597 (22 October 1645); *CCD*, 13a: 340.

[79] Richelieu—Duchess of Aiguillon (1638); Sedan—Duchess of Bouillon (1639); Angers—Goussault (1640), with the abbot of Vaux; Nanteuil—Marchioness of Maignelay (1641); Liancourt—Duchess of Liancourt (1645); Saint-Denis—Marie de Lamoignon and Nesmond (1645); Chars—Herse (1647); Bernay—de Brou (1654); Arras—Aiguillon (with minor contributions from other Ladies) (1656).

The duchess of Nesmond interceded with the queen to fund a house of Daughters in Chantilly in 1655, while Marie Fouquet used her influence with two of her sons, the archbishop of Narbonne and the superintendent of finances, to convince them that they should permit the Daughters to settle in Narbonne, Belle-Isle, and Vaux-le-Vicomte in 1659–60: Dinan, *Women and Poor Relief*, 148.

[80] Du Fay also occasionally funded minor refurbishments at Saint-Lazare during the 1630s. There are several references to the gifts that she and Marillac gave in the letters that de Paul sent to them during the late 1620s and 1630s in *CCD*, 1, *passim*.

impact to support works of their choice. It is true that here again the duchess of Aiguillon stands head and shoulders above others, although the destination of her gifts means that they are beyond the remit of this study.[81] Even so, the sixteen donations that fourteen other women made were extremely substantial.[82] While one of these chose to remain anonymous, twelve were certainly members of confraternities of charity, and eleven of these belonged to the confraternity of the *Hôtel-Dieu*. More remarkably, these eleven were responsible for thirteen, or more than three-quarters, of the sixteen donations. Further, six were widows at the time of gifting, and hence had both the means and liberty to dispense their goods as they saw fit, while just three united with their husbands in making the gifts.

The list's most arresting revelation, however, is the personal proximity of this set of eleven to de Paul. With a handful of others, these formed an inner circle of consoeurs, and six of them either served time as officers or were sisters or daughters of women who did so. The importance of the familial connections should not be underestimated; Élisabeth Merault, for instance, was the sister of an officer (Marguerite) whose tenure coincided with the signing of Élisabeth's contracts for the donation of land in 1644 and 1647.[83] Although the remainder were not officers (or at least are not known to have been), they were still committed members, who over the years often took special responsibility for overseeing particular works which required them to liaise with de Paul. Amongst other duties, Charlotte de Herse, for instance, the widow of a parliamentary president and former ambassador, headed the campaign for aid to the war-torn north-east in the 1640s and early 1650s, which required her to communicate frequently with de Paul regarding transportation of money and goods by his missionaries and so on. She, like the other women, directed donations towards the cost of missions or ordinand retreats. Some gave a particularly personal twist to theirs: Geneviève Goussault requested that her legacy of 1,100 *livres* be spent on decorating an altar at Bons-Enfants and on masses for her soul there, which benefited both the training of seminarians and her eternal health.[84] Evidently, neither she nor her companions handed out cash or land indiscriminately, without thought for recipients or the use to which the income would most likely be put. Each woman's choice of the Lazarists from the

[81] Along with providing funds for a Lazarist house in Rome, Aiguillon made donations in the 1640s, which enabled the Lazarists to establish a skeleton presence in Tunis and Algiers. In 1643, she and de Paul agreed that a portion of her gift of 14,000 *livres* would be used to send Lazarists to Barbary, and she assigned revenues from three coach routes in France to the same purpose in 1647. In 1646 and 1648 respectively, she purchased the offices of consul for Algiers and Tunis, and offered them to the Lazarists to fill. For further details, see Forrestal and Roşu, 'Slavery on the Frontier'.

[82] See Appendices 2 and 3 for the features of the 16 donations.

The crown agreed to provide funding for ordinand retreats in 1643 and 1644, the approval for which no doubt came from Anne of Austria. However, this was an institutional donation, and therefore is not equivalent to the donations under review here.

[83] Marguerite was the widow of Anthoine l'Arche, *sieur de Saint-Mandé*, a former royal councillor and *lieutenant-géneral d'eaux et forêts de France*: ACMP, 'Noms des premières Dames de la Charite, 1634–60' (unpaginated); AN, Y 184, fo. 83v (22 December 1644), Y 185, fo. 34r (2 September 1647).

[84] Goussault made her will while staying at the Daughters' motherhouse shortly before she died: *CCD*, 13b: 121, 390–6; Gobillon, *Mademoiselle Le Gras*, 74.

myriad of meritorious options in Paris was an informed one, for they knew de Paul and the Lazarists' works very well. Equally, this meant that they were often content to trust de Paul to decide precisely where their gift could be put to best use.[85] And, for his part, he was scrupulous in informing them of the results that ensued and to express the Lazarists' gratitude for their generosity. These courtesies were vital to maintaining the women's trust and enthusiasm, as well as being precursors to his invitations 'to continue their good graces'.[86]

All of these donations belong to the years after 1635, and therefore to the years in which de Paul cultivated his ties with the women within the setting of the *Hôtel-Dieu* confraternity. They were quick to grasp the opportunities that the confraternities in general offered as a means to strive for virtue in themselves and others, but they also enjoyed extraordinary privileges that many others could not access, for the support that de Paul provided to them inspired, guided, and undergirded their charitable acts and campaigns. In return, their affinity for the pursuit of what was a common mission of Catholic welfare led them to make common cause with him in other spheres of his work, that is, to extend their resources to the Lazarist missions and clerical formation. As members of the inner circle of the *Hôtel-Dieu* association as well as a core group of Lazarist patrons, these women were therefore not only unusual amongst the collaborators that de Paul gathered in the pursuit of his mission of charity, they were highly exceptional.

[85] See, for instance, Maignelay's complimentary comments about the missionary 'acts of charity' that de Paul's men had performed during their missions around Nanteueil during the 1630s: *CCD*, 2: 110, Claude-Marguerite de Gondi to de Paul, 21 August 1640.

[86] *CCD*, 2: 273, de Paul to Bernard Codoing, 18 March 1642.

10

Affinities, Associations, and Projects of Charity

I

By now, it should be glaringly obvious that de Paul had a penchant for structures that enabled charitable piety to be organized collectively, whether they were for missions, visits to the sick and poor, or sacerdotal formation. Less observable to date has been the fact that his affection for the communal performance of religious acts extended beyond organizations that he founded, promoted, or ran himself. Around 1635, he joined a recently formed secretive grouping called the Company of the Holy Sacrament, and remained an ordinary member until his death. Founded by the duke of Ventadour in 1627, this male association attracted at least 450 clerical and lay members in Paris over the course of its existence to the 1660s, many of social distinction, wealth, and political influence. Its most zealous confreres met regularly to promote their initiatives to Christianize society, that is, to fortify religious discipline and eradicate immoral practices such as prostitution and drunkenness.

For historians of seventeenth-century France, the term *cabale des dévots* can refer only to this shadowy group, which was restored to public view with the discovery of a late seventeenth-century manuscript of its history at the close of the nineteenth century. Shortly afterwards, Raoul Allier rendered the association sensational when he claimed that its impact had been both malign and all-powerful, such was its dominance over religious affairs in Paris. Amongst the participants in its machinations, Allier included de Paul, whose actions he assumed to have been controlled by the Company, and whose missionaries were at its beck and call. De Paul's occasional appearance in the manuscript history, accompanied by his near silence about the group in his correspondence, seemed to feed Allier's claim; de Paul was candid about his links with other groupings, and the absence of the Company from his communications suggested that he sought to hide his relations with it from scrutiny, and its activities from the discovery of outsiders.[1]

While nobody denies that de Paul was a member of Company, it is absurd to suggest that he was its naive instrument or that he, and consequently the Lazarists and the confraternities, were wholly controlled by it. Yet, there remains much

[1] Allier, *Cabale*; Voyer d'Argenson, *Annales*.

which is uncertain about the exact nature of his connection to it: to what extent did de Paul work through the Company, operate independently of it, or even in opposition to it? Where does it fit into the weave of relationships that he cultivated while promoting his mission of charity, and into the activities that he organized or encouraged the Ladies and Lazarists to perform? The answers to these questions do not lie in segregating the Company from other constituent groups and individuals with whom de Paul worked for forensic analysis. Rather, it should be situated relationally amongst them, for two reasons. First, de Paul was in close contact with numerous figures within each group. Second, he was unique in being the only person who had a role in all of them, and this meant that he was also a point of connection linking them. Of course, his centrality to the operations of the Lazarists was greater than the other two: the Company had near absolute autonomy since de Paul was just one of many members in Paris, while the Ladies also enjoyed full governmental powers over their activities.[2] However, as superior general of the Lazarists, it was within de Paul's power to establish collaborations with both, and to attempt to assimilate the work of the Lazarists with their activities and objectives if he wished.

II

In reaching his conclusions about de Paul, Allier assumed that many of the missions that the Lazarists undertook were the products of the 'occult' influence of the Company of the Holy Sacrament. They certainly had a mutual interest in improving standards of piety amongst the faithful, which on occasion led the Company to ask de Paul to organize a mission; for example, in 1649, it paid 60 *livres* to the Lazarists for a mission in Férolles, one of six parishes about which it had received reports of profanities committed against the eucharistic sacrament during the Fronde. De Paul combined this demand with their regular mission in Brie-Comte-Robert.[3] In making this kind of request, the secretive Company deliberately never acted in its own name, but deputed someone to liaise with de Paul, so it can be problematical to distinguish the resulting works from those independently solicited by Company members. Yet it is not impossible. In 1633, for instance, Antoine Lamy approached de Paul to ask that he provide priests to complete a mission at the *Quinze-Vingts* hospital, of which he was director. He and his wife were already closely enough associated with de Paul, as the foundation of a confraternity of charity on their land demonstrates, to make such an invitation independently of the Company.[4]

Overlapping memberships between the Tuesday Conferences and the Company also led Allier to conclude automatically that the missions of the former were always

[2] In Paris, the Company is known to have had at least 182 ecclesiastical and 267 lay members, but probably had many more. By 1660, the Company had 'chapters' in over sixty-four towns and cities across France, with perhaps 4,000 members in total: Tallon, *Compagnie*, 25, *passim*.

[3] Voyer d'Argenson, *Annales*, 58–109.

[4] Lamy also asked de Paul to establish a confraternity of charity in the hospital: Abelly, *Vie*, ii, 256.

Company events. Six of the known Conference members served as its director, while nineteen others were ordinary members.[5] Indeed, it would be surprising were the number lower, for the sacerdotal piety that the Conference prescribed fitted comfortably with the social engagement that the Company advocated. But this led Allier to surmise, for example, that Olier's mission in the Auvergne in 1636 was a Company mission, on the basis that Olier was a member of the Company and that his spiritual director was Charles de Condren, one of its founding members. But even if Condren did recommend it to Olier, as a spiritual director might, there is no evidence to suggest that it became a formal mission of the Company. It is more likely that the origin of the mission can be traced to the Tuesday Conferences, for a number of Olier's fellow confreres joined him in the Auvergne, and the author of the Company's otherwise meticulously minuted seventeenth-century history, René de Voyer Argenson, did not mention this mission (or the mission in the *Quinze-Vingts*) at all when he recounted the Company's activities for 1633 or 1636.[6] On the other hand, there is evidence to suggest that the groups did collaborate on other occasions, with de Paul acting as the organizing force. In 1635, Company members expressed their unease about the levels of ignorance apparent in several villages around Paris. The Company asked de Paul to carry out a mission for this 'great evil', for which he used Tuesday Conference members. Three years later, he cooperated with two of these, François Perrochel and François Renar, when the Company deputed him to investigate its suspicions that masses were being poorly celebrated in Paris. He also agreed, somewhat reluctantly, to lodge a number of vagabond priests at Saint-Lazare, for the upkeep of whom the Company paid.[7]

There is obviously no overlap in the memberships of the Company and the female confraternities of charity, but a significant number of *Hôtel-Dieu* consoeurs had male relatives who were active in the Company, including husbands, sons, and sons-in-laws in the Lamoignon, Fouquet, Lamy, L'Hoste, and Séguier families. They usually worked through its aegis rather than actively cooperating with female family members. When they did, however, de Paul was able to provide the unifying glue. At the *Hôtel-Dieu*, he met the desires of the gentlemen of the Holy Sacrament and the Ladies from the mid-1630s, while also acting as patron to a number of younger ecclesiastics who had come to his attention during retreats and conferences. The quality of the services that the existing hospital chaplains delivered had become a source of concern to the Company at an early stage of its existence, and it deputed three of its members to investigate them in 1636. On hearing their dismal assessments, it asked de Paul to supply priests to meet the demands of ministry. But he proved unwilling to deploy his own missionaries, because they were already stretched to fulfil the demands of their own duties, and because the job was anyway inconsistent with their vocational purpose. He knew too that the tricky question of payment needed to be addressed first. De Paul therefore decided to appeal to the Ladies' officers to consider whether they would pay the necessary stipends. Once

[5] Tallon, *Compagnie, passim.*
[6] Allier, *Cabale*, 138.
[7] Voyer d'Argenson, *Annales*, 58–109.

they acquiesced with an offer of 150 *livres* per priest, he recommended names for the posts, and he maintained responsibility for appointments until his death.[8]

III

The development of the Lazarists' activity in Marseille offers an illuminating case study of the advantages that de Paul was able to garner from cooperation across the associations. During the 1640s, the patronage of members of the Ladies and Company was axiomatic to the institutional expansion of the Congregation in the south; a house was established in Marseille in 1643, and the twenty-nine priests and five coadjutor brothers deployed there to 1660 were responsible for the pastoral care of galley convicts and the completion of missions in its rural surroundings.[9] Marseille's importance as a Mediterranean port also meant that the house was a staging post for operations in north Africa, particularly for the transfer of funds donated by Ladies such as Madeleine de Lamoignon to ransom captive Christians.[10] By the 1650s, de Paul judged it amongst the most important Lazarist foundations in France because of its strategic location in the south and on the Mediterranean, its size, and the range of its residents' responsibilities.

The actions which led to the commencement of these duties were first and foremost the personal initiatives of individual members of the Company and the Ladies. Concurrently, however, for the Holy Sacrament at least, they also represented the official policy of the new branch of the Company in Marseille, founded by Antoine Godeau and Simiane de La Coste in 1639.[11] Equally, although it was not de Paul who instigated the venture, he was characteristically quick to recognize the advantage of responding positively to the overtures made to him to contribute to it. He thus ensured that his Congregation benefited from the devout wishes that drew the chief patrons to pool their resources.

[8] François Renar subsequently added a donation of 100 *livres* to the fund. Unfortunately, the names of the first six appointees are not extant, but some of de Paul's subsequent presentations are, notably those of six that he made in 1642. Of these, most were relatively low-level ecclesiastics. The inclusion of the Irish priest Kilian Calughan suggests that most came to de Paul's notice when they frequented the conferences held on Thursdays at Bons-Enfants, which Irish clerics attended regularly in the 1640s. Calughan's companions in presentation were Charles Rulhiat, Pierre Leclerc, Guillaume Tranchart, Mathurin Menart, and Florent Arnaut: AN, LL267, fo. 278v, and extrait du registre 59, fos 63, 94; *État au vrai du bien et revenue de l'Hôtel-Dieu*, 70; *CCD*, 1: 349, de Paul to Louise de Marillac, 2 November 1636; *CCD*, 13a: 179; Voyer d'Argenson, *Annales*, 58–63.

[9] During the 1650s, the Lazarists taught some novice monks of the abbey of Saint-Victor, Marseille, but this was short-lived. In 1658, the bishop of Marseille, Étienne du Puget, decided to invite the Congregation to run a proposed seminary, but it did not open for a further fifteen years: AN, S6707; AD des Bouches-du-Rhône, Série H, Registre 35, 'Saint-Victor de Marseille'; *CCD*, 7: 69, de Paul to Firmin Get, 18 January 1658; *CCD*, 7: 116, same to same, 8 March 1658.

[10] Amongst her many charitable interests, Lamoignon held the ransom of captive Christians dear, according to her biographer, Jacques Marsolier; on one occasion, she donated 18,000 *livres* to pay the debts for which a merchant was being held captive in Algiers, and she quested regularly to raise money to ransom seventy others: BSG, Ms 4232, Marsolier, 'La Vie de Mademoiselle de Lamoignon', fo. 187r.

[11] Ruffi, *Chevalier de la Coste*, 40–105; Tallon, *Compagnie*, 29.

De Paul's connection to the galleys was long-standing, for he had been their chaplain general since 1619. In the early 1620s, he had organized a number of missions to the galleys in Bordeaux and Marseille, and he and Portail had visited the prisoners lodged in Paris before they departed for the ports. Having witnessed them being 'treated like beasts', de Paul also supervised the transfer of the condemned men from deplorable conditions in the dungeons of the *conciergerie* and other Parisian prisons to a new prison near Saint-Roch church in 1622, enacting a move on which Philippe de Gondi and the archbishop had decided in 1618, before he became chaplain. Subsequently, although the Lazarists' foundation contract stipulated that its members carry out missions for the galley convicts, their rural missions took priority from 1625, and visits and missions to the galleys all but ended for a time. Instead, de Paul deputed other ecclesiastics, such as Capuchins, for the tasks.[12] Furthermore, in Paris, the community of Saint-Nicolas-du-Chardonnet became the principal pastors after the archbishop again transferred the condemned to a new prison, *La Tournelle*, in their parish in 1632: he appointed them to minister in its chapel, preach weekly, and to deliver lessons in catechism twice weekly. At this time, members of the Company of the Holy Sacrament in Paris began to visit the prisoners too, while the Daughters and women of the confraternity of Saint-Nicolas-du-Chardonnet parish partially made up for the Lazarists' absence.[13]

Visiting prisoners was a specialized act of virtue, usually only carried out by the most dedicated and experienced consoeurs who could endure the foul language, filth, and odours that greeted those who came to give spiritual and material consolation to the condemned men. These formed a tiny group of twelve specially deputed women, who committed to visiting not merely the 400 prisoners in *La Tournelle* on a weekly basis, but eight other prisons dotted around the city as well (a task of staggering dimensions that they could not have expected to complete thoroughly). Amongst those most closely involved were Louise de Marillac, and Marie Lamoignon and her daughter-in-law, Madeleine. It was probably Marillac and the senior Lamoignon who wrote the regulations that the visitors followed during these years. The spiritual justification that these offered to inspire the visitors was a condensed version of the teaching found in the confraternal rules, but the directives were tailored specifically for a prison environment. The women's distribution of small pots of food to prisoners gave them a pretext to offer some words of religious instruction, and to exhort them to perform acts of contrition and make a general confession of their sins. The women watched to ensure that the prisoners could attend mass, and that the chapels were decently equipped, while they also distributed small books of devotion. To improve living conditions, they supplied straw, mattresses, coal, and clothing to the condemned, and tried to organize visits by doctors to the sick.[14]

12 BN, Ms 20942, fo. 534r; *CCD*, 10: 103; Forget, 'Des prisons au bagne de Marseille'.

13 *CCD*, 1: 168, de Paul to Louise de Marillac, 1632; for the archiepiscopal ordinance, see AN, MM 292 (2 September 1634); Schoenher, *Séminaire de Saint-Nicolas-Du-Chardonnet*, i, 128.

14 *Mémoire des prisons de Paris*; *Instructions utiles pour les dames*. The latter is the set of regulations that the Ladies adopted.

The duchess of Aiguillon was not amongst the twelve ladies who visited the prisons, but she did donate to the cause. Her anxiety about it became both more pressing and more worldly when she became the administrator of her late uncle's estate; the cardinal's heir was his 15-year-old grandnephew, Armand-Jean du Plessis, duke of Richelieu, whose father had been appointed general of the galleys in 1635, after Cardinal Richelieu pressurized the duke of Retz to sell the office. Armand-Jean held the office from 1643 until his profligacy forced him to sell it in 1661. Until 1656, when he officially matured, his aunt held considerable influence over its functioning, even though he increasingly challenged her control of his assets from 1650.[15] It was fortunate therefore for de Paul that one of Aiguillon's key objectives was to ensure that he should retain the office of chaplain general of the galleys in security and perpetuity; at her request, in 1643 Anne of Austria asked the king to issue a royal ordinance that assigned the office of chaplain general 'permanently to the Superior General of the Congregation of the Priests of the Mission now and to come'. This decree also allowed him to 'entrust this duty' to the superior of the Marseille house 'in his absence'.[16]

In the long term, the Richelieu family's acquisition of the generalship was as crucial for de Paul's ability to establish the Lazarists in Marseille as had Philippe de Gondi's possession of it been to his appointment as chaplain general of the galleys initially. But Aiguillon's action should be understood within the context of her efforts to strengthen her nephew's formal authority over the galleys, and in particular her wish to rationalize the structures of command in the general's interests. Her uncle had used the galley fleet as a vehicle for patronage, appointing members of leading noble Provençal families to positions of command, and asserting personal dominance over the individual galleys, numbering twenty, of the fleet. On his death, the captains, led by the *bailli* of Marseille, Paul-Albert de Forbin, who owned two galleys, reasserted their autonomy, which included challenging the authority of the duke over their commands.[17] At the same time as Aiguillon petitioned that de Paul should be confirmed in his post as chaplain general, therefore, she pleaded with the royal council that orders from the king should go to the duke rather than directly to the galley commanders, so that he could then send these along with his own to the officers in Marseille. She did so in the hope that this would ensure that the general was kept as informed as possible about royal wishes, and could coordinate his orders with the king's. The strategy was designed specifically to challenge the independence of Forbin, whom the duchess accused of countermanding the duke's orders, and of acting as if only he 'might be capable of serving the king'.[18]

Aiguillon's interest was not purely patrimonial, of course. In 1643, she asked de Paul to send five missionaries to give a mission on the galleys in Marseille, and prevailed on the new bishop of Marseille, Jean-Baptiste Gault, a member of the

[15] AAE, Mémoires et Documents, F, 856, fo. 311; Bergin, *Cardinal Richelieu*, 280–4; Mousnier, *Institutions of France*, 53.

[16] *CCD*, 13a: 337–8.

[17] James, *Navy and Government*, 101–7.

[18] AAE, Mémoires et Documents, F, 847, fos 229–30. On Forbin's career, see Petiet, *Bailli de Forbin*.

Company of the Holy Sacrament and the Tuesday Conferences, to add a few more. Afterwards, Gault wrote enthusiastically to his spiritual adviser to recount the events of the six-week mission, and shared that it had convinced many convicts to resolve 'not to offend God anymore, and to take their affliction patiently'. He commented that Aiguillon wished to preserve these results by establishing a permanent mission, a proposal that he was extremely glad to endorse. Gault also confessed that he now hoped to establish a hospital for the galleys, because his compassion had been aroused when he witnessed the sick men on them 'abandoned and despairing' in their pain.[19] He knew, he wrote, that Philippe de Gondi had hoped to build a hospital over twenty years before (it is possible that the prelate had already discussed this with de Paul), but his plan had never progressed beyond the identification of a site. Having aided Aiguillon, the bishop had since written to her to seek a favour in return, and she had agreed to donate 9,000 *livres* for what she called 'this holy intention . . . so agreeable to God'.[20] Gault signed off his letter by revealing that he had also approached a few other 'persons of piety' about the idea. He meant fellow members of the Company in Marseille and in Paris. In Paris, the collective assembly approved it as a 'very useful' endeavour, but left individual members in both cities to pursue it as they saw fit.[21]

Gault died at the end of May 1643 when he unexpectedly caught the plague. By then, however, he had enlisted the Company in Marseille to the hospital's cause, and one of its founders, La Coste, became an indefatigable promoter of it, as well as one of the first administrators. He visited Paris in mid-1643 for meetings with de Paul and Aiguillon to devise the next stage of foundation. They agreed that the Lazarists should take responsibility for it, and de Paul and Aiguillon signed a contract to this effect in July.[22] For his part, La Coste advanced large sums to pay for building works that he oversaw through the 1640s, as well as donating 6,000 *livres* for these.[23] Then, in 1646, Aiguillon successfully petitioned the crown to make the hospital a titular royal foundation. With the queen mother's assent, he granted two arsenals for conversion and 9,000 *livres* annually, as well as a lump sum of 3,000 *livres* for linens and other essential equipment.[24]

Despite the endowment and grants, however, the hospital faced considerable financial hardship. After the galleys moved to Toulon in 1655 the crown did not pay the annual grants, even though the hospital still had around 300 patients. De Paul was repeatedly forced to ask the duchess to intercede with the

[19] Ruffi and other commentators did not realize (or ignored) that Gault was the instigator of this project in the 1640s, but his personal account of events confirms this: Ruffi, *Chevalier de la Coste*, 164.

[20] Albanès, *Gallia Christiana novissima*, cols 624–7, Jean-Baptiste Gault to Charles Guillard d'Arcy, 5 May 1643; Bausset, *Tableau*, 30. Aiguillon's letters promising Gault 9,000 *livres* are printed in Marchetty, *Messire J. B. Gault*, 209, 255.

[21] Voyer d'Argenson, *Annales*, 90–1.

[22] *CCD*, 13a: 335–7. See also Appendix 1.

[23] On his death in 1649, La Coste bequeathed 16,000 *livres* for the foundation of a seminary in Marseille under Lazarist management, but this did not open until 1673: Ruffi, *Chevalier de la Coste*, 121–37, 196.

[24] The crown gave additional annual income of 3,000 *livres* in September 1648, and another lump sum of 4,600 *livres* in 1651: See AN, S6707 for the letters patent, and MM 534, fos 241v–242r.

superintendent of finances, Nicolas Fouquet, for financial support, particularly for the wages of thirteen almoners that he recruited from Bons-Enfants seminary. He realized that her access to the minister was indispensable in appeals of this kind, and admitted that 'we can do very little without her'. Unfortunately, Aiguillon's efforts bore little fruit, as the crown continued to drag its feet; Fouquet's promises to pay up amounted to nothing more than the occasional allocation of token sums for costs, and in 1658 a frustrated de Paul reported that the crown was now refusing to pay even the stipends for the previous two years. Finally, he resorted to his connection with the minister's mother, Madame Fouquet, to pursue the matter, with her maternal influence proving only marginally more rewarding; in 1659, the minister agreed to pay a paltry sum of 2,000 *livres*, which did not go far.[25]

The letters patent for the institution allotted to de Paul the power to appoint its administrators, with the approbation of the general of the galleys.[26] Since two were replaced every two years, this was a significant privilege, and potentially a means of ensuring that de Paul could maintain his influence in the hospital's management. Over the years, he habitually appointed the same men, after passing on his nominations with his opinions on their suitability to the duchess, and later to the duke; for example, in 1656–7, he recommended that Pierre de Bausset (*sieur de Roquefort* and chief medical officer of the military hospital in Marseille) be reappointed, along with his nephew Antoine (lieutenant seneschal of Marseille); Bausset had demonstrated his fitness for the post on other occasions, and de Paul believed both men to be 'among the leading citizens and most upright men in the town'.[27] He must have known also that they were members of the Company of the Holy Sacrament, which added further proof of their integrity of faith and commitment to the convicts. He depended on them to challenge refusals by the galleys' officers to cooperate with the Lazarists' care for the sick in their workforce. This was an ongoing problem, for the loss of any man reduced the manpower available on a galley, and the galley owners were only compensated with payments of 3 *sous* per patient per day. De Paul was acutely aware of the danger of allowing the officers to influence hospital policy, as is apparent in his warning to the duke that he should not appoint the marquis of Ternes to the board of administrators instead of one of the Baussets, because he 'would find a way either to get control of the king's alms or to destroy that good work [of the hospital]'.[28]

[25] *CCD*, 6: 260, de Paul to Firmin Get, 2 March 1657; *CCD*, 6: 265, same to same, 9 March 1657; *CCD*, 6: 279, same to same, 29 March 1657; *CCD*, 6: 392, same to same, 27 July 1657; *CCD*, 6: 431, same to same, 24 August 1657; *CCD*, 7: 109, same to same, 1 March 1658; *CCD*, 7: 410, de Paul to Philippe Le Vacher, 13 December 1658; *CCD*, 7: 437, de Paul to Firmin Get, 27 December 1658; *CCD*, 7: 455, same to same, 17 January 1659; *CCD*, 7: 467, same to same, 7 February 1659; AN, S6707, 'Fondation et Establissement des Prêtres de la Mission dans Marseille', fos 51r, 56r.

[26] AN, S6707; MM 534, fos 241v–242r.

[27] *CCD*, 6: 207, de Paul to Firmin Get, 16 February 1657; *CCD*, 6: 259, same to same, 23 February 1657; *CCD*, 7: 81, same to same, 1 February 1658; *CCD*, 7: 94, same to same, 8 February 1658.

[28] *CCD*, 2: 575, Gaspard de Simiane de La Coste to de Paul, 1645; *CCD*, 7: 93–4, de Paul to Firmin Get, 8 February 1658.

De Paul found, however, that he was not always able to rely on local allies to protect the Lazarists' interests or to hold sway over those administrators who, devout though they might be, did not necessarily share all of his views on the provision of care. They diverged over the features of the missionaries' work in the hospital, the degree of commitment that the missionaries could give to it, and, more broadly, the extent to which spiritual and temporal affairs should be separately administered. De Paul argued for a distinct demarcation, but in reality this was less clear cut because his power to select administrators meant that he himself exercised an indirect role in policy-making in the secular sphere. Specifically, dispute was sparked when the Lazarists purchased a house close to the hospital in which to live and perhaps to establish a small seminary in 1647. Excepting La Coste, the hospital administrators protested strongly against this, because they feared that the purchase signalled that the community would not remain loyal to their hospitaller ministry. They contended that two priests should live at the hospital, devoting their energy exclusively to ministering to the patients, and they put heavy pressure on the superior, Firmin Get, to concede; they also attempted to dictate the terms of service, arguing that it should include time-consuming duties of chant and solemn services in the chapel. In effect, they wished to treat the Lazarists as hospitaller religious like the Brothers of Charity. De Paul made his opposition to this known to La Coste, so that he might relay it locally, and also dispatched Antoine Portail to restate at a meeting with administrators the Lazarists' entitlement to determine what services they would provide. In briefing Portail, he observed that he did not doubt that the administrators wished to 'have the upper hand in everything'. Of this, they should be disabused, for the Lazarists were bound to care first and foremost for the convicts on the galleys, and their work in the hospital was 'merely an accessory' to this priority. Moreover, as they had discovered to their cost in Toul a decade previously, their principal purpose did not lie in the management of hospitals.[29]

The disagreement rumbled on until 1650, when de Paul switched tactic by turning to the source of his own power in the hospital, the duchess of Aiguillon, to win his case. She was the only surviving patron founder of the hospital, and the spokesperson for the duke of Richelieu who approved the administrators' appointments: the threat of her disapproval and the withdrawal of her favour alone were probably sufficient to enable de Paul to face down opposition among them. He also counted on the goodwill of Pierre de Bausset, whom he had recently appointed as an administrator, to rebalance the ranks. On 9 July, he met with the pair in Paris, where they issued decisive instructions to settle the dispute. First, they insisted that it was de Paul's prerogative to decide how many Lazarist priests were to serve in the hospital (two), and de Paul was to decide who they were. Second, they stipulated that the priests were concerned only with spiritual affairs in the hospital, and were not to be pressurized into fulfilling other duties. Third, the superior of the Marseille house was to attend the administrators' meetings, and 'have a deliberative voice

[29] *CCD* , 3: 272–3, de Paul to Antoine Portail, 14 February 1648; *CCD*, 3: 295, same to same, 24 April 1648; *CCD*, 3: 295, same to same, 8 May 1648.

with *les sieurs* administrators' in the resolution and execution of policies.[30] This actually contradicted the second regulation because the superior would now intervene in matters of temporal administration. But it blurred the boundary between the sacred and secular administrations to suit de Paul's ends. He clearly felt that it did not suffice to have sympathetic individuals like Bausset on the board; he needed also to have a Lazarist spokesperson to represent him and the Congregation at meetings. Despite advocating that the spiritual and secular domains should be kept separate, therefore, de Paul, with the backing of his allies, chose to interpret this principle in favour of the spiritual realm, and in defence of the Congregation's autonomy against encroachments by outsiders.

The calling of the duchess to the Lazarists' side in the argument lanced the wound, and relations settled down thereafter into the pattern outlined in the directives. But de Paul's defence throughout bears some similarity to his defence of Lazarist autonomy in the disagreements with episcopal patrons in the same years. However, these particular struggles were *intra-ecclesia*, in that they centred on the location of power in the jurisdictional relationship between a bishop and a congregation of secular missionaries operating in his diocese. In contrast, de Paul's effort to defend his power and the Lazarists' privileges in the hospital in Marseille was directed against intrusion from the secular realm, whose representatives pushed through the jurisdictional boundary to encroach on clerical independence. Like other ecclesiastics, de Paul accepted that the church and the state, the twin pillars of society, were bound in a mutually reinforcing relationship that ensured order in society. He was also fully conscious of, and ready to exploit, the immense benefits that the temporal government brought to his Congregation and to the church in general. But, like many churchmen, he was suspicious of the tendency to undermine their liberty of jurisdiction by subjecting ecclesiastical concerns to secular oversight or diktat. Indeed, he was no doubt cognizant also of the episcopate's public and protracted attempts to protect its jurisdictional freedom and, as the guardian of the French church, to preserve its jurisdictional independence from violation by the crown, particularly through the aggressively Gallican *parlement* of Paris.[31] Within the institutional setting of the galley hospital, de Paul made the same effort, on a smaller scale, to protect his Congregation's right to self-determination.

IV

In these years, there were many categories of needy poor to whom pious Catholics could direct their prayers, money, and time. From the later 1630s, the *Hôtel-Dieu* confraternity and the Company of the Holy Sacrament began to provide aid for those affected by the Thirty Years War in the north-eastern provinces of France. When conditions for the poor there and in Paris itself worsened considerably

[30] Portail also attended the meeting: AN, S6707, 'Fondation et Establissement des Prêtres de la Mission dans Marseille', fos 52v–53v; *CCD*, 13a: 365–7.

[31] Forrestal, *Fathers*, 144–70.

during the 1640s, they redoubled their efforts. The existence of confraternities of charity across the city enabled the consoeurs of the *Hôtel-Dieu* group to spearhead a large-scale campaign of fundraising. It was a small cohort of women, however, who oversaw the mammoth tasks of organizing the collection and distribution of food, clothing, and agricultural tools, and who took the lead in providing examples of personal generosity for their fellows: the duchess of Aiguillon, Madames de Herse, Fouquet, and Traversay, the elder and younger de Lamoignon, and Mademoiselle Viole, who had been the association's treasurer some years earlier (1636–9). All of these were in the core group of consoeurs most closely associated with de Paul. Amongst them, Madeleine de Lamoignon was especially energetic in collecting alms and packing parcels of supplies for the provinces, while she and her elderly mother donated enormous amounts of corn for the cause. After the *Fronde* ended in 1653, Picardy and Champagne remained pitifully affected by the continued conflict between France and Spain, so she led the Ladies' drive to raise alms for the purchase of ornaments and vestments for churches damaged by troops and the upkeep of clergy. Her ingenuity was particularly important in achieving maximum results from minimum resources, as the wealthy of Paris experienced 'disaster fatigue' or found that they could barely maintain their own families with their diminishing assets. Lamoignon organized that nuns in Parisian monasteries be set to work making vestments for clergy and chemises to preserve the modesty of stricken peasants. Noticing that second-hand clothing could also serve this purpose, she introduced collections for garments, and established a boutique in which people could donate and purchase these.[32] Donations to the Ladies' campaign reached 367,500 *livres* by July 1657, a staggering figure which did not include the bulk goods, such as linens, furniture, and agricultural implements, that the Ladies had also distributed.[33]

At the same time, members of the Company of the Holy Sacrament were enacting their own aid campaign. The dominant figures in its organization were Gaston, baron de Renty, and Charles Maignart de Bernières, both of whom spent vast sums from their fortunes on the cause. Together with alms, Bernières donated a total of 80,000 *livres* in aid, of which he gave 35,000 *livres* to the Ladies. Some cooperation with the women was likely, for Renty's wife was a member of the *Hôtel-Dieu* confraternity.[34] However, rather than combining into one, the two campaigns were actually at times subjected to lively competition between their participants. From comments that de Paul made, it can be gleaned that they were vying for a limited range of resources, and that members of the Company sought to limit the Ladies' control of the alms that they collected, demanding that they be

[32] BSG, Ms 4232, Marsolier, 'La Vie de Mademoiselle de Lamoignon', 112–14, 159–60, 412; *CCD*, 5: 519, de Paul to Lambert aux Couteaux, 3 January 1653.

[33] *CCD*, 13b: 427.

[34] Moreover, Renty's conversion to a life of intense devotion had been assisted by his exposure to the Daughters' work in Saint-Paul parish in 1640. From then, he began to offer twice weekly meals for beggars in his own home and to visit the sick poor in their homes and at the *Hôtel-Dieu* to catechize: S. Iure, *Monsieur de Renty*, 165–9; ACMP, 'Noms des premieres Dames de la Charite, 1634–60' (unpaginated); Bessières, *Vincent de Paul, passim*; Féron, *Maignart de Bernières*, 255–6.

handed over to it; no wonder, for at the height of their campaign the Ladies were collecting alms of 16,000 *livres* per month! The duchess of Aiguillon remonstrated with Company members, and forced them to back down, although they still gazed covetously on the women's successes.[35]

De Paul witnessed the associations' rivalry, though he did not act as a peace broker between them on the issue in question. But with the potential for discord between charitable volunteers so possible, despite their pursuit of the same cause, his ability to contribute in other ways to their collaboration and solidarity was worthwhile. He found ways to capitalize on his position in each organization to advance the works of emergency welfare, although his priority lay in facilitating their attainment rather than in leading the entire campaign for assistance. As the head of the Lazarists, the most obvious input that he could make lay in the area of manpower. Under great pressure, the missionaries based in Sedan, Toul, and Troyes operated depots to distribute food and other essentials transported from Paris to the indigent. De Paul also appointed a number of men, most famously Matthieu Regnard, to trek back and forth between the capital and the north-east, carrying money and other goods for the hinterlands of Reims, Rethel, Laon, Saint-Quentin, Ham, Marle, Sedan, and Arras.[36] Yet, it is important not to overestimate the contribution that the Congregation made to this effort, however heroic the actions of those who bore the burden of travel across contested and devastated lands. By 1653, the Congregation could supply only three missionaries to travel to rural areas, and the Company of the Holy Sacrament had begun to rely more on religious orders, who adopted the innovative tactics that the Lazarists had deployed in manning distribution depots.[37]

The reports and letters that crossed de Paul's desk in Saint-Lazare proved vital in deciding the localities to which he should send his men, and provided information to pass to the Ladies about 'the number and needs of the poor' in affected areas.[38] But they also served another purpose, enabling him to partner with the Company and the Ladies to raise the profile of fundraising. It was de Paul who first really grasped the impact that publicity about the dreadful conditions would bring, and he produced a memoir for the Ladies to circulate when collecting alms in order 'to inform people of the affair'. Marillac and the other women made revisions that they thought necessary, and the strategy proved so successful that it spawned a whole series of similar leaflets in the early 1650s.[39] These included summaries of reports received from clerics 'in the field', and each sketched an evocative image of the 'deplorable state of some Churches' in Picardy and Champagne, where priests were forced to celebrate mass 'under canopies of straw . . . without any other altar than a simple plank', and before which a congregation kneeled in mud. They implored Parisians to donate their alms to heal the misery of people who had been abandoned

35 *CCD*, 2: 261, de Paul to Louise de Marillac, 1640–48; *CCD*, 6: 58, de Paul to Jean Martin, 28 July 1656.

36 *CCD*, 13b: 428.

37 *CCD*, 4: 520, de Paul to Lambert aux Couteaux, 3 January 1653; *Magasin charitable*, 13.

38 *CCD*, 6: 58, de Paul to Jean Martin, 28 July 1656.

39 *CCD*, 2: 261, de Paul to Louise de Marillac, 1640–8.

and languished near death, and were driven 'to eat grass and decaying carcasses like beasts'. At the foot of each leaflet, readers were informed that they could donate their alms to the houses of the women most involved in the campaign.[40] Subsequently, in 1655, when Maignart published similar relations for the Company of the Holy Sacrament, he also extracted much of the material (often verbatim) from letters that de Paul had passed to him.[41] He requested that donations should be passed to Herse and Lamoignon, indicating that by this time the Company and the Ladies were cooperating as far as possible in the aid effort, and that the support that de Paul provided to both was extremely valuable. For his part, de Paul acknowledged the Ladies' initiative in the marshalling of resources and the execution of the charitable schemes, and admitted that they 'enlisted' the Lazarists' help to realize their aims. He knew that they gave opportunities and means for him and his men to administer charity that he would have been hard pressed to find otherwise.[42]

V

The achievements of the aid campaign provided an incentive for de Paul and the Lazarists to work with the Ladies on further projects, should the right opportunity arise. In the 1650s, one such appeared to do so when the Ladies tried to involve them in a project to establish a general hospital in Paris which would offer food, shelter, and religious instruction to indigent men, women, and children in a large set of enclosed complexes. The course of events that followed, however, confirm that the women were quite capable of proceeding independently, with an autonomy that left de Paul with the undesirable task of refusing to accept the favour that they bestowed. Indeed, from 1653, the founding of the new hospital had little to do with de Paul directly, and instead became the subject of negotiations between the Ladies, the Company, and parliamentary officials, each of whom harboured differing expectations of the form that its governmental structure should take. As such, de Paul and the Lazarists became embroiled more than ever in the rivalries that existed between branches of the *dévot* community in Paris, and involuntary parties to the ongoing debate over the boundary between the sacred and the secular in public life.

Unlike the *Hôtel-Dieu*, the General Hospital, when it finally opened, was viewed by most members of the civic elite of Paris as a place of confinement, in which the healthy poor could be reshaped to become productive members of society, through training in skills useful to making their livings, exposure to the edifying teaching of catechism, and the practice of regular worship. The scale of the rationalizing project was immense in both cost and infrastructure, and needed to be if it was to answer

[40] The leaflets list Madames de Herse, Fouquet, Traversay, and Mademoiselles de Lamoignon and Viole. Several samples survive in the Bibliothèque Mazarine: *Aux veritable enfans de Dieu*, and *Nouvel advis*.

[41] *Recueil des relations*.

[42] *CCD*, 6: 58, de Paul to Jean Martin, 28 July 1656.

anxiety about the urgent need to take mendicants from the streets. It was the Company of the Holy Sacrament that had first considered it in the 1630s, and it resurrected the suggestion in the 1650s as the number of vagrants in the capital swelled.[43] The Ladies who became involved at this time accepted that the alarming scale of the problem rendered it necessary to introduce a policy of forced incarceration to cope, and that the same methods of visits and fundraising that they had used at the *Hôtel-Dieu* would serve the indigent concerned. Their immediate inspiration was an institute named *Nom de Jésus* in the faubourg Saint-Laurent, which de Paul had recently opened to provide residential care for needy people. Yet even though the consoeurs cited this as a model of care, it differed from their proposed foundation in critical respects, the most important of which was the voluntary nature of the residents' stay. Moreover, the establishment that they envisaged would dwarf *Nom de Jésus* in size, for it housed just forty elderly of both sexes, as well as a clutch of children, who were probably some of the orphaned refugees rescued from the 'ruined villages' of north-east France.[44] It was staffed by Daughters, while Lazarists visited frequently to provide pastoral care.

De Paul may have had it in mind to open *Nom de Jésus* as early as 1644, but it was not until 1647 that he was in possession of a property to house it. Three years earlier, he had purchased a large dwelling and garden for the Lazarists, paying 11,000 *livres* to its owner, Noel Bonhomme. Unfortunately, Bonhomme was being chased by a pack of creditors, and he refused first to leave the property and then to hand over its keys once forced, and even claimed compensation for works carried out on the house and the planting of fruit trees, flowers, and vines during this period. In the short but intense legal battle that de Paul undertook to obtain possession of the house, he had to apply for no less than three parliamentary *arrêts* before the former proprietor surrendered the property; had de Paul 'been able to foresee all these various cavilling points which have been brought against him', he would, he claimed in one of his petitions to the *parlement*, never have troubled with the house at all. Eventually, the residents moved into it in March 1653 after necessary adjustments to accommodation. Then de Paul purchased an adjoining building and garden to provide additional space, costing 3,750 *livres*.[45]

These were enormous sums to risk, and it is by no means certain that de Paul knew that a benefactor would underwrite the venture when he first began to pursue it. Even if he did, it was only in 1653 that he could breathe a sigh of relief when an 'anonymous bourgeois of Paris' finally signed a contract to this effect. Appointing de Paul the director of *Nom de Jésus*, he donated 100,000 *livres* to it, with strict conditions on its use for the purchase price, further building works, furnishings, church ornaments, and residents' upkeep. 60,000 *livres* of the sum should, he

[43] Voyer d'Argenson, *Annales*; McHugh, *Hospital Politics*, 85–6. See also Elmore, 'Origins of the Hôpital Général', ch. 3.

[44] The orphans numbered more than 800 overall. At *Nom de Jésus*, a handful of people entered each year. Complete figures are available only from 1659, but in that year one man and five women entered, and in 1660 three more men were accepted: AN, S6114; *CCD*, 13b: 427.

[45] Documents relating to the purchases and legal case are contained in AN, S6114 and S6601. See also *CCD*, 13a: 351–7.

directed, be invested to produce an annual income of 3,000 *livres*. The benefactor also insisted that he remain anonymous, and de Paul guarded his secret so closely that it has remained intact until now.[46] However, de Paul invested the money in the *cinq grosses fermes des gabelles* and the accrued revenues left a paper trail in which Mathieu Vinot was periodically named. Since his name is entirely absent from de Paul's correspondence, he would otherwise remain elusive, even though he held de Paul and his endeavours in such high regard that he blessed the Lazarists with the most generous donation that they ever received under his superior generalship. The pair are most likely to have become acquainted when de Paul joined the Council of Ecclesiastical Affairs in 1643, for Vinot was a *sécretaire ordinaire* to Anne of Austria between 1640 and 1664.[47]

According to de Paul, *Nom de Jésus* was a place of protection, rather than of involuntary confinement, but he, along with Louise de Marillac, still expected that it would serve the glory of God 'which ordered man to earn his bread by working'. The residents' daily routine was therefore composed of an exacting set of religious obligations and labour, devised to guard against idleness and vice, and to promote habits of dedication and productivity that were pleasing to God, and a grateful use of his gifts. Males and females were kept separate at all times, took their meals in silence, attended prayers twice daily in the chapel, listened to spiritual readings each day, had a session of catechism every evening, sang spiritual songs while busy at work, went to confession and took communion monthly, and left the house only with the sanction of the Daughter in charge. Their daily labour also served a practical purpose. Adults with a trade were given priority of entry, and residents were kept busy with 'useful and productive' tasks such as clothmaking, shoemaking, lacemaking, and sewing when they were not at prayer or taking their meals. The products that they made were sold for the house's upkeep, the adult residents were paid a small wage, and the children learned skills for their future livelihoods.[48]

This was hardly a luxurious existence, although it offered otherwise desperate and destitute people a semblance of security and the dignity of a small salary and trade. However, the primary goal of the institute was not actually 'to maintain their body' but 'to save their soul', and the rule advocated that the residents '[dream] principally to be a good Poor [person], living and dying as a good Poor [person]', trusting that God would provide for their material necessities if they did so.[49] Therein may have been part of its attraction for the Ladies, for those who accepted their station in life while living as honourably as possible would not overturn the prevailing social order. Organizationally too, for women who had encountered the

[46] AN, S6601; MM 534, fos 50r–51v (29 October 1653).

[47] AN, S6685, 'Registre', *passim*, for occasional details of the revenues accruing from the investment, and the naming of Vinot as donor. The register reveals that the investment was returning at least 6,000 *livres* annually around 1660; Griselle, *État de la maison*, 31,117.

[48] See AN, M53, no. 21, for the institutional rule; *Pensées de Louise de Marillac*, 272ff; Sullivan (ed.), *Writings*, 794–5.

[49] AN, M53, no. 21 (unpaginated): 'Ils se souviendront que cest Etablissement n'est pas tant fait pour Entretenir le Corps que pour sauver l'ame . . . songera principalement à ester bon Pauvre, vivant et mourant en bon Pauvre.'

logistical difficulties inherent in providing aid to the masses of sick and poor, a still larger establishment to house them appeared to be the obvious next step in efficiency. And, with older children and the elderly, they decided, could be included the foundlings under their care, as well as any other indigent of the streets.

Not long after de Paul opened *Nom de Jésus*, Madeleine de Lamoignon proposed to the Ladies that it could form a model for a general hospital. After discussing this, they brought the idea to de Paul's notice, but were nonplussed to find that he greeted it with less enthusiasm than they expected. Although he agreed to support their resolution to ask the queen, through the agency of the duchess of Aiguillon, to allow *La Salpêtrière* (situated opposite the *Arsenal*), to house it, he otherwise urged them to proceed with caution. This was not due to his usual desire to practise holy indifference, however. Rather, de Paul must have already known that plans were afoot to develop an institution much larger in scale. The Company of the Holy Sacrament, to whose deliberations he was privy, was lobbying *parlementaires* and ministers to establish a general hospital, and in mid-1653, precisely at the time that the Ladies approached de Paul, the first president of the *parlement*, Pomponne de Bellièvre, decided that a major reform of welfare should be undertaken. He commissioned a member of the Company and parliamentary counsellor, Christophe du Plessis, to investigate if the best option would be to unite existing institutions into a new hospital under a single board of directors. Not coincidentally, the Company authorized du Plessis to take the hospital's foundation as his principal work of piety at the same time, in order to speed the process.[50] It is likely, therefore, that de Paul knew that any venture that the Ladies brought into being in *La Salpêtrière* would soon be absorbed into this. However, although knowledgeable of its potential, he never engaged to any great extent in the campaign his confreres ran to this end.

Meanwhile, setting the Ladies' plan in motion, Aiguillon promised 50,000 *livres* to it.[51] Dedicated as ever to fundraising, Lamoignon managed to convince her friend and relative Angélique Faure, the widow of Claude de Bullion, former superintendent of finances and keeper of the seals, to contribute 80,000 *livres* to the proposal. Bullion insisted that Lamoignon keep her name confidential, and the discovery that it was she who bankrolled the Ladies' campaign is particularly noteworthy because her name is never mentioned in the rollcall of elite women who funded their schemes. Although she was a member of the confraternity of charity in her parish, she did not join the Ladies of the *Hôtel-Dieu*, which is rather surprising given her social stature and financial means. She chose to direct most of her wealth towards missions in New France, and the foundation of a *Hôtel-Dieu* in Montréal.[52] In the case of the General Hospital, Bullion's adamancy that she guard her privacy apparently forced her friend into comic but creative action: she is said to have visited Bullion's home clad in a voluminous skirt, which covered an underskirt

[50] Voyer d'Argenson, *Annales*, 136. [51] Abelly, *Vie*, i, 214.

[52] Madame de Bullion's daughter was married to Pomponne de Bellièvre: AN 766; Bib. Maz., Ms 1792, 'Actes relatif à la Congrégation de S. Jean de Dieu suivie de l'histoire chronologique abrégée de l'établissement des hopitaux de l'Ordre de la Charité en France', 42; Le Blant, 'Notes sur Madame de Bullion'; Simpson, *Marguerite Bourgeoys*, 80–2.

strung about with pockets in which she hid large amounts of money. The volume of cash no doubt necessitated multiple trips to and fro, but it was precisely the kind of escapade that the lively Lamoignon might relish. Thereafter, she pleaded incessantly with others to contribute, reassuring herself that her success in persuading them was worth the accusations of temerity thrown at her.[53]

By this time, Lamoignon, Aiguillon, Herse, and other leading consoeurs knew about the Company's more advanced plans.[54] So did Louise de Marillac, and she became anxious to ensure that the male Company would not block the Ladies' involvement in it, either during the period of foundation or thereafter. If the scheme had been purely a political matter, she reflected, then it would indeed need to be undertaken exclusively by men. But 'if it is considered as a work of charity, the women can undertake it in the manner that they have undertaken the other great works and difficult exercises of charity that God has approved by the benediction that his bounty gave there'. Borrowing the same defence of female leadership in public welfare that de Paul had used, she argued that God had often been served by both sexes through history, and that women like Judith, Ursula, Catherine of Alexandria, and Theresa of Avila had set precedents for such roles. She felt sufficiently assured to recommend a strategy to satisfy all parties. The women should take a full role in founding and running the hospital by organizing the aid offered within it, and should feel able to give their opinions simply and frankly, without being subjected to condescension. Those men involved should not necessarily be members of the Company, since its members were obliged to hide their charitable actions. They should 'give counsel' to the women, and 'act in the procedures and actions of justice that will perhaps be suitable to do in order to maintain all these types of people in their work'. Astutely, therefore, she turned the Company's reputation for secrecy upon itself in order to defend the Ladies' input into the hospital.[55]

Marillac's suggestion also explains why de Paul agreed to assist the Ladies while simultaneously recommending that they proceed slowly. Knowing that, by this stage, the Company was moving steadily closer to its goal, he realized that it was unwise for the women to start a rival campaign unwittingly, and hoped instead that they would be able to join in the existing project in the way that Marillac proposed. Coste assumes that the Company then thwarted the Ladies at every turn in order to deter them, but while there is no doubt that progress was slow, there is no evidence to suggest that this was deliberately orchestrated.[56] In the meantime, a number of

[53] BSG, Ms 4232, fos 199r–206r, 216r.

[54] AD de la Haute-Garonne, Ms 30, fo 51r.

[55] Diefendorf assumes that de Paul kept Marillac in the dark about the Company's plan, while Dinan supposes that she opposed the entire scheme for the hospital from the beginning. But Marillac's reflections in August 1653 prove otherwise, and are also more consistent with the fact that the Daughters of Charity worked in the hospital once it was established: *Pensées de Louise de Marillac*, 286–8: 'Si elle est considérée comme œuvre de charité, les femmes la peuvent entreprendre en la manière qu'elles ont entrepris les autres grandes et pénibles exercices de charité que Dieu a approuvés par la bénédiction que sa bonté y a donnée . . . tant pour conseils . . . que pour agir dans les procédures et actions de justice qu'il conviendra peut-être faire pour maintenir toutes ces manières de gens en leur devoir'; Diefendorf, *Penitence*, 236; Dinan, 'Motivations for Charity', 186.

[56] The halting of restoration work at *La Salpêtrière* in late 1653 on the order of the prince of Condé, chief mason of the city, may simply have been due to the growing expectation that a hospital would be

Ladies did all they could to hasten the decision-making process, by writing letters to this effect to Pomponne de Bellièvre and other *parlementaires*, and promising donations to the enterprise when they met with him.[57] Finally, in March 1656, a royal edict prohibited mendicity in Paris, and established a hospital, comprising six establishments dotted around Paris, including *La Salpêtière* and *Bicêtre* (a dilapidated building in which foundlings had been lodged between 1647 and 1650). The new first president of the *parlement*, Guillaume Lamoignon, headed, with the procurator general, Nicolas Fouquet, a board of twenty-eight *chefs-nés* or directors of the hospital. Four of these were the husbands of *Hôtel-Dieu* consoeurs, and eleven were members of the Company of the Holy Sacrament.[58]

The institution to which the Ladies finally contributed was far greater in scale than that which they had originally visualized, but they held precisely the position in it that Marillac had advocated, even if this was not officially acknowledged in the legislation. Thus, having already spent 3,400 *livres* on beds, linens, and utensils, they now proceeded to raise an additional 240,000 *livres*, to which Viole then added 4,000 *livres*.[59] But the acquisition of this role had not been the extent of their ambition. The Ladies held particular interest in the partners with whom they would work once the institution opened, and were anxious that those they thought most fitted to the provision of charity should be formally invited to exercise their skills there. For priestly ministry, their first choice was the Lazarists, and throughout 1654 and 1655 their president lobbied on their behalf, initially with de Paul and subsequently with leading *parlementaires*. She requested that the Lazarists be appointed as the hospital's spiritual administrators and that their superior general should act as a temporal administrator, with a deliberative voice on the board.[60] Aiguillon did not achieve all of these desires, but when the crown issued the edict for the hospital's foundation it did stipulate that the Lazarists would be responsible for 'the spiritual care and instruction' of the confined.[61] Yet the Lazarists were nowhere to be found in the hospital when it opened in 1657, and despite Aiguillon's professions of dismay, de Paul refused to permit them to take up their appointment. More perplexing again for the Ladies, Marillac committed the Daughters to working in the hospital once it opened, even though the Lazarists still continued to remain aloof. It is possible that the women had simply assumed, rather high-handedly, that de Paul would be delighted to agree with their wishes,

founded under royal sponsorship, and that projected schemes should be put on hold until this was confirmed: *CCD*, 5: 53, de Paul to the duchess of Aiguillon, 9 November 1653; Coste, *Saint*, ii, 296.

[57] Conversely, in a meeting with Pomponne de Bellièvre in May 1655, some of the Ladies, including Aiguillon and the Lamoignon women, threatened to withhold donations if the scheme was not completed 'correctly': AD de la Haute-Garonne, Ms 30, fos 54v, 81r, 93v–94r. The author of this manuscript may have been Jean de Gomont, as clues in the text reveal that the author, like Gomont, was a *parlementaire*, a member of the Company of the Holy Sacrament, and intimately involved in the decision-making process.

[58] *Edict du Roy portant establissement de l'hospital general* (unpaginated).

[59] Archives de l'Assistance Publique, Paris, Ms 108, Foss 1, 67; *L'Hospital general charitable*, 9.

[60] The Ladies also requested that the Daughters of Charity should serve in the sections of the hospital designated for female inmates: AD de la Haute-Garonne, Ms 30, fo. 62r.

[61] *Edict du Roy portant establissement de l'hospital general* (unpaginated).

but to proceed with their appeals in the first place, they must have felt that they had reason to believe that he would accept whatever roles the Lazarists were offered. Why did de Paul reject such great favour and opportunity, at the risk of alienating some of the Congregation's most ardent admirers and patrons?

To account for de Paul's motives, it is worth noting that he was not actually given the chance to turn down the position of temporal administrator. He might well have done so if he had been, since he did not judge the Lazarists' forays into the temporal administration of hospitals fondly. But it is also possible to observe the hand of Pomponne de Bellièvre at work in the disruption of the Ladies' ambition. As Poujol and McHugh note, the new board did not include any ecclesiastic at all. For Poujol, this was a mark of the 'modernism' inherent in the original charter, while McHugh maintains that the only reason that the archbishop of Paris was not listed as an administrator was because the diocese was empty at the time.[62] The absence of a role for de Paul suggests that Poujol may be nearer the mark. Pomponne de Bellièvre, while quite agreeable to the suggestion that the Lazarists should be the spiritual ministers of the hospital, was resolutely opposed to their gaining of secular power within it. He was equally opposed to the granting of a formal clerical title such as rector of the hospital to their superior, because this, he warned, would perhaps lead them to claim that this was a benefice, and as such entitled them to representation on the board then and in the future.[63] This testifies to a desire on his part to place welfare under the governmental control of secular agents, and to limit the contribution of ecclesiastics to the provision of spiritual consolation.

De Paul did not make his decision to decline spiritual ministry at the hospital lightly, for he brooded at length about the invitation before finally resolving to reject it.[64] It is generally taken for granted that his refusal stemmed from his distaste for the involuntary nature of stays there, and it is true that he had never advocated the forcible confining of poor men, women, and children, sick or able, in institutions. Even so, he did not explain his reservations about the hospital in these terms. On the contrary, he made it clear that he was not staunchly opposed in principle to the project. Instead, he stated that he hoped it would succeed, and to prove this, he assisted in its launch by sending Lazarists to partake in the first mission there. He also offered to send more if needed in the future. Subsequently, he successively recommended two priests from the Tuesday Conferences to act as rectors.[65] None of these sound like the actions of a man who recoiled in principle from the establishment or the ethos behind it.

There were those who did, but they were a minority in voicing their objections as the tide of poverty continued to rise in Paris. Notably, the Capuchin friar Yves de

[62] Poujol, 'La Naissance de l'Hôpital Général', 23; McHugh, *Hospital Politics*, 90.

[63] Archives Départmentales de la Haute-Garonne, Ms 30, fos 64r–65v.

[64] ACMP, Robineau, 'Remarques', fos 152r–154r.

[65] These were Louis Abelly and Thomas Régnoust, a doctor of the Paris Faculty: *CCD*, 6: 263, de Paul to Jean Martin, 2 March 1657; *CCD*, 6: 268, de Paul to the duchess of Aiguillon, March 1657; *CCD*, 6: 274, de Paul to Seraphin de Mauroy, 23 March 1657; *CCD*, 6: 275, de Paul to the duchess of Aiguillon, 23 March 1657; Abelly, *Vie*, i, 218.

Paris roundly condemned the hospital in his 1661 publication *Les Œuvres de miséricorde*, in which he also accused the rich of shutting the poor away in order to avert the discomfort they felt when they saw them in ragged bunches on street corners. Poverty was not a crime, he blasted, but it had been turned into one when the indigent were forced into captivity.[66] De Paul might have voiced the same criticism, particularly since he professed as a maxim that Jesus, in whose image the poor were moulded, had lived as a free and virtuous man in poverty on earth. Instead, however, he chose to excuse the Lazarists from the appointment on other grounds. The first of these was practicality, for de Paul observed that he simply did not have sufficient manpower to commit to such an onerous responsibility; no doubt his negative memory of events in Toul during the 1630s offered a salutary reminder of the importance of matching personnel to workload.[67] He was also able to defend his decline on spiritual grounds, because he had excused his men from hospital duties in the past by stating that this type of labour was simply an accessory to their real work of missions. Both reasons were legitimate and sensible. But it is in his concern to protect the Lazarists' mission that the heart of their founder's objections to the hospital can be located.

Unlike many of his contemporaries, de Paul realized that the soaring rates of mendicancy in Paris were a complex and intractable problem that would not be answered by attempts to enclose all of the perpetrators behind high walls. The hospital project was, he commented, a 'vast, very difficult plan', the ambition and scale of which would cause it to act as a plughole down which all resources would drain, to the detriment of every poor person outside the capital. Even as he expressed his hope that it would succeed, he fretted: what, he wondered, would become of the rural poor in need of assistance? Since the hospital was a scheme for the urban poor, it could not satisfy either the material or spiritual needs of those who remained in the countryside, and these would continue to suffer the depredations that he had seen and heard about for decades.[68]

De Paul might also have enquired what would become of the mission of the Lazarists, which he had founded on the call of the poor, if this were to happen. It was feasible that the hospital would distract the attention of donors from the Lazarists, reducing their ability to care for the rural poor, and thereby their ability to live out their vocational purpose. Those Ladies now most involved in the hospital's foundation, funding, and provision of care were some of those who had historically proved the most enthusiastic patrons of the Congregation of the Mission, so this was certainly not a remote concern. Unlike the outspoken Yves de Paris, de Paul could not afford to criticize their latest charitable scheme openly: it would smack of ungratefulness for their generosity in the past and sour relations with them in the

[66] Paris, *Œuvres de miséricorde*, 295–303.

[67] *CCD*, 6: 269, de Paul to the duchess of Aiguillon, March 1657; *CCD*, 6: 275, same to same; *CCD*, 6: 274, de Paul to Seraphin de Mauroy, 23 March 1657.

[68] *CCD*, 6: 263, de Paul to unnamed, March 1657; ACMP, Robineau, 'Remarques', fos 152r–154r. According to Robineau, de Paul described the General Hospital as a 'sponge' which would attract 'gold and money'.

future. Instead, he deliberately calibrated a strategy that broadly endorsed the actions of those Ladies involved in the foundation, while keeping the Lazarists detached from its workings and immersed in their proper ministry. De Paul knew that to focus on the rural poor was to protect the Lazarists, and he was shrewd enough to seek out credible ways of doing so.

PART V

CONSOLIDATION

11

Power to Appoint?

I

Measured in terms of external recognition and rewards, the final two decades of de Paul's life were years of immense achievement. Institutionally, his decision to found the Lazarists in 1625 had proved to be a risk worth taking, as thereafter their resources continued to grow, their infrastructure to develop, and their ministerial work generally to thrive. Personally, de Paul accumulated from 1643 the kind of preferments that testified to the esteem in which he was held, and contributed further to the reputation he was earning in steering the Lazarists' missionary campaigns and clerical training. In June 1643, he joined the royal Council of Ecclesiastical Affairs, commonly known as the Council of Conscience, while shortly afterwards the duchess of Aiguillon appointed him as vicar general of the Benedictine abbeys of Marmoutiers (Tours) and Saint-Ouen (Rouen) and the priory of Saint-Martin-des-Champs (Paris), with substantial rights of presentation to their dependent benefices.[1] Nearly a decade later, de Paul left the Council (October 1652), but he continued in his role of vicar general until a year before his death.[2]

[1] Between 24 October 1650 and 17 June 1652, de Paul also replaced Louis and Claude de Chandenier as vicar general of the abbeys of Saint-Philibert (Tournus) and Saint-Jean-de-Réome (Moutiers-Saint-Jean) in Langres diocese, while they resided with Nicolas Pavillon in Alet. I have been unable to discover any evidence to suggest that de Paul made any presentations to dependent benefices while he stood in for the brothers: AN, Minutier Central, ET/LVI/121 (17 June 1652).

[2] It is widely thought that de Paul was excluded from the Council as a penalty for having strayed into a political matter. He had already done so in 1649 when, travelling at some risk to his personal safety to Saint-Germain-en-Laye, he pleaded with the regent and Mazarin to restore peace to the kingdom during the *Fronde*. By 1651, de Paul, along with others such as Léon Bouthillier, count of Chavigny, adjudged that the principal reason that it was continuing was because Mazarin was such a divisive figure, and he was involved in the negotiations between the chief protagonists, who included the prince of Condé and Gaston d'Orléans, before Mazarin's second exile in Sedan in August 1652. De Paul's extensive relations ensured that he was well informed of events and opinions: on 11 September, he suggested to Mazarin that he might delay his return to Paris until after the king had done so, so that the king could win the hearts of Parisians, and thus convince Gaston and Condé that there was no hope of whipping up more popular support for their cause. Ultimately, this was the strategy that Mazarin undertook, for Louis and his mother returned to the capital on 21 October, while Mazarin did not join them immediately. However, news of de Paul's departure from the Council had reached Cahors by 2 October (after de Paul wrote to inform Solminihac), so it may not have been de Paul's advice which triggered his exclusion from it. He may even have already left by the time that he wrote to Mazarin on 11 September: *CCD*, 4: 414, de Paul to Mazarin, 29 June–17 July 1652; *CCD*, 4: 459–64, same to same, 11 September 1652; *CCD*, 4: 475, Alain de Solminihac to de Paul, 2 October 1652.

These appointments dramatically increased de Paul's access to sources of patronage in the church and royal government, and his retention of the posts for the next decade led many contemporaries to assume he exercised considerable influence through them as a patron of ecclesiastical reform. Indeed, their perceptions have shaped his reputation as a figure endowed with the power to make or break ecclesiastical careers. The staying power of these opinions has withstood the interrogation of Paul Broutin, who argues that, at court, it was de Paul's 'studied humility' which enabled him to achieve his goals while in post. A contemporary court witness, however, was far less convinced; while she admitted that de Paul's humility was genuine, Madame de Motteville contended that it had little effect other than to arouse admiration, for it could not compete with the ambition and self-interest that dominated court politics.[3] However, Broutin and de Paul's biographers choose not to give credence to her view, preferring to recycle tales of de Paul's calm reaction to missiles (such as footstools!) launched at his head by disappointed and disgruntled petitioners as evidence of both his virtue and his power over appointments. This and other colourful stories cannot readily be considered as accurate descriptions of events.[4] Still, there is no doubt that de Paul adopted a strict criterion by which to judge his ambition and success, for he taught that humility opened a door to achievement, and was therefore the means by which he fulfilled his mission imperative to populate the church with devout clergy. But did de Paul really achieve such results through its practice? What other factors affected his ability to exercise the functional powers associated with his new offices, both at court and beyond? More fundamentally, did his acquisition of these honours warrant his reputation as a figure of significant, even decisive, authority in the promotion of clergy within the church?

II

De Paul moved into his posts with trepidation, for, while he recognized their potential, his elevation exacerbated his concerns about the incompatibility of honours with missionary humility. His teachings to the Lazarists in these years

[3] Madame de Motteville's judgement implicitly condemned Cardinal Mazarin in particular, for her dislike of him meant that she rarely allotted any virtue to his actions: Bertaut Motteville (ed.), *Mémoires de Madame de Motteville*, i, 167–8; Abelly, *Vie*, ii, 444; Broutin, *Réforme pastorale*, ii, 469–70.

[4] The 'footstool' tale first appeared in Maupas du Tour's funeral oration in 1660, but was not connected to de Paul's work on the Council. Moreover, the missile was said to be a chair and its thrower a young lady who de Paul had suggested should improve her behaviour. However, Maupas du Tour also referred to insults piled on de Paul by a noble after he opposed his request for a benefice, and these two stories were subsequently amalgamated; Maynard embellished them lavishly in a long scene in which an unidentified duchess lost her temper, and threw a footstool when de Paul objected to her attempts to ensure that her son become bishop of Poitiers and selected Antonio Barberini instead. In separating the threads of this version, it is worth noting that although Poitiers became vacant in 1651, it was Mazarin who chose Barberini, and he did so for political reasons. It is possible, however, that the cardinal asked de Paul to deliver the bad news of this to the male noble mentioned by Maupas du Tour, and that his messenger came under fire when he did so—but this is speculation: Abelly, *Vie*, iii, 157; Maupas du Tour, *Funeral Oration*, 116; Bergin, *French Episcopate*, 526; Maynard, *Vincent de Paul*, iii, 418.

reflect the degree to which this issue occupied his thoughts. As superior general, he was aware that his own ability to embody the core missionary values was of critical importance if he were to retain respect for his authority. His personal sense of identity was intrinsically missionary, shaped by his efforts to meet the goals of evangelization and his mindfulness of the qualities and actions that he needed to master in order to do so. But he generally chose to judge himself to be a poor missionary rather than a good one, an assessment that he made apparent to associates when he began to sign off his letters as 'Vincent Depaul, unworthy priest of the mission', around 1638.[5] It is not coincidental that it was at this time that the Lazarists began to attract greater patronage from high-ranking patrons, and that the public esteem in which de Paul was held as their founder and leader rose rapidly. When pride in praise and achievements threatened, his instinct was to contrast the reality with the ideal, pointing out in chastisement the yawning gulf between them in his own person.

This meant that de Paul's iterations of humility were reflexive, in that they offered a lesson to himself as well as to his confreres that the greater the material compliment the more necessary it was to remain humbly in service to God. So too, his repeated and often exaggerated self-excoriations were efforts to avoid being contaminated by ambition or arrogance, for they reminded him of his faults and inspired renewed resolve to overcome them. For instance, in teaching the Lazarists about preaching, de Paul was partial to insisting that nobody should preach 'like I preach: crying out loud, clapping my hands, leaning halfway out of the pulpit'. In reality he did not, although those who heard him speak testified that he spoke with extraordinary 'force', meaning with passionate or zealous devotion.[6] However, in pointing out his own supposed inadequacies, de Paul was simultaneously able to invite his men to model their conduct on its inverse, an infinitely superior portrait: the Son of God, whose unaffected preaching was born of a 'great and marvellous humility,' and who had moved his audience to a state of loving awe for the goodness and glory of their creator.[7] In humiliating himself before his confreres, de Paul expected to glorify God in their eyes, and to inspire them to emulate his son.

In his twilight years, de Paul took several opportunities to speak to his fellows about the ways in which their missionary humility should guide their encounters with those of superior social status. He claimed to draw heavily from his own experience, recalling his interactions with bishops and lay patrons, and his conversations with courtiers and ministers in the sumptuous surroundings of the royal court. To the authority of bishops, de Paul advised, the missionary should display an attitude of humble submission, and to courtiers an attitude of straightforward sincerity without resort to artifice or 'subtleties or tricks'. What the Lazarist said should come arrow-like 'from the heart'. Of course, to deliberately use the virtue of humility to gain something from a patron could precipitate allegations of hypocrisy or deceit, a danger of which de Paul was also quite aware. But he appeared confident

[5] *CCD*, 1: 523, de Paul to Pierre du Chesne, 28 January 1639. [6] *CCD*, 11: pp. xxi.
[7] *CCD*, 1: 184, de Paul to a Lazarist priest, 15 January 1633; *CCD*, 11: 239–41, 259.

that such charges would only withstand scrutiny if he was not in genuine possession of the virtue, that is, if his thoughts did not accord with his spoken words and action, and if all of these were not 'for God'. Moreover, in invoking positive reactions of good will, trust, and favour, the virtue should function as a worthy tool in achieving God's wishes. De Paul's approach to the cultivation of favour was, consequently, a prime expression of his belief that the example of virtue rebounded positively on those who practised it. Who, he enquired of his confreres, did not like a humble person? In situations where the Lazarists were inferior in either social standing or official authority, their humility offered a means to counter this inequality, and to rebalance interaction: what bishop, de Paul asked rhetorically, for instance, would not choose to respond kindly to a Lazarist endowed with humility?[8]

De Paul's question should not be dismissed as a simple quest to flatter the wealthy and powerful into dispensing favours. His justification for the use of humility delved deeply into his understanding of the function of virtues in human relations, and of the social hierarchies within French society. Being an expression of charity, humility was of course a necessary feature of all intercourse, but de Paul claimed to have learned that it was especially so in instances where a union of amity led to significant gains for the Lazarists' range of activities. He insisted that it was a primary rule of engagement for superiors, indeed a behavioural imperative: 'A missionary who gets down on his knees before Bishops . . . like a valley that draws moisture from the mountains, receives their blessing and benevolence.'[9] In this context, de Paul's advocacy of humility was predicated on his assumption that the bishop enjoyed a privileged position in the hierarchy of ecclesiastical orders. In acknowledging his superior stature and the functional power of government that accompanied it through humble gestures of subjection, the Lazarist would signal that there were no barriers between them which might prevent the bishop from trusting him and no need to second guess his motives. Furthermore, when he recognized the prelate's power over those of inferior status, he was also appealing to the bishop to use it responsibly, that is, to respond in a way which expressed his power positively.

Rhetoric of humility in speech, and expositions of it in acts, had the potential to be particularly noticeable and persuasive in environments where the virtue was valued but seldom in evidence. De Paul recounted that he had learned this from his observation of associates he knew well and greatly esteemed, and who had regularly been the centre of attention at court and in noble households. One of these, François de Sales, had advised him that he had countered the upsurge of pride that threatened to engulf him when he preached before an appreciative audience of high-born men and women in Paris in 1618; instead of encouraging their admiration with a splendid or ostentatious sermon, he had sought deliberately to humble himself by telling the simple story of St Martin. Some were disappointed with the simplicity of his account, but all noted its contrariety to the conventions of 'honour', and it was this which fascinated de Paul. The lesson that he took from it

[8] *CCD*, 12: 142–223. [9] *CCD*, 12: 223.

was that the bishop had carried the 'true spirit of Christianity' to his audience in his humble behaviour, provoking reactions of both consternation and praise because it was so alien to this environment even if praiseworthy in the abstract. In this precise execution of humility, de Sales had demonstrated the influence that the virtue could wield over those who were confronted with it unexpectedly.[10] De Paul also claimed to have experienced the rich harvest that the virtue reaped when in Madame de Gondi's employ. Amidst the grandeur of her household, she had, he recalled, been the epitome of simplicity, conscious always of the need to steer clear of 'sensual or temporal self-interest', and in her humility she had desired only to serve God. There was 'nothing', de Paul noted, 'more pleasing than this to attract good people'.[11] If they believed a person to be good because they believed them to have pure motives, they would trust their words and their actions, even to the point of permitting them the liberty of expressing discontent and even disagreement.

III

Are the claims that de Paul made to his confreres about his own experiences borne out by the evidence of his achievements in office? To answer this, it is necessary to recognize as a preliminary that de Paul's positions on the Council and as vicar general offered different types of opportunity. The Council was an institutional novelty, established to deal with all ecclesiastical affairs under the crown's remit more efficiently, and to consolidate control over its rights of patronage. As an ordinary member of the body, de Paul could air his views on appropriate nominations, in the hope that they would be taken into account by other members, especially the queen and her chief minister, Cardinal Mazarin. Of the two positions, it was the more prestigious, but this was offset by the fact that his ability to exercise influence on appointments through it was also less certain. As vicar general, in contrast, he could expect to use his rights of presentation directly and decisively to promote those whom he held in high regard, albeit with the blessing of the duchess. In this role, he therefore had fewer rivals and obstacles to his decision-making, which made the process of presentation far more straightforward than that of the Council.

Before 1643, de Paul exerted only limited influence on promotions of any kind; he had, of course, appointed Lazarists to office, and had also used his position as superior of the Visitation to appoint members of the Tuesday Conferences to offices in his gift. He selected Blampignon and Gambart to be confessors in the first and second Visitation convent respectively in the 1630s, while he appointed Jacques Charton as the superior of the Magdalens, whom the Visitation sisters supervised, in 1632 (a position that Charton retained until the mid-1640s).[12] Mainly, however, de Paul had encouraged the direction of attention towards

[10] *CCD*, 5: 477–9, de Paul to Jean Martin, 26 November 1655. [11] *CCD*, 12: 142, 144–5.

[12] In 1655, Blampignon repaid the trust that de Paul had put in him to deliver appropriate pastoral care by donating the priory of Bussière-Badil in Limoges diocese to the Lazarists. Rome confirmed the translation in 1658: AN, S6703 (4 June 1658); Bellussière, 'Varia'.

individuals within the group by sending them on missions or to lead conferences at ordinand retreats.[13] These activities gave notice that they were individuals with the kind of pastoral inclination and experience suitable for ecclesiastical posts. In addition, while four members of the Conferences were promoted to the episcopate between 1636 and 1640, none of them needed to rely on de Paul for their promotion, for all had excellent connections at court.[14] Only in Nicolas Pavillon's appointment in 1637 can de Paul's direct influence be isolated, and even here he held it over Pavillon rather than Richelieu or Louis XIII. It was actually Aiguillon who first drew her uncle's attention to Pavillon, after she praised his preaching prowess to him. Richelieu then suggested the young priest to the king as a suitable candidate for the mitre. On de Paul's encouragement, Pavillon accepted Alet when it was offered to him shortly afterwards, and he evidently did so because he trusted his guidance.[15]

While the crown also weighed up social and political considerations in nominating bishops, Richelieu's appreciation for the services to clerical formation that de Paul and his Congregation provided led him to judge that the participation of these men in the Tuesday Conferences was evidence of their readiness and aptness for episcopal preferment. Louis XIII shared this view, and around the time of his death asked de Paul, through his confessor Jacques Dinet, to supply a list of those he judged worthy for episcopal promotion, apparently even remarking that potential bishops should spend time at Saint-Lazare before preferment. This confirms that de Paul's growing reputation as a producer of clergy was key to any sway he held at court at this stage of his career; he noted at the time that everyone, including the king, noticed 'something different about' bishops who had been trained at Saint-Lazare. But he was not alone in being newly permitted to voice suggestions at court at this time; Louis XIII also sought lists of suitable candidates for dioceses from other informed clerical sources when he asked de Paul to produce his.[16] The establishment of the Council was, however, a formal effort to organize such advisory communications, and to give voice to the long-expressed calls of reformers for an improvement in the standard of appointments, in a more efficient manner. With the prospect of a regency to follow the king's death, it was also an attempt to ensure that members of the high nobility would not be able to grab church positions, as they had managed to do in earlier periods of political weakness.

[13] See, for example, *CCD*, 5: 297, Jean-François Mousnier to de Paul, 6 February 1655.

[14] Antoine Godeau was already a respected intellectual, who had been promoted to the *Académie Française* by Richelieu in 1634, while François Fouquet was a member of an upcoming *robe* family heavily beholden to the minister. Felix Vialart was also a member of a family in favour at court, thanks to the services provided by his father, the son of a former master of requests and ambassador to the Swiss: Bergin, *French Episcopate*, 626, 631–2, 713.

[15] Aubery, *Histoire*, 600. Broutin embosses the account by adding that Richelieu sought the agreement of de Paul and the Jesuit Nicolas Caussin for the choice, while Dejean adds that Aiguillon made her recommendation after she heard Pavillon deliver a sermon in the parish of Sainte-Croix-de-la-Bretonnerie. But neither he nor Broutin offers documentary evidence to support their claims: Broutin, *Réforme pastorale*, i, 200; Dejean, *Prélat indépendant*, 8.

[16] *CCD*, 2: 427, de Paul to Bernard Codoing, 17 April 1643; 'Dernier moments de Louis XIII racontés par le père Dinet son confesseur', 232–3.

For her part, Aiguillon's decision to employ de Paul as vicar general rested on a number of presuppositions. She was sure of his integrity and administrative skill, her confidence born of his fulfilment of the conditions under which her family's patronage was granted over the previous decade. She also accepted that he would be in command of the three dossiers she placed in his care, because the different strands of de Paul's work in clerical formation—the Tuesday Conferences, ordinand retreats, missions, and seminaries—provided a pool of potential candidates as well as the means to gather information on their appropriateness for office. Indeed, the actual missions themselves were also an important means of acquiring knowledge about the conditions of benefices, which was indispensable in attempting to match them to potential appointees. The Lazarists had long performed missions in many of the dioceses in which the benefices dependent on the abbeys and priory were situated, and had even done so in many of the parishes on their lists of presentation. For instance, by happy coincidence, Villepreux was a dependent of Marmoutiers and one of the parishes in which the missionaries regularly carried out a mission in fulfilment of the terms of their foundation contract. In 1657, de Paul made a presentation to the cure, which had recently fallen vacant. The successful appointee, Étienne Meslier, travelled from his former parish of Saint-Clément-de-Faucourt in Chartres diocese to take up his new post. This native of Chartres had probably come to de Paul's notice while serving there, for it was amongst the parishes in which the Lazarists had completed missions since the 1620s.[17]

The prestige of the abbeys and priory with which the duchess entrusted de Paul was reflected in their large number of presentations, as well as in the wealth of their endowments. They formed part of the legacy of benefices that her uncle bequeathed to his descendants. During 1642, as he prepared for his death, he passed them to his grandnephew, Armand-Jean, who was under his aunt's care. He held them *in commendam* until 10 September 1652 when he transferred them to his brother Emmanuel, who continued to possess them *in commendam*.[18] They simply enjoyed the revenues that accrued between 1642 and 1659, while de Paul acted as their vicar general.[19] If de Paul had any qualms about representing absentee abbots they are not on record. In any case, perhaps they were assuaged by the opportunities that his positions offered for the promotion of capable clergy: they potentially entailed making presentations to vacancies for approximately 525 parishes, and at least 39 chapels and 3 prebends. Marmoutiers possessed by far

[17] AN, L520 (20 September 1657); Ferté, *Vie religieuse*, 407.

[18] AD de Seine-Maritime, 14H188 (10 September 1652); Sainte-Marthe et al. (eds), *Gallia Christiana*, vii, col. 543; xi, col. 155; Pommeraye, *Histoire*, 337.

[19] In his sole mention of any of the three monastic institutions in question, Coste mistakenly assumes that de Paul became vicar general of Saint-Ouen around 1659. He drew on the memoir of de Paul's secretary Louis Robineau, which alleged that de Paul refused to take the office of vicar general of Saint-Ouen on the basis of his age and declining health, but also in protest against the crown's detention of Emmanuel de Vignerod. However, Vignerod was never detained, and documentary evidence survives to prove that de Paul had made many presentations for Saint-Ouen in preceding years: ACMP, Robineau, 'Remarques', fos 27r–28r; Coste, *Saint*, ii, 242–3.

the greatest number (386 dependent cures, as well as 23 chapels and 3 prebends), while the others shared the remainder fairly evenly.[20] They were scattered through France; for instance, although located in Paris, Saint-Martin had just twenty-two presentations in the diocese, but many more in neighbouring dioceses like Chartres, Meaux, and Orléans, and further north in the three adjoining sees of Beauvais, Amiens, and Noyon.[21] Those of Saint-Ouen were located in six different dioceses, and those of Marmoutiers were in at least thirty.[22]

Judged in seventeenth-century terms of birth and wealth, de Paul was obviously Aiguillon's social inferior, just as he had been Madame de Gondi's. But it was not only his sacerdotal office, contacts, and competence that ensured her goodwill and resources, for de Paul's apparent humility lent an air of purity to his efforts, and for the devout duchess a sense that he would not be deterred in the pursuit of their common goals. Simultaneously, he carefully demonstrated that he knew that the duchess could withdraw her favour should he neglect to admit her authority as patron. Thus, he routinely sought her opinion on the men that he selected, and awaited her approval with deference before formalizing his choices. It was always possible that Aiguillon would wish to promote individuals for secular reasons of loyalty or reward, which might have set her at cross-purposes with de Paul, but in general she appears to have accepted his recommendations because she approved of the criteria that he used to make them.

Undoubtedly, de Paul viewed the vacancies as a means to provide the church with clerics of whose virtue he approved, and with whom he was sufficiently closely acquainted to expect that they would repay his favour by performing their new duties diligently, and perhaps by collaborating with him or the Lazarists. He appointed individuals both as an incentive and a dividend for good behaviour, therefore. For example, in November 1652, he wrote to the duchess to request that she endorse his wish to give Saint-Claire-sur-Epte priory in Gisors, a dependant of Marmoutiers, to Charles de Saveuses, for he could think of no one 'more deserving than he, nor . . . one from which you ought to expect more gratitude'. De Paul was confident of this not only because Saveuses was a Carmelite priest, but because he was an ecclesiastical counsellor in the Paris *parlement*, whom he had recently consulted in relation to a court case over the Norais donation; he may even have been moved to offer him the priory in gratitude for his advice. De Paul was also sure that Saveuses would like to have it because his sister who lived in the area had alerted him to its impending vacancy, probably at her brother's instigation. As soon as de Paul received her letter, he approached Aiguillon to urge her to bear Saveuses

[20] In theory, de Paul's duties should have included overseeing the temporal possessions of the establishments, including leases and rents, but in practice he did not deal with these aspects of their patrimony; instead, the brothers' *intendants* managed these. Saint-Martin held sixty cures and twelve chapels, while Saint-Ouen had sixty-nine cure and four chapels: Pommeraye, *Histoire*, 385.

[21] AN, S*1440 (this is a register of the dependants of Saint-Martin, which dates from the eighteenth century); Pommeraye, *Histoire*, 386.

[22] AD d'Ille-et-Vilaine, G52; AD d'Indre et Loire, H383 and H385; *Pouillé général des abbayes de France.*

in mind when the time arrived to fill the office of prior. Evidently she did, for he was duly appointed shortly afterwards.[23]

Unlike Saint-Claire, the majority of benefices probably did not become available during the seventeen years that de Paul was vicar general, for their incumbents would probably have held office for reasonably long periods of time. However, it is possible to identify twenty selections, eighteen of which were for parish cures, and the majority (fifteen) made between September 1652 and April 1657. A scan of the names and birthplaces of those presented suggests that de Paul tended to choose priests from the dioceses in which the benefices were situated. He probably adopted this tactic on the assumption that the appointee might be less likely to be viewed as an outsider by locals and would perhaps be more knowledgeable about local affairs. In his capacity as vicar general of Saint-Ouen, for example, de Paul made five presentations to the parishes of Saint-Croix-de-Saint-Ouen and Saint-Croix-de-Pelletier in Rouen diocese, with all of the candidates recorded as being priests of the diocese. It is probable, however, that it was during their years away from Rouen that two of these came to de Paul's notice; the first priest, Charles Desmarets, was an Oratorian, and the second, Jean Thirel, had completed his bachelor's degree in theology in Paris.[24] The five men were generally well educated; three had received a university education, while Desmarets would have benefited from a comprehensive theological formation in his Oratorian seminary. Such educational attainments are common enough among other nominees to assume that, if de Paul did not consider them essential prerequisites for nominees, they certainly advantaged them. In general though, where de Paul had encountered the appointees is less easy to determine, since their previous connection to him can only be corroborated in three cases, one of which was the presentation of Saveuses. A second individual was Louis Abelly, a Tuesday Conference member who had just returned from a five-year stint as the vicar general for François Fouquet in Bayonne when de Paul offered him the central Parisian parish of Saint-Josse (a dependant of Saint-Martin-des-Champs), in September 1643.[25]

The third presentation, of Pierre Horcholle, then *curé* of Notre-Dame-de-Neufchâtel (north-east of Rouen), derived from the bonds that he had enjoyed with de Paul through clerical formation and confraternal activism. As a result of these, de Paul displayed a conspicuous desire to assist Horcholle by any means in his power, and in 1650 he greeted Horcholle's request that he do so with pleasure and affection. Indeed, de Paul mentioned that Horcholle had stayed at Saint-Lazare in the past—presumably on retreat—and that it would be a great 'consolation' if he could visit again. Furthermore, he knew that the confraternity that he had personally established in Notre-Dame-de-Neufchâtel in 1634 had flourished since because Horcholle had supported it after he arrived there some years later. With

[23] *CCD*, 4: 507–8, de Paul to the duchess of Aiguillon, 20 November 1652; Vernon, *Charles de Saveuses*, 28, 144.

[24] AD de Seine-Maritime, G1247 (10 September 1643, 20 May 1650, 15 September 1652, 30 August 1653(2)).

[25] AN, S*1440, fo. 72r.

such reciprocal advantages having blessed their relationship, Horcholle now felt able to ask de Paul to find a new parish in which to minister. He suggested a parish in Saint-Malo diocese, and de Paul responded that he would do his utmost to help. Since this was not a parish to which he could present, he intended to work through the Council of Ecclesiastical Affairs.[26] Shortly afterwards, he had to admit defeat, for he discovered through an intermediary that the bishop of Saint-Malo had promised it to somebody else.[27] Turning to another option that Horcholle suggested, he again used a go-between to discover whether this parish might be suitable, only to be told that the *seigneur* with right of presentation had Jansenist sympathies that would prevent him from entertaining any approach from de Paul. So de Paul confided in his friend that he would await 'a better opportunity to serve' him.[28] It finally came in 1657, when an opening dawned amongst the benefices over which de Paul had direct sanction, and for which he did not have to depend on other patrons. In April, he wrote in some excitement to Horcholle to offer him the newly vacant parish of Bruquedalle (dependent on Saint-Ouen). Although slightly embarrassed that its income was a modest 400 *livres* annually, de Paul could not hide the satisfaction that he felt in finally being able to fulfil Horcholle's desire.[29]

IV

De Paul's ability to satisfy men like Horcholle was far less clear cut during his tenure on the Council of Ecclesiastical Affairs. From the historian's perspective, the examination of his activities is complicated by the fact that the minutes of the meetings record only decisions made, rather than the discussion that preceded them; indeed, the content of some of the discussions which led to appointments may never have been put on paper at all, but was expressed only in informal or confidential conversations outside the meetings. Furthermore, some nominations did not enter the minutes. Behind these challenging silences and omissions lurk the obstacles, the ambiguities, and the opportunities with which de Paul contended and of which he availed in seeking to exert his influence on decision-making.

De Paul was one of several members of the Council, all of whom had agendas and objectives which did not necessarily dovetail with his, and his voice was frequently in peril of being lost in the chorus of opinions. Moreover, since Mazarin was obliged to weigh up a multitude of factors in making selections, he was not always inclined to listen to de Paul's. Yet, at the same time, it should not be supposed that conflict between de Paul and Mazarin was always the order of the day. Nominations that stirred up differences of opinion or arguments were more likely to be noted by contemporaries, which can give a misleading impression about

[26] AD de Seine-Maritime, G 1515; *CCD*, 4: 1–2, de Paul to Pierre Horcholle, 1 April 1650.
[27] *CCD*, 4: 40–1, de Paul to Pierre Horcholle, 28 June 1650.
[28] *CCD*, 4: 74, de Paul to Pierre Horcholle, 2 September 1650.
[29] *CCD*, 6: 309–10, de Paul to Pierre Horcholle, 30 April 1657. De Paul's secretary mistakenly addressed the letter to Monsieur Horcholle of Saint-Jacques parish.

their prevalence. *Dévot* pressure was not something that Mazarin could ignore entirely, or that the pious Anne of Austria wished to disregard if she could avoid doing so. There is good reason to assume, therefore, that many appointments were trouble-free, and therefore received little commentary at the time.

De Paul's relationship with the queen regent was different, for she was greatly admiring of the devoutness of this humble priest who appeared before her in patched clothing, and many have assumed that he acted as her director of conscience as a result.[30] But there is no evidence to suggest that he acted in this capacity with any consistency or exclusivity. All of the Council's members were the queen's directors of conscience, and were called this by Mazarin amongst others.[31] In 1643, besides Mazarin, de Paul, and Anne of Austria, these included the chancellor, and three churchmen (Bishop Potier of Beauvais, Bishop Cospeau of Lisieux, and Jacques Charton). After the Council was reorganized in March 1651 it included the marquis of Châteauneuf, the royal confessor, Charles Paulin, and Mazarin's client, Bishop Péréfixe of Rodez.[32] Some at court also wrongly assumed that de Paul was the director of the council, but this was inconceivable, not least because Louis XIII had assigned special care of ecclesiastical affairs to Mazarin on his deathbed. Given the power accruing to those who assigned the vast range of benefices in the crown's remit, this was not a right he was likely to surrender or share easily. In addition, given the cross-section of interests that he was obliged to satisfy on the regent's behalf when making recommendations to her, Mazarin had to attend not only to the *dévot* interests that de Paul represented, but also to the need to reward or encourage the loyalty of political rivals such as Gaston d'Orléans and the prince of Condé. At times, this inserted tension into his relationship with de Paul who, as an ecclesiastic, claimed to have a higher call on the queen's conscience than the minister.

Over time, de Paul came to know, through the full range of his ecclesiastical activities, a selection of individuals who attended court or held positions there. Although none of the women most closely associated with de Paul served in the regent's household, Aiguillon was amongst a number who had influence at court, either through the direct access that their status conferred or their kinship with ministers such as Séguier, Brienne, and Fouquet.[33] Five members of the Tuesday Conferences had roles at court while de Paul sat on the Council, Jacques Charton amongst them, but they obtained them independently of him.[34] Some of de Paul's

[30] See, for example, Defos du Rau, 'Vincent de Paul'.

[31] Chéruel and Avenel (eds), *Lettres du Cardinal Mazarin*, ii, 855, Mazarin to the count of Alais, 7 February 1648 (actually 1647).

[32] Bergin, *French Episcopate*, 509, 523–4.

[33] Few of the queen mother's ladies-in-waiting belonged to the high nobility, members of whom did not serve in her household, unless as chief lady of honour or superintendant: Kleinman, 'Social Dynamics'.

[34] Laurent de Brisacier had begun his career in 1633 as an almoner in Louis XIII's household, before adding the role of councillor of state to his remit in 1648, and briefly acting as preceptor for the young king in 1649; Jean de Maupeou became a royal almoner, thanks to Mazarin's protection, in 1646 while in minor orders, and only joined the Conferences in 1651 after his ordination; Nicolas de Saint-Jean was Anne of Austria's chaplain at Saint-Roch, and one of her *confesseurs du commun* from

connections at court, however, were amongst Mazarin's opponents. These included former Richelieu supporters and former members of the *cabale des importants*, led by Madame de Chevreuse and the duke of Beaufort, who organized an unsuccessful conspiracy to assassinate Mazarin in 1643.

This pair was seconded in their resentment of Mazarin's influence by Philippe de Gondi, and a number of Ladies of the *Hôtel-Dieu*, including Maignelay, Brienne, and, to a certain extent, Aiguillon, although none of these was actively involved in the plot. Through the 1640s, de Paul strayed over the line when he carried messages to the regent on their behalf, but this was not because he was duped into doing so. In order to reduce Anne's dependence on Mazarin, on whom she depended for tutelage in political matters, they targeted her religious scruples together, suggesting that she was attracting scandal by the intimacy of her relationship with him. They further sought to undermine their sharing of common leisure interests, but again on the grounds of concerns about the queen's virtue and salvation; more than once, de Paul attempted to wean Anne from her love of theatre by increasing the pressure placed upon her when the *curé* of the Louvre (the parish priest of Saint-Germain-l'Auxerrois) announced that she was setting a poor example by patronizing actors at the royal palace there.[35] To occupy her time more piously, and to limit the amount that she spent in Mazarin's company, Anne was encouraged to establish a confraternity of charity at court. De Paul enthusiastically drafted statutes, which he envisaged as a directorate for the various groups in Parisian parishes, over which Anne would preside, and through which her ladies-in-waiting, organized in groups of three, would superintend the enterprises in which they were engaged, issuing instructions and funds when necessary.[36] Evidently, de Paul hoped to raise the public status of the confraternities by placing them in a hierarchy of operation topped by a royal foundation, which would also be the means to channel court patronage to them. This ambitious plan was not implemented, however, because Anne, despite her predilection for religious acts, did not commit herself. The proposal may have been one of the issues that Mazarin had in mind when he wrote in annoyance around the close of 1643 that the *dévots* were trying to monopolize the regent's time at his expense, and he may have convinced her not to take it further.[37]

Although rumours of de Paul's disgrace from the Council circulated at court almost as soon as he took his place on it, and surfaced periodically thereafter, he could not have remained in his post until 1652 had not his favour endured. From the crown's viewpoint, one of the principal reasons why he survived was because Mazarin felt that the payoff from his presence was greater than the competition that

1651; Achille Courtin, *seigneur* of Mesnuls, joined the Conferences only around 1655 after he had decided on ordination in the wake of his wife's death: *CCD*, 5: 54, de Paul to the duchess of Aiguillon, 9 November 1653; Bergin, *French Episcopate*, 669; Griselle, *État de la maison*, 97, 104, 133, 381; Guichard, 'Laurent Bouchet . . . Conférences de mardi'.

[35] 'Under the pretext of affection', as Mazarin recorded caustically in his private notebook: BN, Ms Baluze 174, carnet 2, 62 (June–July 1642). The *curé* and de Paul repeated their objections in 1647: Constant (ed.), *Mémoires de Nicolas Goulas*, ii, 202–3; Kleinman, *Anne of Austria*, 164–84.

[36] *CCD*, 13b: 441–2.

[37] BN, Ms Baluze 174, carnet 5, 24.

he provided to his will. There were several grounds for this, two of which were plain and practical: firstly, the number of informants on whom de Paul was able to call for information and opinion was extremely large, and could be used to serve royal requirements. They emanated from all sectors of his work. In the south-west, for instance, de Paul relied on Lazarists for information-gathering, but he also gained knowledge of people and affairs there from prelates such as Alain de Solminihac and Nicolas Pavillon, whose positions offered excellent vantage points from which to investigate when de Paul asked.[38] In the 1640s, Pavillon was in the habit of sending reports to de Paul on the 'principal and more frequent disorders' amongst clergy that he noticed in his region, in the hope that de Paul's seat on the council would enable him to '[procure] on occasion the reform of good order and discipline in the church'. Likewise, in 1646, de Paul learned details from Solminihac's missives about the character and conduct of Bishop Estrades of Périgueux, which led him to stand fast, even if to no avail, against the royal decision to transfer him to Condom (on the strength of his brother's history of military and diplomatic service to Louis XIII and Mazarin). De Paul's informant noted disapprovingly that Estrades had displayed little inclination to reside in his first diocese, despite its shocking state of neglect, and even more regrettably had quickly set his ambitions on Condom, bargaining benefices with Bishop de Cous's nephew in order to persuade him to abandon his desire to succeed his uncle. De Paul informed Solminihac in return that he knew the nephew because he had completed a retreat at Saint-Lazare, but that he had not made a favourable impression, in fact quite the opposite. Thus, Solminihac's exasperated outburst that he could not imagine 'how it is possible to think of giving dioceses to such persons' met with his sympathy.[39]

Secondly, de Paul's years of experience in ministry and institutional management rendered him a skilled collator of data and a diplomatic negotiator, and these skills proved priceless in the resolution of disputes and the implementation of crown policies on matters such as diocesan restructuring. Both the queen and Mazarin were confident in his ability to troubleshoot problems and pursue the crown's wishes even in cases which were particularly politically sensitive. Additionally, de Paul's solid understanding of church governmental laws and customs made it very likely that the crown would depute him to arbitrate with concerned parties and tender solutions.

The most important of the affairs to which de Paul was asked to devote a large portion of his time was the establishment of the new diocese of La Rochelle in the mid-1640s, a scheme which pertained to the rights and range of episcopal government but also carried important ramifications for royal authority in western France. The fall of La Rochelle in 1628 had raised the challenge of how to deal with the former Huguenot stronghold, and Louis XIII had quickly announced that he would create a new Catholic bishopric for the area. This was to be a new version of the older diocese of Maillezais, and the king appointed Henri de Béthune as

[38] *CCD*, 2: 586–7, Nicolas Pavillon to de Paul, 12 July 1645.

[39] *CCD*, 2: 679, Alain de Solminihac to de Paul, 31 July 1646; *CCD*, 3: 229, same to same, 20 August 1647.

bishop of Maillezais in anticipation of the redrawing of boundaries. The proposal was a sensitive issue for neighbouring prelates, however, and it made little headway after a number objected.[40] Then, in 1646, Mazarin decided to resurrect the project, and de Paul was asked to represent the crown in the negotiations. Consequently, by the time that Béthune was nominated archbishop of Bordeaux in November 1646, de Paul had already been interceding with the bishops affected by the plan for at least six months, and it was actually he who secured Béthune's agreement to being transferred to Bordeaux. This may not have been too difficult as it was an obvious promotion, but to sweeten the deal, de Paul agreed with Béthune that he would receive an annual pension and income from benefices near La Rochelle. De Paul wrote to report the outcome of his work to Mazarin in August, who quickly replied that the queen approved it, and asked de Paul to send a letter of appointment to Béthune.

With the see of Maillezais about to be vacated, the crown was at last in a position to create a new diocese, which included La Rochelle itself, as well as parishes that had formerly been in Saintes diocese. Abelly asserted that de Paul recommended to the queen that the current bishop of Saintes, Jacques Raoul de La Guibourgère, should be offered the new diocese. Though short of documentary proof, this claim may contain some truth since de Paul and Raoul had been on cordial terms since the 1630s when the bishop had first invited the Lazarists to carry out missions in Saintes, and their relationship was reinforced when he requested that the Lazarists run a seminary there in 1644. It was also the case that Raoul had previously refused to cooperate with the crown unless he was offered adequate compensation for the loss of a portion of his diocese.[41] De Paul's mediation was therefore key to his change of heart, for even if he cannot be proven to have initially suggested the bishop's translation to La Rochelle, he certainly secured it by persuading him to accept the reconfiguration of diocesan borders, and by bearing the glad tidings that he would be compensated with the honour of becoming the first bishop of the new diocese.[42] As a result, Raoul was temporarily translated to Maillezais in November, and to La Rochelle two years later.[43]

The crown also drew on de Paul's expertise in cases of contention regarding the reform of its monastic benefices and foundations. For these, de Paul reported to the Council on the wellbeing, resources, and membership of a troubled institute or order, or on the nature of a dispute over the future filling and functioning of a benefice. The Council also entrusted him with the responsibility of recommending resolutions, which demanded an adroit ability to evaluate opposing arguments that were often based on conflicting evidence. But success was not always a foregone conclusion. In 1645, the Council deliberated the election of the general of the Premonstratensian order and the abbot of Prémontré abbey, which was the original

[40] Bergin, *French Episcopate*, 33–4.

[41] BN, Ms Baluze, 175, fo. 120r, Jacques Raoul de La Guibourgère to Jules Mazarin, 20 April 1643, and fo. 126r, same to same, 29 June 1643.

[42] Abelly, *Vie*, ii, 453–4; *CCD*, 3: 20, de Paul to Jules Mazarin, 20 August 1646; *CCD*, 3: 34, Jules Mazarin to de Paul, 27 August 1646.

[43] Bergin, *French Episcopate*, 570.

and most prestigious of the order's houses. Simon Raguet claimed to have been elected to these offices, but this was hotly disputed by the abbey's prior and canons, who immediately complained to the papacy that the election procedure had been canonically flawed and was therefore void. Having received a papal bull vindicating their stance in April 1645, they then proceeded to elect a new general, the reform-minded Augustin Le Pellier, only to be abruptly halted when Raguet appealed to the king.[44] In the meantime, both candidates continued to uphold the legitimacy of their elections, by installing their rival supporters in positions of authority in the abbeys and priories of the order. After Charton led a preliminary reconnaissance, the Council deputed de Paul to devise a permanent solution to the conflict. At the close of 1646, he reported back in Le Pellier's favour, but drew attention to the need to entice his competitor to accept this decision. As a result, the Council recommended to the king that he should 'accord the expeditions necessary for the election of... Augustin Le Pellier', on the condition that he pursue reform of the order, and that he offer Raguet compensation to the tune of almost 10,000 *livres*.[45]

Finally, the crown had still more to gain from de Paul's presence on the Council, a fact of which he took both cognizance and advantage. Specifically referring to his personal experience in 1659, he concluded that those who did not always act sincerely at court still liked others to do so.[46] This might be partly because they admired the simplicity and purity of their motives. Yet de Paul also understood that there was more than one way to interpret the value that figures like Mazarin placed on his humble frankness; the presence of an individual who purported to speak as God's advocate lent a sheen of piety to the Council's workings, while also functioning as a shield behind which decisions driven by less elevated motivations could be sheltered. Indeed, the predictability of de Paul's principled opinions would make it easier to do so. In 1645, for instance, Mazarin ignored the duke of Épernon's attempt to restore his family's standing, after losses incurred under Richelieu, by perpetuating its traditional hold over the diocese of Vabres, which two members of the La Vallette-Épernon branch had held since 1600. De Paul knew the duke's candidate slightly but felt unable to assess his suitability on their short acquaintance. He sought information on his piety and capability (including whether he was actually a priest as he claimed!), from Archbishop Montchal of Toulouse, and promised to delay his nomination until he received it.[47] The news was not positive, and de Paul does not seem to have taken La Valette's cause further. But this suited Mazarin, who was not interested in rewarding former victims of Richelieu, and the duke and his relative were left unsatisfied. The individual ultimately appointed to Vabres in April, Isaac Habert, was quite satisfying to both Mazarin and de Paul, for he was a highly regarded theologian, who had already begun publicly to decry Jansenist teaching.[48]

[44] BN, Ms Fr 15721, fo. 294r–v.

[45] BN, Ms Fr 15721, fos 190r, 295r, 300r. A dispute erupted again in 1652 when Le Pellier parted ways with one of his former supporters, the abbot of Cuissy, over the implementation of reforms. De Paul attempted to mediate, but the quarrel continued after he left the Council: *CCD*, 4: 30, de Paul to Augustin Le Pellier, 6 March 1652.

[46] *CCD*, 12: 142.

[47] *CCD*, 2: 555, de Paul to Charles de Montchal, 24 February 1645.

[48] AAE, Mémoires et Documents, France, 851, fo. 120r; Bergin, *French Episcopate*, 503, 637, 651.

V

In contrast to the Vabres case, there were occasions when de Paul's opposition to the interests of family honour and political ambitions went unheeded because the practical requirements of government triumphed over the ideals of religious reform. Furthermore, while Motteville's wry observation that the Council 'served therefore only to exclude those that it did not want to favour' may be an exaggeration, Mazarin certainly sought to control the proceedings of the meetings themselves. As time went on, the Council met less frequently, and even less so again from 1648 when the *Fronde* erupted, but it is evident that even before then many of the decisions about benefices were made outside its meetings, on an informal basis. After early 1648, de Paul attended court for meetings quite rarely, but this was not simply because he disliked going there. It was also because Mazarin increasingly reduced the Council to rubberstamping nominations that he had already decided, and of which he was confident the queen would approve. During his exile, there is little evidence that he relinquished his control; just before he left in March 1651, the pro-Mazarin François de Harlay observed that it would be wise after his departure 'to be on good terms with everyone'. Thus, when he canvassed for the coadjutorship of Rouen soon afterwards, he approached the Council through Charton and the bishop of Lavour, a trusted Mazarine servant, but did not bother to seek de Paul's aid at all.[49]

In some instances, the minister acted to prevail over de Paul, while still providing crumbs to satisfy his desire for devout appointees. From the start, therefore, they locked horns over vacancies, with mixed results for de Paul. Notably, in early 1644 de Paul decided to disagree openly with Mazarin's plan to appoint Louis de La Rochefoucauld to Comminges, and suggested his own candidate, Olier, instead. He focused his opposition on the fact that La Rochefoucauld was not yet a priest, even though he was equipped with a licentiate in canon law, and was already acting as *officialis* for a satisfied Solminihac in Cahors. In terms of social and educational background, as well as administrative experience, he ticked the necessary boxes, but the fact that he was not ordained provided a convenient if genuine excuse for de Paul to oppose his elevation and to recommend Olier instead.[50] However, de Paul's victory was only partial, for while La Rochefoucauld did not meet with the queen's approval, neither did Olier. His disappointment at this soon abated somewhat

[49] BN, Ms Baluze, 327, fo. 1v, François II de Harlay de Champvallon to François de Harlay de Champvallon (archbishop of Rouen), 1 March 1651. The young Harlay received his nomination for the prelateship rather than the coadjutorship in May: Bergin, *French Episcopate*, 525.

[50] De Paul was not resolutely critical of La Rochefoucauld. Less than a year earlier, he had requested that the queen provide him with a canonry, which suggests that he thought he was a young man with excellent potential, but not ready for onerous episcopal responsibilities just yet. After La Rochefoucauld was ordained, Solminihac recommended him to de Paul for the vicar generalship of Périgueux in 1646. He finally became bishop of Lectoure in 1649, no doubt with de Paul's blessing, since he was by then ordained. But, unfortunately, de Paul's faith in the new prelate went unrewarded, because, for reasons which are unclear, he never set foot in his diocese before his death in 1654: *CCD*, 2: 429, Alain de Solminihac to de Paul, 3 May 1643; Bergin, *French Episcopate*, 650.

when the chief minister persuaded the queen to approve a compromise candidate in appeasement: Gilbert de Choiseul was a strongly Gallican and pro-Mazarin cleric, whose brother was captain of the guards in Gaston's household, but he was also an ordained priest known for his piety and intellect (he held a licentiate in theology), and certain to take his duties as a bishop seriously.[51]

This wrangle confirms that a secretary of state's observation that Mazarin could not convince the queen 'to go against the decision of Monsieur Vincent', was not an accurate assessment of the balance of power within the Council in the 1640s.[52] Mazarin understood the impact that de Paul's moral standing might have, and did his utmost to ensure that it was not the factor that determined nominations. De Paul could not, consequently, assume that his humbly and sincerely expressed convictions would suffice, and he also needed to exercise discretion in deciding whether and when to convey his opposition openly. In these circumstances, it is hardly surprising too that he was prepared to resort to tactics by which he could influence decisions as they were being made, and understood that his best hope of influencing appointments often lay in the months before they were tabled at meetings. To do so, he at times endeavoured to work in combination with figures sympathetic to his reform agenda: in regard to Comminges, Mazarin discovered that de Paul was in league with the count of Chavigny and Aiguillon, for neither of whom he cared, to sway the regent in Olier's favour.[53] But, in addition, de Paul deployed the skills which had formed the partial basis for his appointment to the Council in the first place, that is, those of information-gathering. He operated strategically, making deliberate efforts not only to collect information but also to manage it in ways that would uphold his views, enable him to make timely interventions, and apply pressure on those who could affect outcomes or who stood to gain or lose from them. If these tactics of information-gathering and management did not necessarily correspond with Mazarin's objectives, it was de Paul's hope that they would enable him to meet his.

This approach included the fielding of applications that de Paul simply did not wish to assist, as well as those he did. He politely rejected the first type and did not bring them to the Council's attention, but also tended to use his rejections as opportunities to instruct in the virtues of detachment, lack of ambition, and faithfulness to one's true calling in life.[54] But those who aspired to nomination did not always perceive the limits of his influence on the Council in any case, and they were usually reluctant to discount the impact that he could have, should he decide to champion them. Thus, the author Jean-Louis Guez de Balzac sought to win de Paul's support for his diocesan ambitions as soon as he acceded to the Council, because he thought that he was the 'counsellor of Her Majesty's conscience'. In January 1644, he sent de Paul a copy of his latest poem, 'Christus

[51] Bergin, *French Episcopate*, 595–6.

[52] BN, Ms 4200, fo. 141r (8 July 1645); *CCD*, 13a: 150–1.

[53] Chéruel and Avenel (eds), *Lettres du Cardinal Mazarin*, iv, 208–9, Jules Mazarin to Hugues de Lionne, 28 May 1651.

[54] *CCD*, 4: 20–1, de Paul to unnamed, 1643–52; *CCD*, 4: 83, de Paul to unnamed, 1643–52.

nascens', through his friend the poet Jean Chapelain, but then doubted the wisdom of his action, because he worried that the pious de Paul would think that it reeked of ambition and self-promotion. He therefore quickly wrote to Chapelain again, in the hope that he would reassure de Paul that he would rather have 'the charge only of saying the Breviary' than the cares of a diocese.[55] Balzac never won his diocese, nor is there any evidence to hint that de Paul offered him any hope of doing so.

In other cases, however, potential nominees did not require de Paul's sponsorship to have their case heard, for they already had powerful advocates. Knowing this, de Paul attempted in 1646 to thwart Mazarin's wish to reward the services of the president of the Paris *parlement*, Mathieu Molé, with the bishopric of Bayeux for his son, by resorting to a mix of humble persuasion and private intervention behind the scenes, albeit with frustrating results. Initially, de Paul articulated his objections to both the cardinal and the queen by arguing that the recently ordained Molé was inexperienced in ministry, and ill prepared to assume responsibility for this sizable and neglected diocese (although he was highly educated, with a doctorate in canon law). His protests fell on deaf ears, and Mazarin simply dismissed him by retorting that he would ask the nominee to visit de Paul for 'the instructions that you judge necessary for acquitting himself well of this office'. Conceding that the direct approach was not working, de Paul then tried another tack. He went twice to speak personally with the other party involved, Molé, ostensibly on another matter, but really in the hope that he could provoke his conscience to the point that he would tell his son to refuse the nomination. In the course of their first conversation, de Paul managed to find the opportunity to express his fears frankly but humbly, professing that his criticisms of the president's son were inspired purely by his desire to ensure that the church was served by leaders dedicated to God. Molé listened patiently to de Paul's earnest plea, and at their second meeting claimed that it had discomfited him so much that he had tossed and turned in his sleep as he fretted about the implications of what de Paul had said. Yet, even if this was true, the securing of his son's earthly future still won out over de Paul's entreaties: Molé informed him that as a father it was his duty to provide for his children as best he could, and that his son would be surrounded by competent diocesan officials who would make up for his inadequacies.[56]

In early 1648, the Dominican nuns of Proulian priory accused de Paul of dragging his feet in bringing the resignation of their prioress to the notice of his fellow councillors, in order to ensure that her long-time rival was elected as her successor.[57] When de Paul finally did so on 28 October, it caused great confusion, with the crown unwilling to appoint a prioress until certain it was within the king's

[55] Tamizey de Larroque (ed.), *Lettres de Balzac*, 57, Jean-Louis Guiz de Balzac to Jean Chapelain, 23 November 1643; Tamizey de Larroque (ed.), *Lettres de Balzac*, 84, same to same, 21 January 1644; Tamizey de Larroque (ed.), *Lettres de Balzac*, 94, same to same, 15 February 1644. 'Christus nascens' is printed in Balzac, *Œuvres*, ii, 31.

[56] For the quotation, see *CCD*, 2: 615, Jules Mazarin to de Paul, February 1646. See also Abelly, *Vie*, ii, 451–2; Chéruel and Avenel (eds), *Lettres du Cardinal Mazarin*, ii, 899, Jules Mazarin to Mathieu Molé, 21 May 1647; Chéruel and Avenel (eds), *Lettres du Cardinal Mazarin*, ii,924, same to same, 18 July 1647.

[57] When the prioress, Antoinette de Sérillac, resigned in January 1647, she expected her niece to succeed her, but died before she could ensure this. Her opponents grabbed their opportunity by holding an election, which Eléonor Daffis won: BN, Ms 15721, fo. 840r–v.

remit.[58] However, this appears to have been an isolated allegation, for nobody else at the time seems to have contended that de Paul delayed the transmission of information to buy time or buried it altogether so that he could see off decisions of which he would disapprove. Yet the converse assertion can be substantiated without a shadow of doubt: de Paul actively sought to regulate the flow of information in order to accelerate the progress of clerical candidates of whom he approved. For instance, Bergin contends that de Paul exhibited his aversion to Mazarin's desire to have his client François Bosquet installed as coadjutor of Lodève in 1647 (with a view to succession) by drawing attention to dubious clauses in Bishop Plantavit's resignation.[59] But this is a misinterpretation of de Paul's position, for he requested that he should be permitted to investigate them for exactly the opposite reason: he hoped to present the right kind of information, in order to ensure that Bosquet was actually appointed. Not only did de Paul already have a good opinion of his 'merit and ability', he had known about the proposal for his appointment for nearly two years because Nicolas Pavillon had asked him to assist in its accomplishment in 1645. Furthermore, in March 1646, Paul had asked the bishop to investigate a rumour that Bosquet was set to gain the diocese by purchasing a library and garden from Plantavit, which might be construed as simony. Having done so, Pavillon informed de Paul that there was no truth in it, and he sent Bosquet to visit de Paul on a number of occasions in order to reassure him of his integrity. De Paul's subsequent investigation was therefore tactical, designed to quench criticism for the nomination; an official checking of the terms by the councillor widely recognized as the most scrupulous of all was the best means to silence naysayers. Indeed, the speed with which the official query took place testifies to the fact that de Paul already had the information that was needed, for Anne of Austria nominated Bosquet to Lodève just four months after the Council recommended him.[60]

VI

The range of the Council's interests offered de Paul a privileged and near unparalleled vista of royal ecclesiastical affairs. Yet, with so many variables with which to contend in the appointments process, he found it immensely challenging to act as the foremost influence in the making or breaking of a candidate's hopes, whatever means he chose to apply. Indeed, it is impossible to avoid the conclusion that when he did so it was frequently simply because the crown had no major or immediate political reason to refuse the request. Indeed, such politically neutral cases provided

[58] BN, Ms 15721, fo. 840r–v.Unfortunately, the paper trail disappears at this point, and the crown's final response to the rival claims cannot be ascertained.

[59] Bergin, *French Episcopate*, 511–12.

[60] *CCD*, 2: 605, Nicolas Pavillon to de Paul, 28 December 1645; *CCD*, 2: 613, same to same, 5 February 1646; *CCD*, 2: 617–18, same to same, 1 March 1646; BN, Ms Fr 15720, fo. 341r (this is an undated resolution accepting Plantavit's resignation in Bosquet's favour, and was probably written shortly after the Council meeting in December 1647 and before Bosquet's formal nomination in April 1648).

the perfect opportunities for Mazarin and Anne to reward de Paul for his services. He was permitted therefore to assist two former Lazarists, so that they in turn found themselves indebted to him for securing their futures once they departed the Congregation. Realistically, neither could be said to possess any other patron at court, and they faced uncertain prospects, having each spent twelve and three years in institutional life. Immediately after Nicolas Durot left in early 1645, the Council recommended him for a canonry in Saint-Martin-d'Angers, and in August he was nominated to the cure of Landes-Debinusson in Maillezais diocese, left vacant by his relative's death. The speed with which he acquired both benefices implies that de Paul was instrumental in tabling them and in pushing for their enactment. Similarly, although Jean Duhamel's elevation to a canonry at the collegial church of Notre-Dame-de-La-Ronde in Rouen took place eight years after his departure in 1640, it speaks strongly of de Paul's sponsorship in the Council. Duhamel had remained in good standing with de Paul, not least because it was only illness that had caused him to leave in the first place, a decision about which he expressed some regret three years later, and for which he tried to compensate by donating 1,000 *livres* to his former companions. His loyalty to them made it natural that de Paul would assist him subsequently if possible.[61]

Equally, de Paul's decision to speak up for Cardinal de La Rochefoucauld and for the heads of the Congregation of France evaporated the suspicions with which the latter in particular had greeted the Lazarist takeover of Saint-Lazare in the 1630s, so that he enjoyed cordial relations with them by the mid-1640s. La Rochefoucauld and de Paul found common ground in clerical reform first, when the cardinal sought de Paul's advice on 'best practice' in ecclesiastical discipline in 1640, and after this added him to an informal group of ecclesiastics he consulted on important affairs.[62] Over time, their affinity had percolated through to influence de Paul's relations with leading members of the Congregation of France such as Blanchart, so that even de Paul's support for Solminihac's struggle to keep Chancelade abbey independent from the Congregation of France failed to sour relations. De Paul displayed remarkable ability to maintain a credible posture that did not offend anyone in this conflict, and this was due in no small measure to his willingness to act in the cardinal's and the Congregation of France's interests whenever he thought it possible in the Council. He made his greatest overture in early 1644, when, in answer to the elderly La Rochefoucauld's request, he was able to relay to Charles Faure that he had successfully pushed for the approval of the cardinal's

[61] AAE, Mémoires et Documents, France, 851, fo. 191r (Durot); AAE, Mémoires et Documents, France, 851, 852 (unpaginated, but the relevant minute for Durot's second nomination can be found under the date 9 August 1645), and 853, fo. 190r (Duhamel); AN, M211 (18 April 1643); *Notices sur les prêtres, clercs et frères*, i, 457.

[62] De Paul replied to questions posed in writing by Robert Lachau, rector of the Jesuit college in Clermont-Ferrand, where La Rochefoucauld had been bishop and retained an active interest in the formation of diocesan clergy: CCD, 13a: 312–13; Bergin, *La Rochefoucauld*, 108.

The council included experts from a variety of relevant areas, including the judiciary, which was represented by Matthieu Molé, first president of the Paris parliament. Other members in the 1630s and early 1640s included Lezeau and Vertamont, councillors of state, and the Maurist superior general, Grégoire Tarisse: BSG, Ms 712, fo. 82v.

resignation of Sainte-Geneviève abbey without prejudice to its independence. La Rochefoucauld and his niece Madame de Sénécey, who enjoyed access to the queen as governess to Louis XIV, had sought fruitlessly to achieve this for several years, and numerous ambitious courtiers sought the abbey as a prize. De Paul's intercession therefore proved critical, and earned him lasting gratitude from the Congregation.[63]

It helped too, of course, if either Mazarin or the queen actively favoured de Paul's preferences. Having obtained a personal undertaking from the queen that she would choose an apostolic successor for his see in 1646, Solminihac called on de Paul in 1651 to intercede by reminding Anne of her promise. Solminihac's own high standing at court had meant that he was able to present his case in its early stages but his age meant that he subsequently relied on de Paul to see it through in Paris. Most of the mediation in which de Paul engaged to achieve this was conducted outside the confines of Council meetings, and without the knowledge of other Council members. Mazarin was absent from court during much of this time, so de Paul was able to reach the queen without obstacle, but this was not the reason why he was successful in his petition. Though the queen respected his opinion, he also benefited hugely from her desire to fulfil the hope of a bishop of devout reputation and loyal service to the crown. In due course, de Paul passed the good news to Solminihac that the queen had given him permission to choose his successor. Solminihac in turn informed him that he had selected Nicolas Sévin, then bishop of Sarlat, judging that he would be a prelate 'who would be more than just a man', that is, a prelate imbued with the graces necessary to maintain the 'well-being' that he had laboured so long to achieve in Cahors.[64] From thereon, Solminihac depended on de Paul to press his cause with Anne, and he insisted that strict confidentiality should characterize their interaction, to ensure that others could not wreck the negotiations. Furthermore, de Paul devised the arrangement by which Sévin finally succeeded, convincing Solminihac that he should not resign but that Sévin should act as his coadjutor with a view to replacing him as bishop on his death.[65]

Solminihac could be certain that de Paul would endorse his candidate: he had known Sévin even before he became bishop of Sarlat in 1644, because he was a member of the Tuesday Conferences.[66] He was amongst five of the known

[63] La Rochefoucauld's resignation was approved on 30 June 1644: BSG, Ms 712, fos 81r–82r; *CCD*, 12: 360–1, Charles Faure to de Paul, 21 June 1644; *CCD*, 2: 509–10, de Paul to Charles Faure, 26 June 1644.

[64] *CCD*, 4: 222, Alain de Solminihac to de Paul, 2 July 1651.

[65] The nomination was delayed inadvertently as Mazarin and Anne virtually ceased nominations altogether between mid-1651 and May 1652, partly because opportunities to make them were extremely scarce, and partly to encourage people to remain in line. De Paul's departure from the Council in autumn 1652 may further have delayed the final step, and it was another four years before the royal nomination, including de Paul's testimony on Sévin's aptness, was presented in Rome: *CCD*, 4: 152, Alain de Solminihac to de Paul, 25 January 1651; *CCD*, 4: 163, same to same, 1 March 1651; *CCD*, 4: 609, Alain de Solminihac to Anne of Austria, 2 July 1651; *CCD*, 5: 171–3, Alain de Solminihac to de Paul, 26 July 1654; *CCD*, 13a: 181–2; Bergin, *French Episcopate*, 526, 703.

[66] De Paul was amongst those who provided depositions to Rome on the candidate's suitability for post: *CCD*, 13a: 181–2. In 1643, he had also done so for François Perrochel, when he was nominated to Boulogne: *CCD*, 13a: 145–7. See also Blet, 'Vincent de Paul'.

members of the association to receive nominations while de Paul sat on the Council, which accounts for one-third of the total number of nominations made from within the group's ranks as a whole.[67] These were, however, fairly evenly distributed over the two decades, meaning that de Paul's time on the Council did not see a spike in nominations. More importantly again, Sévin's preferment was the only one of the five in which de Paul played such a pivotal role. Their membership of the Conferences and their links with de Paul played a contextual role that enhanced their prospects of preferment, but the additional pressures of political priorities and the influence of alternative patrons proved to be the decisive factors; thus, Louis Fouquet was the brother of Mazarin's client Nicolas Fouquet, while his cousin Jean de Maupeou (nominated to Chalon-sur-Saône in 1659) had been under Mazarin's protection at court since the 1640s.[68] As early as 1643, Solminihac had proposed to de Paul that Philibert de Brandon might be a good match for Périgueux, which required an apostolic man if it was to recover from decades of poor supervision by the ailing Bishop La Beraudière, and he confessed that he had also mentioned this to the late Cardinal Richelieu, to no avail. De Paul probably kept Brandon in mind, only to be disappointed by Estrades's appointment, but he raised his name again as a suitable candidate while Périgueux stood vacant later. Solminihac was eventually able to thank him for managing to draw the queen's approving eye to Brandon at last. The triumph was probably not exclusively his, however, for Brandon was the widower of Chancellor Séguier's niece, and therefore impeccably connected at court.[69]

These were appointments from which de Paul would have taken great pleasure, even if his imprint on their making was largely secondary. But to be able to exercise more privilege, he required not only that vacancies should arise, but also that the routes that led from them to preferment would not be strewn with obstacles in the form of rival candidates and political priorities. De Paul preferred to proclaim that humility alone won over individuals to the side of God's advocate and God's cause, but the reality was that such high-minded ideals of virtuous behaviour stood only a modest hope on their own when pitted against the political bargaining and hard-nosed decision-making that characterized the appointments process. However much de Paul liked to present this as a series of opportunities and means to improve the calibre of clergy in the French church, it was in reality contaminated

[67] In addition, Paul de Gondi, later Cardinal de Retz, became coadjutor of Paris in 1643, and the disputed archbishop of Paris in 1654. De Paul is likely to have expressed support for Gondi's promotion in 1643 (and may have regretted it later), but this is not on record. In any case, it was the ability of the Gondi family to use the opportunity of Richelieu's death to persuade the queen to approve the nomination which was the deciding factor. Gondi's elevation was one of three nominations to coajutorships that the crown granted to high-ranking families in 1643–4, as part of a process of stabilizing the new regime: Bergin, *French Episcopate*, 498–9.

[68] Maupeau probably joined the company around the time of his ordination in 1651. He was consecrated bishop in the church at Saint-Lazare on 9 May 1660. The fifth prelate was Étienne Caulet who was nominated for Pamiers in 1644: *CCD*, 8: 344, de Paul to Louis Rivet, 9 May 1660; Bergin, *French Episcopate*, 669.

[69] *CCD*, 2: 429–30, Alain de Solminihac to de Paul, 3 May 1643; *CCD*, 3: 240, same to same, 21 September 1647; *CCD*, 3: 342, same to same, 22 July 1648.

by the intrusion of other factors and interests. Indeed, while his own appointments as vicar general may have exhibited this less blatantly than his period on the Council, they portrayed a similar syncretism at their cores, for in accepting the posts de Paul enrolled in defending the Richelieu family's patrimony as much as that of the church. Ecclesiastical appointments were political, and those who sought to influence them strayed into the political arena, whatever their reservations about operating in it or adopting its rules of play. De Paul may have entered it for what might be construed as non-political reasons, but he knew that in practice political sensitivity and acuity were vital to meet his objectives there: a reputation for the grace-given virtue of humility was of little use if he did not possess the human qualities of shrewdness and practicality which would enable him to deploy the intelligence that he marshalled in targeted and effective ways. Overall, his accomplishments in the appointments of churchmen were moderate, and those for which he could claim credit owed at least as much to his willingness to adopt these tactics as they did to his cultivation of a humble demeanour.

12

Leaving a Legacy in a Fragmented Church

I

If the final two decades of de Paul's life were years of significant recognition and reward, they were simultaneously ones of stiff challenge. From the early 1640s, the onset of the Jansenist controversy meant that differences in theological opinion in the Catholic reform movement became so profound that he began to fear that he was hearing the death knell of his life's work. The dispute threatened to squander the energy of reform in the church, as the unity of the *dévot* movement fragmented into pro- and anti-Jansenist factions.[1] When de Paul became embroiled in it, he was subjected to attack from Jansenist critics, who called into question the trustworthiness and integrity of his humility and the sagacity of his judgement. In this reading of his hostility to the new movement, de Paul's ignorance seemingly knew no bounds, and neither did the misplaced zeal that inspired his efforts to overcome it.[2] Worse, as the protagonists battled to defend their convictions on issues of faith and discipline, the distinctive missionary ethos and practices of his Congregation were subjected to such searching scrutiny that its future appeared to be set at risk.

Over the course of his involvement in the conflict, de Paul emerged as a dedicated and prominent anti-Jansenist campaigner, heavily engaged in countering its principal ideas and in successive attempts to silence its advocates. Though his critics condemned him as too ignorant to comprehend the refined concepts at stake in the conflict, he articulated plausible theological and pastoral concerns, most of which he identified in the early 1640s when he encountered the teaching enshrined in the keystone publications of the movement. The first of these was the *Augustinus*, produced over many years by the bishop of Ypres, Cornelius Jansen, and printed in 1640, while the second was the equally famous *De la Fréquente communion*, published by Antoine Arnauld in 1643. When the first appeared in print, claiming to perpetuate the theology of the fourth-century church father Augustine, it quickly attracted accusations that its author had distorted the saint's doctrines on grace, sin, free will, and salvation. Simultaneously, however, it earned praise, which reflected the presence of a particularly rigorous approach to moral discipline within the *dévot* movement.[3] Prominent among Jansen's champions was his long-time associate,

[1] Wright, *Divisions*, *passim*.

[2] Gerberon, *Histoire*, i, 392, 422. For a modern repetition of this insult, see Dejean, *Prélat indépendant*, 11.

[3] Arnauld, *Communion*, 587.

Jean Duvergier de Hauranne, the abbot of Saint-Cyran, who encouraged his protégé Arnauld to publish *Fréquente communion* as a vindication of his friend's controversial work. This had a galvanizing effect on the emergence of pro- and anti-Jansenist parties in France, partly because the text was far more accessible in language and style than the extremely scholarly *Augustinus*. Its admirers awarded it a privileged position nearly on a par with the *Augustinus* itself in the nascent canon of Jansenist literature, while its detractors, de Paul amongst them, disliked its unsettling ability to spread its doctrines through a wide audience of readers. Thereafter, public interest was held further captive by a startling train of events, including the papal condemnation of five Jansenist propositions in 1653, the miracle of the holy thorn, and the appearance of Blaise Pascal's *Lettres provinciales* in 1657, which defended Jansenist doctrines by ridiculing Jesuit casuistry in an audience-friendly format.

The opinions expressed in the foundational works were based on a particular understanding of humankind's relationship with God within the material world. For Jansenists like Arnauld, human nature was inherently corrupt; because of the fall, individuals were not able to choose between good and evil, but would invariably be drawn towards sin. Equally, the gap between flawed humans and the divine could only be closed by the infusion of divine grace offered through Christ the redeemer. To access this, individuals had to cultivate an intense routine of solitary prayer and mortification, through which they would become open to the will of God. Because these introspective practices would encourage them to examine their conscience, they would enable them to develop a truly contrite heart. One of the most controversial aspects of this teaching was the recommendation of delayed confession and communion, until individuals reached a state of near spiritual perfection. This represented a strict understanding of redemption, in which forgiveness was not possible for most because they never proved truly contrite.[4] Arnauld's supporters were gratified, therefore, that his composition refuted 'lax' moral teaching, which had become firmly associated with the Jesuits in France by the early 1640s, and instead proposed doctrines and disciplines of austere penitence and infrequent sacramental participation, supposedly based on the practices of the early church. Thus, rather than steps that enabled one to advance in sanctity, confession and the eucharist were confirmations or seals of progress in contrition and sanctity.

De Paul read *Fréquente communion* not long after it was published, and it profoundly shaped his attitude. His reading, he asserted, opened his eyes to the falsity and danger of the opinions that the emerging movement promoted.[5] He adjudged the book to be incredibly dangerous, because it made false theological claims which divided opinions and encouraged Catholics to query magisterial authority. Furthermore, de Paul's pastoral praxis was established on a soteriology that he believed to contrast sharply with Jansenist assumptions about grace and the sacraments. Such a firmly held view enabled him to determine that they were also destined to clash in pastoral care, as theological principles were translated into

[4] Arnauld, *Communion*, *passim*; Orcibal, *Spiritualité*, 114–28, 233–41; Sedgwick, *Jansenism*, 32–3.

[5] BN, Ms Fr 24999, fo. 81r: 'Il n'est point de la part de Dieu.'

practice in the economy of salvation. De Paul's opposition was first and foremost theological, therefore, rather than pastoral, as often assumed. He began by intellectually evaluating the orthodoxy of Jansenist theology, and followed up by judging whether it polluted or purified the pastoral care that his missionaries provided for the rural poor. It was this journey that led to his major interventions in the debate: these were concentrated in the decade between 1643 and 1653, that is, between the appearance of *Fréquente communion* and the publication of the papal bull *Cum occasione*, which condemned five propositions supposedly contained in the *Augustinus*.

De Paul's rejection of Arnauld's teaching also led him to have a tainted opinion of those who had influenced him in its development, especially Arnauld's spiritual father, Saint-Cyran, whom de Paul had once counted amongst his friends. The learned abbot had been a prominent figure in *dévot* circles, and de Paul had originally been introduced to him by Bérulle around 1624. Like others, he was 'ravished' by Saint-Cyran's keen spiritual intellect and arresting conversation.[6] Once de Paul moved to Saint-Lazare, his mounting workload and physical distance from the city centre meant that they did not meet as often, though de Paul continued to hold his friend in high regard and to send clerics such as Caulet and Brûlart de Sillery to him for spiritual sustenance.[7]

During these years, Saint-Cyran became the spiritual director to the nuns of Port-Royale convent, and soon became the subject of whispers about the nature of the sacramental regime that he introduced there. Simultaneously, accusations were fired from another quarter about his loyalty to the royal regime; once he was identified as an associate of Jansen, who had trenchantly condemned French foreign policy in the *Mars Gallicus* in 1636, it was simply a matter of time before he raised the ire of Richelieu. The cardinal was also offended by Saint-Cyran's attacks on the Jesuits, with whom he shared doctrinal and pastoral principles. As a result, he sent him to stew in the *château de Vincennes* for a few years in 1638. To gather incriminating evidence against the abbot, Richelieu ordered an investigation, with which all those closely associated with Saint-Cyran were directed to cooperate. Amongst them was de Paul. As an ecclesiastic, he refused to appear before a lay judge, as was his privilege, but he did make a long deposition over three days at the beginning of April 1639.[8]

The judgements of Saint-Cyran that de Paul offered in response to the series of questions put to him during his deposition were markedly different from those that he made post-1643. They do, however, reveal that he was aware that his extended acquaintance with the abbot might place him under suspicion too, particularly since he was asked to explain the contents of a long letter that Saint-Cyran had sent to him in November 1637; in this, Saint-Cyran referred rather bitterly to a meeting

[6] BN, Ms Fr 24999, fo. 71r; Bib. Maz., Ms 2341, fos 287–91; Barcos, *Défense*, 12.

[7] De Paul also recommended Antoine Singlin, a member of the Tuesday Conferences, to Saint-Cyran, only to lose him to Jansenism, in succeeding years: *Lettre de Mre Jean Du Verger de Hauranne*, 157.

[8] The two major studies of the abbot are still Orcibal, *Duvergier de Hauranne*, and Orcibal, *Spiritualité*.

that they had shortly before, and to points of disagreement that had arisen between them during its course (possibly about vows and penance). De Paul explained the circumstances of their discussion by testifying that he had become aware of 'rumours' that had been circulating about the abbot's theological opinions for some time, and had visited him to warn him about the danger these involved.[9] The rumours had sprung from a number of individuals, principal among them two Tuesday Conference priests, Olier and Caulet, the latter of whom told de Paul that Saint-Cyran had 'peculiar opinions'.[10] Since de Paul had recommended Saint-Cyran to Caulet it was hardly surprising, as a result, that he kept the letter that the abbot had sent to him; he confessed that he did so in case he needed to demonstrate that he did not hold any of the opinions that some alleged were held by its author. Even so, he did not incriminate Saint-Cyran in any way, perhaps because of loyalty to an old friend whom he wished to protect from further punishment, or his failure at the time to appreciate that Saint-Cyran's views might be considered dangerously heterodox.[11]

The allegations that de Paul made about Saint-Cyran subsequent to 1643 reveal, however, a man who had hardened his attitude towards him, to the point that he contradicted the testimony that he had provided in his deposition, and proved unwilling to take anything that Saint-Cyran had said to him in good part. He increasingly distanced himself and the Lazarists from the late abbot, and in doing so protected their good standing while contributing to the vilification of Saint-Cyran, and to the emergence of the Jansenist and anti-Jansenist camps. Despite having put an orthodox gloss on Saint-Cyran's words before, de Paul began to state unequivocally that he had been a latter-day Luther or Calvin, and that he had never held any respect for popes or church councils.[12] In 1639, he had also denied openly that Saint-Cyran had expressed anything but orthodox opinions on contrition and absolution; when asked whether Saint-Cyran had alleged that it was an abuse to give absolution immediately after confession and before the performance of satisfactory penance, de Paul answered that even though the abbot had at times spoken 'of penance before absolution', he had never, as far as he was aware, made this particular claim. It was untrue too, he deposed, that Saint-Cyran maintained that perfect contrition was necessary for the granting of absolution from sins.[13] To illustrate,

[9] *CCD*, 1: 396, Jean Duvergier de Hauranne to de Paul, 20 November 1637; BN, Ms Fr 24999, fo. 72r.

[10] These opinions were apparently on priesthood, but their specific nature is unknown: *CCD*, 13a: 105–6; *Lettre de Mre Jean Du Verger de Hauranne*, 157; Pinthereau, *Reliques*.

[11] Coste, *Saint*, iii, 140; Dodin, 'Monsieur Vincent'.

[12] *CCD*, 4: 184, de Paul to Pierre Nivelle, 1651; *CCD*, 4: 209, de Paul to Nicolas Pavillon and Étienne Caulet, June 1651.

[13] Saint-Cyran made a similar statement on absolution and contrition in his deposition, which he signed after a lengthy interrogation in late May. Indeed, he concluded in this that attrition was sufficient for the granting of absolution, and that contrition was not necessary. Concurrently, however, he did lament briefly that the Lazarists did not attend sufficiently to assessing the dispositions of penitents before they absolved them, a criticism of which de Paul had either not been aware or had not been willing to admit in his deposition. Evidently, the abbot thought them somewhat similar to the Jesuits in this regard, whose approach he deplored, and this hinted at the split to come: *Recueil de plusieurs pièces*, 90.

de Paul had pointed to his behaviour: would a champion of deferred absolution, he quizzed, have sponsored Lazarist missions? Obviously not, yet this was exactly what the abbot had done, knowing that these missionaries habitually administered absolution immediately after penitents confessed their sins.[14] Ten years later, however, de Paul again used assertion and example, but this time to condemn rather than vindicate. In a letter to a Lazarist, he vouched that he had personally seen Saint-Cyran defer absolution until those who confessed performed their penances. This was, de Paul noted, a heretical act, and it stemmed from a heretical belief which he had originally denied the abbot had held.

De Paul issued this particular condemnation in the midst of a piercing critique of the arguments that Arnauld had presented in *Fréquente communion*, and in which he expressly stated that Arnauld and Saint-Cyran were affiliates in advocating deferred absolution.[15] He now consistently coupled the two to prove their joint culpability for heresy, and asserted that their beliefs were utterly destructive of 'Holy Communion'.[16] Refusals to challenge other heresies had in the past, he recalled, almost destroyed the church, so he felt compelled to denounce publicly the destructive errors now in vogue.[17] In order to do so, of course, de Paul first needed to be sure of his theological footing. Though his letters contain numerous references to individual components of Jansenist theology, his most coherent and extensive justification for his antagonism towards it is to be found in a treatise that he penned between 1646 and June 1648. Its scholastic format suggests that he conceived it, not for publication, but as an exercise enabling him first to elucidate Jansenist tenets comprehensively and clearly, and then to marshal the solid evidence and arguments that would counter them.[18] These rested, he affirmed, in the body of magisterial teaching accumulated over centuries, and laid out in Scripture and church councils. It had survived the errors of Pelagius in the fourth century and, more recently, of Michel Baius, whose mistaken ideas had bothered the church like 'malignant illnesses'.

It was the Jansenists' favourite, Augustine, who had combated Pelagius, but de Paul refused to accept that Augustine was their ally. Although the church had agreed with the saintly bishop of Hippo that humans could never hope to save

[14] Saint-Cyran had invited the Lazarists to carry out missions in parishes dependent on his abbey, and had also offered them an abbey in Poitiers so that they could do the same there; however, this transfer did not happen: *CCD*, 13a: 108–9.

[15] *CCD*, 3: 360, de Paul to Jean Dehorgny, 10 September 1648.

[16] Here de Paul had in mind the dual definition of communion, in which it could mean both the eucharistic and ecclesiological body of Christ, the unity of which was represented most vividly when the faithful gathered to celebrate the sacrifice of the mass: *CCD*, 3: 362, de Paul to Jean Dehorgny, 10 September 1648. See also BN, Ms Fr 24999, fo. 71r, for de Paul's comparison of Arnauld and Saint-Cyran with Calvinists.

[17] *CCD*, 4: 185–6, de Paul to Pierre Nivelle, 1651.

[18] The treatise was unfinished, but de Paul wrote that he intended to conclude by specifying the true means of persevering in the ancient beliefs of the church, which would have capped the scholastic structure of the piece. The original manuscript of the treatise was lost in 1987, but an authenticated photocopy is held in the ACMP. I refer to this copy, rather than to the printed reproductions printed in the French and English published correspondence, both of which contain important errors: ACMP, 'Grâce'.

themselves de Paul argued that the Jansenists distorted his soteriological teaching by pretending that Augustine taught that the reception of grace was invincible, that is, irresistible. Rather, de Paul insisted, Augustine had taught, as had Paul before him, that the failure of some to become 'enlightened' lay in their unwillingness to accept the 'chalice of salvation'. Therefore, their poor use of their free will resulted in their damnation; this was not, de Paul went on to confirm emphatically, caused by the absence of grace. As the infallible Council of Trent had confirmed, God granted sufficient grace to everyone; whether they accepted its assistance was their choice.[19] Confidently, he wrote:

> God desires that everyone might be saved, and gives everyone the means for that; but, if they do not observe them, it is not God's fault, but theirs.[20]

God received those who responded to his call with merciful charity. Indeed, de Paul understood catechesis to be instrumental in this interaction, for it was in learning the lessons of sin, mercy, and reconciliation from the humble missionary that the layperson chose to respond to God. The Lazarists' emphasis on daily sessions of instruction during missions reflected de Paul's concern that the sacraments which followed were not dispensed without adequate preparation beforehand. Yet he noted in his treatise that he could not acquiesce with the Jansenists that the grace-giving sacraments should be withheld until one had reached a point of near perfection. This was partly because it was far too demanding for the average Christian to achieve, and partly because he assumed that the sacraments both confirmed progress in submission to God and assisted the individual to achieve it.

It was not just the bishop of Hippo whose teaching was contested during the Jansenist conflict, and in this treatise and elsewhere de Paul proved keen to place other major prelates on the side of orthodoxy. Most notably, he displayed an intensely personal desire to protect de Sales, to whom he owed a spiritual debt, from Jansenist appropriation. On three occasions in the treatise, de Paul justified his perspective with references drawn explicitly from the *Treatise on the Love of God.* He echoed the late prelate's assertion that 'the Grace of God is never wanting to such as do what they can, invoking the divine assistance . . . God never abandons such as he has once justified unless they abandon him first; so that, if they be not wanting to grace they shall obtain glory.'[21] De Paul strengthened his hand by lining up Scripture (Matt. 23: 37), a church father (Augustine), and a council (Trent) behind de Sales, and the section forms the most spiritually arresting part of an otherwise rather dry scholarly treatise. The Salesian analogies that de Paul abbreviated spoke amply of the energizing qualities of grace, for those moved by it: pilgrims awoken from their night's sleep could use the sun to walk safely to their sacred destination, as birds spread their wings and sailors hoisted sails to capture

[19] ACMP, 'Grâce', *passim.* De Paul was referring to session six of the Council (Decree on Justification), especially chapters five to seven: Tanner (ed.), ii, 671–81.

[20] ACMP, 'Grâce', fo. 3v: 'Dieu desire que tout le monde soit sauvé, et donne des moyens à tous pour cela; mais, s'ils ne les observent, ce n'est pas la faute de Dieu, mais la leur.'

[21] De Sales, *Treatise*, 116–17, 179.

favourable winds to follow their routes. Equally, grace could be shunned, just as eyes remained sightless against the illuminating 'rays of the sun' if one obstinately refused to open them.[22]

II

In his treatise, de Paul displayed an intellectual ease attributable to substantial dogmatic learning, and his assembly of evidence and argument would have given him cause enough to resist the flow of Jansenist teaching. However, he had other immediate reasons to do so, for in defending orthodoxy in the church as a whole he understood that he was simultaneously defending his own reputation, and the ministerial security of the Lazarist Congregation into the future. It would be especially dangerous to permit Jansenist partisans any opportunity to deride and dismiss the founder who had devised the ethos that distinguished them within the French pastorate. But this is precisely what leading Jansenists sought to do, in a bid to undermine de Paul's credibility, and to remind the faithful that they should not have confidence in his ability to adjudicate intricate theological problems or matters of pastoral discipline. Specifically, they concentrated their observations on de Paul's humility, endeavouring to turn it into a weapon to destroy his own good standing as well as that of the clerical association that he led.

The first blast of this campaign was to be found in the letter that Saint-Cyran sent to de Paul following their November 1637 meeting, and which became public fodder within a short time. In this, he reproved the excessive humility that made the missive's recipient susceptible to swallowing false rumours. De Paul was, he contended, incapable of understanding and evaluating ideas thoroughly, and was swayed by those who were of greater ability or more forceful in their expression. He went on, with 'astonishment in [his] soul', to accuse de Paul of betraying his own values of gentleness and reservation in being taken in by the falsities uttered by his opponents.[23] Some months later in his deposition, the abbot again condemned de Paul with faint praise, saying that, although prudent and good-willed, he possessed neither the 'knowledge' nor 'understanding' to adjudicate 'matters of doctrine and learning' properly.[24]

Antoine Arnauld shared his director's disparaging assessment of de Paul's intellectual resources and prowess, but he was less merciful in his expression. He also extended the criticisms to the Lazarists as a whole. Like other priests of the Paris diocese, Arnauld completed a ten-day retreat with them before his ordination in 1641, which offered him the opportunity to experience their teaching methods and evaluate the content of their training. He found little to commend.

[22] De Sales, *Treatise*, 116–17, 178–80, 182; ACMP, 'Grâce', fos 3v–4r.

[23] *CCD*, 1: 393, Jean Duvergier de Hauranne to de Paul, 20 November 1637.

[24] *Recueil de plusieurs pièces*, 30: '. . . il croit ledit sieur Vincent prudent, mais qu'il se peut tromper par faute de lumieres & intelligence dans les choses de la doctrine & de la science, & non faute de bonne volonté; & qu'il le tient homme de bien'.

From Bons-Enfants, he wrote to Saint-Cyran to express his disdain for the absence of serious theological dissection and reflection there. Although Arnauld admitted that the retreat leaders were pleasant enough, he felt that he was not nourished by the teaching on offer. To compensate, he wrote, he had made a specific request to be allowed to read the New Testament, rather than the books of meditation normally assigned to retreatants. In Arnauld's judgement, these filtered biblical teaching to the point that it was insubstantial and unsatisfying to a man accustomed to the 'solid meat' of advanced theological subjects. Moreover, he preferred to rely on his director even while under the Lazarists' supervision, for he promised to send him a copy of one of the subjects of meditation, so that he could indicate to him what was 'not proper' for him to reflect on.[25]

These opinions made their way further into public sight during de Paul's lifetime when an anonymous Irish Jansenist, writing under the pseudonym Clonsinnil, published his *Deffense des Hibernois disciples de S. Augustin* in 1651. In this he avowed that de Paul had the humility to admit 'that he does not understand anything in the matter of grace', and that he left the more demanding tasks of theological reflection to others. Over time, this kind of backhanded praise was to become standard fare in Jansenist commentary on de Paul, and Saint-Cyran's nephew and noted controversialist Martin de Barcos would incorporate it into his 1668 work *Défense de feu Mr. Vincent de Paul.*[26] It inferred that, even though de Paul's men served the rural poor humbly on their missions, the simplicity of their methods and teaching misled them. The Jansenists traced this failing back to their superior general: his personal limitations were institutionalized in their formation and activities, where scarcely any emphasis was placed on their theological training because they were so busy with 'good works'. As a result, they possessed, the Jansenists asserted, neither the knowledge nor the tools to teach the faith correctly. Indeed, they claimed scornfully that all the Lazarists had time to read were two books by the Jesuit Martin Becan (van der Beeck). One of these was the *Summa Theologiae Scholasticae*, while the other was the *Manuale Controversarium*, a work of controversy refuting Protestant doctrines, including those relating to predestination.[27] This 'book for the ignorant', Barcos caustically observed, embodied what was most superficial in Jesuit learning, that is, a lack of profundity, which made it a subject of derision amongst those capable of evaluating it correctly.[28]

For these observers, de Paul's mistake was to attempt to compensate for his intellectual inadequacies by submitting to the judgement of Jansenist enemies, particularly the Jesuits. His excessive humility rendered him obsequious in his deference, and empowered them to be arrogant or even tyrannous. This was itself a

[25] *Œuvres de Messire Antoine Arnauld*, i, 17–21, Antoine Arnauld to Jean Duvergier de Hauranne, 15 September 1641.

[26] Barcos, *Défense*, 4, 9, 70.

[27] The *Summa* was a compendium based largely on the Jesuit Francisco Suarez's commentary on Thomas Aquinas. First published in 1612, two editions had been published in France by this time, in 1625 and 1634. The first French edition of the *Manuale* was published in 1624: Becan, *Summa*; Becan, *Manuale*.

[28] Barcos, *Défense*, 85–6; Clonsinnil, *Deffense*, 13.

vice, as both Bernard of Clairvaux and Thomas Aquinas had pointed out centuries before.[29] Indeed, at least one fervent Jansenist who knew de Paul would ultimately push this further, to throw suspicions on the sincerity of his humility at all. Looking back from a distance of twenty years, Claude Lancelot argued de Paul used the virtue as a ruse, deliberately hiding his inferiority 'under a veil of affected humility'. To prove this, he repeated Arnauld's assertion that the Lazarists' approach to spiritual pedagogy was akin to feeding milk to babies, in order to condemn their superior general as being intolerant of solid foods, which required that he be nourished in the language of the church and accustomed to discerning what was good. Lancelot then presented the most incriminating construal for what appeared to be the most innocent of words and actions: he mockingly recounted that during their famous meeting of 1637, Saint-Cyran had asked de Paul to define the church. In answer, de Paul had recited a line from the catechism that his missionaries used to instruct children. This enabled Lancelot to brand him as intellectually simplistic and immature but also deliberately duplicitous in dodging the difficult questions.[30]

In recalibrating the qualities and application of humility through these damning criticisms, Jansenists cut to the heart of de Paul's missionary ethos. For his part, he realized, therefore, that it was imperative that he retain his personal claim to humility if his ability to oppose the new movement was not to be compromised. After all, if he was thought to feign humility he would be guilty of hypocrisy; if he was excessively humble, he would be culpable of servile obsequiousness and poor judgement. If either extreme were true, how could his views on Jansenism or anything else of religious importance be trusted? The answers to these questions had considerable implications for de Paul's ability to combat the movement. By the 1640s, he was in a position to exploit a breadth of positions and acquaintanceships to do so. Since his detractors could not challenge his actual possession of offices, they sought to raise suspicions of his virtue that would lead to questions about his ability to act through them. This was because de Paul's ability to collaborate depended on the willingness of other parties to assume that the humility that he expressed in his other areas of Lazarist mission work was just as evident in his straightforward expression of opposition to Jansenism. In other words, they had to accept that the virtue that proved his probity in one sphere of action did the same when applied in another, or at least that it did not cause him to err in judgement.[31]

Humility was simultaneously a collective as well as an individual missionary value, which de Paul expected to transcend his own person as one of the five 'faculties of the soul of the Congregation'. As an authentic signature of Lazarist ministry it lay at the centre of his mission strategy for the conversion of souls.[32] The Jansenists' critique of humility therefore worked against the ethos of his association,

[29] Thomas Aquinas, *Summa Theologica*, II, II, 161, 6, accessed 23 June 2016, <http://www.sacred-texts.com/chr/aquinas/summa/sum418.htm>.

[30] Lancelot, *Mémoires*, 326.

[31] See, for example, the comments of the Minim Simon Martin on the example that de Paul offered to sinners. Martin published a French translation of Luis de Grenade's *Guide des pécheurs* in 1645: *CCD*, 2: 580, Simon Martin to de Paul, 1645.

[32] *CCD*, 13a: 438.

firstly by attempting to cast the judgement of the man who had shaped it into disrepute, and secondly by throwing doubt on the legitimacy of the strategies themselves. To claim humility as de Paul did was to stake a claim for salvific truth, in terms of both the purity of doctrine and the legitimacy of pastoral practices that he advocated. De Paul fought Jansenism, therefore, because he believed that its victory would leave the Lazarist missionary bereft of his understanding of his purpose in the history of salvation. If so, there would be little to motivate him to carry out selfless acts of ministry, endure long weeks of toil in rural parishes, or surrender the comforts of family life. Without it, the Congregation, still so youthful, would be rendered redundant in the church, reduced to an organization built on futile hopes of missionary charity.

For de Paul, this understanding was all the more pertinent in a decade when the details of a rarefied theological dispute dominated public discourse, for it warned against the dangers of an intellectual indulgence that did not contribute to the Lazarists' spiritual health or the common ecclesiastical good. As a result, he alluded to the Jansenists' faults on many occasions when he warned his men about the toxic effects of knowledge paired with pride. Not long after *Fréquente communion* appeared, he reminded them, in the words of St Paul, that knowledge without humility inflated the ego, but was ultimately profitless because it did not result in acts of loving virtue.[33] Consequently, if Arnauld disapproved of the formation methods that he experienced as Bons-Enfants, de Paul was equally disappointed with his lack of regard for the value of pastoral experience in tempering extreme theological opinions. It was, of course, in de Paul's view, necessary to structure the retreats so that they suited the needs of future parish priests, and this required training in basic moral theology and common pastoral functions. But, in de Paul's opinion, Arnauld possessed a dangerously restricted outlook, in which his cerebral musings on theological concepts were divorced from practical theology. In the same year that he sojourned at Bons-Enfants, Arnauld had successfully defended his doctoral thesis at the Sorbonne, and shortly afterwards published his first books.[34] In exasperation, de Paul asked a Lazarist priest:

> Is it not insufferable blindness, in a matter of such importance, to prefer to the universal practice of all Christendom the ideas of a young man who, when he did his writing, has no experience in the direction of souls?

Moreover, since 1643, Arnauld had given spiritual direction to the nuns of Port-Royal, but de Paul clearly did not think that this type of pastoral experience equipped him to understand the needs of ordinary parishioners. Worse, he thought that Arnauld did not practise what he preached to others. De Paul declared frostily to the same correspondent that if he paid attention to Arnauld's book 'not only would I renounce Mass and Holy Communion forever in a spirit of humility, but I would even have a horror of the Sacrament'. He then sarcastically pointed out that Arnauld's own conduct was duplicitous, for although he was eager to disparage

[33] *CCD*, 11: 116; 1 Cor. 8: 1.

[34] The first was *Théologie morales des Jésuites*, which was quickly followed by *Fréquente communion*.

other ecclesiastics, such as de Paul, for celebrating the mass frequently, he was to be found at the altar daily. It was also indicative of supreme vanity, for the Jansenist who celebrated mass routinely was apparently sure that he had attained the virtue needed to approach it. With these well-aimed darts of censure, de Paul tried to capture the higher ground of true virtue, pointedly denying the presence of genuine humility in those who sought to use this virtue to deny the validity of his opposition to them.[35]

III

While the best hope for the Jansenists' mudslinging lay with those who shared their theological sympathies, it became apparent as time passed that those who shared de Paul's objections to their wider convictions were not convinced by their efforts on this front. They did not grow to regard his humility negatively, and remained willing to place trust in his words and actions of opposition and to unite with him regardless. Indeed, some of them were even ready to assume that de Paul's humility confirmed his theological competence because it proved that his judgement was unclouded by sinful motives or prejudices. It was partly for these reasons that anti-Jansenist authors such as Léonard de Marande and the playwright Charles Desmarets de Saint-Sorlin began to ask de Paul to scour their anti-Jansenist texts for errors before publication in the early 1640s, and that he vouch for their theological proficiency and integrity.[36] Of course, they also sought de Paul's endorsement because his positions and public profile might increase their readership and maximize the credibility of their work, but they still would not have done so had they believed his image to be damaged in the public eye. Indeed, de Paul's reputation as an informed anti-Jansenist was actually enhanced considerably by these approaches. His familiarity with new texts augmented his ability to act as a spokesperson for the anti-Jansenist camp,[37] and even meant that he was positioned to identify areas of debate that warranted new intervention from appropriate scholars; in 1656, for instance, he suggested to the Jesuit Annat that he should compose a refutation of the miracle of the holy thorn, the resulting cures from which Jansenist apologists

[35] *CCD*, 3: 358–67, de Paul to Jean Dehorgny, 10 September 1648.

[36] Léonard de Marande sent manuscript copies of his many anti-Jansenist works to de Paul to examine before he published them; the most famous was his *Inconveniénts d'état procédans du Jansénisme*, addressed to Antoine Arnauld. Likewise, on Desmarets's request, de Paul read his *Délices de l'Esprit* in manuscript, and was amongst the 'several wise and pious Theologians, experts in the knowledge of interior matters' whom Desmarets mentioned as having read and approved it: *Délices de l'Esprit*, especially the *epistre* and *protestation* (unpaginated); Desmarets, *Quatrième partie*, 222–3.

[37] De Paul provided a further example of this cross-fertilization in using two as yet unpublished texts refuting the Jansenist argument on the equality of Peter and Paul to produce his 1646 treatise. These were probably the work of Isaac Habert, whom de Paul deemed 'one of the most learned theologians that we have', and with whom he was to develop closer contact over the next few years: *CCD*, 3: 73–4, de Paul to Girolamo Grimaldi, 4 October 1646.

insisted on presenting as vindications of the truth of their doctrines and proof that they held the favour of God.[38]

As he began to assert his own views, however, de Paul discovered that his ability to combat Jansenism was complicated by the split emerging within the broader reform movement. The network of relations that he had developed through missions and clerical formation provided obvious opportunities to align with those who shared his opinion of Jansenism and to persuade others to his view, but it quickly became apparent that his associates were dividing along party lines in much the same way as other *dévots*. As a result, he could still play to his strengths, by attempting to cooperate with individuals, but he could not assume that a shared history of religious endeavour would override or compensate for differences in outlook regarding Jansenist ideas.

De Paul did not find his most active allies amongst the women with whom he worked in charitable activities. This is not because they were all sympathetic to Jansenist teaching, but is representative, rather, of the parameters of the public debate itself, which was a heavily intellectualized and gendered affair. With the exception of the nuns of Port-Royal, few women engaged openly or formally in it, and it was instead overwhelmingly dominated by male clerics, including the episcopate and members of the Sorbonne.[39] Arnauld's position as a doctor of the Sorbonne ensured that the Jansenist conflict in the university became a highly personalized affair, with the doctors splitting into pro and anti-Arnauld factions. Just as importantly, the pastoral implications of the dispute were also subject to clerical expertise, which meant that lay people were supposed to take direction from their religious teachers. De Paul reiterated this throughout the affair, writing with growing urgency through the late 1640s that a lack of decisive guidance from the clergy could mean that umpteen members of the faithful would suffer damnation.[40]

As time passed, de Paul's fears seemed to be borne out; not only did the Jansenists refuse to relinquish their views, they planted doubts about frequentation of the sacraments in the minds of large numbers of laypeople. Indeed, some of those who had contributed to charitable works stemming from de Paul, including the duchess of Liancourt and her husband, were persuaded to their views; in 1655, this climaxed dramatically in the refusal of a confessor in Saint-Sulpice parish to absolve the duke because of his affiliation with Jansenism. As a result, de Paul's hopes that insistent dissemination of true doctrine and appropriate devotional practices would win out against error shrank; referring to the Liancourts' refusal to abandon their Jansenist sympathies in 1657, he commented pessimistically that, despite all efforts to convert them, they remained in their 'wretched, deplorable state', which was akin to 'a state of hell'. They could not 'extricate themselves from this state,

[38] Annat finally wrote two pamphlets on the subject: Abelly, *Vie*, ii, 496; Annat, *Rabat-joie*; Annat, *Défense de la vérité catholique*.

[39] In private, however, some women could be highly exercised by the theological issues pertaining to the conflict, as Hillman's case study of the devotional culture of an informal cohort of eight female, aristocratic, and spiritual friends, which included the duchess of Liancourt, demonstrates: Hillman, *Female Piety*, 79–87.

[40] ACMP, 'Grâce', fo. 1r; *CCD*, 3: 365, de Paul to Jean Dehorgny, 10 September 1648.

regardless of what is said to them'.[41] De Paul might have hoped to influence them because they enjoyed a common bond in the promotion of charity: Madame was a member of the confraternity at the *Hôtel-Dieu* in Paris, while the couple had expressed their religious sentiments together in their patronage of the Daughters in Liancourt parish from 1645.[42] But these links did not prove robust enough to convince them to follow de Paul's lead.[43]

Similar differences of opinion became a regular feature of de Paul's other relationships. Members of the Tuesday Conferences, many exceptionally theologically literate, did not display the uniformity of spirit that de Paul desired of the group; though formally united in their quest to nurture priestly virtues and devotional discipline, this bond did not guarantee agreement in relation to Jansenism, particularly as both sides of the debate insisted on their loyalty to the pursuit of priestly sanctity. Some of the confreres remained publicly aloof from the furore, but the division was nonetheless pronounced. Those who stood alongside de Paul often acted in unison with him; on de Paul's invitation, Louis Abelly, a prominent critic of Jansenist writings who was known especially for publishing works supporting the pope's power to issue authoritative judgements of the contested doctrines, led a number of conferences at Saint-Lazare in which he deconstructed core Jansenist teachings in 1648.[44] These were attended by Tuesday Conference members, but also by Lazarists and some seminarians, a number of whom de Paul feared were vacillating over the new ideas. Amongst the Conference confreres present was Hippolyte Féret, who had hitherto 'been caught up in these new opinions'. De Paul noted with satisfaction the impact that Abelly's words had on his attitude: having listened and reflected carefully, he abruptly turned from these ideas, and redirected his energy towards their defeat.[45] Likewise, confrere Laurent Bouchet resolved during his retreat at Saint-Lazare in 1650 to 'work strongly to smother in its birth the new sect' of Jansenists who claimed 'to be assured, by a certitude of faith, that they have the Holy Spirit with them'. He had his opportunity when de Paul engaged him to speak with Abelly on the perils of Jansenism at ordinand retreats in 1655.[46] Another member's refutations found their way into print, even if only after his death. This was principally due to Abelly, who published his life of François Renar in 1659, six years after he had passed away. During the course of

41 *CCD*, 11: 355. 42 AN, S6169.

43 It might be expected that the couple's split over Jansenist affiliations would destroy their relationship with de Paul and Marillac, but this did not happen. In 1657 de Paul invited the duchess to become the primary protector of the Daughters of Providence on the death of their founding patroness, Marie de Poulaillon; at precisely the time that he was lamenting the Liancourts' state of damnation elsewhere, he was informing Madame that God wanted her 'to be, for time and for eternity, one of the principal instruments . . . to preserve the purity and hoiness of many virgins': *CCD*, 6: 551, de Paul to Jeanne de Liancourt, 18 October 1657.

44 De Paul forwarded one of these to the Lazarirst Edme Jolly in Rome so that he could present it to Pope Alexander VII: Abelly, *De l'obèissance*; Abelly, *Défense de la hiérarchie*; *CCD*, 7: 499, de Paul to Edme Jolly, 4 April 1659.

45 *CCD*, 3: 329, de Paul to Jean Dehorgny, 25 June 1648.

46 Bibliothèque de Chartres, Ms 457 (sixth day, unpaginated): 'De travailler fortement a étouffer dans sa naissance la nouvelle secte . . . qui règne dans Paris et se multiplie tous les jours, ainsi qui dissent être assurés, par une certitude de foi, qu'ils ont le Saint-Esprit avec eux.'

composition, Abelly discussed the possibility of publishing anti-Jansenist maxims that Renar had composed with a number of 'friends', probably de Paul and other Tuesday Conference members. Finally, they decided that Renar's maxims should be made accessible to a general audience, and they were published at the same time as Abelly's laudatory life.[47]

Both Féret and Bouchet had spent periods in the episcopal households of confreres who subsequently earned notoriety for their support of Jansenism; in the mid-1640s, Féret lived in Alet where Pavillon was bishop, and Bouchet was attached to the household of Caulet in Pamiers. Both returned to Paris in 1646. It was in Alet, Féret subsequently confessed, that he had first been tempted by Jansenist ideas, and only the influence of de Paul and Abelly had rescued him from their allure.[48] The company of the Tuesday Conferences also contained a number of other known partisans, including Claude Tristan, who was successively archdeacon and vicar general of Beauvais, a hotbed of Jansenism governed by Nicolas Choart de Buzenval.[49] The three prelates, along with Antoine Arnauld's brother, Henri, bishop of Angers, refused to sign the anti-Jansenist formulary issued by the Assembly of Clergy in 1657 without reservations that contradicted it by distinguishing between *droit* and *fait*.[50] In this, they were supported by a number of Conference members who had also by then been raised to episcopal office; though Godeau, the Fouquet brothers, and Vialart did not share their penchant for Jansenist doctrines, they objected firmly to the suggestion that a bishop should not be permitted to exercise his doctrinal judgement over an issue that was open to interpretation.[51] Similar variation in attitudes can be identified amongst de Paul's other associates in diocesan missionary and clerical training. Bishops Perrochel (a Conference member) and Solminihac proved dogged adversaries of Jansenism. However, a history of Lazarist missions or the existence of a Lazarist house in a diocese were not generally sound indications of the affiliations of its bishop, or of de Paul's ability to affect a prelate's posture. He hoped that the goodwill generated by the Lazarists' services would assist his overtures to prelates on Jansenism, yet bishops like Nivelle and Raoul de La Guibourgère refused to allow their gratitude or their personal liking of de Paul to affect their judgements on this matter of faith.

With the onset of Jansenism uncovering the hidden distinctions amongst churchmen, it might, as a result, be supposed that de Paul's hitherto warm

[47] Pastorally orientated, the maxims advocated penitential disciplines that contradicted Jansenist directives on infrequent sacramental reception, delayed absolution, and public penance, which Renar argued were far too rigorous and 'rough' for 'poor sinners'. Abelly wrote the preface for this volume, and there recounted the history of its publication: Renar, *Maximes*.

[48] *CCD*, 3: 329, de Paul to Jean Dehorgny, 25 June 1648; Joseph Guichard, 'Laurent Bouchet . . . L'Anti-Janséniste'.

[49] Others included Buisson and Singlin, both of whom, according to Bouchet, left the company once they had plumped for the 'party of the demon': Bibliothèque de Chartres, Ms 596, t. xviii, 279.

[50] Antoine Arnauld devised a distinction between *droit* and *fait* to allow Jansenists to subscribe to the Formulary in 1657. This was to enable them to declare that they accepted the pope's condemnation of the five propositions (*droit*), but believed that he was mistaken regarding their presence in the *Augustinus* (*fait*): Cognet, *Jansénisme*, 64.

[51] Vialart did oppose the expulsion of Arnauld from the Sorbonne in 1656, however: Forrestal, *Fathers*, 127–9; Gres-Gayer, *Jansénisme*, 311.

relationships with bishops like Caulet and Pavillon would turn glacial during this period. However, his approaches to known Jansenists, and willingness to preserve personal relations with them, were utterly at odds with his campaigning to defeat the teachings that they championed, and they are indicative of the tactical choices with which he was faced from the early 1640s. One reason for his effort in this domain was his awareness that it would be foolish to bite the hands that fed the Lazarists or to deny the faithful the chance to enjoy the group's ministrations. Thus, de Paul continued to permit his confreres to execute missions for Henri Arnauld, and even expressed his hope that the prelate's invitation to the Lazarists to establish a house in his diocese would come to fruition.[52] Another was his realization that it was sensible to retain communication in case it would lead to an opportunity to exercise influence at some point. In 1656 and 1657, de Paul did not permit the hazard of contagion to prevent him from inviting Caulet and Pavillon to return to Saint-Lazare to speak at ordinand retreats, because he wanted to speak to them privately about their intransigent attitude to the formulary.[53]

V

For de Paul, the defeat of Jansenism was not simply a matter of keeping his options open, however valuable this might prove. Achieving this ambition depended on his ability to align with those, like the intellectually talented Abelly and Boucher, who could best help him to get the results he wanted. In the Council of Ecclesiastical Affairs, hostility towards the disciples of Augustine was almost universal, with the exception of the elderly Bishop Potier, and it quickly became common knowledge when de Paul declared his opposition in one of its meetings in 1643. The Council provided one venue in which he could encourage the government to lean on leading Jansenists, and from 1648 onwards he joined his colleagues there in advising the queen to use her influence to ensure that papal censures of Jansenist teaching would be respected when they were issued, despite the potential conflict with Gallican liberties that might arise.[54] He also had a particular ally on the Council in Jacques Charton, who was a confrere of the Tuesday Conferences as well. Even so, de Paul was not the major petitioner for the anti-Jansenist cause before the queen and minister, and did not act as an intermediary for key figures

[52] *CCD*, 6: 410, de Paul to Henri Arnauld, 8 August 1657.

[53] De Paul's contradictory attitude extended further down the hierarchy, to men such as the Oratorian Claude Séguenot. His translation into French of Augustine's treatise on virginity, with commentary, was censured by the Sorbonne in 1638, and he was imprisoned in the Bastille for nearly four years. De Paul knew him as a 'dangerous' Jansenist, but allowed René Alméras to stay with him in Tours in 1660: *CCD*, 3: 293, Jean-Jacques Olier to de Paul, April 1648; *CCD*, 6: 389, de Paul to François Caulet, 24 July 1657; *CCD*, 8: 413, de Paul to René Alméras, 4 August 1660; *CCD*, 438–9, Claude Séguenot to de Paul, 12 August 1660; Séguenot, *Sainte Virginité*; *Censura Sacrae Facultatis Theologiae Parisiensis*.

[54] The pope had already censured Barcos's works, and the campaign to ensure that all Jansenist heresies were condemned was under way: *CCD*, 3: 319, de Paul to Jean Dehorgny, 25 June 1648; BN, Ms Fr 24999, fo. 82r.

like François Hallier who travelled to Rome in 1651 to seek papal condemnation of the five propositions: the rabidly anti-Jansenist confessor to the king, the Jesuit Jacques Dinet, acted as Hallier's main representative at court while he was in Rome, while Hallier asked Olier to speak to Mazarin on such issues as the need to ensure that *Cum occasione* was registered in *parlement*.[55]

This fact should not be taken to mean, however, that de Paul played a negligible role in the hunt for victory over the Jansenists, but, rather, that the Council was not where he proved busiest or most effective. While in Rome Hallier wrote intermittently to de Paul, who received his updates with great interest. This was because, outside the Council, he and Charton were to be found together in a select but loose circle which coalesced by 1648 to combat Jansenism by petitioning the pope to issue a bull of condemnation. It was yet another Tuesday Conference member, Hippolyte Féret, who instigated the creation of this informal grouping, although he was not part of it. Sometime early in 1648, Féret suggested to Abelly that de Paul should combine with other prominent figures in Paris to form what he called 'a secret congregation to defend the ancient truths'. Abelly must have passed this idea to de Paul, for within a short time of its floating, the latter met with ecclesiastics strategically positioned in prominent ecclesiastical institutions, and highly proficient in theology, at Saint-Lazare. Although this nucleus of activists was not officially a committee, it did function somewhat like an ad hoc one over time.[56] Along with de Paul and Charton, its first affiliates included Coqueret and Nicolas Cornet, then syndic of the Sorbonne. Numbers grew moderately, to include in the next five years the Grand Master of the College of Navarre, Jean Péreyret; Robert Duval, the nephew of de Paul's late adviser André Duval, and his successor as *professeur royal* in the Sorbonne; Martin Grandin, the principal of the College of Dainville and professor of theology at the Sorbonne. It is also likely that Hallier joined with them for a period.[57] With the exception of de Paul, these men were doctors of the Sorbonne, which became a major centre for the conflict around this time. De Paul could not participate directly in the debates and votes that took place in the faculty, but his relations with those who could encouraged him to participate in the background activities that sought to determine their course. In return, his own importance to the grouping lay in the extensive and priceless contacts that he brought to it, which reached far beyond any that he developed in the university, and were vital in the campaign to have Jansenism condemned.

University affairs became the covert focus of de Paul's attention at the turn of the decade. The occasion for this was the *affaire des Hibernois*, an episode in which Paul sought to manipulate events within the university despite his outsider status, and which had its roots in the links that he had encouraged between the Lazarists and

55 BSG, Ms 1452, fos 1r–2v, M? Aubery (on behalf of François Hallier) to Jacques Dinet, 16 June 1653; BSG, Ms 1452, fos 119r–120v, François Hallier to Jacques Dinet, 16 June 1653. Abelly quoted part of this letter in his *vie* of de Paul, but did not include the proposal that Olier should speak to the minister: Abelly, *Vie*, ii, 583–5.

56 *CCD* translates the French 'congrégation' as committee: *CCD*, 3: 318–29, de Paul to Jean Dehorgny, 25 June 1648.

57 ACMP, Robineau, 'Remarques', fo. 56r.

Irish clerical students from the late 1640s. These came under pronounced public scrutiny in early 1651, after twenty-seven Irish clerical students signed a declaration against the 'new dogmas', in which they affirmed their adherence to the Tridentine decrees and those of earlier councils on grace. On the instigation of the university rector, Jean Courtin, the academic council insisted that the students revoke their signatures, and avoid intervening in matters of doctrinal judgement in the future, a privilege to which they had no right. At this point, the students appealed to the Faculty of Theology and the *parlement*, both of which sided with them, albeit following heated debates in the Faculty chamber. There, the new syndic, Hallier, proved one of their staunchest defenders.[58]

Although the Irish comprised a number of theologically literate figures, such as Thomas Mede (who probably composed the declaration), it was unusual for students who stood low in the university's ranks to carry out such a provocative act. Grès-Gayer remains uncertain about the origin of the events and the objectives of those involved, but it is not difficult to find the hand of de Paul and his partners behind it, and to deduce that they orchestrated the event in order to flush out Jansenists and their sympathizers in the university.[59] De Paul may not have instigated the declaration, but it is extremely unlikely that it would have seen the light of day without his approval. The students sent a copy of it to him as soon as they had signed it, and a few days before they sent it to the university. This suggests that they wanted to have his blessing for its contents and for their wish to send it before they actually took this step. But none of this happened out of the blue. For some time the students had been connected to de Paul through several of the fifteen Irish ecclesiastics who had joined the Lazarists since 1638. Furthermore, Bons-Enfants had been providing support for exiled Irish clerics living in Paris, since they did not have a college similar to those found in Louvain, Salamanca, and elsewhere. They had attended regular conferences held on Thursdays there over the years, and in the late 1640s de Paul had permitted an Irish Lazarist, George White, to run special conferences for his fellow countrymen there.[60] This was the venue in which the declaration was hatched.

In this process, de Paul used the links that already existed between the Lazarists and the Irish to play on the latter's vulnerable status as a group of exiled clerics in need of favour and opportunities for promotion. With his knowledge, White used the conferences to instil orthodox loyalties in the participants, which was especially important since a number of Irish theologians were already regarded as partisans of Jansenism.[61] His activity fitted neatly into the broader pattern of conferences run under Lazarist auspices, which saw de Paul ensure that their contents were tailored to producing ecclesiastics convinced of orthodox doctrines and alert to the supposed falsehoods of Jansenism. Moreover, when the declaration emerged from the

[58] Grès-Gayer, *Jansénisme*, 93–5; Wall, 'Irish Enterprise'.

[59] Grès-Gayer, *Jansénisme*, 91.

[60] Furthermore, de Paul had long taken an interest in the Irish mission, and had even sent six missionaries to Ireland on the request of Propaganda Fide five years before: Forrestal, 'Irish Entrants'. See also Boyle, 'Hibernia Vincentiana', and Boyle, *Vincent de Paul.*

[61] O'Connor, *Jansenists*, 173–238.

conferences, rumours surfaced that White, with de Paul's authorization, had promised them that the signatories could hope for de Paul's favour if they put their names to it.[62] The allegation was not simply Jansenist sour grapes, for it is given credence by the fact that, very soon afterwards, de Paul used his credit with the Congregation of France to intervene with the superior of Sainte-Geneviève on behalf of Thomas Mede. Evidently, adherence to de Paul's orthodoxy paid dividends. Mede had been a ringleader within the student group, and was one of the two principal appellants of the university's decision before the Faculty. For de Paul, Mede's evident loyalty to doctrinal purity also indicated his reliability and vigilance. This led him to suppose that this 'very good man' should be positioned to use these qualities sentry-like, by being appointed an examiner at masters level in the university.[63]

De Paul's most energetic efforts in the campaign culminated some time after this episode. Well before 1648, he had begun to use his extensive list of associates to gather and disseminate information that he thought valuable to the anti-Jansenist cause. Not only did this necessitate that he concentrate on exchanges with those who were positively disposed to sharing information on Jansenist sympathizers, it also demanded that he work with those who were best positioned regionally to cooperate with him. From an early stage, individual bishops proved crucial conduits of information from the provinces, but even amongst the informants as a whole Alain de Solminihac took the lead place. In the mid-1640s, he grew increasingly concerned about the advance of Jansenism in the south-west, especially in Toulouse, where he warned de Paul in 1650 that the university's professors had begun to teach suspect doctrines, perhaps emboldened by the fact that the bishop of Comminges had preached on them three times in the city. The town, he predicted darkly, 'will cause us trouble'.[64] This meant that he relished the fact, as he put it, that he and de Paul had 'joined battle at last'.[65]

Not long after he reported on heterodoxy in Toulouse, Solminihac responded enthusiastically when de Paul asked him to sign a letter from French bishops to Innocent X, which asked that he should examine five Jansenist propositions.[66] De Paul had neither compiled the propositions nor suggested the letter, both tasks having fallen to Isaac Habert after he had produced seven propositions for censure by the Sorbonne in 1649.[67] There, the syndic François Hallier had used his authority to ensure that the Sorbonne formally condemned them.[68] De Paul was, however, deeply involved in assembling a team of signatories for the plea, and assumed particular responsibility for this within the 'committee' of ecclesiastics with whom he was working in Paris. On his request, Solminihac agreed to act as an

62 Thus, Clonsinnil intimated that the students had been used by de Paul, and that they realized that if they did not sign they could expect to be shunned in the future: Clonsinnil, *Deffense*, 2, 13–14.

63 De Paul asked the superior, Antoine Sconin, to recommend the appointment to the then chancellor of the university, Jean Fronteau, who was also a member of the Congregation of France. Although he did not refuse to appoint Mede, Fronteau was ousted as chancellor because he supposedly displayed Jansenist leanings in September 1652: *CCD*, 4: 241–2, de Paul to Antoine Sconin, 9 August 1651.

64 *CCD*, 3: 591, Alain de Solminihac to de Paul, 15 February 1650.

65 *CCD* 4: 160, same to same, 13 February 1651.

66 *CCD*, 4: 607–8, French bishops to Pope Innocent X, 1651.

67 Ceyssens, 'Isaac Habert'.

68 Ceyssens, 'François Hallier'.

advocate in the south-west, and to approach four other bishops about following his example in signing.[69] Simultaneously, and all the while keeping Solminihac informed, de Paul targeted other bishops that he knew well through Lazarist activities or their membership of the Tuesday Conferences or both; these were prelates such as Pavillon, Caulet, Raoul de La Guibourgère, Nivelle, Desclaux of Dax, and Béthune of Bordeaux. In writing to them, sometimes more than once, de Paul employed a humble tone as he apologized for taking the 'liberty' to send the petition to those who were superior in ecclesiastical status, but he coupled this with reminders that they were duty bound as protectors of their flocks to seek a decisive statement of orthodoxy from their own hierarchical superior, the pope.[70] He was not, however, sufficiently confident to proposition bishops with whom he did not enjoy an established connection. In these cases, he appealed to those he did know to act as his intermediary with their peers: having successfully sought Desclaux's signature, for instance, he requested that the prelate persuade his neighbour, Dolce of Bayonne, to do the same.[71]

Between January and August 1651, de Paul and Solminihac delightedly recorded the rising number of signatures, which eventually numbered eighty-eight. De Paul was the principal solicitor of perhaps twenty of them.[72] Along with his successes, however, he had notable disappointments. He made the mistake of asking Caulet to encourage Daffis of Lombez to sign, which might explain why his name does not appear amongst those who eventually did. Nor did that of Bishop Raoul de La Guibourgère; he had invited the Lazarists to his former diocese of Saintes for missions and to run the diocesan seminary, and was also indebted to de Paul for his appointment to La Rochelle in 1646, but this history was not enough to convince him to comply with de Paul's appeal to sign the letter.[73] De Paul met similar failure in courting Nivelle, despite sending the letter to him twice, and emphasizing that sixty of 'his learned and zealous peers, including the bishop of Cahors', had already signed it. Insistently but ineffectively, the appeal reminded its reluctant recipient of the high stakes at issue: 'the glory of God, peace in the Church and, I venture to say, in the State as well'.[74] Two other bishops linked to de Paul through the Tuesday Conferences or a seminary actually reacted even more negatively to the letter, by joining nine of their colleagues in appending their signatures to a letter addressed to the pope, which stated that the propositions should first be examined by a council of French bishops. In these cases, it was possible that sympathy with Jansenist ideas or Gallican sensitivity about the independence of the French church and its episcopate, or a combination of both, were at play.[75]

[69] *CCD*, 4: 160, Alain de Solminihac to de Paul, 13 February 1651.

[70] For an example, see *CCD*, 4: 182–6, de Paul to Pierre Nivelle, 23 April 1651.

[71] *CCD*, 4: 202, de Paul to Jacques Desclaux, 21 May 1651.

[72] *CCD*, 4: 160, Alain de Solminihac to de Paul, 13 February 1651; *CCD*, 4: 179, de Paul to Jacques Dinet, 14 April 1651. See also BN, Baluze 123, fo. 75r, for an incomplete list of signatures.

[73] *CCD*, 4: 179, de Paul to Jacques Dinet, 14 April 1651.

[74] *CCD*, 4: 183, de Paul to Pierre Nivelle, 23 April 1651.

[75] These were Bishops Vialart and Delbène: *CCD*, 4: 160, Alain de Solminihac to de Paul, 13 February 1651; *CCD*, 4: 179, de Paul to Jacques Dinet, 14 April 1651. For the letter of the eleven bishops, see Rapin, *Mémoires*, i, 380–2. For a detailed analysis of the Gallican claim that bishops

Once the letter was dispatched, de Paul continued to confer with Charton, Duval, and the others regarding its outcome. Their discussions took on greater urgency when a trio of Jansenist agents travelled to Rome in late 1651 to plead their case before the pope, and centred on whether it was necessary to send a delegation there to counter them.[76] It appeared opportune, indeed essential, to respond in kind, but opinion was not initially unanimous that this was the best way to proceed. Both Duval and Cornet expressed concern that a papal condemnation of Jansenist teaching might prove so all encompassing that it would muddy rather than clarify the waters. With his gaze firmly set on the reputation of the French church, Grandin noted that pleading to Rome gave the impression that the French church was in disarray, but still preferred to take this course, especially since this would curtail the Jansenists' ambition to appear 'to the eyes of everyone as the defenders of truth since their adversaries would not have dared to appear to enter in dispute with them'. De Paul had already expressed the same view in his correspondence on a number of occasions, so he was now fully in favour of proceeding in this way, as a result.[77] At this point too, the question of funding became pertinent, for the costs of travel, accommodation, paperwork, and gifts commensurate with such an enterprise would be onerous and sustained. Here de Paul stepped in, agreeing to supervise the collection of funds. He had ready resort; those with whom he cooperated in this venture were based in two Parisian parishes, which is significant enough, but at least two were also members of the Tuesday Conferences. In the parish of Saint-Sulpice, the *curé* Jean-Jacques Olier and another Sulpician, Alexander de Bretonvilliers, supervised the collection of donations, and the priestly community in Saint-Germain-l'Auxerrois did likewise. There the *curé* was Jean Colombet, but, more importantly, it was the home of Laurent Bouchet.[78]

It was much to de Paul's relief when Innocent X finally issued the papal bull in 1653. His judgement did not, of course, resolve the dispute for it entered a new phase when its opponents began to distinguish between *fait* and *droit* in order to deny its application to *Augustinus*, and the Sorbonne doctors took to arguing over the expulsion of Antoine Arnauld from their ranks. Yet, although de Paul remained staunchly antagonistic to Jansenism, he gradually began to retreat from the public arena of battle, preferring to intervene privately to persuade old associates like

could, individually or collectively, judge spiritual issues that were not already defined articles of faith, see Forrestal, *Fathers*, 127–38.

[76] René Rapin later suggested that it was the *curé* of Saint-Germain-l'Auxerrois, Jean Colombet, who suggested that a deputation was necessary, which is possible but uncorroborated. In any case, it was certainly these men who actually brought it into being: Rapin, *Mémoires*, i, 430–1.

[77] The activists also agreed to petition the court for letters of introduction to the French ambassador around this time. De Paul mentioned that this request had been successful in a letter to Hallier during the summer: *CCD*, 4: 394, de Paul to François Hallier, 21 June 1652.

[78] There is no conclusive evidence to suggest that Bretonvilliers and Colombet were, like Olier and Bouchet, members of the Tuesday Conferences, but this link via fundraising with de Paul raises the possibility that they were. The fact that the memorial service for de Paul's death was organized by members of the conference in Saint-Germain-l'Auxerrois parish makes it even more credible. In addition to these 'modest efforts', de Paul offered the delegation bed and board at the Lazarists' house in Rome, although they did not take advantage of this: Arsenal, Ms 2009, 192–3; *CCD*, 4: 394, de Paul to François Hallier, 21 June 1652; *CCD*, 4: 430, de Paul to unnamed, May 1652–May 1653.

Caulet and Pavillon to submit to the bull after it was published. In effect, he continued to perform the functions for which he had always been most valuable, that is, to align tactically with those of similar disposition to his and to persuade others to his opinions, using the associative ties that he had nurtured as he developed the structure and works of the Congregation of the Mission. Jansenists had not begun to target de Paul as one of their chief adversaries merely because of the vehemence with which he rejected their doctrines. His approach to conversion and redemption offered a public alternative, indeed a reproach, to their own, and the links that he cultivated through his efforts to sanctify clerics and laity were the basis for and means of his actions against them. Even so, these connections of reciprocal favour regularly proved fallible in their ability to permit de Paul to ally and persuade. Any victories that he won were the outcome of the goodwill that bishops and other clerics had developed towards him when he and his missionaries served their ecclesiastical needs. But they owed just as much to a shared belief that their soteriology and pastoral care were superior to Jansenist imperatives; without this, de Paul had no hope at all of co-opting them to his cause.

Conclusion

I

In seventeenth-century France, the Catholic reform movement produced more than its fair share of advocates for the promotion of religious devotion, virtue, and discipline within society. Few proved more active or persistent in their pursuit than Vincent de Paul, whose degree of involvement has led many to assume that he was not only the quintessential representative of the Catholic Reformation in France, but its principal architect as it matured. This study's close analysis of his wide-ranging activities disproves both contentions, for it underscores heavily the variety of opinions and operations that gave the movement its character and import, while also offering unprecedented insights into the ways in which de Paul engaged with them in order to influence its direction. In reality, de Paul stands out amongst a host of distinguished peers, not because he controlled the path and products of the reform movement as a whole, but because he succeeded in articulating and applying traditional teachings and existing practices in new, enterprising, and systematic ways. It was beyond any single individual to determine the direction and outcome of the Catholic Reformation in France, but the environment from which it arose offered an abundance of opportunities to innovate, to organize, and to support religious sensibilities. De Paul managed to carve a particularly distinctive and popular manifestation of religious activism within it, turning a personal vocational imperative to evangelize into a congregation of secular missionaries, which was—crucially—endowed with multifaceted features of pastoral care. The Lazarist Congregation stood, therefore, at the heart of an enterprise geared towards the reform of contemporary religious practices. Its prominence rested, furthermore, on de Paul's marked ability to exploit the potential for association and collaboration that lay amongst a cross-section of his contemporaries, who, for a variety of reasons, became well disposed to his efforts to realize his goals.

De Paul's engagement over the course of forty years or so with the broad range of Lazarist interests means that the exploration of his experience also casts vital light on the evolution of the reform movement as a whole. After all, his career spanned the principal decades of the drive for renewal in France, and his activities throughout contributed to the broad pattern of creativity, growth, consolidation, and fragmentation that characterized it. In devising and implementing his vision for the Lazarists, de Paul was, at the same time, influenced by his environment, so that the qualities of the vision itself were affected deeply by ideas and practices that he borrowed from the intellectual richness of his surroundings. In France the seeds of the reform movement were sown well before de Paul arrived in Paris. Like others, he was touched over time by the questing spirit of renewal which moved individuals and groups to implement ideas and practices that would re-energize and reorganize the church for a new era, while he went on too to play a role in the breakdown of unity amongst *dévots* during the 1640s. By this time, he was a well-established public figure, and one increasingly surefooted in dealing with the demands involved in expanding and managing a clerical institute. The contrast between the young man who had found himself in a predicament over the abbey of Saint-Léonard in the early 1610s and the savvy individual who withstood the efforts of the bishop of Narbonne to dictate contract terms that were not to his liking in the 1650s could not be starker. In the early 1610s, de Paul displayed all the characteristics of an ambitious and needy young cleric on the make; by the late 1650s, he was a veteran negotiator, and a seasoned assessor of the types of resources and relations on which the Congregation's works could be built. Critically too, de Paul had come to redefine his ambitions, so that they were situated within an institutional framework for mission rather than that of personal promotion and livelihood. As a result, he could regard honours bestowed on him, such as his position on the royal Council of Ecclesiastical Affairs, as opportunities for him to fulfil his Lazarist duty to reform the French clergy.

II

As de Paul began to engage with the resources, ideas, and people that shaped his understanding of pastoral care from the early 1600s, he slowly began to pick his way towards a less conventional clerical career. Indeed, while in Paris he already displayed signs of the astuteness that would later lead him to forge attachments with figures and families who had something significant to offer to his mission causes—a defining feature of his efforts to promote the Lazarists' interests from the 1620s. In particular, the fact that de Paul managed to capture the attention and ultimately the patronage of Pierre de Bérulle was pivotal to his future, for it meant that he headed towards gains that would bear their greatest results years later in the foundation, structure, ethos, and practices of the Congregation of the Mission. Bérulle's Oratory offered the example of a congregational model of clerical life, but his influence over de Paul's early appointments provided still more: opportunities to develop a rural pastoral strategy, to whet his vocational appetite to serve the rural peasantry, and to access the lavish lay patronage that would endow the association in which he would satisfy it.

That all of these were effectively in place by the late 1620s testifies to the inspirational and fertile nature of the religious environment from which de Paul emerged, but also to his ability to take advantage of it. Yet however deeply one searches, it is not possible to identify a 'grand strategy' on his part at this stage. Indeed, throughout his career, de Paul was to be at times reactive and at others proactive, and it is by means of this choreography that he was gradually able to develop the structure and features of the Lazarist works. Thus, while his connection to the Gondi provided potential access to material supports, it might have resulted in nothing more than the conventional duties of a cleric in a noble household and sinecures had he not been able to couple it with a visionary strategy of missionary evangelization. In using the Gondi endowment to establish his new clerical association, de Paul displayed the talents of an ecclesiastical entrepreneur, for this momentous step in turn permitted him to put his formula of catechetical instruction, sacramental provision, and confraternal charity into action on missionary campaigns. He did so to even greater effect when he split the Lazarists' expression of their missionary call into three dimensions, thereby turning the Congregation into the centrepiece of his quest to invigorate devotion and virtue in the church. For de Paul, this diversity enlarged the field of operation, and created a multitude of possibilities for influencing religious life amongst different sectors of the population. He was not, of course, unique in wanting to improve the piety of the faithful, the standard of clergy, or the provision of charitable welfare, for these had proved to be concerns to a greater or lesser extent of many Catholics in the decades since Trent, including some in France. Nor was de Paul wholly original in using the formal structures of a clerical community, seminaries, or confraternities to do so, for much larger clerical groups such as the Jesuits and Oratorians were already experimenting with each of these in their work. However, his approach was uniquely coherent. The pastoral agenda in each type of structure was determined by the primary virtue of charity, meaning that de Paul placed the religious care of a wide variety and number of people under its unifying banner.

It is remarkable that antipathy to Protestantism exercised such a minimal direct influence on this pastoral agenda, given the often actively hostile attitude of *dévots* to the faith and its members. This is not to suggest that de Paul did not share the negative opinions of some of his associates, such as Bérulle, or that his wish to improve rural religious discipline was not inspired at least partly by the desire to ensure that the Protestant religion could never make inroads amongst the faithful again. But, after the 1610s, de Paul mentioned Protestantism only occasionally, and barely engaged with ventures that other *dévots* established to convert its adherents. Indeed, from the earliest years of the Lazarists' work, he granted little credence to controversy as a means of evangelization, and his distinctive views on the best means to convert Protestants earned the Congregation handsome patronage from the crown. This is symptomatic of the heterogeneity of opinions on this and other issues amongst *dévots*, as well as of the multiple spiritual influences that were available to de Paul in developing the Lazarist ethos and practices. He drew some of these from *dévot* figures, as well as from the wider corpus of church teaching ranging from Augustine to Louis of Granada. But he was particularly judicious in mining the thought of a figure who was fast becoming a popular spiritual hero for the devout of Paris, even if there is no reason to doubt his genuine admiration and affection for him: the teaching of the late bishop of Geneva offered a sound underpinning to de Paul's understanding of the ways in which different categories of the faithful could express the virtue of charity, and more specifically of how they could do so within the different areas of Lazarist missionary work. Moreover, as de Sales was already publicly admired and celebrated, de Paul's friendship and spiritual association with him provided precisely the kind of attention and credibility that he needed in order to make fruitful connections.

Most significantly, de Paul placed the Lazarists themselves at the core of his evangelizing drive, viewing them as instruments of charity as they converted rural peasants, trained the priests who would care for them, and founded confraternities. In deciding on the virtues that would form the quintet of institutional values that enabled their charity, de Paul could pick from a wide range of possibilities. He decided to place special stress on humility as both a core attribute and a tool of conversion, advocating that it should be a key determinant of the Lazarists' conduct and interaction with peasants, patrons, and courtiers. His choices point to the supreme versatility and flexibility that marked out his evangelizing programme, in which virtues related to charity could be prioritized in order to give special shape to specific tasks, such as evangelization of the poor or care of the sick.

More broadly, in invoking charity for those who became associated with the Lazarists' work, de Paul expected that it would realize other benefits. First, it enabled them to practise the virtue too. Rural parishioners could emulate the Lazarist missionary's charity when they responded freely to his call to convert; those who gave financial support to the Lazarists' work, occasionally laboured on their missions, or contributed advice and mediation (of the kind offered by Marie de La Trinité in Troyes), engaged in acts of charity that contributed to their own salvation and that of others. De Paul habitually notified benefactors of both the incentives and the rewards of charity, and the specific references that they made to them in their contracts, conference notes, or letters indicated that individuals like Brûlart and Boucher were receptive to his message. Likewise, de Paul resorted to the confraternities of charity in order to offer a new venue in which to exercise charity. Their rules provided the consoeurs with inspirational direction appropriate to their sex, by urging them to serve Christ in their lay female vocation. Along with the emphasis that de Paul placed on spiritual equality and sisterliness, he remained sensitive to the power of social categories and conventions to influence the ways that members engaged with each other and with the works of charity. He used his knowledge in ways that played to the strengths (and aspirations) of particular types of member. This was especially productive for his dealings with the confraternity of the *Hôtel-Dieu* of Paris. To rally its ranks of socially elevated women in challenging times of want, de Paul frankly encouraged them to mould themselves in the shape of ancient heroines, so that they could take their rightful place to the fore of public welfare.

III

The popularity of the *Hôtel-Dieu* and other confraternities in Paris was partly due to de Paul's ability to use his position as the ecclesiastical superior of the Visitation to form active links with other admirers of de Sales. But, crucially, this led to gains in other areas of his work: those with whom de Paul shared a common Salesian sympathy extended their devotional generosity to his efforts to build a community of clerics whose pastoral work was expressly influenced by de Sales's teaching. Even more importantly, the provision of opportunities to pursue charity in different ways provided a framework for bonding; charity was to unite its practitioners across the Lazarist works, from those who responded to the Lazarists on mission to those who paid to give them the opportunity to do so. In attempting to establish these bonds, therefore, de Paul relied on spiritual affinity, so that the missionary enterprise would be held together by an infrastructure of mission houses, seminaries, endowments, donations, and formal confraternal structures, and by activists united by a sense of common virtue and devout goals in the long term. Indeed, this was the main way in which de Paul hoped to compensate for his personal distance from most members of the confraternities in Paris, since the message of charity that he wished them to absorb was enshrined for perpetuation in the rules of the association itself.

Shared sympathies or goals did not invariably ensure, however, that projects went smoothly or were fully implemented. Most notably, de Paul appears to have held misgivings about the remit ascribed to the new General Hospital in Paris in the late 1650s, even though he prudently kept these quiet in order to maintain smooth relations with women who had been essential allies in developing the Congregation of the Mission. Indeed, the motivations that inspired his associates to cooperate with him in meeting religious goals were never either singular or simple, as many of his relationships with patrons demonstrated. In the later 1630s, leading patrons Cardinal Richelieu and the duchess of Aiguillon were inspired by a shifting and related set of familial, political, and religious concerns when bestowing the gifts that allowed de Paul to install the Lazarists in Richelieu, Luçon, and Marseille. In these cases, despite delays and temporary setbacks, the collaboration went smoothly, with the result that Richelieu and Marseille had become two of the most important Lazarist foundations by the time that de Paul died. At times, however, de Paul's plans took unexpected turns when they met an obstacle thrown up by competing objectives: for the future direction of the Lazarists' work, this was never with more portentous implications than in Cahors, when de Paul caved in to Bishop Solminihac's wish to confine the Lazarist community to the management of his seminary and a parish, rather than allow them to assume their usual responsibility for missions. This set a precedent whose consequences would become apparent only in the generations after de Paul's death, and which came about not because he desired it, but because someone who was not a Lazarist did. In this case, Solminihac wanted a seminary whose personnel were devoted to the training of large numbers of diocesan clergy, and did not feel any onus to help the Lazarists to meet their obligations as missionaries to the peasantry.

On the flipside, Solminihac was, however, a figure of influence amongst bishops in the south-west, who helped de Paul to expand the Lazarists' presence in the region, and to gather the kind of valuable information by which he might affect decision-making on the Council of Ecclesiastical Affairs. Theirs was a relationship that was years in the making, and indicative not merely of de Paul's willingness to put great effort into cultivating connections that only gradually achieved results, but also of his ability to provide bishops and others with what they wanted. In the

1630s, de Paul assisted Solminihac in problems relating to Chancelade, before eventually acting as his intermediary with the queen in relation to his resignation and replacement in Cahors—all in addition to his provision of Lazarists to run the bishop's much longed-for seminary. Similarly, for other prelates, the way in which de Paul developed the Lazarists' specialist works meant that he could provide missionaries and seminary administrators for those who sought to improve religious discipline in their dioceses. Even those who were not motivated specifically or overtly by the same Salesian impulses that inspired de Paul, therefore, could use the Lazarist services that were their end products to implement their pastoral programmes.

Over time, de Paul's decision to augment the original purpose of the Lazarist Congregation to include clerical formation repaid him handsomely. In expanding the group's activities to include first retreats and then seminaries, he increased the numbers who could become subject to its pastoral attention. Just as importantly, he provided an incentive for new patrons to emerge. From 1643, the majority of new houses were founded by prelates, which meant that the Lazarists joined with the senior members of the French ecclesiastical hierarchy in the implementation of a common agenda to improve religious standards amongst clergy and laity. In this again, the advantages of the broad nature of the missionary enterprise for reform are apparent, for it was sufficiently versatile to suit many requirements. Indeed, de Paul played a critical role in ensuring that institutional reform measures became a major characteristic of the French Catholic Reformation over time, while still doing his part to retain the interest and active involvement of non-episcopal Catholics, which had featured from the start, in it.

Although he did not originally set this out as its express purpose, yet another of de Paul's initiatives in the domain of clerical formation, the Tuesday Conferences, played some role in this process. This company was initially formed to provide spiritual guidance to its clerical members as well as training for the ecclesiastical posts to which they might subsequently rise. It became a pool of collaborators from which de Paul might draw to promote his pastoral interests, not so much in the area of seminaries, but certainly in those of Lazarist missions and anti-Jansenism. Despite the members' common vow to take Jesus as their model for living, it was never likely that even those who strived for excellence in their vocations would agree on every aspect of theology, particularly those that were ambiguous. In addition, it was also unlikely that they would all select the Lazarists for their missions and seminaries, for other factors such as familial pressure, financial restrictions, or governmental priorities often determined their choices. The number who did choose the Lazarists for these was, however, sufficiently large to make it worthwhile for de Paul to continue to direct the group until his death.

Equally, however, it should be remembered that, although the resources that emanated from prelates like Raoul de La Guibourgère, Grangier de Liverdi, and the Fouquet brothers inaugurated a new phase of Lazarist expansion, this kind of high-level support and promotion of the Congregation's works was far from novel. From the very beginning, de Paul had succeeded in attracting sponsorship from the uppermost echelons of French society, the members of which could offer the kind of financial backing, offices, connections, and public endorsement that were essential if his association was to find a secure and prominent position in the church. Thus, over time, the goods of female members of the nobility as well as those of bishops featured prominently amongst the major endowments and donations de Paul accepted on the Lazarists' behalf. Further, by virtue of the preferential treatment that the Gondi and Richelieu families offered, in particular, de Paul and the Lazarists came to the attention of the royal family itself, and ultimately, therefore, to the point whereby they were able to access the prized patronage in the crown's possession.

In developing the infrastructure for the Lazarists' works, de Paul was also enabled by the monarchy's administrative structures and mechanisms, because so many of the assets and income that major donors gave to the Congregation derived from *rentes*, coach routes, and royal grants, as well as from ecclesiastical sources such as diocesan incomes. Simultaneously, the growth of the Lazarists contributed moderately to the expansion of the administrative state itself, adding to the development of a more complex fiscal administrative system by further intertwining public and private resources in its financial networks. Equally, it meant, of course, that the material wellbeing of the Lazarists and their pastoral interests were heavily dependent on the institutions of the developing Bourbon state as well as on the support of the king's subjects. Their reliance grew further when the royal family was added to the list of major Lazarist patrons, and might be seen to place de Paul in an invidious position as a result.

For some scholars of Jansenism, de Paul's relations with the *grands* of the political establishment compromised his integrity, independence, and discernment, and left him unwilling to question the crown's policies in regard to the movement and its principal protagonists.[1] In contrast, de Paul claimed that he entered the minefield of secular politics only for affairs that bore on the health of the church.[2] This justification for clerical involvement was far from exceptional, although many issues could be deemed to have possible repercussions for the church's wellbeing, particularly in a realm where so much of the institution's patrimony was in the monarch's gift. To be fair, de Paul's opposition to Jansenism derived primarily from his theological and pastoral concerns about the implications of its teaching. Still, the dovetailing of his view with the crown's hostility to the movement can be situated within a broader perspective that reveals the strategy that de Paul adopted for his causes. He understood that patronage was essential to the advancement of the Lazarists and of their mission, and that he needed to provide services to those in positions of political, ecclesiastical, and social power if he was to gain their approval and backing. When he did so, and when he authorized the Lazarists to follow suit, he and they profited handsomely, gaining a foothold in Sedan, for instance, in return for becoming accomplices in the reunion of the principality with the Bourbon monarchy.

[1] See, representatively, Dejean, *Prélat indépendant*, 11.

[2] *CCD*, 2: 495, de Paul to Guillaume Gallais, 13 February 1644.

In spite of the mutual benefits summarized above, de Paul discovered that piety and politics were often uneasy bedfellows in his relations with the crown. This was nowhere more obvious than in the procedures of the Council of Ecclesiastical Affairs, his time on which demonstrated not only the extent to which he had been integrated into the government's ecclesiastical decision-making, but also the restrictions on his ability to promote clerical reform there. While on this body, de Paul displayed considerable political acuity in navigating his way, because he acknowledged that humility, shrewdness, and pragmatism were not mutually exclusive qualities, and that his value to the crown lay in his ability to employ all of them in the appointments process. He could also call on his skills and resources for the collation and management of information, which suited a government that wished to exert greater control over royal patrimony and was dependent on knowledge of it to extend its authority over the king's subjects. In doing so, de Paul proved a productive servant of the realm. But he certainly did not enjoy a similar level of success in using the same skills and resources to reduce or cancel out the effects of political ambition or expediency. Indeed, while he could be proactive in seeking to set the agenda for appointments, he was frequently forced to react to the machinations not only of Mazarin, but also of others outside the Council itself, such as Mathieu Molé, to guard what he saw as the church's interests and health.

Even so, the overall effect of de Paul's time on the Council was positive if measured in terms of royal favour, for his contributions to the appointments process drew him and therefore the Lazarists further into the royal fold for the future. This was a bargain that had to be struck if other of his causes, such as the campaign to defeat Jansenism and the expansion of Lazarist works, were to be pursued with real hope of success. It was also one of the greatest and most persistent challenges of de Paul's efforts to shape religious belief and behaviour. De Paul built the Congregation by cultivating links with those who could contribute the kinds of intellectual and material resources that would underpin its growth. The long-term workings of the wider enterprise of missions, clerical formation, and assistance to the sick and poor depended greatly on his ability to establish institutional collaborations and organized devotional charity. And the extraordinary degree of interconnectedness and functional association that all of this entailed meant that he had to pay heed to both idealism and pragmatism if he was to avoid either of two extremes, that is, of missing out on new opportunities or of selling out to them.

APPENDIX 1

Lazarist Houses Established in France, 1625–1660

Date	Location	Patron Founder(s)	Endowment	Conditions
1624[a]	Paris	Archbishop de Gondi (Paris)	College of Bons-Enfants[b]	
1632	Paris	Adrien Le Bon, prior of Saint-Lazare	Former priory of Saint-Lazare, and possessions	Pensions totalling 5,600 *livres* annually for religious
1635	Toul	Bishop Chrétien de Gournay (Toul)	Church, house, and hospital	Two parish cures; care of the hospital
1637	Troyes	Noel Brûlart de Sillery; Bishop René de Breslay (Troyes)	House in Troyes; *Hôtel de Troyes*, Paris; 19,400 *livres* in cash and *rentes*; revenue from *aides et vins* (then *c.*1,800 *livres* annually)	Six priests and two brothers; quinquennial missions in nine parishes of Order of Malta; missions in diocese; annual ordinand retreats (seminary added in 1643)
1637	Notre-Dame de la Rose	Marie Wignerod de Combalet, duchess of Aiguillon; Bishop Barthélemy Delbène (Agen)	13,500 *livres* from Orléans coaches (*c.*1,000*livres* income annually); house	At least three priests for missions; care of shrine
1638	Richelieu	Cardinal Richelieu	46,400 *livres*; 5,500 *livres* annually; properties in Richelieu; revenues from Saint-Nicolas-de-Champvant priory	Twenty priests; parish cure; ordinand and clerical retreats; five-yearly missions in Poitiers and Lucon
1641 (closed 1654, reopened mid-1660)	Crécy-en-Brie	Louis XIII; Pierre de Lorthon (secretary to Anne of Austria)	Use of royal *château*; annual income of 8,000 *livres*; offices of *regrattier* in Lagny-sur-Marne	Eight priests and two brothers for missions
1641	Luçon	Cardinal Richelieu	4,850 *livres* for purchase of residence	Missions
1643	Sedan	Louis XIV; Archbishop Léonor d'Estampes de Valençay (Reims)	74,000 *livres*; 2,500 *livres* annually; agricultural produce	Eight priests and two brothers; care of cure of Sedan and curacy of Balan; missions in Sedan and rest of Reims diocese

(*continued*)

Continued

Date	Location	Patron Founder(s)	Endowment	Conditions
1643	Marseille	Marie Wignerod de Combalet, duchess of Aiguillon	14,000 *livres*, with *c.*1,400 *livres* annually from the Rouen coaches	Four missionaries for the galleys (including five-yearly missions) and parish missions; pastoral care of convicts in hospital
1643	Cahors	Bishop Alain de Solminihac (Cahors)	2,000 *livres* annually; 18,000 *livres*	Four priests and two brothers; Saint-Étienne parish cure; seminary; missions (missions revoked)
1644	Montmirail	Pierre de Gondi, duke of Retz	*Hôtel de la Chaussée*	Missions
1644	Saintes	Bishop Jacques Raoul de la Guibourgère (Saintes)	House; 1,200 *livres* annually	Four Lazarists for seminary and missions
1645	Saint-Méen	Bishop Achille de Harlay (Saint-Malo)	Saint-Méen monastery; 1,131 *livres* 10 *sous* in revenue and produce annually	Five priests for missions and seminary; care of shrine
1645	Le Mans	Martin Lucas (provost of Notre-Dame-de-Coëffort (Le Mans)	Provostship of Notre-Dame-de-Coëffort; houses; agricultural land	Seminary; missions; pastoral care at *Hôtel-Dieu*
1650	Agen	Bishop Barthélemy Delbène (Agen)	Sainte-Foy and Saint-Pierre-de-Montmagnerie priories; land parcel	Three priests and two brothers for seminary
1650 (closed 1651)	Périgueux	Bishop Philibert de Brandon (Périgueux)	House	Seminary; missions
1652	Montauban	Bishop Pierre de Murviel (Montauban); Bishop Pierre de Bertier (Montauban)	House	Seminary; missions; care of Saint-Aignan cure and sanctuary
1654	Tréguier	Bishop Balthazar Grangier de Liverdi (Tréguier); Michel Thepault de Rumelin, *grand pénitencier* (Tréguier)	1,000 *livres* annually; 7,700 *livres*; small properties and three *chapellenies*	Three priest and one brother for missions
1654	Agde	Bishop François Fouquet (Agde)	House	Seminary; missions
1659	Meaux	Bishop Dominique Séguier (Meaux)	25,000 *livres*	Seminary; missions
1659	Narbonne	Bishop François Fouquet (Agde)	House	Seminary; missions; care of Maiour cure

[a] This list does not include the supposed houses of Alet and Montpellier, often counted amongst the foundations of this period: for further information, see Ch. 8, n. 30 (Alet), and n. 21 (Montpellier).

[b] Counted with Saint-Lazare as one establishment from 1633.

APPENDIX 2

Endowed Lazarist Missions in France, 1625–1660

Date	Patron Founder(s)	Value	Site(s)	Number of Missionaries	Schedule	Stipulations or Alterations
1625	Philippe-Emmanuel and Marguerite de Gondi	45,000 *livres*	Rocheport, Commerges, Euville, Folleville, Joigny, Montmirail, Dampierre, Villepeurx, Plessis-Ecouis; galleys		Quinquennial	
1629	Louis Callon, *curé* of Aumale	45,000 *livres*	Rouen diocese, especially Aumale deanery	2	Biennial	
1632	Nicolas Vivian, *maître des comptes*	10,000 *livres*	Jurisdictions of Bordeaux, Toulouse, and Provence *parlements*			1636—a further 200 *livres*
1633	Elie Laisné, *sieur de la Marguerie*	200 *livres* annually	Angoulême (Blanzac town, and Ivrignas, Aubeuille, Champagne, and Plassas parishes)	3	Quinquennial	1637—a further 100 *livres*; 1642—a further 166 *livres* 13 *sous*
*1634	Catherine Vigor and Antoine Lamy, *auditeur* in *chambre des comptes*	148 *livres* 13 *sous* 4 *deniers* annually from *rentes* on *décimes*; initial payment of 297 *livres* 6 *sous* 8 *deniers*	Gentilly, Ferreux	5	Sexennial	1640—altered to octennial
1639	Claude Chomel, *conseiller de roi, trésorier et payeur de la gendarmerie de France*	100 *livres* annually, from *rentes* of 1,800 *livres*	Villemandé (Paris diocese)		Quinquennial	Plaque for donor in Saint-Lazare church

(*continued*)

Continued

Date	Patron Founder(s)	Value	Site(s)	Number of Missionaries	Schedule	Stipulations or Alterations
*1641	Élisabeth Brouilly, *dame de La Becherelle*	100 *livres* annually	Buvarde parish (Soissons diocese)		Quinquennial	
1646	Nicolas Desguerrons, priest	900 *livres*	Arcys-sur-Aubre parish (Troyes diocese)			
*1651	Marie Lamoignon	2,000 *livres* in *rentes*, then producing income of 100 *livres* annually	Baville, Breüilpont, Couberon, and other places as necessary		Sexennial	
1655	Laurence Teyrac de Paulian, baroness of Castelnau	18,000 *livres* in *rentes* from Aix or *pays de Provence*	Six parishes in Marseille	2/3	Quinquennial	Low masses for the benefactor
*1656	Marie Camus	500 *livres* in *rentes*	Missions in six parishes (Tanlay, Vanlay, Savoisy, Châteauneuf, Boiscommun, and Nibelle)		Sexennial	

Note: This is a list of known endowments for specific mission sites. It excludes Lazarist houses which had obligations for formal missions attached to them.

* Donation by a member of the Ladies of Charity of the *Hôtel-Dieu* (Paris)

APPENDIX 3

Other Significant Donations for Lazarist Works in France, 1625–1660

Date	Donor	Donation	Purpose	Other Stipulations or Alterations
1632	Jean Billard, resident of Saint-Paul parish, Paris	600 *livres* in *rentes*		
1632	Martin Parmoutier, *curé* of La Queue-en-Brie	3,000 *livres* in *rentes*		
1634	Pierre de Glanderon, canon of Saint-Denis, Paris	1,000 *livres*		
*1635	Charlotte de Herse	Two farms in Mespuits and Fréneville		
*1637	Madeleine de Lamoignon	Annual revenue from *rentes* of 300 *livres*		
*1638–43	Charlotte de Herse	6,000 *livres* × six years	Ordinand retreats	
*1639	Geneviève Goussault	1,100 *livres*	Altar and masses at Bons-Enfants	
1640	Noel Brûlart de Sillery, commander of the Troyes temple of the Order of the Knights Hospitaller of Saint John of Jerusalem and Malta	80,000 *livres* in *rentes* from *fermes des aides* of Angers, with revenue then 10,000 *livres* annually		
1640	Anonymous widow	25,000 *livres*; modest (unspecified) amount of annual revenue		
1641	Pierre Le Pelletier, *auditeur* in *chambre des comptes*	6,600 *livres*		Daily mass in perpetuity at Saint-Lazare

(*continued*)

Continued

Date	Donor	Donation	Purpose	Other Stipulations or Alterations
1642	Cardinal Richelieu	1,000 *écus*	Maintenance of twelve seminarians at Bons-Enfants	
1643	Jean Duhamel, former Lazarist	1,000 *livres*		
1643	Jean Coqueret, principal of College of Grassins	5,000 *livres*	Maintenance of ordinands of French dioceses	
*1644	Élisabeth Merault and Jacques Norais, *sieur d'Orsigny, conseiller notaire* and *secrétaire honoraire du roi*	120 *arpents* of land in Saclay		Annual pension for the couple; acquisition lost in 1658
1644	Louis Toutblanc, secretary to duke of Retz	Two farms in Courbetost (Montmirail)		
1645	Marie Vignerod de Combalet, duchess of Aiguillon	10,000 *livres*	Building of premises for ordinands at Saint-Lazare on site of former infirmary	
1645	Nicolas Hennequin de Vincy, *seigneur* of Fey and Vincy	11,700 *livres*		Annual pension of 585 *livres*
*1647	Élisabeth Merault and Jacques Norais, *sieur d'Orsigny, conseiller notaire*, and *secrétaire honoraire du roi*	7.25 *arpents* of land in Saclay		Acqusition lost in 1658
1650	Charlotte-Marquerite de Gondi, marchioness of Maignelay	18,000 *livres* in *rentes*, with revenue then 1,000 *livres* annually	Ordinand retreats in Paris	Exchanged for 175 *arpents* of land at Plessis-Trappes in 1651, with the annual rental income paying for ordinand retreats
1650	François Vincent, former seminarian at Bons-Enfants, cleric of Meaux diocese	Three houses in Nully-Saint-Front parish; 26 *arpents* of land in Nully, Maubrey, and Alilly		Perpetual retreat at Saint-Lazare; masses in perpetuity
1650	François Voisin, priest, *seigneur* of Villebourg, *ancien conseiller du roi au grand conseil*	7,000 *livres*	Training of clergy at Bons-Enfants and Saint-Lazare	1,500 *livres* to be used for 'propagation of the faith' in Ireland

1651	Jean Lanier, Lazarist brother	2,700 *livres*		
1651	Jean Le Féron, priest of Paris diocese, living in Saint-Étienne-du-Mont parish	18,000 *livres*		
1653	Robert Le Féron, cleric at Bons-Enfants	10,800 *livres*		
*1653	Madelaine Roussel	3,600 *livres*	Missions	200 *livres* pension annually for donor until her death; this sum to be used for missions thereafter
*1653	Marie Souplet and Nicolas Le Camus, former secretary of Michel de Marillac, *chevalier*, *conseiller ordinaire du roi*, and *maître des requêtes ordinaire*	Farm in Grigny (Essone)		
1653	Mathieu Vinot, *secrétaire ordinaire* to Anne of Austria	100,000 *livres*	Reimbursement of purchase price of *Nom de Jésus* properties; refurbishments to same; upkeep of residents at same	
1654	Antoine Galert, doctor in theology, residing at Mont Saint-Hilaire, Paris	2,400 *livres*		Annual pension of 200 *livres*
1655	Louis de Chandenier, priest, resident at Saint-Lazare shortly before death in 1660 (possibly with intention of joining Lazarists)	Saint-Pourcain-sur-Sioule priory (Auvergne)	Ordinand retreats at Saint-Lazare	First transferred to Edme Menestrier and then united to Lazarists (March 1660)
1655	Claude Blampignon, prior of Bussière-Badil priory, Limoges diocese	Bussière-Badil priory		
*1657	Marie Fouquet	Annual revenue from *rentes* of 2,800 *livres*	Missions (including in Barbary)	
1658	Nicolas Pignay, priest	Twenty-five *boiselées de terre*, and *c.*3,000 *livres*	The upkeep of the Lazarist house in Luçon[a]	
1659	Nicolas Étienne, Lazarist priest	36,000 *livres*	Missions (to be expanded to include Madagascar and elsewhere outside France after his death)	Daily mass for donor and family

Note: This is a list of known donations of this kind.

[a] See also Ch. 7, section IV.

* Donation by a member of the Ladies of Charity of the *Hôtel-Dieu* (Paris).

Bibliography

MANUSCRIPT SOURCES

Archives Communales de Châtillon-sur-Chalaronne
GG96, GG105, GG121.

Archives des Affaires Étrangères, Paris
Mémoires et Documents, France: 84, 830, 847, 851–3, 856.

Archives de la Congrégation de la Mission, Paris
In this category, the term 'copy' designates a certified transcription, photocopy, photograph, or scanned copy of an original document.

'Acte d'Association et Premier Règlement des Dames de la Confrérie de la Charité de Châtillon-lès-Dombes' (copy).
'Acte de l'établissement de la Confrérie de Montmirail'.
'Déposition du Frère Chollier, d'après le registre des missions'.
'De la Compagnie de M[ss] de la Conférence qui s'assemblent une fois la semaine à S. Lazare'.
Dossier 'Agen'.
Dossier 'Cahors'.
Dossier 'La Rose'.
Dossier 'Saint-Méen'.
'Érection de la Confrérie de la Charité de Châtillon' (copy).
'Jean Coqueret to Geneviève Goussault, 8 June 1633' (copy).
'Barthélemy Donadieu de Griet to Geneviève Goussault' (copy).
'Livre de la Charité des Pauvres de Chastillon pour Damoiselle Charlotte de Brye Dame de Burnan' (copy).
'Noms des premières Dames de la Charité, 1634–60'.
Paul, Vincent de. 'De la grâce' (copy).
Paul, Vincent de. 'Sermon sur le catéchisme'.
Paul, Vincent de. 'Sermon sur le [*sic*] communion I'.
Paul, Vincent de. 'Sermon sur le [*sic*] communion II'.
'Processus S. C. Rituum in causa beatificationis venerabilis servi Dei Vincentii a Paulo'.
'Reconnaissance d'une dette de M. Vincent envers Jacques Gasteaud' (copy).
'Règlement de Bons-Enfants 1645'.
'Règlement de la Charité de Femmes de Châtillon-lès-Dombes'.
'Règlement de l'association de la Charité de Courboin'.
'Règles du Séminaire'.
'Règles du Directeur du Séminaire'.
Robineau, Louis. 'Remarques sur les actes et paroles de feu Monsieur Vincent de Paul notre très Honoré Père et Fondateur'.
'Supplique de Marguerite de Silly, 25 septembre, 1618' (copy).
'Testament de Claude Gilbert, curé de S. Pierre et S. Denys de Montmartre, 9 octobre 1695'.

Archives de l'Assistance Publique, Paris
108–9.

Archives Départementales de Charente-Maritime
B1522.
E1203.
3E1203.

Archives Départementales de l'Ain
3E 23463.

Archives Départementales de la Loire
H702.

Archives Départementales de l'Aube
5G1, 5G249.

Archives Départementales des Bouches-du-Rhône
Série H, Registre 35, 'Saint-Victor de Marseille'.

Archives Départementales des Landes
GG1, Série H (subsérie E2 (registre 2)).

Archives Départementales d'Ille-et-Vilaine
G52.

Archives Départementales d'Indre et Loire
G1291.
H383, H385, H699–702, H705–6, H708.

Archives Départementales de la Gironde
C3831.
G619.

Archives Départementales de la Haute-Garonne
30.

Archives Départementales de la Marne
2G270, 2G275, 2G278.

Archives Départementales de la Seine-Maritime
G6, G133, G723, G1247, G1515, G9574.

Archives Départementales de la Vienne
1H18 103.

Archives Départementales de Meurthe-et-Moselle
G125, G155.

Archives Départementales du Rhône
1G 48 [28], 1G 87 (registre 8).
4G 121 (registre 81).

Archives des Carmélites de Clamart
Duval, Robert. 'La Vie de Mre André Duval Prêtre, Docteur de Sorbonne, Professeur royal en Théologie, Doyen de la Faculté, et l'un des trois premiers Supérieurs de l'Ordre de N.D. du Mont Carmel de la Réforme de Ste Térèse en France'.

Archives Nationales, Paris
766.
E1691.
H^{3} 2554.
H^{5} 3288.
KK180.
L426, L520, LL267.
M53, M105, M209–12, M213: 'Mémoires sur la fondation de Monsieur de Gondy comte de Joigny et de la dame son épouse'.
MM 292, MM 475, MM 534, MM 536, MM 538, MM 623.
Minutier Central: ET/XLV/32 (pièce 68), ET/LI/505, ET/LIV/260, ET/LVI/121, ET/LXXXIV/52, ET/LXXXIV/54, Registre 184.
S160, S6114, S6169, S6373a–6373b, S6579, S6597, S6601, S6617, S6681a, S6685, S6691, S6698, S6703, S6706, S6707: 'Fondation et Établissement des Prêtres de la Mission dans Marseille', S6708, S6710–19, S6849–50.
S*1140.
Y 174, Y 176, Y 180, Y 184–5, Y 193.
Z^{2} 4584, Z10 10 241.

Archives of the Congregation of the Mission, Krakow
'Autographes de Saint Vincent et de ses premiers compagnons', no. 152.

Archivio Segreto Vaticano, Rome
Congregatio Vescovi e Regolari, Reg. Episcoporum, 79 (1635).

Archivio Storico de Propaganda Fide, Rome
Acta 6.
Scritture originali riferite nelle congregazioni generali: 83, 89, 129–30, 198–9, 387.

Bibliothèque de l'Arsenal, Paris
2009.
5416.

Bibliothèque Mazarine, Paris
1792.
2214, 2341, 2430, 2453: 'La Vie du vénérable Serviteur de Dieu Messire Adrien Bourdoise Premier Prestre et Instituteur de la Communauté et Séminaire de Saint Nicolas du Chardonnet à Paris', 2489: 'Mémoire pour servir à la vie de madame de Miramion depuis sa naissance jusques à vingt-cinq ans'.

Bibliothèque Municipale de Chartres
453 (t. viii), 457.
596.

Bibliothèque Municipale de Laon
Carton 12, no. 126.

Bibliothèque Municipale de Mâcon
294.

Bibliothèque Nationale, Paris
4200.
20942.
Baluze: 123, 174–275, 327.
Clairambault: 1136, 1140, 1157.
Dupuy: 625, 835.
Français: 2786, 14428 (i), 15720–1, 19831, 24999.
Nouvelles acquisitions françaises: 6210, 9787, 22326.

Bibliothèque Sainte-Geneviève, Paris
14H188.
611–14: Claude Molinet, 'Histoire des chanoines réguliers de l'Ordre de S. Augustin de la Congrégation de France depuis l'origine jusqu'en 1670', 624.
701, 712.
1452.
3250, 3278.
4232: Jacques de Marsolier, 'La Vie de Mademoiselle de Lamoignon'.

PRINTED PRIMARY SOURCES

Abelly, Louis. *Lettres de S. François Xavier: de la Compagnie de Jésus, apôtre du Japon* (Paris 1638).
Abelly, Louis. *De l'obéissance et soumission qui est due à N.-S. Père le Pape en ce qui regarde les choses de la foi* (Paris 1654).
Abelly, Louis. *Défense de la hiérarchie de l'Église et de l'autorité légitime de N. S. P. le Pape et de nos seigneurs les évesques contre la doctrine pernicieuse d'un libelle anonyme mis depuis quelque temps en lumière par les ennemis de la paix et de la vérité, avec quelques réflexions sur la relation des délibérations de la dernière assemblée générale du Clergé de France touchant la constitution de N. S. P. le Pape Innocent X* (Paris 1659).
Abelly, Louis. *La Vie du vénérable servant de Dieu Vincent de Paul*, 3 vols (Paris 1664).
Abelly, Louis. *La Vie du vénérable servant de Dieu Vincent de Paul*, 2 vols (Paris 1668).
Acta ecclesiae mediolanensis (Milan 1583).
Amelote, Denis. *La Vie du Père Condren* (Paris 1643).
Annat, François. *Défense de la vérité catholique touchant les miracles contre les déguisements et artifices de la réponse faite par MM. de Port-Royal à un écrit intitule* Observations nécessaires sur ce qu'on dit estre arrivé à Port-Royal au sujet de la Saincte Espine; par le sieur de Sainte-Foy, docteur en théologie (Paris 1657).
Annat, François. *Rabat-joie des Jansénistes ou observations nécessaires pour ce qu'on dit être arrive au Port Royal au sujet de la Sainte Epine* (n.p. n.d.).

Aquinas, Thomas. *Summa Theologica*, II, II, 161, 6 <http://www.sacred-texts.com/chr/aquinas/summa/sum418.htm>.

Argenson, René de Voyer d'. *Annales de la Compagnie du Saint-Sacrement*, edited by Dom H. Beauchet-Filleau (Marseille 1900).

Arnauld, Antoine. *De la fréquente communion. Où les sentiments des pères, des Papes, et des Conciles, touchant l'usage des Sacrements de Pénitence et d'Eucharistie, sont fidèlement exposez: Pour servir d'adresse aux personnes qui pensent sérieusement à se convertir à Dieu; & aux Pasteurs et Confesseurs zelez pour le bien des âmes* (Paris 1643).

Arnauld, Antoine. *Théologie morales des Jésuites* (Paris 1643).

Arnauld, Antoine. *Œuvres de Messire Antoine Arnauld, docteur de la maison et société de Sorbonne*, 43 vols (Paris 1775–83).

Aubery, Antoine. *Histoire du Cardinal de Richelieu* (Paris 1660).

Aux véritable enfans de Dieu (n.p. n.d.).

Balzac, Jean-Louis Guez de. *Œuvres complètes*, 2 vols (Paris 1665, reprinted Geneva 1971).

Balzac, Jean-Louis Guez de. *Lettres de Jean-Louis Guez de Balzac*, edited by Philippe Tamizey de Larroque (Paris 1873).

Barcos, Martin de. *Défense de feu Mr. Vincent de Paul instituteur et premier supérieur général de la Congrégation de la Mission, contre les faux discours du livre de sa vie publiée par Mr. Abelly, Ancien Évêque de Rodez, et contre les Impostures de quelques autres Écrits sur ce sujet* (Paris 1668).

Batterel, Louis. *Mémoires domestiques pour servir à l'Histoire de l'Oratoire*, edited by Auguste-Marie-Pierre Ingold, 5 vols (Paris 1902–11).

Bauduen, Marc de. *La Vie admirable de très-haute très-puissante très-illustre & très-vertueuse dame Charlote Marguerite de Gondy, marquise de Magnelais. Où les ames fidèles trouveront dequoy admirer, & des vertus solides à imiter* (Paris 1666).

Bausset, Pierre de. *Tableau de la vie et de la mort de Messire J.-B. Gault, évêque de Marseille* (Paris 1643).

Beaunier, André. *Recueil historique, chronologique, et topographique de archevêchés, évêchés, abbayes, prieurés etc. en France*, 2 vols (Paris 1726).

Bécan, Martin. *Summa Theologiae Scholasticae*, 4 vols (Mainz 1612).

Bécan, Martin. *Manuale controversarium hujus temporis* (Mainz 1623).

Bérulle, Pierre de. *Correspondance de Cardinal Pierre de Bérulle*, edited by Jean Dagens, 3 vols (Paris 1937–9).

Bérulle, Pierre de. *Œuvres complètes de Bérulle*, edited by Michel Dupuy (and Blandine Delahaye), 12 vols (Paris 1995–2012).

Binsfeld, Pierre. *Enchiridion theologiae pastoralis* (Douai 1630).

Boulenger, Louis. *Abrégé de la vie et de la mort de Messire Charles de La Saussaye, curé de Saint-Jacques-de-la-Boucherie* (Paris 1622).

Calmet, Augustin. *Histoire ecclésiastique et civile de Lorraine* (Nancy 1728).

Camus, Jean-Pierre. *Homélies panégyriques de Sainct Charles Borromée* (Paris 1623).

Camus, Jean-Pierre. *Le Noviciat cléricale* (Paris 1643).

Camus, Jean-Pierre. *L'Esprit du bien-heureux François de Sales, évesque de Genève*, 3 vols (Paris 1840).

Canfield, Benet of. *Renaissance Dialectic and Renaissance Piety: Benet of Canfield's Rule of Perfection*, translated by Kent Emery Jr. (Binghamton, NY, 1987).

Canisius, Peter. *Summa docrinae christianae* (Ingolstadt 1555).

Canisius, Peter. *Catechismus minimus* (Ingolstadt 1556).

Canisius, Peter. *Parvus catechismus catholicorum* (Vienna 1558).

Censura Sacrae Facultatis Theologiae Parisiensis, lata in librum qui inscribitur, De la saincte Virginité, Discours traduit de Sainct-Augustin, avec quelques remarques (Paris 1638).

La Compagnie des Filles de la Charité aux origines: Documents, edited by Elisabeth Charpy (Paris 1989).

Chastenet, Léonard. *La Vie de Mgr Alain de Solminihac évesque baron, et comte de Caors, et abbé régulier de Chancellade* (Cahors 1665).

Chroniques de l'ordre des Carmélites de la réforme de Sainte Thérèse depuis leur introduction en France, 5 vols (Troyes 1846–65).

Clonsinnil, M. de. *Deffense des hibernois disciples de S. Augustin* (Paris 1651).

'Codex Sarzana', edited and translated by John Rybolt. *Vincentiana* 3–4 (1991): pp. 303–406.

Collection des procès-verbaux des assemblées générales du clergé de France, edited by Antoine Duranthon, 9 vols (Paris 1767–8).

Collet, Philibert. *Explication des statuts, coutumes et usages observes dans la province de Bresse, Bugey, Valromey et Gex* (Lyon 1698).

Collet, Pierre. *La Vie de St Vincent de Paul*, 2 vols (Nancy 1748).

Complaintes et regrets des pauvres sur le tombeau de la Reine Marguerite, duchesse de Valois (Paris 1615).

Corbinelli, Jean. *Histoire et preuves généalogique de la Maison de Gondi*, 2 vols (Paris 1705).

Coste, Hilarion de. *Les Éloges et les vies des reines, princesses, dames illustres en piété, en courage et en doctrine*, 2 vols (Paris 1630).

Coste, Hilarion de. *Les Éloges et les vies des reines, princesses, dames illustres en piété, en courage et en doctrine*, 2 vols (Paris 1647).

Cousturier, Philippe Le. *La Vie de feu Mr Robert Guériteau, docteur en théologie, prêtre, chanoine en l'église Notre-Dame de Mantes, curé de Sainte-Croix en la même ville* (Paris 1651).

Delville, Guillaume. *Petit Abrégé de l'institut de la Congrégation de la Mission* (Douai 1656).

'Dernier moments de Louis XIII racontés par le père Dinet son confesseur'. *Le Cabinet historique* 12 (1886): pp. 232–3.

Desfontaines, Pierre-François Guyot, Jean du Castre d'Auvigny, and Louis-François-Joseph de La Barre. *Histoire de la ville de Paris*, 5 vols (Paris 1735).

Desmarets, Jean. *Délices de l'Esprit: Dialogues. Dediez aux beaux esprits du monde* (Paris 1658).

Desmarets, Jean. *Quatrième partie de la réponse aux insolentes apologies de Port-Royal* (Paris 1668).

Decrees of the Ecumenical Councils, edited by Norman P. Tanner, 2 vols (London and Georgetown 1990).

'Documenti inediti per la storia della Congregazione della mission, presso l'archivio della S. D. "de Propaganda Fide" I', edited by Angelo Coppo. *Annali della Missione* 79, nos 3–4 (1972): pp. 222–55.

'Documenti inediti per la storia della Congregazione della mission, presso l'archivio della S. D. "de Propaganda Fide" II', edited by Angelo Coppo. *Annali della Missione* 80, no. 1 (1973): pp. 37–65.

Drelincourt, Charles. *Dialogues familiers sur les principales objections des missionaires de ce temps par Charles Drelincourt* (Paris 1648).

Du Mans, Martial. *Almanach spirituel pour la ville et fauxbourgs de Paris* (Paris 1650).

Du Tour, Henri de Maupas. *La Vie de la vénérable Mère Jeanne Françoise Frémiot* (Paris 1644).

Du Tour, Henri de Maupas. *Oraison funèbre à la mémoire de feu Messire Vincent de Paul instituteur fondateur et supérieur général des Prêtres de la Mission* (Paris 1661).

Du Tour, Henri de Maupas. *The Funeral Oration for Vincent de Paul*, edited and translated by Edward R. Udovic (Chicago 2015).

Duval, André. *La Vie admirable de Sœur Marie de l'Incarnation, Religieuse converse en l'Ordre de Nostre Dame du mont Carmel, & fondatrice d'iceluy en France, appelée au monde la Damoiselle Acarie* (Paris 1621).

Duvergier de Hauranne, Jean. *Lettre de Mre Jean Du Verger de Hauranne à un ecclésiastique de ses amis touchant les dispositions à la prêtrise* (Paris 1647).

Édict du Roy portant establissement de l'hospital général pour le renfermement des pauvres mandians de la ville et fauxbourgs de Paris (Paris 1656).

Erasmus, Desiderius. *Novum Instrumentum omne* (Basel 1516).

État au vrai du bien et revenue de l'Hôtel-Dieu et de la dépense journalière (Paris 1651).

Félibien, D. Michel. *Histoire de la ville de Paris*, 5 vols (Paris 1722).

Gaufreteau, Jean de. *Chronique Bordeloise*, edited by Jules Délpit, 2 vols (Bordeaux 1878).

Gerberon, Gabriel. *Histoire générale du Jansénisme*, 3 vols (Amsterdam 1700).

Gobillon, Nicolas. *La Vie de Mademoiselle Le Gras, fondatrice et première supérieure de la Compagnie des Filles de la Charité, servantes des pauvres malades* (Paris 1676).

Godeau, Antoine. *Lettres de M. Godeau, évesque de Vence, sur divers sujets* (Paris 1713).

Gondi, François-Paul de. *Œuvres du Cardinal de Retz*, edited by Alphonse Feillet, Jules Gourdault, and François Régis Chantelauze, 10 vols (Paris 1825, reprint 1997).

Goulas, Nicolas. *Mémoires de Nicolas Goulas, gentilhomme ordinaire de la chambre du Duc d'Orléans*, edited by Charles Constant, 3 vols (Paris 1899).

Granada, Louis of. *La Guia de Pecadores* (Badajoz 1555).

Granada, Louis of. *Guide des pécheurs*, translated by Simon Martin (Paris 1645).

Granada, Louis of. *Summa of the Christian Life: Selected Texts from the Writings of Venerable Louis of Granada, O.P.*, translated by Jordan Aumann, 3 vols (Saint Louis 1954).

Habert, Germain. *La Vie du Cardinal de Bérulle, instituteur et premier Supérieur General de la Congrégation de l'Oratoire de Iesus-Christ nostre Seigneur* (Paris 1646).

Hersent, Charles. *Le Sacré Monument dédié à la mémoire du très puissant et très invincible monarque, Louis le Juste* (Paris 1643).

Instructions utiles pour les dames qui désirent rendre la charité aux pauvres prisonniers (n.p. n.d.).

Iure, Jean Baptiste S. *La Vie de Monsieur de Renty* (Paris 1652).

Kempis, Thomas à. *The Imitation of Christ*, translated by E. M. Blaiklock (London 1979).

Lancelot, Claude. *Mémoires touchant la vie de M. de Saint-Cyran*, edited by Denis Donetzkoff (Paris 2003).

Le Magasin charitable, du mois de janvier 1653 (Paris 1652).

Les Mémoires de R. P. Dom Bernard Audebert, edited by Léon Guilloreau (Paris 1911).

L'Estoile, Pierre de. *Journal pour le règne d'Henri IV*, edited by Louis Raymond Lefèvre and André Martin, 3 vols (Paris 1948–58).

'Lettre inédite d'un ami de Saint Vincent de Paul', edited by Bernard Koch. *Bulletin des Lazaristes de France* 173 (avril 2000): pp. 102–7.

L'Hospital général charitable (Paris 1657).

Livre-Journal de Pierre de Bessot, edited by Tamizey de Larroque (Périgueux 1893).

Loyola, Ignatius of. *The Spiritual Exercises*, translated by George E. Ganss (Saint Louis 1992).

Luther, Martin. *Luther's Works*, edited and translated by Theodore G. Tappert et al. 55 vols (Saint Louis 1955–86).

'Madame de Gondi: A Contemporary Seventeenth-Century Life', edited and translated by Barbara Diefendorf and John Rybolt. *Vincentian Heritage* 21, no. 1 (2000): pp. 25–43.

Manifeste de Monsieur le duc de Bouillon à la reyne régente (n.p. 1643).

Marande, Léonard de. *Inconveniénts d'état procédans du Jansénisme avec la réfutation du Mars françois par M. Jansénius* (Paris 1654).
Marchetty, François. *La Vie de Messire J. B. Gault, évêque de Marseille* (Paris 1650).
Marillac, Louise de. *Pensées de Louise de Marillac, Damoiselle Le Gras* (Paris 1899).
Marillac, Louise de. *Spiritual Writings of Louise de Marillac*, edited and translated by Louise Sullivan (New York 1991).
Mazarin, Jules. *Lettres du Cardinal Mazarin pendant son ministère*, edited by Pierre-Adolphe Chéruel and Georges d'Avenel, 9 vols (Paris 1872–1906).
Mémoire des prisons de Paris, dont la Compagnie des Dames, où Madame la première président de la Moignon est supérieure, prend soin depuis longtemps (n.p. n.d.).
Motteville, Françoise Bertaut de. *Mémoires de Madame de Motteville*, 4 vols (Paris 1886).
'Notes et Documents'. *Mission et Charité* 8 (1962): p. 495.
Nouvel Advis important sur les misères du temps (n.p. n.d.).
Oraison funèbre de haute et puissante dame Charlotte Marguerite De Gondy, Marquise de Maignelay. Prononcée en la présence de Monseigneur l'Archevesque de Corinthe, Coadiuteur de Paris, célébrant Pontificalement dans l'Église des Prestres de l'Oratoire de Iésus (Paris 1651).
Paris, Yves de. *Les Œuvres de miséricorde* (Paris 1661).
Paul, Vincent de. *Saint Vincent de Paul: Correspondance, entretiens, documents*, edited by Pierre Coste, 14 vols (Paris 1920–5).
Paul, Vincent de. *Saint Vincent de Paul: Correspondence, conférences, documents*, edited by Jacqueline Kilar et al. 14 vols (New York 1985–2014).
Péréfixe, Hardouin de. *Hippolyte Feret prestre, docteur en théologie, curé de Saint Nicolas du Chardonnet, vicaire général de monseigneur l'illustrissime & reverendissime père en Dieu messier Hardouin de Péréfixe* (Paris 1665).
Pinthereau, François. *Les Reliques de Messire Iean Du Verger de Hauranne, abbé de Saint Cyran, extraites des ouvrages qu'il a composez & donnez au public* (Louvain 1646).
Pommeraye, François. *Histoire de l'abbaye royale de Saint-Ouen* (Rouen 1662).
Rapin, René. *Mémoires du P. René Rapin de la compagnie de Jésus sur l'église et la société, la cour, la ville et le jansénisme, 1644–1669*, edited by Léon Aubineau, 3 vols (Paris 1865).
Recueil de plusieurs pièces pour server à l'histoire de Port-Royal, ou supplément aux Mémoires de Messieurs Fontaine, Lancelot, et du Fossé (Utrecht 1740).
Recueil des relations contenant ce qui s'est fait pour l'assistance des pauvres: Entre autres ceux de Paris, & des environs, & des provinces de Picardie & Champagne, pendant les années 1650, 1651, 1652, 1653 & 1654 (Paris 1655).
Regulae seu Constitutiones commune Congregationis Missionis (Paris 1658).
Renar, François. *Maximes tirées de la doctrine des conciles, et des saints pères, opposes à celles du Livres de la fréquente Communion, et à la conduit de quelques nouveaux Directeurs* (Paris 1659).
Richelieu, Armand de. *Lettres, instructions diplomatiques et papiers d'état du Cardinal Richelieu*, edited by Georges d'Avenel, 8 vols (Paris 1853–77).
Robineau, Louis. *Remarques sur les actes et paroles de feu Monsieur Vincent de Paul notre très Honoré Père et Fondateur*, edited by André Dodin (Paris 1991).
Ruffi, Antoine de. *La Vie de M. le Chevalier de la Coste* (Aix 1659).
Sacra Rituum Congregatione Eminentissimo, & Reverendissimo D. Card de La Tremoille Parisien (Rome 1717).
Sacra Rituum Congregation Eminentissimo, & Reverendissimo D. Card. Paulutio Parisien (Rome 1723).
Sales, François de. *Œuvres complètes de Saint François de Sales, évêque et prince de Genève*, 16 vols (Paris 1821).

Sales, François de. *Treatise on the Love of God*, translated by Henry Benedict Mackey (London 1884).
Sales, François de. *Œuvres de Saint François de Sales*, 26 vols (Annecy 1892–1932).
Sales, François de. *Introduction to the Devout Life*, edited and translated by John K. Ryan, 2nd edn (New York 1989).
Séguenot, Claude. *De la sainte virginité, discours traduit de S. Augustin, avec quelques remarques pour la clarté de la doctrine* (Paris 1638).
Solminihac, Alain de. *Alain de Solminihac: Lettres et documents*, edited by Eugène Sol (Cahors 1930).
Testament de Monsieur le Cardinal Duc de Richelieu (Paris 1643).
'The Primitive Common Rules of the Congregation of the Mission', edited and translated by John Rybolt. *Vincentiana* (May–June 2008): pp. 205–30.
The Constitutions of the Society of Jesus, edited and translated by George E. Ganss (St Louis 1970).
Troisième advis important sur les misères publiques du Blésois, du Berry, de la Touraine, du Maine, partie de la Champagne et autres lieux (n.p. n.d.).
'Two Unpublished Documents of Saint Vincent de Paul', edited and translated by John Rybolt. *Vincentian Heritage* 28, no. 1 (2008): pp. 1–8.
Vernon, Jean-Marie de. *La Vie de Messire Charles de Saveuses, supérieur et restaurateur des Ursulines de Magny* (Paris 1678).

REFERENCE WORKS

Charbonnier, Pierre, and Abel Poitrineau. *Les Anciennes Mesures locales du Centre-Ouest d'après les tables de conversion* (Paris 2001).
Dictionnaire de la noblesse, edited by François Aubert de la Chesnaye-Desbois, 19 vols (Paris 1866–76).
Gallia Christiana, edited by Denis Sainte-Marthe et al., 16 vols (Paris 1715–1899).
Gallia Christiana novissima: Histoire des archevêchés, évêchés & abbayes de France d'après les documents authentiques recueillis dans les registres du Vatican et les archives locales, edited by Joseph Albanès, 7 vols (Valence 1899–1920).
Hélyot, Pierre. *Dictionnaire des ordres religieux, ou Histoire des ordres monastiques, religieux et militaires et des congrégations séculières de l'un et l'autre sexe, qui ont été établis jusqu'à présente*, edited by Jacques Paul Migne, 4 vols (Paris 1847–63).
New Catholic Encyclopaedia, 18 vols (New York 1967–2001).

SECONDARY SOURCES

Allier, Raoul. *La Cabale des dévots* (Paris 1902).
Alliot, Gervais. *Le Pouillé général des abbayes de France et bénéfices qui en dépendent* (Paris 1826).
Archer, E. *The Assistance of the Poor in Paris and in the North-Eastern French Provinces, 1614–1660, with Special Reference to the Letters of St. Vincent de Paul* (Ph.D., University of London, 1936).
Audiat, Louis. *Le Diocèse de Saintes au XVIIIe siècle* (Paris 1894).
Baccrabère, Georges. 'La Pratique religieuse dans le diocèse de Toulouse aux XVIe et XVIIe siècles'. *Annales du Midi* 74 (1962): pp. 287–319.
Battiffol, Louis. *Le Cardinal de Retz: Ambitions et aventures d'un homme d'esprit au XVIIe siècle* (Paris 1927).

Bayley, Peter. *French Pulpit Oratory 1598–1650* (Cambridge 1980).

Bellussière, F. de. 'Varia', *Bulletin de la Société Historique et Archéologique du Périgord* (1886): pp. 66–8.

Benedict, Philip. 'The Catholic Response to Protestantism: Church Activity and Popular Piety in Rouen 1560–1600'. In *Religion and the People, 800–1700*, edited by James Obelkevitch (Chapel Hill, NC, 1979): pp. 168–90.

Bergin, Joseph. *Cardinal Richelieu: Power and the Pursuit of Wealth* (New Haven and London 1985).

Bergin, Joseph. *Cardinal de la Rochefoucauld: Leadership and Reform in the French Church* (New Haven and London 1987).

Bergin, Joseph. *The Rise of Richelieu* (New Haven and London 1991).

Bergin, Joseph. *The Making of the French Episcopate, 1589–1661* (New Haven and London 2004).

Bergin, Joseph. *Church, Society and Religious Change in France, 1580–1730* (New Haven and London 2009).

Bergin, Joseph. *The Politics of Religion in Early Modern France* (New Haven and London 2014).

Bessières, R. P. *Au temps de Saint Vincent de Paul: Deux grands méconnus précurseurs de l'action Catholique et sociale. Gaston de Renty et Henri Buch* (Paris 1931).

Bigonneau, Michel. 'Les Études de Saint Vincent de Paul à Toulouse'. *Bulletin de la Société de Borda* 385 (1982), pp. 521–4.

Bireley, Robert. *The Refashioning of Catholicism, 1450–1700* (Houndmills 1999).

Black, Christopher. *Italian Confraternities in the Sixteenth Century* (Cambridge 1989).

Blant, Robert Le. 'Notes sur Madame de Bullion, bienfaitrice de l'Hôtel-Dieu de Montréal après 1587–26 juin 1664'. *Revue d'histoire de l'Amérique française* 12 (1958): pp. 112–25.

Blet, Pierre. 'Vincent de Paul et l'épiscopat français'. In *Vincent de Paul. Actes du Colloque International d'Études Vincentiennes* (Rome 1983): pp. 223–58.

Bleynie, Magdeleine. *Madame de Villeneuve* (Paris 1946).

Bois, Louis-Édouard. *Vie de l'illustre serviteur de Dieu Noël Brûlart de Sillery* (Paris 1843).

Bois. Louis-Édouard. *Le Chevalier Noël Brûlart de Sillery* (Quebec 1871).

Bonneau, Alfred. *Madame de Beauharnais de Miramion: Sa vie et ses œuvres charitables, 1629–1696* (Paris 1868).

Bonnot, Isabelle. *Hérétique ou saint? Henri Arnauld évêque janséniste d'Angers au xviie siècle* (Paris 1983).

Bosseboeuf, Louis-Auguste. *Richelieu et ses environs* (Tours 1890, reprinted Paris 1990).

Bossy, John. 'Catholicity and Nationality in the Northern Counter-Reformation'. *Studies in Church History* 18 (1982): pp. 285–96.

Boyle, Patrick. 'Hibernia Vincentiana or the Relations of St. Vincent de Paul with Ireland'. *Irish Ecclesiastical Record* 14 (1903): pp. 289–316.

Boyle, Patrick. *St. Vincent de Paul and the Vincentians in Ireland, Scotland and England, AD. 1638–1909* (London 1909).

Brejon de Lavergnée, Matthieu. *Histoire des Filles de la Charité, xviie–xviiie siècles: la rue pour cloître* (Paris 2011).

Brémond, Henri. *Histoire littéraire du sentiment religieux en France depuis la fin des guerres de religion jusqu'à nos jours*, 12 vols (Paris 1916–36).

Brian, Isabelle. *Messieurs de Sainte-Geneviève: Religieux et curés, de la Contre-Réforme à la Révolution* (Paris 2001).

Brockliss, Laurence. *French Higher Education in the Seventeenth and Eighteenth Centuries: A Cultural History* (Oxford 1987).

Broutin, Paul. *La Réforme pastorale en France au xviie siècle*, 2 vols (Paris 1956).

Bruté, Jean. *Chronologie historique de MM. les curés de S. Benoît de 1181–1751* (Paris 1752).

Bugelli, Alexandrette. *Vincent de Paul: Une pastorale du pardon et de la réconciliation. La Confession générale* (Fribourg 1997).

Casagrande, Giovanna. 'Confraternities and Lay Female Religiosity in Late Medieval and Renaissance Umbria'. In *The Politics of Ritual Kinship: Confraternities and Social Order in Early Modern Italy*, edited by Nicholas Terpstra (Cambridge 2000): pp. 48–66.

Cassan, Michel. 'Laïcs, Ligue et Réforme Catholique à Limoges'. *Histoire Économie et Société* 10 (1991): pp. 159–75.

Certeau, Michel de. 'L'Illettré éclairé dans l'histoire de la lettre de Surin sur le Jeune Homme du Coche (1630)'. *Revue d'Ascétique et du Mystique* 44 (1968): pp. 369–412.

Ceyssens, Lucien. 'François Hallier'. *Bulletin de l'Institut Historique Belge de Rome* 40 (1969): pp. 157–264.

Ceyssens, Lucien. 'L'Antijanséniste Isaac Habert (1598–1668)'. *Bulletin de l'Institut Historique Belge de Rome* 42 (1972): pp. 237–305.

Chalumeau, Raymond. 'Saint Vincent de Paul et les Missions en France au xviie siècle'. *XVIIe Siècle* 41 (1958): pp. 304–27.

Chalumeau, Raymond (pseud. Jules Melot). 'Saint Vincent de Paul, pèlerin de Rome'. *Mission et Charité* 28 (1967): pp. 322–5.

Chantelauze, Raymond. *Saint Vincent de Paul et les Gondi* (Paris 1882).

Châtellier, Louis. *The Europe of the Devout: The Catholic Reformation and the Formation of a New Society*, translated by Jean Birrell (Cambridge 1989).

Chevrières, Jean Darché de. *Le St Abbé Bourdoise*, 2 vols (Paris 1884).

Clossey, Luke. *Salvation and Globalization in the Early Jesuit Missions* (Cambridge 2008).

Cloysault, Edme. *Recueil de vies de quelques prêtres de l'Oratoire*, 2 vols (Paris, 1882).

Cochois, Paul. *Bérulle et l'école française* (Paris 1963).

Cognet, Louis. *La Spiritualité française au xviie siècle* (Paris 1949).

Cognet, Louis. *Le Jansénisme* (Paris 1964).

Collins, James. *The State in Early Modern France*, 2nd edn (Cambridge 2009).

Combaluzier, Fernand. 'L'Abbaye de Saint-Léonard de Chaumes et Saint Vincent de Paul (14 mai 1610–29 octobre 1616)'. *Annales de la Congrégation de la Mission et les Filles de la Charité* 106 (1941): pp. 249–65.

Confraternities and Catholic Reform in Italy, France, and Spain, edited by John Patrick Donnelly and Michael W. Maher (Kirksville, Mo. 1999).

Congar, Pierre. 'Fabert à l'œuvre à Sedan'. *Annales Sedanaises d'Histoire et d'Archéologie* 45 (1961): pp. 26–35.

Coste, Pierre. 'Histoire des cathédrales de Dax'. *Bulletin de la Société de Borda* 2 (1908): pp. 121–242.

Coste, Pierre. *Le Grand Saint du grand siècle: Monsieur Vincent*, 3 vols (Paris 1931).

Dagens, Jean. *Bérulle et les origines de la restauration Catholique (1575–1611)* (Bruges 1952).

Darche, Jean. *Le Saint Abbé Bourdoise: Réformation du clergé et promoteur du séminaires en France*, 2 vols (Paris 1883–4).

Darricau, Raymond. 'L'Évêque dans la pensée de Saint Vincent de Paul'. *Divus Thomas* 84 (1981): pp. 161–88.

Davis, Natalie Zemon. 'Poor Relief, Humanism, and Heresy: The Case of Lyon'. In *Society and Culture in Early Modern France* (Stanford, Calif. 1974): pp. 17–64.

Deffrennes, Pierre. 'La Vocation de Saint Vincent de Paul: Étude de psychologie surnaturelle'. *Revue d'Ascétique et de Mystique* 13 (1932): pp. 60–86, 164–83, 294–321, 389–411.

Degert, Antoine. *Histoire des séminaires français jusqu'à la Révolution*, 2 vols (Paris 1912).

Dejean, Étienne. *Un prélat indépendant au xviie siècle: Nicolas Pavillon évêque d'Alet (1637–1677)* (Paris 1909).

Delumeau, Jean. *Catholicism between Luther and Voltaire: A New View of the Counter-Reformation* (London 1977).

Deroo, André. *Saint Charles Borromée, cardinal réformateur, docteur de la pastorale, 1538–1484* (Paris 1963).

Deville, Raymond. L'École française de spiritualité, 2nd edn (Paris 2008).

Devos, Roger. 'Le Testament spirituel de sainte Jeanne-Françoise de Chantal et l'affaire du visiteur apostolique'. *Revue d'Histoire de la Spiritualité* 48 (1972): pp. 453–76.

Devos, Roger. 'Le Testament spirituel de sainte Jeanne-Françoise de Chantal et l'affaire du visiteur apostolique'. *Revue d'Histoire de la Spiritualité* 49 (1973): pp. 199–226, 341–66.

Dewald, Jonathan. *Pont-St-Pierre, 1398–1789: Lordship, Community, and Capitalism in Early Modern France* (Berkeley 1987).

Diefendorf, Barbara. '"Give us back our children": Patriarchal Authority and Parental Consent to Religious Vocations in Early Counter-Reformation France'. *Journal of Modern History* 68, no. 2 (1996): pp. 265–307.

Diefendorf, Barbara. *From Penitence to Charity: Pious Women and the Catholic Reformation in Paris* (Oxford 2004).

Diefendorf, Barbara. 'Henri IV, the *Dévots* and the Making of a French Catholic Reformation'. In *After the League: Politics and Religion in Early Bourbon France*, edited by Alison Forrestal and Eric Nelson (Basingstoke 2009): pp. 157–79.

Dinan, Susan. 'Motivations for Charity in Early Modern France'. In *The Reformation of Charity: The Secular and the Religious in Early Modern Poor Relief*, edited by Thomas Safley (Boston 2003): pp. 176–92.

Dinan, Susan. *Women and Poor Relief in Seventeenth-Century France: The Early History of the Daughters of Charity* (Aldershot 2006).

Dodin, André. 'Saint Vincent et l'approbation des Litanies du Saint Nom de Jésus'. *Annales de la Congrégation de la Mission et les Filles de la Charité* 104 (1939): pp. 200–2.

Dodin, André. 'Monsieur Vincent et Jean Duvergier de Hauranne'. *Les Deux Abbés de Saint-Cyran: Chroniques de Port-Royal* 26–28 (1977–9): pp. 55–72.

Dodin, André. *L'Esprit Vincentien: Le secret de Saint Vincent de Paul* (Paris 1981).

Dodin, André. *Monsieur Vincent parle à ceux qui souffrent* (Paris 1981).

Dodin, André. *François de Sales, Vincent de Paul: Les deux amis* (Paris 1984).

Dodin, André. *Vincent de Paul and Charity: A Contemporary Portrait of his Life and Apostolic Spirit*, edited by Hugh O'Donnell and Marjorie Gale Hornstein, translated by Jean Marie Smith and Dennis Saunders (New York 1993).

Dodin, André. *Saint Vincent de Paul et la charité*, 2nd edn (Saint-Germain-du-Puy 1998).

Dompnier, Bernard. 'La Congrégation Romaine "de Propaganda Fide" et les compagnies de prêtres missionnaires (1627–1664)'. In *Vincent de Paul: Actes du Colloque international d'études Vincentiennes* (Rome 1983): pp. 42–63.

Dompnier, Bernard. 'La Compagnie de Jésus et la mission de l'intérieur'. In *Les Jésuites et l'âge Baroque*, edited by Luce Giald and Louis de Vaucelles (Grenoble 1996): pp. 155–79.

Dulaure, Jacques Antoine. *Histoire physique, civile et morale de Paris depuis les premiers temps historiques jusqu'à nos jours*, 7 vols (Paris 1823–8).

Dupuy, Michel. *Bérulle et le sacerdoce: Étude historique et doctrinal* (Paris 1969).

Du Rau, Joseph Defos. 'Saint Vincent de Paul orateur et homme d'État'. *Bulletin de la Société de Borda* 297 (1960): pp. 149–63.

Duvignacq-Glessgen, Marie-Ange. *L'Ordre de la Visitation à Paris au xviie et xviiie siècles* (Paris 1994).

Ellington, Donna Spivey. *From Sacred Body to Angelic Soul: Understanding Mary in Late Medieval and Early Modern Europe* (Washington DC 2001).
Elmore, Richard. 'The Origins of the Hôpital Général de Paris' (Ph.D. diss., University of Notre-Dame, 1975).
Evennett, Henry Outram. *The Spirit of the Counter-Reformation* (Cambridge 1968).
Faillon, Étienne-Michel. *Vie de M. Olier fondateur du séminaire de Saint-Sulpice*, 3 vols, 4th edn (Paris 1873).
Farr, James. *Authority and Sexuality in Early Modern Burgundy, 1550–1730* (Oxford and New York 1995).
Favreau, Robert. *Le Diocèse de Poitiers* (Paris 1988).
Féron, Alexandre. *La Vie et les œuvres de Charles Maignart de Bernières (1616–1662)* (Rouen 1930).
Ferrari, Anne. *Figures de la contemplation: La <rhétorique divine> de Pierre de Bérulle* (Paris 1997).
Ferté, Jeanne. *La Vie religieuse dans les campagnes parisiennes (1622–1695)* (Paris 1962).
Fillon, Benjamin. *Une fondation de Saint Vincent de Paul à Luçon* (Fontenay 1848).
Finley-Croswhite, Annette. *Henri IV and the Towns: The Pursuit of Legitimacy in French Urban Society, 1589–1610* (Cambridge 1999).
Fitzgibbon Adams, Mara Catherine. *Poor Relief as Catalyst: Female Activism and Confessional Identity in Seventeenth-Century France* (Ph.D., University of Iowa, 2006).
Flynn, Maureen. *Sacred Charity: Confraternities and Social Welfare in Spain, 1400–1700* (Ithaca, NY, and London 1989).
Foissac, Adrien. *Le Premier grand séminaire de Cahors* (Cahors 1911).
Forman, Marcelle. 'Henri Louis Chasteigner de la Rocheposay, Évêque de Poitiers, 1612–1651'. *Bulletin de la Société des Antiquaires de l'Ouest et des Musées de Poitiers* 3 (1955): pp. 165–231.
Fouqueray, Henri. *Histoire de la compagnie de Jésus en France des origines à la suppression (1528–1762)*, 5 vols (Paris 1910–22).
Forget, Mireille. 'Des prisons au bagne de Marseille: La charité à l'égard des condamnés au xviie siècle'. *XVIIe Siècle* 90–1 (1971): pp. 147–74.
Forrestal, Alison. *Fathers, Pastors and Kings: Visions of Episcopacy in Seventeenth-Century France* (Manchester 2004).
Forrestal, Alison. 'Vincent de Paul as Mentor'. *Vincentian Heritage* 27, no. 2 (2008): pp. 7–16.
Forrestal, Alison. 'Irish Entrants to the Congregation of the Mission, 1625–60'. *Archivium Hibernicum* 62 (2009): pp. 37–149.
Forrestal, Alison. 'The Making of a Catholic *Dévot*'. In *Politics and Religion in Early Bourbon France*, edited by Alison Forrestal and Eric Nelson (Basingstoke 2009): pp. 180–99.
Forrestal, Alison. 'Vincent de Paul: The Principles and Practices of Government, 1625–60'. *Vincentian Heritage* 29, no. 2 (2009): pp. 50–67.
Forrestal, Alison. 'Venues for Clerical Formation in Catholic Reformation Paris: Vincent de Paul and the Tuesday Conference and Company'. *Proceedings of the Western Society for French History*, 38 (2010): pp. 44–60.
Forrestal, Alison. 'Catholic Missionaries in a Territory of Reunion: The French Crown and the Congregation of the Mission in Sedan, 1642–1647'. In *Frontier and Border Regions in Early Modern Europe*, edited by Steven Ellis and Raingard Eβer (Hannover 2013): pp. 157–74.
Forrestal, Alison, and Felicia Roşu. 'Slavery on the Frontier: The Report of a French Missionary on Seventeenth-Century Tunis'. *Reformation and Renaissance Review* 14, no. 2 (2012): pp. 170–211.

Forster, Marc. *The Counter-Reformation in the Villages: Religion and Reform in the Bishopric of Speyer, 1560–1720* (Ithaca, NY, and London 1992).

Forster, Marc. *Catholic Revival in the Age of the Baroque: Religious Identity in Southwest Germany* (Cambridge 2001).

Fosseyeux, Marcel Martin. 'Contribution à l'histoire du monastère Sainte-Marie du faubourg Saint-Antoine au xviie siècle'. *Bulletin de la Société de l'Histoire de Paris et de l'Île-de-France* 37 (1910): pp. 184–202.

Gayon-Molinié, C. 'Saint Vincent de Paul et le diocèse de Dax'. *Bulletin de la Société de Borda* 385 (1982): pp. 517–20.

Gentilcore, David. '"Adapt yourselves to the people's capabilities": Missionary Strategies, Methods and Impact in the Kingdom of Naples, 1600–1800'. *Journal of Ecclesiastical History* 45, no. 2 (1994): pp. 69–96.

Gres-Gayer, Jacques. *Le Jansénisme en Sorbonne, 1643–1656* (Paris 1996).

Gres-Gayer, Jacques. *Le Gallicanisme de Sorbonne: Chroniques de la Faculté de Théologie de Paris (1657–1688)* (Paris 2002).

Griselle, Eugène. *État de la maison du roi Louis XIII, de celles de sa mère, Marie de Medicis, de ses sœurs, Chrestienne, Élisabeth et Henriette de France* (Paris 1912).

Guichard, Joseph. 'Laurent Bouchet: Ami et disciple de Saint Vincent de Paul. V—Les conférences de mardi'. *Annales de la Congrégation de la Mission et les Filles de la Charité* 100 (1935): pp. 781–809.

Guichard, Joseph. 'Laurent Bouchet: Ami et disciple de Saint Vincent de Paul. VI—L'Anti-Janséniste'. *Annales de la Congrégation de la Mission et les Filles de la Charité* 101 (1936): pp. 31–50.

Guichard, Joseph. 'Laurent Bouchet: Ami et disciple de Saint Vincent de Paul. Appendice'. *Annales de la Congrégation de la Mission et les Filles de la Charité* 101 (1936): pp. 429–57.

Guillaume, Marie-Joëlle. *Vincent de Paul. Un saint au grand siècle* (Paris 2015).

Gueriteau, L.-D.-C. *Opuscules biographiques: Vie de Jean Coqueret. Vie du Docteur André Duval. Vie de Robert Gueriteau* (Pontoise 1909).

Gutton, Anne-Marie. *Confréries et dévotion sous l'Ancien Régime: Lyonnais, Forez, Beaujolais* (Lyon 1993).

Hanlon, Gregory. *Confession and Community in Seventeenth-Century France: Catholic and Protestant Coexistence in Aquitaine* (Philadelphia 1993).

Hayden, Michael, and Malcolm Greenshields. *Six Hundred Years of Reform: Bishops and the French Church, 1190–1789* (Montreal and London 2005).

Health Care and Poor Relief in Counter-Reformation Europe, edited by Ole Peter Grell and Andrew Cunningham, (London 1999).

Health Care and Poor Relief in Protestant Europe, 1500–1700, edited by Ole Peter Grell and Andrew Cunningham (London 1997).

Hickey, Daniel. 'Le Rôle de l'état dans la réforme Catholique: Une inspection du diocèse de Poitiers lors des Grands Jours de 1634'. *Revue Historique* 624 (2002): pp. 939–61.

Hillman, Jennifer. *Female Piety and the Catholic Reformation in France* (London 2014).

Hodson, Simon. 'Sovereigns and Subjects: The Princes of Sedan and Dukes of Bouillon in Early Modern France, *c.*1450–1652' (D.Phil., Oxford University, 1999).

Hoffmann, Philip. *Church and Community in the Diocese of Lyon, 1500–1789* (New Haven 1984).

Holt, Mack. 'Patterns of *Clientèle* and Economic Opportunity at Court during the Wars of Religion: The Household of François, Duke of Anjou'. *French Historical Studies* 13 (1994): pp. 305–22.

Hsia, Ronnie Po-chia. *The World of Catholic Renewal, 1540–1770* (Cambridge 1998).

Ingold, Auguste-Marie-Pierre. *Essai de bibliographie Oratorienne* (Paris 1880).

Jacques, Émile. *Philippe Cospeau: Un ami-ennemi de Richelieu, 1571–1646* (Parish 1989).

James, Alan. *The Navy and Government in Early Modern France, 1572–1661* (Woodbridge 2004).

Johnson, Trevor. 'Blood, Tears and Xavier-Water: Jesuit Missionaries and Popular Religion in the Eighteenth-Century Upper Palatinate'. In *Popular Religion in Germany and Central Europe, 1400–1800*, edited by Robert Scribner and Trevor Johnson (Houndmills 1996): pp. 183–202.

Julia, Dominique. 'L'Expansion de la Congrégation de la Mission de la mort de Vincent de Paul à la Révolution française'. In *Vincent de Paul: Actes du Colloque International d'Études Vincentiennes* (Rome 1983): pp. 362–419.

Julia, Dominique, and Willem Frijhoff. 'Les Oratoriens de France sous l'ancien régime: Premiers résultats d'une enquête'. *Revue d'Histoire de l'Eglise de France* 65 (1979): pp. 225–63.

Kamen, Henry. *The Iron Century: Social Change in Europe, 1550–1660* (London 1971).

Kettering, Sharon. *Patrons, Brokers and Clients in Seventeenth-Century France* (Oxford 1988).

Kettering, Sharon. 'Clientage during the French Wars of Religion'. *Sixteenth-Century Journal* 20, no. 2 (1989): pp. 221–39.

Kleinman, Ruth. *Anne of Austria: Queen of France* (Ohio 1985).

Kleinman, Ruth. 'Social Dynamics at the French Court: The Household of Anne of Austria'. *French Historical Studies* 16, no. 3 (1990): pp. 517–35.

Klevgard, Paul. 'Society and Politics in Counter-Reformation France: A Study of Bérulle, Vincent de Paul, Olier and Bossuet' (Ph.D. diss., Northwestern University, 1971).

Koch, Bernard. 'Châtillon-lès-Dombes: Compléments'. *Bulletin des Lazaristes de France* 164 (juillet 1998): pp. 145–58.

Koch, Bernard. 'Châtillon-lès-Dombes et les Femmes'. *Bulletin des Lazaristes de France* 165 (octobre 1998): pp. 200–16.

Koch, Bernard. 'Châtillon-lès-Dombes et Saint Vincent'. *Bulletin des Lazaristes de France* 163 (avril 1998): pp. 73–93.

Koch, Bernard. 'Les Dernières années de Saint Vincent et de Sainte Louise'. *Bulletin des Lazaristes de France* 174 (juillet 2000): pp. 144–82.

Koch, Bernard. 'Drawing Up the Common Rules of the Congregation of the Mission'. *Vincentiana* 52, no. 5 (2008): pp. 413–28.

Krumenacker, Yves. *L'École française de spiritualité* (Paris 1998).

Lajeunie, E. J. *Saint François de Sales. L'homme, la pensée, l'action*, 2 vols (Paris 1966).

La Première communion: quatre siècles d'histoire, edited by Jean Delumeau (Paris 1987).

Laven, Mary. *Virgins of Venice: Broken Vows and Cloistered Lives in the Renaissance Convent* (London 2003).

Lebeuf, Jean. *Histoire de la ville et de tout le diocèse de Paris*, 7 vols (Paris 1883–93).

Le Bras, Gabrielle. *Études de sociologie religieuse*, 2 vols (Paris 1955).

Lebrun, François. 'Les Missions des Lazaristes en Haute-Bretagne au xviie siècle'. *Annales de Bretagne et des Pays de l'Ouest* 89, no. 1 (1982): pp. 15–38.

Lecanu, Auguste-François. *Histoire de Clichy-la-Garenne* (Paris 1848).

Leviste, Jacques. *Le Château du Fey et la seigneurie de Villecien depuis le xvie siècle précédé de Saint Vincent de Paul et les seigneurs de Villecien* (Villeneuve-sur-Yonne 1990).

Lewis, Mark. 'The Development of Jesuit Confraternal Activity in the Kingdom of Naples in the 16th and 17th Centuries'. In *The Politics of Ritual Kinship: Confraternities and Social Order in Early Modern Italy*, edited by Nicholas Terpstra (Cambridge 2000): pp. 210–27.

Lindberg, Carter. *Beyond Charity: Reform Initiatives for the Poor* (Minneapolis 1993).

Llewellyn, Kathleen. *Representing Judith in Early Modern French Literature* (Farnham 2014).

Luria, Keith. *Territories of Grace: Cultural Change in the Seventeenth-Century Diocese of Grenoble* (Berkley and Oxford 1991).

Luria, Keith. 'Rituals of Conversion: Catholics and Protestants in Seventeenth-Century Poitou'. In *Culture and Identity in Early Modern Europe*, edited by Barbara Diefendorf and Carla Hesse (Ann Arbor 1993): pp. 65–81.

Luria, Keith. *Sacred Boundaries: Religious Coexistence and Conflict in Early Modern France* (Washington DC 2005).

MacCulloch, Diarmaid. *Reformation: Europe's House Divided, 1490–1700* (London 2004).

McHugh, Timothy. *Hospital Politics in Seventeenth-Century France: The Crown, Urban Elites and the Poor* (Aldershot 2007).

Maher, Michael. 'How the Jesuits Used their Congregations to Promote Frequent Communion'. In *Confraternities and Catholic Reform in Italy, France and Spain*, edited by John Patrick Donnelly and Michael W. Maher (Kirksville, Mo., 1999): pp. 75–95.

Maher, Michael. 'Confession and Consolation: The Society of Jesus and its Promotion of the General Confession'. In *Penitence in the Age of Reformation*, edited by Katherine Jackson Lualdi and Anne T. Thayer (Aldershot 2000): pp. 184–200.

Maillet-Rao, Caroline. *La Pensée politique des dévots: Mathieu de Morgues et Michel de Marillac* (Paris 2015).

Manning, Ruth. *Breaking the Rules: The Emergence of the Active Female Apostolate in Early Seventeenth-Century France* (D.Phil., Oxford University, 2006).

Marboutin, Jean-Robert. *Sainte-Livrade, Notre-Dame de Villamade, Notre-Dame de La Rose* (Agen 1942).

Martène, Edmond. *Histoire de la Congrégation de St Maur*, edited by Gaston Charvin, 10 vols (Paris 1928–56).

Martin, A. Lynn. *The Jesuit Mind: The Mentality of an Elite in Early Modern France* (Ithaca, NY, and London 1988).

Martin, Catherine. *Les Compagnies de la propagation de la foi (1632–1685)* (Geneva 2000).

Martin, Eugène. *Histoire des diocèses de Toul, Nancy & de Saint-Dié*, 3 vols (Nancy 1902).

Mathieu, Robert. *Monsieur Vincent chez les Gondy, les missionnaires et les Filles de la Charité à Montmirail* (Châlons-sur-Marne 1966).

Mauduit, Jean. *Saint Vincent de Paul* (Paris 1960).

Mauzaize, Jean. *Histoire des Frères Mineurs Capucins de la province de Paris (1601–1660)* (Blois 1965).

Mauzaize, Jean. *Le Rôle et l'action des Capucins de la province de Paris dans la France religieuse du xviie siècle*, 3 vols (Paris 1978).

Maynard, Michel Ulysse. *Saint Vincent de Paul: Sa vie, son temps, ses œuvres, son influence*, 4 vols, 3rd edn (Paris 1886).

Merki, Charles. *La Reine Margot et la fin de Valois, 1553–1615* (Paris 1905).

Mesnard, Jean. *Pascal et les Roannez*, 2 vols (Paris 1965).

Mezzadri, Luigi. *Fra giansenisti e antigiansenisti: Vincent Depaul e la Congregazione della Missione (1624–1737)* (Florence 1977).

Mezzadri, Luigi, John Rybolt, and José-Maria Román. *The Vincentians: A General History of the Congregation of the Mission*, translated by Robert Cummings, 6 vols (New York 2009–15).

Milstein, Joanna. *The Gondi: Family Strategy and Survival in Early Modern France* (Farnham 2014).

Monval, Jean. *Les Frères hospitaliers de Saint Jean de Dieu* (Orléans 1936).

Morgain, Stéphane-Marie. *Pierre de Bérulle et les Carmélites de France: La querelle du gouvernement, 1583–1629* (Paris 1995).

Morgain, Stéphane-Marie. *La Théologie politique de Pierre de Bérulle (1598–1629)* (Paris 2001).

Morgain, Stéphane-Marie. 'L'Installation des Carmes Déchaux à Toulouse en mars 1623, de la Ligue au catholicisme royal'. *Revue d'Histoire de l'Église de France* 89, no. 2 (2003): pp. 363–83.

Mortier, Daniel Antonin. *Histoire des maîtres généraux de l'Ordre des Frères Prêcheurs*, 7 vols (Paris 1914).

Mousnier, Roland. *The Institutions of France under the Absolute Monarchy, 1598–1789*, translated by Brian Pearce (Chicago 1979).

Murnaghan, Kevin. 'Simple Monsieur Vincent'. *Colloque* 3 (1980): pp. 11–15.

Nelson, Eric. *The Jesuits and the Monarchy: Catholic Reform and Political Authority in France (1590–1615)* (Aldershot 2005).

Niclas, Jean-Charles. *La Famille de Gondi-Retz au tournant des xvie et xviie siècles: Étude de l'héritage d'une famille ducale à l'époque de la réforme Catholique* (Thèse de l'École de Chartes 1996).

Notices sur les prêtres, clercs et frères défunts de la Congrégation de la Mission, 10 vols (Paris 1881–1910).

O'Connor, Thomas. *Irish Jansenists, 1600–70* (Dublin 2008).

O'Malley, John. *The First Jesuits* (Cambridge, Mass., 1993).

O'Malley, John. *Trent and All That: Renaming Catholicism in the Early Modern Era* (Cambridge, Mass., 2000).

Orcibal, Jean. *Jean Duvergier de Hauranne: Abbé de Saint-Cyran et son temps (1581–1638)* (Louvain and Paris 1947).

Orcibal, Jean. *La Spiritualité de Saint-Cyran avec ses écrits de piété inédits* (Paris 1962).

Paglia, Vincenzo. *La pietà dei carcerati: Confraternite e società a Roma nei secoli xvi–xviii* (Rome 1980).

Parturier, Gaston. *Saint Vincent de Paul et les dames en son temps* (Lyon 1945).

Pérez-Flores, Miguel. 'De l'Equipe missionnaire à la Congrégation de la Mission'. *Mois Vincentien* (juillet 1984): pp. 71–118.

Perouas, Louis. 'La "Mission de Poitou" des Capucins pendant le premier quart du xviie siècle'. *Bulletin de la Société des Antiquaires de l'Ouest et des Musées de Poitiers* 7 (1964): pp. 349–62.

Petiet, Claude. *Le Roi et le Grand Maître: L'Ordre de Malte et la France au xviie siècle* (Paris 2002).

Petiet, Claude. *Le Bailli de Forbin: Lieutenant-Général des galères* (Paris 2003).

Petot, Patrick. *Alain de Solminihac (1593–1659): Prélat réformateur de l'Abbaye de Chancelade à l'évêché de Cahors*, 2 vols (Turnhout 2009).

Peyrous, Bernard. 'Saint Vincent de Paul et le renouvellement des missions paroissiales'. *Bulletin de la Société de Borda* 385 (1982): pp. 568–84.

Peyrous, Bernard. *La Réforme Catholique à Bordeaux (1600–1719)*, 2 vols (Bordeaux 1995).

Pierre, Benoist. *Le Père Joseph: L'Éminence Grise de Richelieu* (Paris 2007).

Pioger, André. *Un orateur de l'école française, Saint Jean Eudes (1601–1680)* (Paris 1940).

Pluyette, Charles. *Unrecteur de l'Université de Paris au xve siècle: Jehan Pluyette et les fondations qu'il institua* (Paris 1900).

Pollmann, Judith. *Catholic Identity and the Revolt of the Netherlands, 1520–1635* (Oxford 2011).

Poole, Stafford. 'The Formative Years of a Saint: Vincent de Paul: 1595–1617'. *Vincentian Heritage* 13, no. 2 (1992): pp. 81–111.

Poole, Stafford. 'The Origins of the Congregation of the Mission: Memory, Myth and Reality'. *Colloque* 27 (Spring 1993): pp. 153–85.

Poole, Stafford, and Douglas Slawson. 'A New Look at an Old Temptation: Saint Vincent de Paul's Temptation and Resolution to Serve the Poor'. *Vincentian Heritage* 11, no. 2 (1990): pp. 125–92.

Poujol, Robert. 'La Naissance de l'Hôpital Général d'après des documents inédits (Papiers Minachon, Assistance Publique de Paris)'. *L'Hôpital de Paris* (Paris 1982): pp. 11–34.

Pregnon, L'Abbé. *Histoire du pays et de la ville de Sedan depuis les temps les plus reculés jusqu'à nos jours*, 3 vols (Charleville 1856).

Prévost, Arthur. *Saint Vincent de Paul et ses institutions en Champagne méridionale* (Bar-sur-Seine 1928).

Prunel, Louis. *La Renaissance Catholique en France au xvii*[e] *siècle* (Paris 1928).

Pujo, Bernard. *Vincent de Paul: The Trailblazer*, translated by Gertrud Graubart Champe (Notre Dame, Ind., 2003).

Rapley, Elizabeth. *The Dévotes: Women and Church in Seventeenth-Century France* (Montreal and London 1990).

Régnier, Louis. *L'Église Notre-Dame d'Écouis, autrefois collégiale* (Paris 1913).

Religious Orders of the Counter-Reformation, edited by Richard DeMolen (New York 1994).

Richet, Denis. 'Sociocultural Aspects of Religious Conflicts in Paris during the Second Half of the Sixteenth Century'. In *Ritual, Religion and the Sacred*, edited by Robert Forster and Orest Ranum (Baltimore 1982): pp. 182–212.

Richet, Denis. *De la Réforme à la Révolution* (Paris 1991).

Roche, Maurice. *Saint Vincent de Paul and the Formation of Clerics* (Fribourg 1964).

Román, José María. 'L'Année 1617 dans la biographie de Saint Vincent de Paul'. *Mois Vincentien* (juillet 1984): pp. 12–28.

Román, José María. *Saint Vincent de Paul: A Biography*, translated by Joyce Howard, 2nd edn (London 1999).

Ropartz, M. S. 'Dom Germain Morel: Histoire de la sécularisation de l'Abbaye de Saint-Méen'. *Mémoires de la Société Archéologique des Côtes du Nord* 3 (1911): pp. 177–204.

Rybolt, John. 'From Life to the Rules: The Genesis of the Rules of the Daughters of Charity'. *Vincentian Heritage* 12, no. 2 (1991): pp. 173–99.

Rybolt, John. 'Saint Vincent's Daily Prayers, and the Development of Common Daily Prayers in the Congregation of the Mission'. *Vincentian Heritage* 31, no. 1 (2012): pp. 47–69.

Safley, Thomas. *The Reformation of Charity: The Secular and the Religious in Early Modern Poor Relief* (Boston 2003).

Salinis, A. de. *Madame de Villeneuve, née Marie Lhuillier d'Interville, fondatrice et institutrice de la Société de la Croix*, 2nd edn (Paris 1918).

Sauzet, Robert. 'Prédication et missions dans le diocèse de Chartres au début du xviie siècle'. *Annales de Bretagne et des Pays de l'Ouest* 81, no. 3 (1974): pp. 491–500.

Sauzet, Robert. *Contre-réforme et réforme Catholique en bas-Languedoc: Le diocèse de Nîmes aux xvii*[e] *siècle* (Louvain and Paris 1979).

Schneider, Robert A. *Public Life in Toulouse 1463–1789: From Municipal Republic to Cosmopolitan City* (Ithaca, NY, and London 1989).

Schoenher, Pierre. *Histoire du séminaire de Saint-Nicolas-du-Chardonnet*, 2 vols (Paris 1909).

Secret, Bernard. 'Saint François de Sales et les missions à l'intérieur'. *XVII*[e] *Siècle* 41 (1958): pp. 304–16.

Sedgwick, Alexander. *Jansenism in Seventeenth-Century France: Voices from the Wilderness* (Charlottesville, Va, 1977).

Selwyn, Jennifer. '"Schools of Mortification": Theatricality and the Role of Penitential Practice in the Jesuits' Popular Missions'. In *Penitence in the Age of Reformations*, edited by Katherine Jackson Lualdi and Anne T. Thayer (Aldershot 2000): pp. 201–21.

Selwyn, Jennifer. *A Paradise Inhabited by Devils: The Jesuits' Civilizing Mission in Early Modern Naples* (Aldershot 2004).

Sérouet, Pierre. *Jean de Brétigny, 1556–1634: Aux origines du Carmel de France, de Belgique et du Congo* (Louvain 1974).

Sheppard, Lancelot. *Barbe Acarie, Wife and Mystic: A Biography* (London 1953).

Simpson, Patricia. *Marguerite Bourgeoys and Montreal, 1640–65* (Montreal 1997).

Smith, Seán Alexander. *Fealty and Fidelity: The Lazarists of Bourbon France, 1660–1736* (Abingdon 2015).

Sol, Eugène. *Le Vénérable Alain de Solminihac abbé de Chancelade et évêque de Cahors* (Cahors 1928).

Tallon, Alain. *La Compagnie du Saint-Sacrement* (Paris 1990).

Taylor, Larissa. *Soldiers of Christ: Preaching in Late Medieval and Reformation France* (New York and Oxford 1992).

Terpstra, Nicholas. *Lay Confraternities and Civic Religion in Renaissance Bologna* (Cambridge 1995).

Terpstra, Nicholas. 'Ignatius, Confratello: Confraternities as Modes of Spiritual Community in Early Modern Society'. In *Early Modern Catholicism: Essays in Honour of John W. O'Malley, S.J.*, edited by Kathleen Comerford and Hilmar Pabel (Toronto 2001): pp. 163–82.

The Politics of Ritual Kinship: Confraternities and Social Order in Early Modern Italy, edited by Nicholas Terpstra (Cambridge 2000).

Tingle, Elizabeth. 'The Origins of Counter-Reform Piety in Nantes: The Catholic League and its Aftermath, 1585–1617'. In *Politics and Religion in Early Bourbon France*, edited by Alison Forrestal and Eric Nelson (Basingstoke 2009): pp. 203–20.

Trochu, François. *S. François de Sales (1567–1622): L'Episcopat*, 2 vols (Lyon 1942).

Urban, Charles. *Nicolas Coëffeteau* (Paris 1893).

Vance, Sylvia P. *The Memoirs of the Cardinal de Retz* (Tübingen 2005).

Vautier, A. 'Saint Vincent de Paul chanoine d'Écouis'. *Petites Annales de St Vincent de Paul* 48 (décembre 1903): pp. 356–64.

Veghel, Optat de. *Benoît de Canfield (1562–1610): Sa vie, sa doctrine et son influence* (Rome 1949).

Viennot, Éliane. *Marguerite de Valois: Histoire d'une femme, histoire d'un mythe* (Paris 1993).

Viguerie, Jean de. *Une œuvre d'éducation sous l'ancien régime: Les Pères de la Doctrine Chrétienne en France et en Italie (1592–1792)* (Paris 1976).

Villain, Étienne-François. *Essai d'une histoire de la paroisse de Saint-Jacques-de-la-Boucherie* (Paris 1758).

Wall, Thomas. 'Irish Enterprise at the University of Paris (1651–1653)'. *Irish Ecclesiastical Record*, 64 (1944): pp. 94–106, 159–71.

Williams, Charles. *The French Oratorians and Absolutism, 1611–1641* (New York 1989).

Wittberg, Patricia. *The Rise of Fall of Catholic Religious Orders: A Social Movement Perspective* (Albany, NY, 1994).

Worcester, Thomas. *Seventeenth-Century Cultural Discourse: France and the Preaching of Bishop Camus* (Berlin 1997).

Wright, Anthony D. *The Counter-Reformation: Catholic Europe and the Non-Christian World*, 2nd edn (Aldershot 2005).

Wright, Anthony D. *The Divisions of French Catholicism, 1629–1645: 'The Parting of the Ways'*, (Farnham 2011).

Zardin, Danilo. 'Relaunching Confraternities in the Tridentine Era: Shaping Consciences and Christianizing Society in Milan and Lombardy'. In *The Politics of Ritual Kinship: Confraternities and Social Order in Early Modern Italy*, edited by Nicholas Terpstra (Cambridge 2000): pp. 190–209.

Index

In this index, the abbreviation 'app' refers to appendix.